TO BE
DISPOSED
BY
AUTHORITY

D0269453

AUTHOR

NOVICK

ACCESSION NUMBER

77681

HOUSE OF COMMONS LIBRARY

House of Commons Library

54056000554979

PROGRAM BUDGETING

Program Analysis and the Federal Budget

PROGRAM BUDGETING

PROGRAM ANALYSIS AND

THE FEDERAL BUDGET

———

DAVID NOVICK, Editor

HARVARD UNIVERSITY PRESS
CAMBRIDGE, MASSACHUSETTS

© Copyright, 1965, 1967, by The RAND Corporation
All rights reserved
Second Edition
Distributed in Great Britain by Oxford University Press, London
Library of Congress Catalog Card Number 66-14451
Printed in the United States of America

PREFACE

Issues of United States foreign and domestic policy, as well as the subproblems of each issue, are frequently presented as unsolvable because we have no way to reduce the alternatives they pose to a simple calculus of gain and loss that is generally understood and accepted. For example, there are widely divergent views on the desirability of America's aiding underdeveloped countries rather than its own less well-developed areas. Even given the desirability of aid (either to foreign countries or within the United States), serious disagreements still remain on how such aid should be structured and administered.

When federal activity was relatively small and the government's revenue requirements were low, only a comparatively small group of people were directly concerned about the problems of choice and the methods used in making the choices. Wars, of course, affected this situation, but it was not until the depression of the 1930's and the period following World War II that a drastic change occurred. The federal government's policies and actions are now major factors in world affairs and in the affairs of each state and local government and every enterprise within the country. They demand of the nation's resources about one-sixth of the gross national product. A continuing need exists, therefore, to analyze both policy and the means of implementation, a need to consider the range of available alternatives and the resources that each of them requires.

While it is indeed difficult to reduce these matters—either the few very large ones or the multitude of smaller ones—to simple issues, a great deal can nevertheless be done to improve the basis for decisionmaking. One step is improvement in the methods of framing the problems and organizing the available data. A second and perhaps more important step is more effective analysis of the information needed to produce better plans or recommendations. The product of these efforts will facilitate the reason, judgment, experience, and intuition of the decisionmaker.

The reasons for making resource allocations on a national scale are not hard to find. First, all requirements, whether for national security or for public welfare, are at best relative. The lack of absoluteness, to say nothing of the lack of clear criteria and adequate information with which to decide among alternatives, subjects to uncertainty the whole process of determining appropriate national objectives and fixing resource allocations. This uncertainty compounds so rapidly that it is impossible to project with any great accuracy the amounts of resources that a program begun now will require five, ten, or fifteen years in the future. Indeed, a program viewed only in terms of a single and parochial set of objectives can have an almost limitless requirement for resources. Moreover, in light of the limit on total resources, even the best program is bound to fail if its requirements are not set at an annual level that can reasonably be met now and sustained in the future.

Herein lies the need for a new approach. Whereas this allocation process is essentially a political one, it can be illuminated by the continuous assembling and analyzing of statistical data on the nature and capability of the economy and the objectives and needs of the nation.

Program budgeting, the subject of this book, provides such an approach. It focuses on the decisionmaking process, particularly the problems of data and analysis. Its first effort is simply the rational ordering of inputs and outputs, in which the initial emphasis is on the identifiable outputs—major objectives of government processes. It then attempts to order the inputs—government activities produced by manpower, material, real estate—so that comparisons among wide ranges of alternatives are feasible and meaningful.

Program budgeting starts with the structuring of the problem and ends with analysis of the data. Among the analytical tools, cost-benefit or cost-utility analysis that compares benefit or utility (outputs) with resources or costs (inputs) is a most prominent one. Since the objective is to improve the decisionmaking that occurs in real life, not in the philosopher's fancy, program budgeting pays special attention to questions of organization and administration, and the politics and pressures of the workaday world.

This book concentrates on the program aspects of the budget. It purposefully avoids problems of fiscal policy, revenue, and related issues in order to explain in greater detail than would otherwise be possible the theory of program budgeting; and it presents a limited number of illustrative examples of how this concept, now applied in the Department of Defense, can be adapted to other areas of the federal government. (Implicitly, the concept is also proposed for state and local government and for private business.)

Thus, when such special subjects as education and transportation are considered in terms of program budgeting, the treatment is intended to be suggestive only and to stimulate research rather than to report on a completed study. The object of these illustrations, as of the entire effort, is to broaden discussion among legislators, government administrators, businessmen, students, and teachers in order to help improve the understanding and accelerate the application of the principles of program budgeting.

The material presented here is the product of eleven authors. Assignment of chapters was made on the basis of knowledge and interest concerning the specific subject matter. The book was under discussion by this group for over a year, and there were two major conferences. It is, therefore, a series of papers organized around a common theme and in terms of a continuous and broad exchange of views rather than a collection of individual essays. No attempt has been made, however, to sacrifice individuality to uniformity except in terms of the most elementary editing principles.

Each writer has had an opportunity to review the work of all the others, not only for the purpose of incorporating the ideas of his associates into his own writing but also so that he might express his views on the way in which his colleagues have handled their parts of the subject matter. The final responsibility for each chapter is that of the author. Duplication and overlap were not considered undesirable when, in the opinion of the writer of that chapter, the treatment of a particular subject area required it. Similarly, there has been no effort to achieve a single point of view or to insist on a standard form for illustrations, either in terms of time periods covered or the use of expenditures as compared with appropriations or other budget categories.

Although the individual chapters have been produced by separate authors, Chapters 1 through 3 and 10 through 12 represent the general background and treatment of program budgeting.

Chapters 4 through 9 are illustrations of the application of the concept to separate fields of federal activity.

The book is divided into three parts. Part I discusses the government decisionmaking process and the role of budgeting in that activity. It traces the efforts that have been made in past years to improve the budgetary process in the federal government and develops the conceptual framework for program budgeting. It considers the use of cost-utility analysis and other analytical techniques and their role in program budgeting.

In Part II the development of program budgeting in the Department of Defense is described, and examples are given of ways in which this concept might be adapted to other areas of the federal government. The treatment in these other activities—space, transport, natural resources, education, and health—is intended to be suggestive only and to stimulate research rather than to report on completed studies.

Part III of the book deals with implementation and operation of the program budget. It considers some potential problems and limitations involved in the implementation of program budgeting and suggests ways in which these might be met. Finally, there is a discussion of the application of an operating federal program budget in terms of its usefulness to the executive branch, the legislative branch, the states, and private economists and political scientists.

Some may find this three-part organization advantageous in that it permits the reader to get a general orientation in Part I and then to turn to the specialized chapter in Part II that fits his special interest. On completing the application of the program-budgeting chapter in Part II, he can then turn to the problems of implementation and orientation if he believes that the concept should be applied in his specialized field.

In addition to its work for the United States Air Force and other governmental agencies, The RAND Corporation regularly sponsors with its own funds research in areas of importance to national security and public welfare. The present study is the product of such Corporation-sponsored research undertaken by the RAND Cost Analysis Department. All of the authors are either full-time employees or consultants at RAND. The RAND employees are: David Novick, Head, Cost Analysis Department; Stephen M. Barro; Gene H. Fisher; and Milton A. Margolis. The consultants to RAND are: Melvin Anshen, Columbia University; Marvin Frankel, University of Illinois; Werner Z. Hirsch, University of California, Los Angeles; Roland N. McKean, University of California, Los Angeles; John R. Meyer, Harvard University; Arthur Smithies, Harvard University; and George A. Steiner, University of California, Los Angeles. Each individual's contribution to the study is identified in the Table of Contents.

Numerous individuals in the Bureau of the Budget, the Office of the Secretary of Defense, other federal government departments and agencies, our universities, and at RAND gave generously of their ideas and time to facilitate the work of the eleven authors. To all of them we are greatly indebted.

This idea could not have become a finished product if Dr. J. Y. Springer and Elizabeth Ridgman of RAND's Cost Analysis Department had not been continuously available for and exceptionally competent in the numerous activities that attend the development and production of a work of this kind. All of us, especially the editor, gratefully acknowledge their most valuable, special contributions.

David Novick, Head
Cost Analysis Department

The RAND Corporation
Santa Monica, California
March 1, 1965

CONTENTS

PART III: IMPLEMENTATION AND OPERATION

TABLES

FIGURES

Chapter 4

Chapter 7

Chapter 8

Chapter 11

Introduction

THE ORIGIN AND HISTORY OF PROGRAM BUDGETING

BY DAVID NOVICK

In many respects the history of program budgeting may be said to have started with President Johnson's news conference of August 25, 1965, when he spoke as follows.

"This morning I have just concluded a breakfast meeting with the Cabinet and with the heads of Federal agencies and I am asking each of them to immediately begin to introduce a very new and very revolutionary system of planning and programming the budgeting throughout the vast Federal Government, so that through the tools of modern management the full promise of a finer life can be brought to every American at the lowest possible cost.

"Under this new system each Cabinet and agency head will set up a very special staff of experts who, using the most modern methods of program analysis, will define the goals of their department for the coming year. And once these goals are established this system will permit us to find the most effective and the least costly alternative to achieving American goals.

"This program is designed to achieve three major objectives: It will help us find new ways to do jobs faster, to do jobs better, and to do jobs less expensively. It will insure a much sounder judgment through more accurate information, pinpointing those things that we ought to do more, spotlighting those things that we ought to do less. It will make our decisionmaking process as up to date, I think, as our space-exploring programs.

"Everything that I have done in both legislation and the construction of a budget has always been guided by my own very deep concern for the American people, consistent with wise management, of course, of the taxpayer's dollar. So this new system will identify our national goals with precision and will do it on a continuing basis. It will enable us to fulfill the needs of all the American people with a minimum amount of waste.

"And because we will be able to make sounder decisions than ever before, I think the people of this nation will receive greater benefits from every tax dollar that is spent in their behalf." (*The New York Times,* August 26, 1965.)

Writing in *The Annals,* May 1967, Bertram Gross and Michael Springer of the Maxwell School, Syracuse University, described this event as "potentially the most significant management improvement in the history of American Government." Since hundreds of government officials—federal, state, and local—and dozens of managers of financial and industrial organizations are either trying to become familiar with the concept or install it in their companies, it seems appropriate to provide background information on the origin and history of the Planning-Programming-Budgeting System (PPBS).

In a sense, one might say that certain elements of program budgeting are as old as civilization. To a greater or lesser degree, every rational person makes some plans for allocation of his limited resources, has certain goals or objectives, and considers alternative means of achieving them. The concepts and methods of program budgeting as it is understood and practiced today, however, are of relatively recent origin. It has two roots. One is in the federal government itself, where program budgeting was introduced as part of the wartime control system by the War Production Board in 1942. The other—an even longer and older root—is in industry.

Program Budgeting in the Federal Government

I shall start with the origins in the federal government, because with these I was closely involved and am therefore more familiar. In the early summer of 1940 President Roosevelt created the National Defense Advisory Commission, which was to assist our friends or "allies-to-be" in facilitating their war efforts. To provide such help, a variety of new or expanded production efforts and a number of new construction projects were undertaken. In all of them, from the building of ships and shipyards to the construction of new factories, one item of demand was common—overhead cranes.

As a result, by late 1940 the first of what would become our World War II controls was introduced—a limitation order controlling the schedule of distribution and use of overhead cranes. It was followed over the next year and a half by a series of orders, which copied the pattern of control of industrial production and distribution that had been used in World War I. There was a limitation order dealing with aluminum because aircraft demands had made this metal in short supply. There were orders dealing with various alloying materials because of increases in hard steel demands for military equipment. There were orders stopping the production of pleasure automobiles to cut back the use of materials such as chromium and components such as ball bearings. And so on. The result was that by the summer of 1941, even before the war had started, a traffic jam had developed in our control system.

Furthermore the military were using authority that had been given them to place priorities for deliveries of finished products such as tanks, aircraft, and ships. At the same time the civilian supply agency was exercising its authority to place priorities on steel, copper, aluminum, and other materials for essentials such as milk pails or medical and hospital supplies. A great many priorities were issued, which soon started to outstrip available supply. It became apparent that this way of doing business—separate controls for each situation—was not likely to work. In the early fall of 1941 a scheme that I had developed, known as the Production Requirements Plan and designed to deal with the priority and allocation problem on an across-the-board basis, was put into effect. Shortly after Pearl Harbor it was made a mandatory nation-wide system.

However, the Production Requirements Plan had been designed as a stopgap measure. Since the military did not know what was required to build their ships and planes and tanks, and since they did not have a schedule that could identify delivery in appropriate time periods, nor any way of effectively controlling the dollar volume of contracts placed, the need had been essential to identify these fundamentals. The Production Requirements Plan was designed to identify the material and component requirements for contracts that were being placed by the military and, probably more important, to measure the inventories and capacities of America's producing industry. It was an interim step on the road to a program budget in that it provided the first overall picture of the United States' needs and resources for war.

From this experience we learned that we could not look at one thing at a time—be it airplanes, ships, or stainless steel milk pails on the demand side; or steel, aluminum, overhead cranes, and ball bearings on the supply side. As a consequence, by early 1942 the War Production Board was looking at the total of military requirements and the total of war-essential civilian requirements in terms of a series of identifiable groupings, and these groups were being studied by use of the analytical tools then available.

The essential features of the situation can be explained rather simply. Although we needed all the airplanes that we could get, all of them were not equally important. At some point, roller bearings for the two-thousandth B-17 were less important than roller bearings for a refrigerator in a municipal hospital. At some point, the one-thousandth tank of a certain type was less important than the stainless steel pails needed for milk to be supplied to either soldiers or civilians. The War Production Board thus learned the need for weighing and evaluating, which led to the introduction in late 1942 of the Controlled Materials Plan.

The Controlled Materials Plan was actually the first program budget used in the federal government. It usually is not so identified because the budgeting was done in terms of copper, steel, aluminum, and other critical material rather than dollars, whereas for most people budgeting is associated with dollars. However, in choosing the media of exchange—copper, steel, and other critical items—the board recognized that, in 1942, dollars were less meaningful than physical resources. Currency could be created by fiat and without restraint, whereas materials of the type labeled as controlling were limited in quality and their supply could be increased only by slow, usually resource-demanding expansion.

For the balance of World War II, therefore—from 1943 through 1945—the system of production in the United States and the distribution of output from that system were effectively controlled through the Controlled Materials Plan. The Plan is called a program budget because it had the following characteristics:

I. Major goals were identified in terms of
   A. United States or allied combat needs
   B. Essential civilian requirements
   C. Other essential military or civilian demands
   D. Aid to friendly nations
   E. Economic warfare

II. Each major goal was identified in program objectives; for example
   A. United States military
      1. Combat theater equipment and supplies
      2. Combat support
      3. Zone of interior activities
III. Program objectives were further defined in program elements; for example
      1. Combat theater equipment and supplies
         a. Aircraft
            (1) (Further defined by type and model)
         b. Tanks
            (1) (Broken down into size and purpose categories)
         c. Automobiles
            (1) (Identified as trucks, jeeps, personnel vehicles, etc.; trucks further defined into size and use categories)
IV. Programs crossed service lines so as to identify land sea, and air forces as well as essential non-military contributions to identified objectives.
 V. The time horizon was extended: a budget was prepared every three months (or quarter) and was projected for sixteen periods (four years), that is, the next quarter and the fifteen succeeding ones.
VI. Alternatives were examined and systematic analysis was made of both supply and requirements. Sometimes this meant resources were augmented by stopping production, as in the outstanding example of gold mining, which provided additional labor and equipment for other mining activities. In other cases essential needs were met by "freezing" inventories and controlling distribution, as in the case of passenger automobiles. In every case the action was the result of analysis.

The systematic analysis was not necessarily systems analysis in the breadth and depth now identified with such studies, but under the Controlled Materials Plan cost-effectiveness analysis was performed, even if it did not have the sophistication that is expected today. In terms of the state of the art of the time, the analytical and related methodology used in our World War II Controlled Materials Plan can be properly identified as the kind of analysis required by a program budget.

The next steps in the federal development of a program budget took place in the Bureau of Reclamation, the Coast Guard, a few other government agencies, and at the RAND Corporation. Early in its history RAND decided that the traditional standards for choosing among preferred means of warfare for the future—for example, increased altitude, speed, or payload of aircraft—were not the only ones, and in a series of studies it expanded the criteria into what is now known as weapons systems analysis. The first of these studies was completed in 1949. In it a number of new factors were introduced—social, political, and economic—so that the study aims went beyond what the specific piece of equipment would do and added considerations such as demands on the U.S. economy or impact on the economy of the enemy. In view of the wide range of considerations in systems analysis, it was determined that the only way to bring this heterogeneous group together was through the common denominator of the dollar.

At that time RAND looked to the Air Staff for its data, and the dollar data were made available in the traditional form; that is, budget and financial information was conveyed in terms of equipment, construction, personnel, and the like. Although there had already been some efforts in the Air Staff to develop a means for looking at weapons systems, these had not proceeded very far. As a consequence, the traditional budget and financial data were something less than satisfactory for weapons systems analysis as developed at RAND.

If one wanted to do a systems analysis showing a comparison between various types of bombers—for example, the proposed B-47 and B-52 as against the existing B-29, B-36, and B-50—the data just were not available. When RAND decided that it would have to engage in a more detailed analysis of the economic requirements of the proposed weapons systems, it began to examine closely the available sources of information. After several years it became apparent that these would not provide the answers if they were maintained in the existing and traditional form. Thus, in 1953 a RAND publication (Novick, *Efficiency and Economy in Government Through New Budgeting and Accounting Procedures,* R-254) proposed that the first program budget be applied to the Air Force.

It also suggested that the methodology could be extended to all military activities.

The Air Force accepted this document with something less than complete enthusiasm, and the idea was discussed for many years. Although the Air Force did not endorse the idea, neither did it prohibit or in any way interfere with RAND's further consideration of the concept. In consequence, RAND continued study and publication of ideas that are now associated with the program budget, culminating in 1960 in the appearance of two documents: Hitch and McKean's *The Economics of Defense in the Nuclear Age,* (Cambridge: Harvard University Press) and my *New Tools for Planners and Programmers* (The RAND Corporation, P-2222). These were brought to the attention of persons in the incoming Kennedy Administration who generally agreed that they might offer one way of facilitating the treatment, analysis, and study of one large segment of the United States budget, namely, the military components. In 1961, the initial effort was launched in the Defense Department, where it has continued since that time. Although program budgeting in the Department of Defense has been the subject of various types of criticism, most of it has been complimentary.

Program Budgeting in Industry

In 1959, after I had been writing about the PPBS for more than five years, I had a visitor who said he had only recently become familiar with the Novick proposals. On reading the material, he had decided that I would be interested in his experiences along the same lines. He had with him a set of documents—General Motor's Budget and Finance Procedures for 1924.

The visitor was Donaldson Brown, who had retired in 1946 as Chairman of the Finance Committee of General Motors and who was until 1965 a member of the Finance Committee of DuPont. According to Mr. Brown, by the time DuPont made its investment in General Motors, DuPont was already using something very much like a program budget system. And this type of planning and budgeting was one of the major innovations in General Motors after the takeover.

The 1924 documents included a basic feature of the PPBS method, which is to identify major objectives, to define programs essential to these goals, to identify resources to the specific types of objectives, and to analyze systematically the alternatives available. This feature may be simplified by illustrating it in the automobile industry. At General Motors it means not only dividing available resources between Chevrolet and Cadillac divisions and the other major lines that General Motors produces but also within the Chevrolet line, identifying objectives in terms of price classes and categories of cars to be offered, setting up specific programs for each, and then calculating the resources required and the *potential* profits and losses under various conditions. Businesses that are now introducing or thinking of introducing the Planning-Programming-Budgeting System also face the problem of thinking through once again their objectives and goals, examining the alternative programs available for accomplishing them, and choosing among them. For a company this approach means analyzing all of the interdependent activities in achieving a specific goal—looking at the whole, not just a series of parts.

The word "potential" expresses one of the major factors in the program budgeting system. That is, the concept deals explicitly with uncertainty. In the typical budget proposal a relatively short period of time is considered—one year—and in handling it, one is confidently assumed to have complete knowledge about what will transpire. The truth of the matter is that even within so short a span of time as a year, events do not work out exactly as planned. There is an element of uncertainty. One major feature of the system introduced in General Motors was the fact that they were planning not only for next year's automobile but for the ones to be marketed in the second, third, fourth, and fifth years. This meant they had to deal with uncertainty in terms of four, five, or more years in the future.

In the current time period at General Motors, next year's model or the automobile for year I is a fixed thing with only a slight possibility of change. The article for the year after that, or year II, is almost a fixed thing because commitments must be made to long lead-time items as much as eighteen months in advance. Even the automobile for year III is fairly well developed at this point in time, and they are planning automobiles for years IV and V. In other words, General Motors continuously has five model years in planning, as well as one model in production. They look at all these years in terms of all of the possible alternatives they can develop with respect to projected market conditions, kinds of competition, changes in income for their customers, and the like. This leads to a broad range of studies or systematic analyses. They at the same time treat the capital investment program, because by and large they cannot make capital investments for an automobile sooner than year VI. In fact, if a change requiring investment in new plant is to be made for an earlier period of time, they must take into account the extraordinary additional costs that will be involved.

It should be pointed out that the concept of systems analysis, which is closely identified with program budgeting, did not really originate in program budgeting per se. Systems analysis always has been a part of the work of competent engineers and engineering firms. Probably the greatest innovations in systems analysis were initiated in the 1920's in the Bell Laboratories. Actually, in many respects the Bell Lab's method of analysis then and today bears a close resemblance to what we called "weapons systems analysis" in the Defense Department or in other organizations such as RAND.

There is one major distinction which is worth noting. That is, that the engineers (and this includes the Bell Laboratories) oriented their thinking largely, and sometimes exclusively, to the hardware or the equipment considerations.

Although they sometimes introduced economic, social, and political aspects, they treated these in a very primitive way. And the great significance of the change that we call weapons systems analysis today is the broadening of both the nature and content of the analysis.

In all of this, quantitative aids are of great importance, and we want to quantify as much as we can. But as has been stated repeatedly by Mr. McNamara; by Mr. Hitch, when he was Assistant Secretary of Defense (Comptroller); and by Mr. Enthoven, the first Assistant Secretary of Defense (Systems Analysis); computers and quantitative methods are not decisionmakers. They are, instead, aids to the decisionmaking process. They are aids in illuminating the issues. Today, most of us realize that we are not talking about computers as the decisionmakers in the PPB process. In fact, it is "anything but."

It is recognized that as important as, and in many cases more important than, quantitative considerations, are problems of a qualitative nature for which we do not have numbers. This does not mean that analysis is not possible just because we cannot quantify. On the contrary, there are many ways of analyzing qualitative problems, and it is an essential ingredient of this process that we undertake to do a substantial amount of qualitative analysis in addition to the quantitative work.

In August 1965, President Johnson said that this system, which has been so successful in the Defense Department, was now to be applied to all the executive offices and agencies of the United States Government. Even though there is a long history of program budgeting, even though it originated outside the federal establishment, even though there are some twenty-five years or more of history that one can ascribe to the activity within the federal establishment, the truth of the matter is that the problem now being faced—the application of the PPB concept to new areas of interest —is a new and very difficult one. One of the major problems is to identify the missions, the objectives, or the goals. For the U.S. Government these must be defined not only for the federal establishment as such, but also for each of the offices and agencies that make up the entire executive department. The same situation prevails at state and local government levels.

Identifying end objectives, designing alternative ways of achieving the objective, and choosing between them on the basis of systematic analysis are the hallmarks of program budgeting.

PART I

GOVERNMENT DECISIONMAKING AND
THE PROGRAM BUDGET

ABBREVIATIONS

ORGANIZATIONS

AEC	Atomic Energy Commission
AID	Agency for International Development
CCC	Commodity Credit Corporation
DOD	Department of Defense
FAA	Federal Aviation Agency
GSA	General Services Administration
HEW	Department of Health, Education, and Welfare
ICC	Interstate Commerce Commission
JCAE	Joint Committee on Atomic Energy
JCS	Joint Chiefs of Staff
JSOP	Joint Strategic Objective Plan
MATS	Military Air Transport Service (Air Force)
MOL	Manned Orbiting Laboratory
MSTS	Military Sea Transportation Service (Navy)
NASA	National Aeronautics and Space Administration
NIH	National Institutes of Health
OART	Office of Advanced Research and Technology (NASA)
OMSF	Office of Manned Space Flight (NASA)
OSD	Office of the Secretary of Defense
OSR	Office of the Secretary of Resources
OSSA	Office of Space Science and Applications (NASA)
OTDA	Office of Tracking and Data Acquisition (NASA)
PHS	Public Health Service
SAC	Strategic Air Command
TVA	Tennessee Valley Authority

TERMS

AICBM	anti-intercontinental ballistic missile
ALBM	air-launched ballistic missile
CEP	circular error probability
FY	fiscal year
GNP	gross national product
ICBM	intercontinental ballistic missile
LAPM	low-altitude penetrating missile
LEA	long-endurance aircraft
NOA	new obligational authority
PCP	Program Change Proposal (system)
PERT	Program Evaluation and Review Technique
R&D	research and development
SST	supersonic transport
UHF	ultra high frequency

Chapter 1

THE FEDERAL BUDGET AS AN INSTRUMENT FOR MANAGEMENT AND ANALYSIS

BY MELVIN ANSHEN

In the operating life of organizations the budgetary process is a unique activity. It is related to the complete administrative range from analysis through planning to management and control. In its end product, the budget, it summarizes (1) the problems to which analysis has been applied, (2) the analytic concepts and techniques brought to bear on those problems, (3) the information relevant to their solution, (4) the proposed (ultimately, the determined) decisions, and (5) the administrative structure through which performance of the approved budget will be executed, controlled, and appraised.

If, as many students of the managerial process assert, what management is all about is making and implementing decisions, then the budget is perhaps the most essential management tool. It organizes, influences, facilitates, and expresses management thought and management action. It must, therefore, be related to organizational objectives, policies, practices, and structure. Rationally designed, it contributes powerfully to the effective and efficient accomplishment of managerial tasks. Carelessly constructed or ill-coordinated with administrative requirements, it cannot fail to be a principal cause of bad decisions and weak execution.

These propositions are applicable equally to all types of organizations, whatever their character and purpose. Resources are rarely, probably never, equal to needs. It is the essence of decisionmaking, therefore, to choose among alternative ends and to ration scarce means to their accomplishment. At this level of description, no significant distinction exists between profit and nonprofit organizations, or between private and public organizations. All require the ordering of goals, the analysis of their relative contributions to the great aims of the total undertaking, the development of plans, the measurement of alternative resource inputs and their relation to progress toward objectives, rational choice of feasible ends, allocation of means, monitoring of progress, and appraisal of results. The budgetary process is the activity through which this work is done. The budget is the instrument through which the process is made operational.

In the context of these observations, this book examines the federal budget of the United States as an instrument for planning resource allocations. The aim of the book is to be both critical and constructive. It examines the design of the budget in the light of its actual and potential uses and identifies the ways in which the budget fails to serve these needs effectively. Against this background it presents a general set of proposals for improving the design that promises to be both effective and feasible. The heart of the proposals is the application in the nondefense parts of the federal budget of a concept—called the *program budget*—that was installed in the Department of Defense in 1961.

USES OF THE FEDERAL BUDGET

The primary operational use of the federal budget is as an instrument for aggregating and displaying annually the expenditure proposals of the executive branch as a basis for appropriation decisions by the Congress. While the budget presentation contains an estimate of income, developed from forecasts of the general level of economic activity and existing or proposed taxes, its more significant content in a managerial sense is its statement of estimated expenditures in terms of amounts and objectives. A related purpose is to serve as the control medium through which spending decisions are administratively implemented and financial accountability is assured.

The same budget design now serves both the decision and implementation objectives. There is no compelling need to employ a common budget structure for these purposes, however, provided the decision structure can be readily translated into the implementation structure by way of an appropriate crossover net. Thus a revision of the budget submittal and decision structure would not require an accompanying reorganization of the executive departments. Indeed, there may be good reasons for revising the former without disturbing the latter.

The fundamental problem resolved through the budgetary process is the familiar one of distributing scarce resources (as measured in money terms) among a variety of competing claims. At this basic decision level the task facing public officials, both executive and legislative, does not differ from the task facing corporate officers, or even individual citizens, who try to manage their means to serve their ends. In all these settings, budgeting is concerned with deciding on the allocation of scarce and reasonably well-defined inputs to attain objectives that range from well- to ill-defined. This involves three interrelated operations. First, it is necessary to determine the most efficient way to attain given objectives. Second, it is necessary to determine the optimal set of concurrent objectives. Third, it is necessary to determine the optimal size of the total budget. The last decision lays down the ultimate bounding constraint that squeezes the allocation judgment.

A good budget system supports and informs judgment in making these determinations. It does this by providing information that is relevant to the required decisions. Relevancy may be defined by the following criteria: (1) aggregation of information in totals that illuminate meaningful decision alternatives and aid rational comparisons among them; (2) with respect to each alternative objective, identification and summation of all pertinent input requirements, both current and future; (3) organization of information in detail that facilitates efficiency measures of inputs in relation to outputs, means in relation to ends, investment in relation to payback. (Such efficiency measures are often referred to as *cost-effectiveness* or *cost-utility analysis*.)

A good budget system does more than serve the needs of public officials, of course. The federal budget is the prime source of information on the magnitude and direction of government spending. This information is essential for those in the private sector of our society who are concerned with understanding, predicting, and exploiting the economic significance of public expenditures. A host of business decisions are influenced by judgments about the present and future impact of public spending—in the financial markets, in commitments on plant size and location, in product development, in research, in the exploration of international opportunities, and many other areas.

For all these uses, how budget information is organized for public decisionmaking can illuminate or obscure its significance for private analysts. Beyond the obvious economic applications, we should also recognize that the effective performance of a

democratic enterprise society is greatly assisted by widespread
understanding of how public decisions are made and what they
mean. Here, again, a clear relationship of means to ends, inputs to
outputs, is a primary requirement.

TYPICAL BUDGET PROBLEMS

The significance of these general observations can be suggested
by a review of some typical nondefense budget problems. As an
introduction to the discussion in later chapters, it will be helpful to
note the variety and complexity of administrative issues that are
raised even within the scope of a few illustrative problems. Present
claims compete against each other, both relatively and absolutely.
Present claims compete against future claims. Present investments
may yield long-term benefits, although with no realizable payback
in the early years. Ongoing activities and established clienteles
compete with new activities and vaguely identified beneficiaries.
Working through all these issues are the information requirements
for analysis, planning, decision, implementation, and control.

Consider, as one example, the problem of budgeting for activities
designed to alleviate poverty and rooted unemployment. The related social diseases of poverty and unemployment have been diag-
nosed as complex phenomena traceable to such varied causes as
economic recession, technological change, obsolete skills, insufficient education, racial prejudice, immobility of labor, and inadequate supply of information on distant job opportunities. Economic
and social analysts have recommended an equally varied assortment of remedial measures. Some federal activities—public works,
aid to depressed areas, surplus food distribution, retraining in
wanted skills, and many others—are already in being, supported by
present appropriations. Proposals lie on the table for larger commitments, as well as for new activities. Against these claims are arrayed, of course, not only the total mass of the nondefense discretionary budget (excluding interest on the debt and commitments
under existing legislation to farmers, veterans, etc.), but also proposals for budget support to activities that aim at related economic
and social problems, such as assistance for the improvement of
mass transit facilities in choked metropolitan areas. Looming over
all is some concept of total federal budgetary capability within the

revenue projections of the tax structure, the economics and politics of the aggregate revenue-expenditure balance, the constraints of the financial cost of the national security commitment, and the claims of other federal programs.

What are the significant budget questions in this problem structure? Consider the following:

1. What is the present budget commitment to relevant ongoing activities?

2. What increment gains in positive contributions to problem resolution might be attributed to added budget commitment?

3. What significant minimum or threshold budget levels would underwrite useful activity in problem areas currently untouched by ongoing programs?

4. What feasible stepped-up rates of program activity can be identified?

5. What budget costs should be associated with them?

6. Can operationally meaningful differentiation be made between the effectiveness of various approaches to the elements of the total poverty and unemployment problem?

7. If so, can such differentiation be related to dollar costs, near- and long-term?

Questions of broader import are also pertinent:

1. Are skill retraining efforts better or worse investments than public works?

2. Are they better or worse than subsidies or other special incentives to attract new industry?

3. Or, at an even more fundamental level, is a dollar invested in an attempt to rehabilitate a mature, technologically displaced, educationally handicapped, unemployed man a better commitment than a comparable dollar invested in supporting the educational and technical preparation of his son for employment in a different line of work in another part of the country?

The questions may look unreasonable, even unanswerable. But the fact is that they are implicitly answered in any budget decision in the defined problem area. The only significant issue is whether the answer rests on intuition and guess, or on a budget system that presents relevant information so organized as to contribute to rational analysis, planning, and decisionmaking. Even a partial and qualified contribution would be valuable, of course. As all managers know, most decisions are made in situations of partial ignorance and uncertainty. The critical factor is the extent to which information specifically organized around the decision requirements can be employed to limit the area of uncertainty and define its general characteristics. An important complication in this instance has been the fact that federal activities related to the relief of poverty and unemployment are sponsored and administered by several executive departments (Labor; Commerce; Agriculture; Health, Education, and Welfare). Until the Office of Economic Opportunity was established, there was no machinery for coordinating these activities, or even, except in gross aggregates, for measuring the total investment. Finally, there was no analytical structure that would facilitate a rational study of cost-effectiveness results. The Office of Economic Opportunity is now charged with these responsibilities, and the creation of a comprehensive program budget by that agency would appear to be an essential first step.

Consider, as a second example, the problem of budgeting for federal support of fundamental and early stage applied research in a specific area of human disease. Among the unavoidable questions that demand explicit or implicit answer are the following:

1. Given some approximate ceiling to the total medical research share of the federal budget, what proportion should be assigned to efforts to discover the causes and cure of this disease?

2. Assuming that the research program will have value only if pursued continuously through an extended period of time, what are the potential second-, third-, and nth-year investments required to sustain a viable path of discovery?

3. What related research activities, present or potential, can be identified and their level of expenditures balanced with the proposed new commitment?

On a broader front, some of the questions are:

1. What are the research resources (human and physical, public and private, military and civilian) on which the proposed program will draw?

2. Will the net effect of a substantial new research program in this area be little more than an inflation of ongoing research efforts, with increments in one program supplied by decrements in another?

3. And at still another level of analysis, what standards of performance can be established that will permit even crude measures of payback on the investment through time?

The responses to these questions, it should be noted, have significance not only for the executive and legislative branches of the federal government, but also for private research and educational institutions. These organizations are rationally compelled to coordinate their long-run activities with federally sponsored research within the context of a grand design for the extension of human knowledge, subject to the constraints of their own individual human and budget resources. In short, federal budget decisions are interlinked with private budget decisions. Improvement in the federal budgetary process will lead to improvement in the private budgetary process, with a consequent gain in the efficiency of the total allocation of a critically scarce resource among competing needs.

Consider, as a third example, the problem of making a meaningful summation of total foreign aid and development expenditures as a basis for (1) assessing the aggregate U.S. commitment, (2) analyzing the relative effectiveness of the component parts in achieving defined objectives, (3) coordinating country-by-country assistance programs, and possibly (4) appraising and amending the grand strategic design in terms of America's worldwide interests and goals. International assistance activities are funded in several executive departments. In some locations, as in the Agency for International Development, they are specifically identified as to magnitude and objective. In others, they are mingled with domestic programs and objectives (as, for example, in agricultural price-support activities). Some programs are of a one-time character; others involve capital investments that will be brought to fruition through a term of years; still others are indeterminate in length, but for strategic reasons must be extended as quasiguaranteed for a stipulated number of years. Many of the programs are significantly related to private investment overseas. Some involve contingent underwriting of private risk ventures through a variety of contractual or implicit guarantees.

Rational analysis, planning, and management of this country's total international security, developmental, and commercial effort would call for a budget structure in which the multitude of related programs is identified as to objectives and magnitudes. For most of them, only gross approximations can be attempted within the present budget design. Informed management performance is severely limited as a result of this structural deficiency. The handicap is directly experienced in the domain of public administration. It spreads by indirection through private business and the work of economic and policy analysts.

CHARACTERISTICS OF A USEFUL BUDGET STRUCTURE

The characteristics of a federal budget structure that would effectively serve public and private users of budget information can be identified against the background of these problems and the preceding general description of the budget's clientele and their responsibilities.

First, the budget design should facilitate meaningful measurement of the total money costs of accomplishing defined objectives. In the military budget, for example, this would mean a statement of the full costs of a proposed new missile system: research and development, investment, and operation; these would be further identified in terms of submarines (if water-based) and crews and weapons, special training and special bases, and maintenance and repair, together with the necessary tools and parts. Moreover, a package of current costs would not suffice. The statement should project the total cost stream through forecastable time.

Second, the budget structure should facilitate the comparison of alternative ways to accomplish a given objective. A military example might be the comparison of the full time-phased costs of a submarine-based missile system with a comparable cost display for a land-based missile. A nonmilitary example would be the comparison of the full time-phased costs of two approaches to the problem of relieving geographic pockets of idle resources: (1) by retraining workers and creating inducements for the in-migration of new industries; (2) by relocating workers at places where employment opportunities exist, with or without retraining.

Third, the budget presentation should clearly identify the future cost implications inherent in near-term financial commitments. Those who allocate scarce funds should be made aware of the prospective expenditure stream and thereby helped to avoid entrapment in the familiar seduction of modest first-year costs.

Fourth, the budget design should facilitate comparison of cost inputs and achievement outputs when related segments of a single program are administered by different management units. An example might be hospital services under the direction of the Veterans Administration versus hospital services under another jurisdiction.

Fifth, the budget design should delineate the objectives of discrete spending commitments in such terms that significant cost-effectiveness (cost-utility) analysis can be carried out. There are obvious limitations on our ability to define measurable goals, or even measurable progress toward such goals, in some areas of federal expenditure. Nevertheless, the budget design should seek continually to expand the area of informed analysis and imaginatively explore concepts and techniques that help to convert qualitative into quantitative goals and common service into allocatable activities.

Sixth, the budget design should make it possible to aggregate related expenditures wherever they occur in the government's sprawling administrative structure. The Congress appropriates money for research in many departmental budgets, as it does for foreign aid. These separate appropriations are not readily brought together at present. But there is no reason why an effective budget drawn up to assist rational decisionmaking should not identify such activities wherever they occur and permit their aggregation so that both legislators and private citizens can recognize the total size and multiple locations of the identified commitment.

Seventh, a budget that effectively meets the foregoing criteria should go far toward serving another important need—that of generating economic data on federal inputs to the national economy by meaningful activity segments. This would help private analysts to understand and interpret the direction and influence of federal spending and thereby improve the efficiency of private investment through a more rational administration of commitments in relation to present and future federal programs. At the same time, others whose interest is in social performance would find a flow of information relevant to their work in defining and predicting problems and thereby organizing resources for their alleviation and solution.

DEFECTS IN THE PRESENT FEDERAL BUDGET STRUCTURE

The present federal budget design is largely the product of a historical response to the need to safeguard the integrity of appropriations against careless, ill-informed, or maleficent administrators in the executive departments. It is an instrument for the control of spending. It was not designed to assist analysis, planning, and decisionmaking, and it does not work well for that purpose. It is a conventional comptroller's budget, not a manager's budget.

The foregoing statement should not be read simply as a proposition of general criticism. The implementation of appropriation decisions without divergence, distortion, or deceit is an important element in the maintenance of democratic institutions. The people must control the public purse through the judgments of their elected representatives and the performance of their civil servants. This is the foundation of public confidence and trust.

But honest and faithful execution of appropriation decisions is not enough. What about the quality of those decisions whose undeviating performance has been ensured? Is a democracy effectively administered if it does not clearly identify its objectives and its resources and rationally allocate scarce means to ensure preferred ends? A budget appropriately designed to meet the requirements of a rational decision process will not, of course, automatically ensure the making of rational decisions. But it can be a powerful influence in that direction. It can identify and factually illuminate the significant alternatives, and it can do this, with at least rough accuracy, in terms of costs as well as in terms of results. Furthermore, it can do this without weakening the important contribution of the budgetary instrument to financial responsibility.

To identify the existing nondefense budget, therefore, as one primarily designed to ensure honesty in the executive departments is to cite one important characteristic of good budget structure, and equally to recognize the omission of another important characteristic—its contribution to informed and rational performance of the managerial function. The two characteristics are not mutually exclusive. Rather, they should be viewed as complementary.

If we direct our attention to the managerial potential of the present budget—specifically to its employment as an instrument for analyzing, planning, deciding, controlling, and evaluating—its defects become obvious. Because it is the product of a desire to ensure financial responsibility within an executive department's structure that evolved haphazardly through the vagaries of history and politics, it is not aligned with the requirements of a rational decision process. It presents requests (and consequent appropriations) in terms of direct objects of expenditure, such as "personnel" or "vehicles." Rarely can these objects of expenditure be related in any meaningful way to specific administrative programs, even when these programs fall within the scope of a single executive department. When, as is often the case, related objectives are pursued in more than one department, only with the greatest difficulty and only in terms of the grossest aggregates can such activities be summed or compared. Probably even more important is the fact that the present budget does not project future cost estimates for current or proposed activities. One sees data only for three fiscal periods: last year (actual), this year (estimated), and next year (the budget). Thus the projection lacks the dimensions needed for rational decision.

The critical nature of this deficiency must not be lightly assessed. Business managers have long ago learned that they cannot make resource decisions in such an information vacuum. When a proposed new venture is being appraised, managers demand a comprehensive and detailed layout of all costs associated with the total commitment. They demand forward projection of the cost stream in the most realistic feasible terms. Lacking this, they are helpless to compare alternative investments, equally helpless to calculate the return on any single investment. Individual decisions that involve substantial financial burdens, such as the purchase of a house or an automobile, usually involve comparable knowledge of total costs extended forward through the period of acquisition and operation or use. In neither case, of course, will the information ordinarily be thoroughly complete or precise. But the demand is for best approximations, periodically refreshed and improved through appraisal of performance against estimated targets. This kind of information should be available to the executive and legislative branches of the federal government as a basis for making reasoned expenditure proposals and appropriation decisions in the nondefense sector of the budget.

Without it, the decisions taken lose in clarity and purpose. Responsible officials lack the information needed to (1) choose among alternative goals when available resources are insufficient to undertake the achievement of all goals concurrently, (2) measure the total immediate cost of activities designed to achieve any single goal, (3) identify currently the implicit future costs of present program decisions, (4) chart with confidence the probable future course of the expenditure side of the budget in total and significant detail, or (5) evaluate the efficiency and effectiveness of the performance of ongoing programs by comparing costs with achievements.

It is easy to cite these direct handicaps to management of the public resources. The indirect handicaps are less visible, but not less important in their influence on the quality of public administration. For example, one common result of the presentation in the budget of current expenditures for ongoing activities, without forward estimates of related costs, is heavy pressure to maintain established activities in which substantial costs have already been incurred, and equally to resist the initiation of new programs. The combination of the familiar economic influence of sunk costs with the equally familiar political influence of vested interests is likely to generate an almost irresistible pressure to maintain the status quo. Further, since population growth and the Parkinson syndrome are likely to push toward expansion of ongoing activities (while counterpressures are fueled only by sporadic economy drives that tend to founder when they meet democratic logrolling), the perpetuation of established programs is the common experience. Farm price supports are a classic example of this unhappy situation, but by no means the only one that might be cited. The general effect can be, and often is, serious delay in responding to critical economic and social needs.

A second indirect result of the present budget structure is a lack of reasonable standards of efficiency and effectiveness in the use of resources. Without defined and time-phased objectives, it is difficult to be critical of administrative performance. To level a charge of waste or malperformance at the managers of a public program is, of course, one of the more popular pastimes of any administration's loyal opposition. But it is a rare experience to find such a charge documented by the kind of precise cost-effectiveness measures that are the common test of the quality of management performance in a well-run organization. Those who take a professional view of management responsibility—and contrary to popular folklore, there are many public administrators who share this attitude—are even more concerned about the absence of the kind of information that would enable a manager to assess the progress and quality of his own performance and, as appropriate, to initiate corrective action before outside criticism can even start.

Serious as these two indirect handicaps of an inadequate budget structure undoubtedly are, there is an even more important effect that disturbs many who study the role of government in our complex industrial society. This is the absence of stimulus to examine the possibilities and feasibilities of translating into actual performance the general philosophical proposition that a central responsibility of a democratic government is to provide or do those things that people need but cannot supply or do effectively for themselves. Like any well-designed tool, a budget is more than an instrument for assisting in the accomplishment of predetermined tasks. It helps to extend, strengthen, and organize a manager's mental reach, to support his ability to contemplate new tasks and to assess their feasibility and desirability in relation to alternatives. A good budget structure, in short, could contribute significantly, if indirectly, to the development of an environment in which those who control our political institutions could meaningfully appraise and debate the great objectives of the American society and our ability to attain them within a balanced assortment of public and private activities. Just as the computer has enormously enlarged our capacity to attack problems that in an earlier age could not even be defined, so a budget rationally designed for management use would open new dimensions of administrative potential. Experienced private managers in large corporations have seen this effect as they have improved their own decisionmaking instruments based on information organized for management use. The effect in the area of public administration would be comparable. It should, of course, be emphasized that a well-designed budget, like a high-powered computer, is a neutral tool. It will serve with equal effectiveness those who would shrink the scope of federal action and those who would expand it. A good budget structure has no politics.

The problems created by the present budget structure are not confined to the management of resources in the public domain. To a much greater extent than is commonly recognized, information reported through the federal budgetary process serves important uses in private industry and in university and other nonprofit research centers. The information deficiencies of the present budget affect the performance of analytical, planning, and decisionmaking activities throughout our society.

With a federal budget aggregating roughly one-sixth of the national income, the gross influence of the government's expenditures is, of course, substantial. The size of the budget and its surplus or deficit position are significant inputs to forecasts of the level of general economic activity. More subtle but no less important effects can be traced to the composition of the budget: the principal division between the defense and civilian sectors, the commitments to international aid, farm price supports, space programs, research activities, education, transportation, housing, relief of the helpless and underprivileged, etc. These expenditure patterns can be strong clues to the character of the demand for products and services in both item and geographic detail. When such budget patterns are extended forward for several years, their meaning may be even more significant and their use by private managers more important. Because long lead times are often involved in the translation of resource commitments into end-product availability, knowledge of the probable approximate size of specific federal programs three to five years in the future can serve to improve the quality of private investment decisions. The net result would be a significant advance in the total efficiency of the nation's economic performance as measured by the ratio of inputs to outputs. The planning horizons of private managers would be extended, and the validity and operational confidence of business planning would be correspondingly strengthened.

Against this background one can trace a substantial, although not readily measured, loss in the quality of private economic performance to existing defects in the information yielded by the federal budget.[1] This loss is experienced in misplaced or delayed investment of resources, in added uncertainties in private economic planning, and in a general lowering of the threshold of confidence

[1] See also David Novick and G. H. Fisher, "The Federal Budget as a Business Indicator," *Harvard Business Review*, vol. 38, no. 3 (May–June 1960), pp. 64–72.

on the part of private managers with respect to the rationality and quality of public administration.

Although redesign of the federal nondefense budget structure in the manner proposed in this book would by no means resolve all the difficulties commonly met by economic analysts, it would contribute importantly to progress in the federal portion of the public sector. Another hopeful result might be to encourage comparable progress in the organization of information for the state and local portions of the public sector. Still a third might be to stimulate and support efforts to refine and upgrade data for the private sector. In the long run we might anticipate a valuable gain in understanding the dynamic behavior of the national (and international) economy, with consequent benefits for both private management and public policy.

Research on the social performance of the American economy has also been limited by information deficiencies originating in part in the federal budget. We have only a partial understanding of the relation between the problems associated with the growth of metropolitan areas and federal spending for such objects as urban housing and mass transportation. Private, as well as public, response to ill-serviced needs is impeded, misdirected, or delayed as a result. The present rising concern with such issues as unemployment, urban and rural slums, the quality and content of education, and the occupations and health of retired persons or those displaced from regular employment reflects awareness of both the major problems in the fabric of our society and the limited knowledge of the dynamics of their cause and cure. Whatever the character of the solutions that may evolve through responses to these difficult challenges, whether through private or public action, a federal budget articulated through objective programs, with grouping of related activities and forward projections of funding requirements, can give significant help in formulating plans, appraising costs, and controlling performance against realistic standards.

PROBLEMS OF A PROGRAM BUDGET

The principal recommendation of this book—to introduce into the nondefense areas of the federal government the kind of program analysis that has been installed in the Department of Defense as an integral part of the planning, programming, and budgeting process—is not a simple proposal for easy innovation. Many problems will have to be resolved in developing the design of the recommended programs. Many others will arise in the early phase of the program budget's operation. Some of these problems are conceptual in character, some are operational, while still others are related to political or bureaucratic considerations. The principal difficulties are described in summary form below. They are treated in greater detail throughout the following chapters, together with suggestions for their study and solution.

The initial conceptual problem that must be resolved in achieving even a preliminary blueprint of the grand design of a program budget is the identification of major programs. The central issue is, of course, nothing less than the definition of the ultimate objectives of the federal government as they are realized through operational decisions. Set in this framework, the designation of a schedule of programs may be described as building a bridge between a matter of political philosophy (what is government for?) and the administrative function of assigning scarce resources among alternative governmental objectives. The unique function of a program budget is to implement the conclusions of a political philosophy through the assignment of resources to their accomplishment. The main advantage claimed for the program budget is that it promises to do this more effectively and more efficiently by (1) providing a framework for more clearly defining the alternatives among which choices must be made and (2) creating an information system that will assist in measuring costs in relation to accomplishments.

In the private sector of the economy, the corporate officer is familiar with a parallel problem. A good information system should be related to a firm's decision requirements. In fact, the best information systems are designed specifically to serve management's chosen decision pattern. The prime questions are: What decisions does management have to make in running the business? What information does management need to make these decisions rationally? These are not easy questions, and good answers are developed only through time and flexible experimentation.

There is a dearth of satisfactory standards and ordered, relevant information on performance to be used in appraising efficiency in most areas of federal activity. In consequence, we have generally lacked a clear articulation of management choice. Experienced professional managers will readily see in this situation a more important category of efficiency: not, Are we doing this particular action economically? rather, Should we be doing this action at all, considering what other actions must be omitted if we devote resources to this one? These critical questions cannot be answered —indeed, cannot even be asked—until all activities are laid out in meaningful terms, and until groupings and the resources necessary to their accomplishment have been estimated through an extended period of time.

The first step in the design of a program budget for nondefense activities, therefore, must be a thorough research of the decision process in the federal government. This is a matter of concept and not of organization structure. We have already noted that the bureaucratic organization of the federal establishment (the departments, agencies, offices, etc.) is largely the result of a historical response to political pressures and short-term expediencies. Except accidentally, it does not reflect a rational management decision process that is broadly related to the great ends of democratic government and specifically related to a schedule of alternative programs that express those great ends in terms that can be handled through the decision process. The question of whether a new program budget would be assisted in its operation through a changed bureaucratic structure is an interesting but entirely separate issue, which is not a necessary part of the present discussion.

Complex problems will be discovered in the course of the proposed study since the ultimate product of the research should be, not a description of the decision process as it exists, but rather the delineation of the decision process as it rationally should be. Some of the most difficult matters will undoubtedly result from the fact that in a number of areas no clear objectives have ever been laid down. This undesirable condition has prevailed in the field of international aid and investment, but it can also be found in many domestic areas, including, among others, agriculture, transportation, education, and unemployment.

A related conceptual problem will have to be dealt with concurrently. It is by no means obvious, in advance of careful study, whether a good program structure should be based on components of specific end objectives (e.g., the accomplishment of certain land reclamation targets), on the principle of cost separation (identifying as a program any activity the costs of which can be readily segregated), on the separation of means and ends (Is education a means or an end in a situation such as skill-retraining courses for workers displaced by automation?), or on some artificially designed pattern that draws from all these and other classification criteria. Although it is a basic argument of this book that the prime influence in program-structure design should be the requirements of a rational decision process, the identification of those requirements is a large and difficult undertaking. It should be anticipated that initial concepts will have to be amended and adapted on the basis of operating experience in the years following the introduction of a program budget system. In this connection it is useful to observe that private business organizations have become familiar with comparable problems and have typically made provision for periodic review and flexible adaptation of information systems in response to the changing needs of a dynamic decision process. Firms that have introduced computers in their decision processes, for example, have found it desirable to make substantial changes in the information systems that feed and support the new decision potential opened up by computers.

With the evolution of some concept of a rational decision process will come the principal guidelines for a workable program system. A number of operational problems will promptly become visible. For example, certain broad activity categories that might appear to be rationally grouped for program-budget purposes are presently carried on in more than one government department. International economic activities offer one illustration of this situation. Activities related to the development and protection of natural resources offer another. Support of education is a third. Techniques will have to be worked out for identifying such related expenditure clusters and for bringing them together for making major allocative decisions. Because there may be persuasive reasons for not disturbing the existing patterns of administrative responsibility in the departments and agencies concerned, it will also be necessary to develop a translation grid that will facilitate the delegation of spending authority back to the responsible administrative units. This is no simple matter, and one should anticipate certain bureaucratic resistance. The threat of opposition is not limited to the public bureaucracy. Each administrative unit is likely to have developed its own clientele in the private sector (those served or in some way advantaged by the work of the public unit). Additional strength for direct and indirect resistance will be found among such client groups.

A second operational problem will arise in connection with the program budget's requirement that cost estimates be projected forward for a number of years in all cases where the cost stream is an essential ingredient of a rational decision in allocating resources. Five years might be taken as a reasonable general requirement. Legislators and public administrators have limited experience in doing this. In the case of most large new activities, for example, the common practice has been to estimate and request funding for only first-year costs, with little more than guesses or vague projections for later time periods. This has been done, of course, not only in the interest of avoiding difficult analysis of future requirements, but also to take advantage of "camel's nose" tactics in gaining acceptance of proposals with relatively modest entrance expenses. Full exposure of such matters is a significant part of the case for the program budget. Rational choice in allocating scarce resources demands knowledge of more than going-in costs. But the implementation of this requirement will have to cope with the existing lack of experience in the development of such cost projections, in addition to the bureaucratic opposition from those who prefer to avoid showing high long-term price tags for their recommended projects.

Closely related to the foregoing will be the need to develop staff expertise in cost estimating and analysis in the executive departments, in the Bureau of the Budget, and, probably, in the staffs of certain congressional committees. The possibility of using a program budget as an effective instrument for analysis, planning, and control will depend directly on the quality of the data fed into the total operation. Only rigorous and persistent review of estimates against the test of actual performance will compel the necessary purification of cost data without which the program budget exercise is more game than management performance.

A third operational problem with strong bureaucratic overtones can be anticipated in the need to bring meaning and reason to the aggregation of program components presently implemented in different organizational units. The activation of a program budget is more than an exercise in simple arithmetic. The character, composition, and magnitude of a program oriented toward a defined objective must be determined through coordinated analysis and planning. The Bureau of the Budget would, of course, have an important contribution to make in bringing this about. But the Bureau has a complex role to play in the federal establishment. Its leadership has not commonly found it feasible to attempt to usurp the normal administrative responsibilities of line management in the executive departments. It may suggest, encourage, and assist in the coordinating process that a working program budget would require. But this would leave important problems of accommodation to administrators in the departments. How they might accomplish this in the context of considerations of historic associations, status, prestige, client relationships, congressional relationships, and other pressures is not likely to be the result of simple rules and working procedures. We are face-to-face here with the common organization difficulty that the goals of a total enterprise are not necessarily consistent with the goals of individual units within the enterprise, or with the goals of individual administrators. There is no reason to be overwhelmingly discouraged by this problem, however. Many large organizations have tackled it successfully.

As indicated earlier, this recitation of problems that will probably accompany the formulation and installation of a program budget in the nondefense sectors of the federal government is illustrative and incomplete. The problems are brought to the reader's attention at the outset of the book simply to ensure a proper balance of potential gain and potential effort in the presentation of our fundamental recommendation. They are treated more fully in subsequent chapters, especially in Chapter 11.

INFORMATION AND DECISION IN MANAGEMENT PERFORMANCE

One final comment is in order about the relation of the program-budget proposal to the quality and efficiency of management performance. As a tool for analysis, the program budget represents a considerable advance over the existing budget structure. It should be recognized, however, that its virtues are those of a tool. It will broaden the reach of those charged with decisionmaking responsibility. It will sharpen their grasp of the critical elements in the resource-allocation problems that confront them. It will illuminate questions of choice among alternatives. It will facilitate measures of performance. However, it will *not in itself* provide answers to problems or make decisions for managers. It will not displace management judgment, wisdom, or experience. It will not determine objectives. It will not judge performance. In short, it will enlighten major decision issues and help managers to manage better.

In doing this, the program budget will also contribute to management performance, and to economic and social analysis, in the private sector of the economy. But, again, its assistance will be in the form of providing more and better information for administrative and analytical applications. The size of the positive contribution will be determined, not by the information array made available through the program budget, but by the imagination and skill of those who discover how the information can be used to enlarge and illuminate the problems that they already face and to define new problems that the present information flow has failed to identify.

Chapter 2

CONCEPTUAL FRAMEWORK FOR THE PROGRAM BUDGET

BY ARTHUR SMITHIES

The need for program budgeting arises from the indissoluble connection between budgeting and the formulation and conduct of national policy—or the policy of a state, a city, or a town, as the case may be. Governments, like private individuals or organizations, are constrained by the scarcity of economic resources at their disposal. Not only the extent to which they pursue particular objectives but the character of the objectives themselves will be influenced by the resources available. On the other hand, the extent to which the government desires to pursue its objectives will influence the resources it makes available to itself by taxation or other means. Planning, programming, and budgeting constitute the process by which objectives and resources, and the interrelations among them, are taken into account to achieve a coherent and comprehensive program of action for the government as a whole. Program budgeting involves the use of budgetary techniques that facilitate explicit consideration of the pursuit of policy objectives in terms of their economic costs, both at the present time and in the future.

To be more specific, a modern government is concerned with the broad objectives of defense; law and order; health, education, and welfare; and with economic development, together with the conduct of current business operations, notably the Post Office. No government, whatever its resources, can avoid the need for compromise among these objectives. No country can defend itself fully against all possible external threats. It takes certain risks with respect to defense for the sake of increasing the domestic welfare of its citizens. It must also compromise between the present and the future. The more actively it promotes defense and welfare at the present time, the more it may (under certain conditions) retard the long-run economic development of the country by curtailing both private and public investment in the future. The country will be frustrated in the pursuit of all its objectives if it neglects the effective maintenance of law and order. Yet compromises are made in this area also. No country supports a police force that will detect every crime, and no country enforces every law up to the limit.

Moreover, the character of each major program will depend on the total resources the government can appropriate to its purposes. A small country (at the present time) cannot afford nuclear weapons. Few countries can, or at any rate do, attempt to educate as wide a segment of their population as does the United States. However, countries may vary in their willingness to pursue their national objectives. With much smaller natural resources, the Soviet Union is prepared to make efforts comparable to those of the United States in both the fields of defense and education.

The task of making the necessary compromises among various objectives is the function of planning, programming, and budgeting. To make those compromises, it is necessary that the various government activities be expressed in terms of a common denominator, and the only common denominator available is money. It is difficult to compare the relative merits of an additional military division and an additional university. It is often more feasible to compare the relative merits of spending an additional billion dollars in one direction or the other. But to make that comparison it is necessary to know how much an additional billion dollars will add to military strength and how much to university education. While defense and education cannot be measured in simple quantitative terms, quantitative information can throw light on the consequences of spending money in various directions.

There are, however, a multitude of ways in which money can be spent on defense or education. To make intelligent comparisons, each of these major functions must be broken down into meaningful subfunctions. Modern defense at least requires considerations in terms of strategic forces and limited war forces. Education must be broken down at least into primary, secondary, and tertiary education. Major programs should thus be considered in terms of subprograms, and at the end of the scale one reaches the manpower, material, and supplies used by the government in support of these activities. Such considerations and calculations should lead to the concept of resources (money) used in "optimal" or preferred ways to achieve policy objectives.

Some government decisions relate only to the immediate future in the sense that if they turn out to be wrong, they can be readily reversed. Others, however, relate to a distant future that can be only dimly foreseen. Pure research in particular is in this category, since its consequences are, in the nature of the case, unknown. But governments nevertheless must make critical decisions with respect to the resources they devote to particular kinds of research as well as to research in the aggregate. At a lower order of difficulty, critical decisions with respect to transportation, resource development, and the development of weapon systems relate to the next decade rather than the next year. All budgeting is essentially a matter of preparing for the future, but modern budgeting involves long-range projections into a highly uncertain future.

The basic point of view of this book is that a government can determine its policies most effectively if it chooses rationally among alternative courses of action, with as full knowledge as possible of the implications of those alternatives. The requirement of choice is imposed on it by the fact that any government is limited by the scarcity of resources. It is fundamental to our culture that rational choice is better than irrational choice. The government must choose not only among various courses of government action, but also between the government's total program and the private sector of the economy. The task of choice is not rendered easier by the fact that a substantial part of the government's program is designed to affect the future performance of the private economy. The primary purpose of program budgeting is to facilitate the making of these difficult choices.

Planning, programming, and budgeting is the focus of the process of comparison and coordination. In line with the foregoing paragraphs it involves:

1. Appraisals and comparisons of various government activities in terms of their contributions to national objectives.

2. Determination of how given objectives can be attained with minimum expenditure of resources.

3. Projection of government activities over an adequate time horizon.

4. Comparison of the relative contribution of private and public activities to national objectives.

5. Revisions of objectives, programs, and budgets in the light of experience and changing circumstances.

These operations are inherent in any planning, programming, and budgetary process. Program budgeting involves more explicit recognition of the need to perform them than has been traditional. It also involves the application of new analytical techniques as an aid to the exercise of the human judgment on which choices must ultimately rest.

It should be clear from this statement of the budgetary problem that the traditional distinction between policymaking and budgeting, or between setting of goals and deciding on how to attain them, is inadequate and misleading. Although the government can have a general desire and intention to defend the country, it cannot have a defense objective that is operationally meaningful until it is aware of the specific military implications of devoting resources to defense; and as part of that awareness, it should know the consequences of using defense resources in alternative ways. The question of allocative efficiency is thus intimately bound up with the question of the determination of goals. An adequate programming system must serve both purposes.

Governments can differ by temperament and institutional arrangements in the relative weights they give to the formulation and pursuit of goals, and the attainment of efficiency in the sense of minimizing costs of particular activities. A "crash program" devised with scant attention to efficiency may reach the moon in 1970. Preoccupation with efficiency may delay the successful event until 1980. However, crash programs can fail utterly, through lack of consideration of factors that would emerge in deliberate analysis.

Even in World War II, however, the overriding condition of scarcity placed limits on the pursuit of military abundance. As mobilization proceeded, competition between military output and civilian supply became acute. While many public and private investment projects could be deferred, supplies of canned foods, clothing, and transportation for the noncombatant population had to be maintained for the sake of the war effort itself. Basic materials—notably steel, copper, and aluminum—and manpower were closely allocated. Special programs were set up for rubber and petroleum. Even though allocation through financial controls receded into the background, the need for efficient allocation asserted itself strongly in other ways.[1] On the other hand, the successful strategy of World War II consisted of producing more of everything that was needed, so that military commanders could concentrate on military victory unhampered by the limitations of scarcity.

The United States, nevertheless, had options denied to most other countries. The political radical can deride preoccupation with efficiency as a delaying tactic. Conservatives can emphasize it for the same reason. Other countries have less freedom of choice. The plans of many of the underdeveloped countries have been frustrated through failure to pay attention to the elementary economics of choice. Considerations of comparative advantage have been ignored for encouraging indiscriminate *import* substitution. Public enterprises have been inefficiently planned and operated. As a result of such experiences, realization is dawning that, from the point of view of development, the basic principles of efficient allocation cannot be ignored.

Since all governments are confronted with the problem of scarcity, the logic of the decisionmaking process is independent of the form of government, even though outcomes may differ widely. All governments are concerned with defense, welfare, development, and law and order. In an authoritarian government initial preferences among these objectives depend on the ambitions and values of a central authority. But authority is constrained by resource limitations and by the fact that any authority is less than absolute in its ability to enforce its will on the people. Recent events in Russia and China emphasize the point.

In a democratic government the process is more indirect. Democracies also depend on leadership, but they depend on democratic consent. Leaders must educate and respond to public opinion. They must propose programs that will serve the national interest and also maintain them in power. Whichever of these objectives is uppermost in their minds, the basic task of allocation remains; and its performance reflects the combined judgment of the leadership and the public concerning the contribution of government expenditures to national objectives. The thesis of this book rests on the

[1] See David Novick, Melvin Anshen, and W. C. Truppner, *Wartime Production Controls* (New York: Columbia University Press, 1949).

assumption that society benefits to the extent that such choices are made in the light of the fullest possible information concerning their implications.

PROGRAM BUDGETING IN THE FEDERAL GOVERNMENT

For half a century there has been dissatisfaction in the United States with traditional budgetary methods, and some notable improvements have been made. A brief survey of that history will help to indicate the possibilities, as well as the difficulties, of further improvement.

Traditionally, budgeting has been conducted in terms of executive departments and their subdivisions. The traditional method of reviewing a department budget is to scrutinize proposed increases or decreases in objects of expenditure, with particular emphasis on personnel of various grades, and with emphasis on supplies and equipment as the activities of the department dictate. Such a system has advantages from the point of view of administrative control and, in highly simplified situations, could meet the requirements set out above. To the extent that every department or subdivision performed an identifiable function, the total expenditures, and particularly changes in them, might serve as rough indicators of the government's program. In the pre-World War II Army, numbers of officers and men were better indicators than they are today. In the Department of Justice, changes in the number and grades of lawyers in the various divisions are some indication of changes in the orientation of the policy of the Department. If such indicators are relied on, the task of the budget reviewer is simply to see to it that the Army does not house itself too comfortably or that the lawyers do not have too many secretaries.

The traditional method is not and never has been adequate. The name of a department or a bureau is not sufficient to describe what it does. Nor are numbers or types of personnel employed an adequate measure of the functions they perform. Furthermore, the traditional budget period of a single year throws little light on the significance of expenditures whose effects may be spread over the next decade.

The inadequacies of the traditional system, however, have long been apparent. As early as 1912, President Taft's Commission on Economy and Efficiency recommended drastic changes in existing procedures. The Commission stated:

The best that a budget can do for the legislator is to enable him to have expert advice in thinking about policies to be determined. His review of the economy and efficiency with which work has been done should be based on facts set forth in the annual reports of expenditures which would supplement the budget.

To the administrator [i.e., the head of an executive department] the advantage to be gained through a budget is the ability to present to the legislature and to the people, through the Chief Executive or someone representing the administration, a well-defined, carefully considered, lucidly expressed welfare program to be financed, and in presenting this, to support requests for appropriation with such concrete data as are necessary to the intelligent consideration of such a program.

To the Executive [i.e., the President] the advantage to be gained lies in his ability to bring together the facts and opinions necessary to the clear formulation of proposals for which he is willing actively to work as the responsible officer. To the people the advantage is the fact that they are taken into the confidence of their official agents. Therein lie the practical use and purpose of the budget.

Consequently, the Commission proposed, first, a comprehensive executive budget (which had not previously existed); second, a classification of the budget in terms of programs or functions, and also a classification based on the distinction between capital and current items; and third, thorough and systematic review of the budget *after the fact*. These innovations were to be added to the traditional budget and resulted in a proposal of extraordinary complexity.

Although the Commission laid the foundation for all subsequent reforms, the political climate of the time did not permit action. In fact, nothing was done until 1921, when the drive for economy after World War I produced the Budget and Accounting Act of that year, which required the President to submit a comprehensive executive budget and set up the Bureau of the Budget as the staff agency to assist him. The comprehensive budget was an essential step in achieving the comparison of alternatives in the executive branch, but the act left departmental budgets and procedures for preparing them unchanged.

Further progress toward a program budget was delayed until after World War II, when the movement again gained impetus—a generation after the Taft Commission. In 1949 the Hoover Commission recommended that "the whole budgetary concept of the federal government should be refashioned by the adoption of a budget based upon functions, activities, and projects: this we designate a 'performance budget'." The recommendation was made a legislative requirement by the National Security Act Amendments of 1949 and the Budgeting and Accounting Procedures Act of 1950. The Second Hoover Commission in 1955 recommended a "program budget" and proposed improvements in the government accounting system that would facilitate budgeting on a cost basis.

The result has been significant change and improvement in the presentation and format of the federal budget, and the change in format has produced a significant change in the methods by which the budget is prepared and considered both in the executive branch and Congress. The old "greensheets" of detailed personnel requirements, which once formed the central pivot of budget examination, have now receded into the background and are included merely as an appendix to the President's budget.

In the immediate postwar period and, of course, before, personal services were the heart of the matter. Budget examination in both the executive branch and Congress consisted mainly of "marking up" the greensheets. Even for a construction agency such as the Navy's Bureau of Ships, procurement of material appeared as a one-line item in the President's budget, while details of personal services occupied three hundred lines. Classification by activities was rudimentary; and at the present time in many bureaus the budget for each bureau is classified by objects and not by significant activities.

The recent changes in classifications are by no means formalities. They reflect changes in the approach of budget officers and congressional committees to their tasks of review and appraisal. Able and conscientious efforts are being made throughout the government to appraise activities in terms of their effectiveness in promoting national objectives. In this respect the idea of program budgeting has been accepted in principle. The main problem at the moment is not to inject a new idea but to improve on what has already been done, and there is still abundant room for improvement.

In two major respects there is still need for reconsideration or revision of previous practice. In the first place, programs or activities are still propounded and considered mainly within the limits of the existing bureaus or departments in which they occur. Even if two or more bureaus or departments conduct activities that are essentially complementary or competitive, those activities are not considered together. To take some obvious examples: In agriculture, the price-support program has to contend with a wheat surplus. At the same time, its research program is devising methods for increasing wheat production! At the departmental level, the failure to achieve coordination among the water resource programs of the Department of the Interior, the Corps of Engineers, and the Department of Agriculture has been a long-standing embarrassment to the government. The President's Message on the budget, however, is arranged in terms of major programs that cut across department lines. For instance, all expenditures in natural resources are grouped as a single major program, irrespective of what department conducts them. But this does not mean that decisions are made in a similar way or that information has been or can be obtained in the form essential to the appropriate decisions.

A second major defect of the present budget is its short time span of one year. It is still mainly concerned with appropriations and expenditures for the succeeding year and contains figures only for the year just completed and estimates for the current year and for the year to which it relates. This may be adequate for many administrative activities, but as pointed out above, it is thoroughly inadequate for procurement of long lead-time items and for construction projects. Whether projections over a number of years should be published in the formal budget is an open question. But there can be little doubt that they should be available to the executive and congressional authorities who review the budget.

The defense budget is a special case that will be discussed in detail in Chapter 4. At this stage it will suffice to indicate with great brevity what has been done since World War II. Despite the creation of the Department of Defense in 1947, the defense budget consisted essentially of budgets for the three separate Services. The total arrived at by the President and the Secretary of Defense was shared among the Services according to some fairly arbitrary formula rather than by consideration of the contribution of the Services to the defense program as a whole or by consideration of programs that cut across Service lines.

In 1949 Congress ordered so-called performance budgets to be submitted for each Service. Prior to that time, budgets had been prepared for the Army and the Navy based on estimates made by their technical services. In the Army, for instance, separate budgets were prepared for the Quartermaster Service, the Transportation Service, the Ordnance Service, etc. Such an arrangement had little merit from the point of view of determining requirements with reference to the mission of the Army. The new performance budget adopted a different classification system, which is now in use. The major headings are Military Personnel; Operation and Maintenance; Procurement; Military Construction; and Research, Development, Test, and Evaluation.

From the point of view of relating the budget to national strategy, this arrangement has little apparent advantage over the old one. A budget constructed on these lines does not permit the Secretary of Defense or the President to tell what provision is being made to increase the capacity to defend the United States, to engage in operations in Asia, etc. However, this budget is an improvement in some respects. It corresponds to major areas of general staff responsibility.

Moreover, it also makes some distinction between the present and the future. Military personnel and operation and maintenance are mainly concerned with current operations. Procurement and construction mainly relate to the investment in equipment for the future, while research and development relates to the more remote future. Thus, if each of the Services had a clear-cut mission, a projection of the present budget over, say, a five-year period could give a coherent picture of military costs for each mission. There would still remain the vital problem of assessing the military effectiveness of the cost incurred.

In 1961 a major change was made by adding a programming system to the existing budget system. Since then decisions have been made on the basis of five-year programs relating to the Department of Defense as a whole, regardless of Service distinctions.

These decisions are subsequently translated into the existing annual budget categories for each Service. During the process of translation and compilation of the budget, minor but not major revisions are made. The President's budget is presented both on a program basis and on a conventional basis for the budget period. The five-year projections are not published for general use. The major programs are Strategic Retaliatory Forces, Continental Air and Missile Defense Forces, General Purpose Forces (including most of the Army and the Navy), Airlift and Sealift Forces, Reserve and National Guard Forces, Research and Development, and General Support. In addition, Retired Pay, Civil Defense, and Military Assistance are included as separate programs.

Budget and program procedures in the Defense Department are the subject of Chapter 4. For the present we shall be concerned with the logic of the program structure that has been adopted, as a complicated and revealing case study of the nature, the possibilities, and the limitations of program budgeting.

WHAT IS A PROGRAM?

In the federal government the terms "program," "performance," "activity," and "function" are all used more or less interchangeably. Although there may be shades of difference among them, there is no consistent pattern.[2] Research, for instance, may be designated by some organizations as an activity and by others as a program. "Program" and "performance" are often used synonymously. The federal budget often uses the expression "program and performance." The performance budget of the Defense Department does not correspond to the present program structure. These ambiguities and inconsistencies of language reveal the ambiguities of the underlying situation. As we shall see, there are a number of criteria for the designation of an operation as a program. The defense program structure itself reveals a variety of criteria that will be discussed in a moment. Meanwhile, light may be shed on the problem by beginning with a hypothetical example outside government.

[2] For other discussions of this point, see Don S. Burrows, "A Program Approach to Federal Budgeting," *Harvard Business Review*, Vol. 27, No. 3 (May 1949), 272–285; David Novick, *Which Program Do We Mean in "Program Budgeting"?* P-530 (Santa Monica, Calif.: The RAND Corporation, May 12, 1954).

Consider the question of the organization of a highly integrated automobile manufacturing corporation that produces not only automobiles but also rubber, iron, and steel. The objective of the corporation is to maximize its profits. But it is hard to imagine that the corporation would conduct operations simply by reference to that objective. If it produces several brand names, it is likely to have a separate program and separate organization for each of them. Each brand name presumably is intended to appeal mainly to a separate section of the market. Or the company may put brands in active competition with each other, as General Motors does.

Programming of final products is hardly likely to be sufficient. Increased demands from the top for rubber and steel do not immediately evoke increases in supply, which may not be forthcoming unless capacity to produce steel and rubber has been built in anticipation of increased demand for automobiles. Consequently, the corporation would probably have both a steel and a rubber program that would attempt to anticipate final demands. Moreover, there would be no point in having separate steel and rubber programs for each of the final products. Errors could be avoided and economies achieved by having single organizations supply steel and rubber to the several final product divisions. Furthermore, those concerned with the manufacture of final products are unlikely to be expert in steel and rubber technology. Effective division of labor commends a vertical division of functions.

The long-run future of the organization will depend on the research and development it conducts. Some research and development may be connected with specific brands, the production of which can be anticipated; in that event it can be included in the final product programs. But some research is of common benefit to all final products, and some will relate to models of the future that will come into production beyond the horizon of any feasible production plans. Consequently, a separate research program is likely to be called for.

It should be noted from this example that the question of programming and that of organization are closely connected. A central management might control the entire operation, in which case the separate programs would aid it in its thinking about its problems. What is more likely is that the need to program will also pattern the administrative shape of the organization and will dictate some decentralization of authority.

Another example from outside government, very different from the corporation, is a liberal arts college. Its objectives are not to make money, nor directly to equip its students to make money. It does not measure its success by the incomes subsequently earned by its alumni—although it is not entirely uninterested in that subject. For objectives it must rely on general statements, such as the advancement of knowledge and equipping its students for citizenship in a free society. Such general statements do not tell it what to teach or what to investigate. And it would not accept the view that its function is simply to teach students what they want to learn. Yet the resources of the college are limited. It must allocate its resources.

The college solves its problems by setting up programs that it believes will throw light on its objectives. It thinks of its faculty as being concerned broadly with science and the humanities, and with teaching and research within these categories. While it cannot define its objectives *precisely*, it believes that their attainment will be furthered by its performance in these areas. The college begins with some allocation and then from year to year considers reallocations that it believes will further its (undefined) objectives. It may be able to make reasonably sensible choices among alternative courses of action, even though its objectives are not clearly defined.

In pursuing its policies, the administration of the university is subject to a number of constraints. It has to persuade its students to accept the relative emphasis it gives to science and the humanities, and its faculty to accept the allocation between teaching and research. Otherwise, it may lose both students and faculty in competition with other institutions. The programming problems of the college are not unlike those of government in fields such as defense or welfare. When government undertakes to produce the marketable goods, its problem is closer to that of private business.

Let us now examine the new program structure of the Department of Defense. Although we do not know precisely why that particular structure was adopted, it is instructive to guess at the possible reasons. The structure clearly derives from the strategic doctrine that distinguishes between general war and limited war, and from the view that the use of large strategic weapons for limited purposes is "unthinkable." It implies that one of the main programming tasks is to achieve the most effective balance between strategic and limited war forces.

Strategic Retaliatory Forces qualifies as a program for a number of reasons. First, it is directly related to a major objective of defense policy, and in principle, requirements for these forces can be calculated from knowledge of the enemy threat and of the capability of our own weapons. Second, the program can be neatly broken down into a number of program elements, such as Polaris, Minuteman, manned bombers, etc. These elements are to some degree substitutes[3] for one another, so that there is a problem in determining a preferred mix. Third, the program cuts across Service lines. The program concept thus serves as an instrument of coordination of the Services.

Continental Defense could be regarded as an element of strategic deterrence. Its main purpose at present is to protect and to warn the strategic forces; and when force requirements are reduced, the better the forces are defended. However, if extensive and effective defense of cities ever becomes a reality, Continental Defense, although still linked to strategic concepts, would have more meaning as a separate program.

General Purpose Forces occupies about 85 per cent of the budget and includes the forces designed to meet nonstrategic attacks in the Western Hemisphere, in the Far East, in Southeast Asia—in fact, all over the world. The threat is not clearly defined, and neither are the requirements for meeting it. Clearly this program is of a very different character from the other two and does not lend itself as readily to analysis in terms either of its components or of its specific contribution to defense objectives. One possibility of improvement that suggests itself is that the program should be broken down on a regional basis; but this meets with the serious objection that forces can be transferred from one region to another, and one cannot predict whether threats will appear in isolation, in sequence, or simultaneously.

Airlift and Sealift is logically a component of General Purpose Forces. It is designed to increase mobility and hence permit economies with respect to the size of forces. It is presumably considered

[3] There are also complementarities that tend to complicate the total problem.

as a separate program because its components, airlift and sealift, should be considered as substitutes for each other, and the best mix should be achieved.

Research and Development includes certain items that are identified with particular mission area programs when these items are in the advanced stages of development and when they can appropriately be directly related to mission areas. Otherwise, Research and Development is properly considered separately when it is conducted for purposes beyond the horizons of other programs.

General Support, a large item that includes nearly 30 per cent of the total budget, includes not only items such as general overhead, which by its nature cannot and should not be allocated to specific programs, but also an amount that has not yet proved feasible to allocate.

Other programs, such as *Reserves* and *Military Assistance,* have presumably been considered separately for administrative or political reasons.

These comments on defense programming are not intended to disparage the important advances that have been made. They are intended, rather, to indicate the difficulties and the variety of criteria involved in breaking up a highly complicated operation into neat program categories.

Many difficulties in devising a satisfactory program system arise in the field of international relations (apart from defense); and because of the complexity of the problem, budgeting and programming in this area are still unsatisfactory. In the first place, the objectives of foreign policy are diverse, complicated, and amorphous. Only a few years ago the situation seemed simpler. Foreign policy appeared to consist of containing Russian expansion in Europe, ostracizing China, and promoting economic development elsewhere. With that degree of simplification, three major programs suggest themselves: political and military means to implement the first two, and economic aid to implement the third. At the present time, Russia must be distinguished from its European satellites; our allies trade with China; Russia and China are active in the underdeveloped countries; and for our part, sharp distinctions must be drawn among Asia, Africa, and Latin America. Foreign programs must be devised with the realization that a simple foreign policy doctrine is not available.

A second major difficulty is that foreign policy cuts across departmental lines; not only the Department of State and the Department of Defense, but the Agency for International Development, the Department of Agriculture, the Department of the Treasury, the Department of Commerce, the Tariff Commissions, and a growing number of international agencies are concerned with it. Moreover, especially in the economic area, there is an intimate relationship between foreign and domestic policy. A serious depression in the United States would be more harmful to underdeveloped countries than calling off the entire aid program.

A third difficulty, which is closer to the province of this book, is the age-old conflict between the regional and the functional point of view. Or more specifically, should a regional or country breakdown be the primary classification, with the functional breakdown secondary, or should it be the other way around? Emphasis on the functional approach tends to center authority in Washington and creates confusion in the field. Emphasis on the country approach may produce coherence in the field and confusion in Washington. Advocates of either emphasis are encountered with strong counterarguments. Administration must be based on one approach or the other. But for the purpose of planning for the future, perhaps both should run in awkward double harness.

Quite different problems and approaches occur in connection with the programming of resource development, such as power, navigation, and flood control. Such activities are designed mainly to improve the economic performance of the country in the future. Unlike defense or foreign policy, they are intended to produce economic benefits. The difficulties arise because they must be formulated in the context of a mixed economy, and in most cases there are direct or indirect private alternatives that are not subject to government planning. (Even though navigation is the exclusive province of the government, there are private transportation alternatives to inland waterways.)

The programming method used by the government should attempt to assess the costs and benefits of individual projects, in comparison with private and other public alternatives. The program, then, consists of the most meritorious projects that the budget will accommodate. Meritorious projects excluded from the budget provide arguments for increasing its size, in the same way that excluded defense or foreign aid activities provide a case for increasing those segments of the budget.

There are difficulties inherent in the specific project approach. The attempt is to apply profit criteria to public projects analogous to those used in evaluating private projects. This involves comparison of monetary values of present and future costs and benefits. But in many important cases, such as urban highways, recreation parkways, free bridges, and flood control dams, the product of the government's investment does not directly enter the market economy. Consequently, evaluation requires imputation of market values. For example, the returns on a bridge have been estimated by attempting to value the time saved by users. Such measurements necessarily contain a strong element of artificiality.

In other cases the purpose of government investment is to alter the character of the market economy, either for the nation as a whole or for particular regions within it. In such instances returns should be measured in terms of the market values that will exist as a result of the investment, rather than those that prevail before it is undertaken. This difficulty has led economists and planners to attempt to construct "shadow" prices as a basis for their measurements.

In still other cases the government undertakes investments that require a longer view of the future than private enterprise is willing to undertake. It is therefore prepared to accept a lower rate of return than that yielded by private investment in other directions. But how much lower the return should be is not revealed by market prices.

These remarks indicate that project evaluation cannot be achieved entirely by objective economic analysis. In most cases there is a strong political element in the choice of projects. To serve the national interest, such choices should be made in the light of overall policies with respect to economic development. Attempts to build up such policies from the consideration of particular projects seem to give undue scope for the influence of particularistic political interests and do not appear to add to the formulation of inherent national objectives. The question is therefore raised whether, in fields such as transportation and natural resources, overall programs should not be formulated into which particular projects can be fitted.

If so, what should such programs contain? Description of an area as an activity or a program implies that its components are more closely in competition with each other than they are with elements outside the program. Should urban transport be placed in competition with international transport more closely than with other aspects of urban development? Should international transport be regarded as a component of transportation, or of foreign trade, or of both? In much current discussion it seems to be taken for granted that transportation is a natural program category. But that conclusion is by no means obvious.

Similar problems and difficulties arise in connection with other fields, such as education, health, and welfare. Some aspects of education and health are designed to increase the economic effectiveness of the labor force. Others are designed to enrich the social and intellectual lives of individuals. Education in particular is held essential for the political health of the country. Possibly the economic aspects of education and health should be considered not only as components of education and health generally but also as parts of a national manpower program.

In the United States in particular there is a further major difficulty connected with activities in the resource and welfare fields. The activities of the federal government are designed to supplement those of the private economy, or to supplement and stimulate state and local governments. Should plans in these areas relate to the nation as a whole, covering the activities of the private economy and all levels of government? To what extent should the federal government attempt to implement such overall plans by controls over the private economy or conditional grants-in-aid to other levels of government? Presumably, our belief in the competitive market economy and our commitment to the federal system preclude thoroughgoing resort to central planning and control in any important area. The federal government is thus faced with a dilemma with which it must live as best it can.

This discussion shows that designation of activities as programs is no easy or trivial matter. The way in which a program structure is set up for the government as a whole, or for any major segment, can have a profound effect on the decisions that are reached, so that the design of programs should be regarded as an important part of the decisionmaking process. The following paragraphs indicate some of the criteria that should be taken into account.

1. An important criterion for a program structure is that it should permit comparison of alternative methods of pursuing an imperfectly determined policy objective. Thus, the need for public assistance can be clarified and analyzed by breaking down the problem into the needs arising from old age, economic dependence, physical disability, and unemployment. Limited resources prevent provisions for all cases under these categories. Despite the absence of a clear-cut concept of social welfare, a satisfactory comparison among these various categories must be formed.

2. Even though objectives may be clearly defined, there are usually alternative ways of accomplishing them. Thus, in the Defense Department, Airlift and Sealift is designated as a separate program, largely because a requirement can be accomplished by various combinations of air and sea transport.

3. Programs may also consist of a number of complementary components, none of which can be effective without the others. A health program requires doctors, nurses, and hospitals in the right proportions.

4. A separate program may be needed where one part of an organization supplies services to several others. Economies are to be expected if a department has a single computer operation rather than separate ones in each bureau. Since the acquisition of computer facilities will have an appreciable lead time, departmental planning is likely to require that computers be budgeted as a separate program, even though they are far removed from the end objectives of the department.

5. An organization's objectives may require it to adopt overlapping structures. This need is evident in foreign affairs, where both geographical and functional programs are required. It is also evident within the country, where regional as well as national requirements must be considered.

6. A further criterion relates to the time span over which expenditures take effect. The uncertainties of the future usually preclude firm estimates of requirements for government services beyond a limited period, say, five years. Yet research and development and investment must be undertaken to provide for a longer-run future. Even where such activities can be identified with some major program, they should be dealt with as separate subprograms because the uncertainties of the longer-run future should affect the

character of the activities undertaken. In other cases such long-range activities may not be identifiable with any current end-product program. In that event it is obvious that they should be dealt with separately. In fact, differences in time spans of various activities may be the leading characteristic of an organization's program structure. A growing undertaking may think primarily in terms of the division of its functions among production, investment, and research and development.

The need for programming arises from the limitations of human beings and the obstinacy of the physical environment. In the first place, it is not sufficient to invoke the Constitution and seek to promote the general welfare. The general welfare can only be understood in terms of components and by choosing among them. Second, the process of relating ends to means is immensely complicated in a modern society. The process must be broken down into a hierarchy of optimizations and sub-optimizations. Third, results cannot be achieved instantaneously, and frequently long lead times are involved. Moreover, resources once committed to a purpose are not readily transferable elsewhere. Consequently, programming is required.

A general distinction between the final and intermediate programs of an organization may be useful. Final programs can be regarded as those that contribute directly to its general objective. Intermediate programs are operations singled out for treatment as programs that contribute to final programs in the immediate or remote future. Thus, in the Department of Defense, strategic forces, general purpose forces, and possibly air defense can be considered final programs, while all the others are intermediate. From the point of view of the government as a whole, however, defense becomes the final program, and its components are intermediate.

PROGRAM PREPARATION, APPRAISAL, AND ANALYSIS

Preparation

Up to this point in the discussion, programming and budgeting have not been distinguished from each other, and program budgeting has been regarded as a process that pays due regard to policy objectives, costs, and time dimensions. We must now modify these simplifications and regard programming and budgeting as different but complementary components of the same operation. Every organization, in or out of government, finds it necessary to have an annual budget that represents a detailed and feasible plan of action for the ensuing year. Every organization, however, must look beyond the next year, even to make coherent plans for that year. Programs and budgets should clearly be consistent with each other. Departures of the budget from the program call for revisions of the program, and program revisions call for changes in the budget (except where minor adjustments in the budget for the next fiscal year are made to reflect purely technical financing requirements, in which case there may be no significant impact on the program).

In some instances budgeting and programming may be identical processes. In the Antitrust Division of the Department of Justice, for instance, the basic cost factor is the number and types of lawyers employed. The requirement derives from the vigor of the government's enforcement policy and the nature of the cases that fall within its net. Antitrust cases cannot be disposed of in one year; consequently, budgeting must look beyond a single year. Apart from the fact that typewriters and secretaries can be adequately dealt with on an annual basis, there is unlikely to be any difference between the requirements of effective programming and effective budgeting.

In other cases, programming and budgeting methods should differ markedly. Consider, for instance, the federal prison system. The system should program for a number of years because it must have a cell for every prisoner. The number of prisoners will depend on future crime rates and enforcement policies. If techniques of detention, punishment, and correction remain the same, the program and its cost can be derived from the expected number of prisoners, changes in price levels, wage rates, conviction costs, etc. Further refinements should take into account change in prison methods that could lead to economies or increased costs: changes in length of sentences, the effects of civil rights legislation and of abolition of capital punishment, etc. Program estimates of this character require human abilities, research methods, and procedures far different from those required to produce a detailed estimate of cost for the *ensuing year*. Although next year's budget should be derived from the program and be consistent with it, it should also be separate.

In contrast to the prison system, programming for defense is vastly more complicated. Defense consists of a number of major programs that are in competition with each other for the resources available for defense, and whose program elements are in competition with each other. The President and the Secretary of Defense should be able to decide whether an increase in one area should result in contraction in another or an increase in the total size of the budget. Changes in external threats, technology, management techniques, and strategic doctrine all demand that programs be subject to continual revision. Consequently, it is clear that programming in defense and other agencies responsible for interrelated programs should be a highly centralized operation, carried out by flexible methods and capable of rapid revision. But the centralized operation should not be permitted to occur in a vacuum. Its success will depend heavily on the extent to which ideas and experience at all levels of the Department can be fed into it.

Ideally the process of revision should be continuous and comprehensive. Every year should, in principle, be the first year of a new program. The need for comprehensive revision derives from the fact that the elements of a program are frequently highly interdependent. Revision of any one element should call for reconsideration of all others. In practice, comprehensiveness may be too costly in time, effort, uncertainty, and confusion. However, the built-in tendencies toward rigidity in any system must be guarded against. In this respect a centralized programming system is likely to be more flexible than a conventional budget system, which is particularly responsive to the forces of inertia throughout the organization.

The need for flexibility has an important bearing on the time span that programs should cover. The very existence of a program implies some loss of flexibility. By reason of having adopted it, the organization reduces its freedom to do something different in future years, since a conscious act of revision is required. On the other hand, investment projects, to say nothing of research and development, undertaken now must be based on some view of a highly uncertain future. Time spans should be long enough but not unnecessarily long.

The dilemma could be partially resolved if programs could be expressed in terms of ranges rather than single figures. If the ranges included genuine upper and lower limits, it would become clear that projection beyond a limited period was not operationally meaningful. Ranges and more elaborate methods for taking uncertainty into account have been frequently advocated but rarely adopted. One approach is to program for limited time horizons but to recognize that important items in the program will yield their benefits beyond the horizon. The imposition of a horizon and the knowledge that there is something beyond it should stimulate the design of projects that could be adapted to conditions that at the present time can be only dimly foreseen.

Appraisal

Both the usefulness and the feasibility of programming depend on one's ability to appraise and analyze past and current experience. The directions and techniques of future policy depend critically on the quantitative and the qualitative data derived from the past, present, and near future. Rational planning can be applied to new departures, such as ballistic missiles, only to the extent that they are comparable with something done in the past. The cost utility of missiles could be appraised initially only by comparison of their expected performance with that of the manned bomber. Now that missiles exist, new generations can be compared with their predecessors, as well as with manned bombers.

Fortunately for the ordinary conduct of life, dramatic breaks with the past are rare. One example is the decision to construct the atomic bomb. It may have been thought at the time that the destructive power of high explosives afforded a basis for comparison, but subsequent experience has shown how naïve were simple and vulgar criteria such as "a bigger bang for a buck." Once the world became imprisoned in the atomic age, however, the feasibility of rational calculation began to assert itself within that world.

We are now at the dawn of the space age. Rational processes do not tell us whether we should go to Mars at all or how soon we should get to Mars. Once we are there, we may be able to think more clearly about other space ventures. Even though the adoption of space exploration as a goal may not be a matter of rational calculation, problems of efficiency arise as soon as the goal is adopted. The resources that the government is prepared to devote to its pursuit are limited by competing claims on the budget. The efficiency with which the operation is carried out may mean the difference between success and failure, given the constraint on available resources. Even though the objective differs from anything that has been undertaken in the past, experience with the design of research, development, and investment in other areas that were once new can be highly useful and relevant.

Consequently, a successful decisionmaking process depends heavily on systematic and thorough accumulation of evidence about the past as a guide to the future. A knowledge of the past is necessary not only to provide experiences analogous to those of the present but to point to methods of improving on past performance. Although this point may seem obvious, it nevertheless needs emphasis. Governments seem prone to two kinds of error in this connection. On the one hand, past experience is simply reproduced through failure to analyze its relevance for the present. A striking example is provided by the Korean War mobilization—both in the pattern of government organization and in the long-range strategy, such as building up an industrial base. Preparations for the long-run future (as distinct from merely fighting the Korean engagement) showed remarkably little awareness of the nature of nuclear war—although we were already in the atomic age. The reason is that those who were called upon to organize the Korean undertaking had little to go on except their World War II experience. No systematic attempts had been made to appraise that experience and adapt it to future requirements. But governments also tend to make the opposite kind of mistake by failing to recognize that history does afford instances of problems closely analogous to those of the present. The United States is not exempt from these tendencies. The government does not preoccupy itself extensively with historical analyses.

In the budgetary area, narrowly defined, recording one aspect of the past has been an important preoccupation. Budgeting has been traditionally associated with accounting. But government accounting systems have been largely designed to check on the honesty of officials and to limit their exercise of discretion. This type of accounting has in turn been reflected in traditional methods of budgeting for the future. As in business, the government in recent years has recognized the need for cost accounting. Improvements have been most marked in the corporation area. They are far less evident among the regular departments and agencies. But it is doubtful whether any accounting system per se will provide all the cost information needed for adequate program analysis.

Reporting on costs, however, is only one side of the problem. Equally important, and far more difficult, are the questions on the benefit side. How well is a long-range research program succeeding? Is public health being improved, or is it deteriorating? Does the fact that we have no war mean that potential enemies are being deterred by our forces? How do we compare a world with foreign aid with a world without it? Can such questions as these be answered systematically? Or must detailed information on costs be associated with crude intuition on benefits? This last may be true: the assessment of benefits depends largely on judgment and intuition rather than on precise measurement.

Analysis

When attention moves from the past to the future, two major questions arise separately or in combination. First, how effective is a program in attaining its intended objective? Second, can existing program results be accomplished at lower cost? These questions attempt to draw a distinction between the *effectiveness* of a program in achieving its objective and the *efficiency* with which it is carried out. For instance, it may be possible to consider the effectiveness of the antitrust program under the present organization of the division. It should also be possible to decide whether the same results could be more efficiently achieved by reorganizing the division. For instance, efficiency might be increased by having fewer senior lawyers and more assistants, or vice versa.

The distinction between effectiveness and efficiency, when it can be made, is useful for analytic purposes. But in important instances, the distinction is arbitrary, and possibly misleading. Consider an analogy from the market economy. If an automobile is perfectly standardized, it is possible to consider separately the demand for it and the cost of production. But suppose a new technology produces a different kind of car that has greater consumer appeal. The distinction between efficiency and effectiveness becomes much more difficult. If the technology produced helicopters that displaced automobiles, the distinction might be meaningless. In these circumstances, total value produced must be compared with total costs. The number of cars loses significance as a precise measurement. It becomes instead an index of automobile transportation. As such, of course, it may have significant uses.

Likewise in government the feasibility of distinguishing between effectiveness and efficiency depends on the possibility of quantitative measurement of programs. Such measurement is possible in a limited number of cases. Electric power can be measured in kilowatts. Volume of mail handled may be a useful measure of the activities of the Post Office, although the citizen may disagree as he waits impatiently for his mail. Again, the number of miles of highway constructed is a measure, but one wants to know where the highways lead. The number of children educated is a significant figure but is not a measure of either the quantity or quality of education.

In other areas, notably defense and law and order, this type of cardinal measurement is clearly impossible. Nevertheless, it may still be possible to apply the criterion "more or less" to a program. Even though strategic deterrence cannot be measured in precise units, it still seems meaningful to say that deterrence has increased, decreased, or remained the same. If this is possible, the efficiency of the program at any level can be examined separately.

The possibility of ordinal measurement can be increased if trade-off relationships can be established among various program components. The effectiveness of Airlift and Sealift will depend on the numbers of troops transported and the speed of the operation. Experience and analysis may show that transporting 100,000 men in one month is preferable to transporting 150,000 in two months. One may, therefore, be able to say that Airlift and Sealift has increased or decreased, even though the composition of the program has changed materially.

The concepts of efficiency and effectiveness have been emphasized because they serve to indicate the areas in which objective analysis may be possible and those where it is not. The efficiency concept implies that measures taken to achieve economies will not affect the attainment of the objectives of the program when it is carried out at a given level. Consequently, efficiency can be dealt with by analytical methods. The relatively new techniques of operations research and cost-effectiveness analysis (as usually conceived) are all concerned with efficiency questions.

The distinction between effectiveness and efficiency must, however, be used with extreme care. Measures that purport to increase efficiency may have pronounced effects, good or bad, on effectiveness. Government economy campaigns, for instance, often reduce effectiveness, sometimes intentionally, in the guise of eliminating waste. On the other hand, the elimination of undeniable waste may improve the effectiveness of government operations generally. With respect to particular programs, increasing the number of students per teacher will affect the quality of education. On the other hand, removal of cumbersome equipment from aircraft on grounds of efficiency may have unforeseen beneficial effects in terms of range and maneuverability. Where such possibilities exist, questions of cost and effectiveness become thoroughly intermingled.

Economic factors probably dominate the cost side of the government's activities, but there are noneconomic costs as well. Probably the most decisive objection to a civil defense program has been not its economic costs but the destruction of social values that it might involve. The destruction of the beauty of the countryside by superhighways, and of cities by freeways, represents noneconomic costs that are too infrequently recognized. In some cases the final purpose of a program, insofar as the government is concerned, is to produce outputs with economic value. Government production of marketable electric power is a clear-cut example. But as was pointed out above, the purported economic evaluation of many government activities necessarily involves political judgments concerning critical elements in the evaluation.

Many government activities are designed to yield both economic and noneconomic returns. Education is a good example. One of its objectives undoubtedly is to produce an enterprising and skilled labor force that will contribute to economic prosperity. Another is to preserve and enlarge the cultural heritage of the country and, hopefully, to sustain its capacity to govern itself, despite technological advance. Another example is public health. Reduction of working time lost by sickness is one of its benefits. But measures to reduce suffering in old age are not undertaken for economic reasons. The idea of economic measurement has great attractiveness because of the analytic possibilities that it offers, especially to economists. But it is a perversion of human values to push it into areas in which it does not belong.

Even where the effectiveness of programs can be measured in terms of money, that is not the end of the story: programs must be undertaken or not undertaken in competition with other programs that are not so measurable. The President, for instance, may have to decide whether to spend his marginal billion dollars on a new (measurable) dam or on new (nonmeasurable) hospitals for the aged. Such decisions are necessarily political. Also within major programs choices are frequently political rather than technical. There is no purely technical basis for deciding the relative emphasis that should be given to strategic deterrence compared with limited-war capabilities. In agriculture, the decision to support agricultural incomes at some desired level is a political rather than a technical matter.

Some authorities feel that political choices can best be made if politicians listen merely to voices in the air, observe straws in the political wind, or regard their occupation as an amusing bargaining game. Our position is that political choices can be improved if politicians are aided by information and technical analysis concerning the probable consequences of their acts. The technician may be able to point out that some courses of political action will not yield the results desired. For instance, in a poor country overemphasis on welfare, compared with development, may destroy the country's chances of both welfare and development.

Ultimately, decisions are made by individuals, groups, or legislative bodies exercising their informed judgment. One can hope that such decisions will be improved if they are made in the light of all available evidence and the evidence is marshaled in an orderly way. Furthermore, such procedure may help to avoid the political bargaining and logrolling that mars rather than makes the political process.

There is a useful parallel to be drawn between political and legal processes. The decisions of judges or juries cannot be appraised by objective standards. They depend on adversary procedures that follow well-established rules. If those rules are violated, decisions are upset on appeal. Otherwise, they stand.

A programming approach to government decisionmaking can be thought of as an adversary process. Decisionmaking is arranged so as to permit the competition of ideas, in the light of which decisionmakers make choices among relevant alternatives.

PROGRAMMING AND ORGANIZATION

Our discussion has indicated that there is a close connection between programming and organization. Programs cannot be formulated or carried out unless they are under the direction of a responsible authority. Also, programs cannot be compared and related to each other except by a superior authority responsible for all of them. The question then arises whether the considerations that determine the best program structure for the government are an equally good guide to its organizational structure. Or are there additional or alternative criteria that should govern its pattern of organization? Because differing programming and organizational structures are found to give rise to conflict, there should clearly be no unnecessary incompatibility between them.

At the highest executive level, there is no incompatibility. The President is the head of the administrative executive branch, and since the Budget and Accounting Act of 1921 it has been definitely established that he is responsible for recommending a comprehensive program to Congress.

There should be a strong presumption that the responsibilities of executive departments should be determined by program criteria. Each department should be assigned responsibility for closely related programs that serve the same general objective. The department head in his recommendations to the President should be personally responsible for achieving the best comprehensive program within the scope of his jurisdiction. Within departments, the organization of bureaus, divisions, and sections should be organized on a programmatic basis unless there are good reasons for departing from that rule.

Unfortunately, the problem is not as simple as this. There are good reasons why the requirements of effective administration may diverge from those of effective programming. There are also reasons—not necessarily good—why in fact programming cuts across administrative lines rather than coincides with them:

1. The existing organization of the government has deep historical roots that the strongest President (to say nothing of Congress) is reluctant to disturb violently. Although Presidents have been repeatedly granted reorganization powers, they have been disinclined to use those powers to make major changes.

2. There may be strong arguments for not disturbing the historical situation, even though contemporary programming requirements seem to demand it. There are many proponents of the virtues of competition among the military services, provided the competition is given coherence by a programming system. Moreover, today's programming structure may not be suitable for tomorrow. Stability in the organization may be worth the price of some inconsistency with the structure that contemporary logic seems to require.

3. When overlapping program structures are required, the organization cannot do full justice to both of them. This difficulty is particularly evident when the regional-functional issue arises.

4. A particular activity may be concerned with more than one program, in which case it cannot be assigned without question to one department. The Corps of Engineers is an essential part of military defense, even though its main peacetime concern is civil works. It should not necessarily be transferred to the Department of the Interior, even though that transfer might improve resource programming. The Department of Agriculture has important international as well as domestic activities. Those activities should not necessarily be transferred to the Department of State. International agricultural programs may be evolved more effectively in an agricultural rather than a foreign service environment.

5. The organization required for effective administration of programs may differ from that required for effective formulation. Good administration may require setting up a separate research department, even though all the research done in it can be identified with other programs. Efficiency may be increased by having scientists working together, under the supervision of scientists, rather than by having them scattered through a departmental bureaucracy. In the case of the Post Office, questions relating to

construction, mail deliveries, and technical improvement can be formulated on a functional and nationwide basis. Yet the administration of the Post Office must necessarily be decentralized on a regional and local basis. Furthermore, a single general counsel's office, a single supply organization, and a single car pool is likely to be enough for one department—simply on grounds of administrative efficiency.

These examples suffice to indicate that apart from the forces of tradition and inertia, the criteria for programming and those for effective organization do not coincide, and may diverge materially. Conditions will differ from department to department. In some instances programming may be a highly centralized operation only indirectly concerned with administration. In simpler situations there need be no incompatibility. In still others, programs are intended to overcome the organizational incongruities that cannot feasibly be altered.

The distinction between programming and administration is not as clear-cut as it may appear at first sight. Administration does not consist simply in carrying out directives. In fact, successful administration implies the exercise of discretion by administrators, hopefully in the direction of measuring the efficiency of their operations. Their operating experience should be brought to bear on future program and policy decisions. Moreover, a powerful administrator has his own ideas concerning future policy, and he may not willingly accept the views of planners and programmers. Or he may have useful ideas to contribute. It is hard to conceive of the three military Services carrying out their missions successfully if they had no ideas on national strategy. A central planning organization is unlikely to be successful if it is insulated from operating experience.

Where programming and administration diverge, the way in which the organization as a whole works depends largely on the means employed to ensure that administrators in fact carry out programs. The mere announcement of a program, however well conceived, is not enough. The world is full of national planning organizations that have remarkably little influence on powerful departments. The critical factor is the head of the organization. Without his authority and support, departments or bureaus are likely to go their own way. Moreover, programming can be a potent instrument for increasing the authority of the department head, as Defense Department experience has shown. In fact, some uneasy critics of Defense Department programming allege that that is its main purpose.

Our main concern in the present discussion is the role that the annual budget can play in synchronizing administration with program decisions. The structure of the budget and the financial controls embodied in it can make for harmony or discord. If, for instance, appropriations are made to separate bureaus, as they used to be, the bureaus acquire a large degree of autonomy and freedom from central control. On the other hand, if appropriations are made to the Secretary of a department and he is free to allocate them at his discretion, he is provided with a powerful instrument of coordination. These matters will be discussed in the next section.

PROGRAMMING AND THE ANNUAL BUDGET

Most governments, as well as other organizations, find it necessary to have an annual, or at most a biennial, budget, even though a coherent program may require projections over a much longer period. Governments are concerned with the immediate impact of their budgets. They may attach importance to a budgetary rule, such as a requirement of budget balance, or they may be concerned with the short-run economic impact of the budget. Furthermore, governments require budgets to be prepared with a degree of detail that would be meaningless if extended over a number of years. Although much has been done since 1950 to eliminate irrelevant detail from the budget, effective administration still requires an impressive amount of detail. Thus, the budget is to be distinguished from a program with respect to both its detail and its time horizon. The need for greater detail also means that the budget should be prepared by methods that differ from, but are consistent with, those used in programming.

If programs were reviewed annually in the manner we have proposed, the annual budget process could result in a more appropriate estimate of the costs of the first year of the continually updated program.

The traditional method of preparing the annual budget has been to begin with initial requests from organization units in terms of their objects of expenditure. In some cases this operation has broken down under its own weight. In defense, for instance, budget preparation is in fact largely centralized, even though all installations go through the motions of the traditional method. In other and simpler situations, where there is no conflict between programs and organization, budget and program preparation can be part of the same operation.

In general, budgeting should be associated with both the programming process and the traditional organization unit method. For the program itself to be realized it must be supported by the financial administration and control of the conventional budgetary process. On the other hand, the methods of cost estimation by use of generalized estimating methods that are necessary for a central operation are not precise enough for the preparation of administrative budgets. These methods cannot always be satisfactorily used to provide precise estimates of requirements for personnel, office supplies, foreign travel, and the like. Moreover, commitment to factors such as those implied by military tables of organization tends to prevent improvements in organization, though it may prevent Parkinsonian expansion.

One possibility would be to use centralized methods to arrive at a first approximation to the budget on a program basis. Tentative allocations among organization units could then be made. The detailed budgets would then be submitted in the form of revisions to the initial allocations. These revisions would become the basis of a second approximation to the budget submitted by the department to the President and by him to Congress.

A more radical departure from traditional budget practice would be to rely entirely on centralized methods for the preparation of the President's budget. This would mean that both the President and Congress would have to consider the budget in programmatic terms, through lack of any other kind of information.

After the budget was enacted by Congress, the various bureaus would then submit their budgets as part of a separate administrative budget process. This would be an internal affair whereby the Secretary of the department arrived at a final allocation of funds.

This suggestion may not be as radical as it sounds. Already, in the Department of Defense, money is to a significant degree allocated through an internal funding program after enactment of appropriations. This is necessary because the detailed estimates that go into the budget are already out of date when the budget goes into operation one year later.

Objection would be raised, however, that elimination of detail from the budget would deprive Congress, as well as the Bureau of the Budget, of an opportunity to review matters such as personnel, which has always been one of its main preoccupations. The answer to this objection is that Congress could still require full reporting by organization units. It could review performance after the fact, and the impressions made by this review would naturally influence attitudes toward appropriation ratios for the future. In fact, appropriation hearings now are as much concerned with review after the fact as with consideration of next year's estimates. Progress in the direction suggested here is not out of the question.

Appropriations should, in general, be made for major programs and perhaps for some of their major subdivisions, and within programs separate appropriations would probably be desirable for research and development, construction, major procurement, and current operations. Those for current operations could be made for obligation within the financial year. For long lead-time items, however, longer term funding would be necessary to facilitate effective programming. In fluid situations, where the program structure is and should be subject to change, a more stable appropriation structure may be desirable. The Department of Defense retains its old appropriation structure side by side with its new program system. Whether this should be a transitional or a permanent arrangement remains to be seen.

Designation of appropriations for such purposes, however, does not settle the question of how the funds are allocated within a department. There can be no question but that appropriations should be made to the Secretary of the department and that he should have considerable freedom to transfer funds among closely related activities. Where programs cut across departmental lines, appropriations can be made either to the head of the major department concerned, or to the President.

The need for freedom to transfer has already been recognized. Before World War II, there were more than 2,000 separate appropriation items in the federal budget. By the Act of 1950 the President was given authority to simplify the budget, and consequently by 1955 the number of items for the whole government had been reduced to 375, implying a great increase of freedom to transfer among activities. Agreement to this change represents recognition by Congress that it cannot achieve economy by highly specific appropriations. Rather it must rely on the discretion of administrators to achieve economy in a time sense.

The question that is still unsettled is how funds should be allocated within departments. Here there are two broad alternatives: consumer allocation and supplier allocation. With consumer allocation, the final user of the goods gets the money initially and "purchases" from the supplier. The supplier gets money only for working capital and long-run capital purposes. With supplier allocation, the supplier gets all the money but is required to supply on requisition to the user—without a financial transaction taking place. Under the first system, the commander of a fleet would get the money and would purchase from the naval supplying bureaus. Under the present system the money is allocated to the bureaus and they supply ships, men, guns, and ammunition to the fleets.

Commanders of fleets and armies in time of war have more important concerns than finance. But in other areas, including many defense activities, the principle of consumer allocation has important advantages. It gives the ultimate user some freedom to choose among alternatives and, hence, to economize. He also has a financial opportunity to influence the type of product supplied to him. Although he is not allowed to make a personal profit, he has some of the incentives of a private business man.

Supplier allocation, on the other hand, tends to neglect questions of cost effectiveness and, hence, to encourage inefficiency. In the absence of compelling reasons to the contrary, such as those already noted, the consumer principle is generally preferable. Applying that principle means that funds should be allocated initially to the directors of final programs. They should purchase from organization units or from the directors of intermediate programs. Funds provided directly to the latter would be for capital purposes. With such a system, financial controls could help implement program decisions and achieve coordination in the face of inevitable divergences between the organizational and programming structures.

Annual budgeting has always involved a dilemma. The principal interest of those concerned with fiscal policy has been the total level of expenditures, which in conjunction with the yield of taxation leads to surpluses, deficits, or budget balance. Yet the primary instrument of control available to the government has been the granting of obligational authority, or appropriations. An appropriation gives an administrator authority to incur obligations either by the letting of formal contracts or by making more informal commitments to spend money.

Especially where procurement and construction are concerned, expenditures made in any year result largely from earlier obligations and from still earlier grants of obligational authority. Similarly, obligational authority granted this year may produce expenditures only in future years. Consequently, efforts by the President or Congress to regulate annual expenditures are frequently frustrated because control actions are not taken long enough in advance. Or else those efforts must be concentrated on the obligations that do result in expenditures in the very near future.

Program budgeting could assist annual budgeting by giving a time profile of the government's activities. Ideally, programs should be prepared for a number of years in advance in terms of the obligational authority to be requested, the obligations to be incurred, and the expenditures to be made in each of the future years. In these circumstances future expenditures could be foreseen and a more firm basis for control would exist.

Some critics of the present budgetary process have urged that attention should be focused on still another concept: costs incurred during the year rather than cash expenditures. Such costs would emphasize resources consumed during the year—for example, equipment spares and spare parts used in a maintenance activity, regardless of the year in which they were procured. Thus account would be taken of beginning and year-end inventories. Costs incurred may give a clearer picture of program progress than do expenditures. On the other hand, cash expenditures may be more relevant for fiscal policy. Choice between these concepts is of secondary importance, however, compared with the need to relate them to prior obligations and appropriations.

CONCLUDING COMMENTS

The effectiveness of the programming-budget system will depend strongly on the staff arrangements made to carry it out. The first point to emphasize is that the entire operation must be the personal responsibility of the executive head of the organization. No one at a lower level has the authority or the right or the ability to acquire the knowledge required to perform the necessary tasks of coordination. This point was explicitly and emphatically recognized with respect to the President in the Budget and Accounting Act of 1921. The Budget Bureau has no authority except as a Presidential staff agency. To underline the point, the Budget Director is not subject to Senate confirmation. Similarly, at the departmental level the Secretary must be responsible for both programs and budgets for the same reasons.

The second point to stress is that programming, budgeting, and review after the fact are separate but highly interrelated operations. Programming is concerned with policy objectives, long-range projections, and analytic methods that go far beyond the scope of traditional budgetary procedures. Programming, however, may remain merely a useful academic exercise unless it is implemented through the budget, which should provide an essential link between policy and administration. Finally, both programming and budgeting depend in essential ways on the information that can be obtained only through perceptive reviews of past performance, which require the exercise of analytic skills going far beyond usual concepts of government accounting.

A conceptual framework for program budgeting will not in itself achieve the desired results. The objectives can only be achieved through the exercise of a wide variety of human skills of the highest caliber.

Chapter 3

THE ROLE OF COST-UTILITY ANALYSIS IN PROGRAM BUDGETING

BY GENE H. FISHER

From the discussion in the previous chapters it may be inferred that program budgeting as envisioned in this book involves several essential considerations. The primary ones may be summarized under three main headings: structural (or format) aspects, analytical process considerations, and data or information system considerations to support the first two items.

The *structural* aspects of program budgeting are concerned with establishing a set of categories oriented primarily toward "end-product" or "end-objective" activities that are meaningful from a long-range-planning point of view.[1] In such a context emphasis is placed on provision for an extended time horizon—some five, even ten or more, years into the future. These characteristics are in marked contrast with conventional governmental budgeting, which stresses functional and/or object class categories and a very short time horizon.

Analytical process considerations pertain to various study activities conducted as an integral part of the program-budgeting process. The primary objective of this type of analytical effort is to systematically examine alternative courses of action in terms of utility and cost, with a view to clarifying the relevant choices (and their implications) open to the decisionmakers in a certain problem area.

Information system considerations are aimed at support of the first two items. There are several senses in which this is important, the primary ones being (1) progress reporting and control and (2) providing data and information to serve as a basis for the analytical process—especially to facilitate the development of estimating relationships that will permit making estimates of benefits and costs of alternative future courses of action.

---

[1] In many instances end products may in fact be *intermediate* products, especially from the point of view of the next higher level in the decision hierarchy.

The present chapter is concerned primarily with the second of the items listed above: analytical process considerations. That an analytical effort is an important part of program budgeting (at least as practiced in the Department of Defense) is made clear in a recent statement by Secretary of Defense McNamara:

As I have pointed out in previous appearances before this Committee, in adding to a Defense program as large as the one we now have, we soon encounter the law of diminishing returns, where each additional increment of resources used produces a proportionately smaller increment of overall defense capability. While the benefits to be gained from each additional increment cannot be measured with precision, careful cost/effectiveness analyses can greatly assist in eliminating those program proposals which clearly contribute little to our military strength in terms of the costs involved.

This principle is just as applicable to qualitative improvements in weapons systems as it is to quantitative increases in our forces. The relevant question is not only "Do we want the very best for our military force?", but also, "Is the additional capability truly required and, if so, is this the least costly way of attaining it?"

Let me give you one hypothetical example to illustrate the point. Suppose we have two tactical fighter aircraft which are identical in every important measure of performance, except one—Aircraft A can fly ten miles per hour faster than Aircraft B. However, Aircraft A costs $10,000 more per unit than Aircraft B. Thus, if we need about 1,000 aircraft, the total additional cost would be $10 million.

If we approach this problem from the viewpoint of a given amount of resources, the additional combat effectiveness represented by the greater speed of Aircraft A would have to be weighed against the additional combat effectiveness which the same $10 million could produce if applied to other defense purposes—more Aircraft B, more or better aircraft munitions, or more ships, or even more military family housing. And if we approach the problem from the point of view of a given amount of combat capability, we would have to determine whether that given amount could be achieved at less cost by buying, for example, more of Aircraft B or more aircraft munitions or better munitions, or perhaps surface-to-surface missiles. Thus, the fact that Aircraft A flies ten miles per hour faster than Aircraft B is not conclusive. We still have to determine whether the greater speed is worth the greater cost. *This kind of determination is the heart of the planning-programming-budgeting or resources allocation problem within the Defense Department* [italics supplied].[2]

[2] From the introduction of the Statement of Secretary of Defense Robert S. McNamara before the Committee on Armed Services on the Fiscal Year 1965–1969 Defense Program and 1965 Defense Budget, January 27, 1964, *Hearings on Military Posture and H.R. 9637*, House of Representatives, 88th Cong., 2d Sess. (Washington, D.C.: U.S. Government Printing Office, 1964).

Numerous analytical approaches may be used to support the total program budgeting process. Here we shall focus on one of them: cost-utility analysis. Before turning to this subject, however, a few of the other types of analysis should be noted briefly.

In terms of the types of problems encountered in the total program-budgeting process, one might think of a wide spectrum going all the way from major allocative decisions on the one hand to progress reporting and control on the other. Major allocative decisions involve such questions as, Should more resources be employed in national security in the future, or in national health programs, or in preservation and development of natural resources, etc.?[3] Ideally, the decisionmakers would like to plan to allocate resources in the future so that for a given budget, for example, the estimated marginal return (or utility) in each major area of application would be equal. But this is more easily said than done; and at the current state of analytical art, no one really knows with any precision how the "grand optimum" might be attained. In the main, the analytical tools now available (particularly the quantitative ones) are just not very helpful in dealing directly with such problems. Intuition and judgment are paramount.

At the other end of the spectrum—progress reporting and control—the main problem is to keep track of programs where the major decisions have *already been made*, to try to detect impending difficulties as programs are being implemented, and to initiate remedial actions through a feedback mechanism when programs are deemed likely to get out of control in the future. Numerous techniques are available for dealing with these types of program-management problems. Examples are the following: financial and management accounting techniques;[4] network-type systems for planning, scheduling, progress reporting, and control;[5] critical-path methods (within the framework of a network-type system);[6] Gantt

[3] For example, see Arthur Smithies, *Government Decision-Making and the Theory of Choice*, P-2960 (Santa Monica, Calif.: The RAND Corporation, October 1964).

[4] See Robert N. Anthony, *Management Accounting* (Homewood, Ill.: Richard D. Irwin, Inc., 1960), chaps. 13–15.

[5] One example is the so-called PERT system. For a description, see *USAF PERT, Volume I, PERT Time System Description Manual*, September 1963, and *USAF PERT, Volume III, PERT Cost System Description Manual*, December 1963 (Washington, D.C.: Headquarters, Air Force Systems Command, Andrews Air Force Base, 1963).

[6] See James E. Kelly and Morgan R. Walker, "Critical-Path Planning and Scheduling," *Proceedings of the Eastern Joint Computer Conference* (Ft. Washington, Pa.: Manchly Associates, Inc., 1959), pp. 160–173; and F. K. Levy, G. L. Thompson,

chart techniques for program planning and control;[7] and various program management reporting and control schemes developed in recent years in the Department of Defense to help program managers in the management of complex weapon system development and production programs.[8]

The area between the ends of the spectrum is a broad and varied one, offering the opportunity for applying a variety of analytical techniques. These techniques are focused primarily toward problem areas short of dealing with determination of the "grand optimum," although they can be of real assistance in sharpening the intuition and judgment of decisionmakers in grappling with the very broad allocative questions. Technically, this is called "suboptimization," and it is here that the analytical efforts are likely to have the highest payoff.[9]

In cases where a wide range of alternative future courses of action needs to be examined in a broad suboptimization context, the main subject of this chapter, cost-utility analysis,[10] may well be the most useful analytical tool. However, in other cases where the suboptimization context is much narrower and a wide range of alternatives is not available, the problem may be one of examining relatively minor variations *within* an essentially prescribed future course of action. The suboptimization context may be relatively narrow for numerous reasons—severe political constraints, lack of new technology to provide the basis for a wide range of alternatives, etc. Here, something akin to capital budgeting[11] techniques may be most appropriate.

---

and J. D. Wiest, *Mathematical Basis of the Critical Path Method,* Office of Naval Research, Research Memorandum No. 86 (Pittsburgh, Pa.: Carnegie Institute of Technology, May 30, 1962).

[7] L. P. Alford and John R. Bangs, *Production Handbook* (New York: Ronald Press, 1947), pp. 216–229.

[8] For a good example, see *Systems Data Presentation and Reporting Procedures (Rainbow Report),* November 1, 1961 (with revisions as of March 9, 1962), Program Management Instruction 1–5 (Washington, D.C.: Headquarters, Air Force Systems Command, Andrews Air Force Base, 1962).

[9] For a discussion of suboptimization, see Charles Hitch, "Suboptimization in Operations Problems," *Journal of the Operations Research Society of America,* vol. 1, no. 3, May 1953, pp. 87–99; and Charles J. Hitch and Roland N. McKean, *The Economics of Defense in the Nuclear Age* (Cambridge, Mass.: Harvard University Press, 1960), pp. 396–402.

[10] Sometimes called "systems analysis"; e.g., see Roland N. McKean, *Efficiency in Government Through Systems Analysis* (New York: John Wiley & Sons, Inc., 1958).

[11] For example, see Joel Dean, *Capital Budgeting* (New York: Columbia University Press, 1951); Harold Bierman, Jr., and Seymour Smidt, *The Capital Budgeting Decision* (New York: The Macmillan Co., 1960); and Elwood S. Buffa, *Models for*

In many instances the above-mentioned techniques may have to be supplemented by other methods. For example, in numerous major decision problems it is not sufficient to deal only with the *direct* economic consequences of proposed alternative future courses of action, ignoring their possible indirect or spillover effects. In such instances it may well be vitally important to consider indirect economic effects either on the economy as a whole or on specified regions or sectors of the total economic system. Certain transportation problems involve considerations of this type.[12] Also, in the case of certain national security and space decisions, especially in the higher echelons of the decision hierarchy, it is often necessary to consider possible regional or industry sector economic impacts associated with alternative weapon system development and procurement choices.[13] One way to deal with such problems is through the use of macroeconomic models that attempt to take into account key interactions among important components of the economic system: for example, interindustry (input-output) models for the economy as a whole[14] and various types of regional models dealing with parts of the total national economy.[15]

Thus it is clear that numerous analytical methods and techniques exist that may be used to support various facets of the total program-budgeting process. We have dealt with this point at some length to emphasize that the subject of this chapter, cost-utility analysis, is not the only analytical tool that might be used in program budgeting.

Let us now turn to our central theme. In the following paragraphs cost-utility analysis is discussed in somewhat general and abstract terms. Illustrative examples are presented later in this

---

Production and Operations Management (New York: John Wiley & Sons, Inc., 1963), chaps. 13 and 14.

[12] For example, see Brian V. Martin and Charles B. Warden, "Transportation Planning in Developing Countries," *Traffic Quarterly* (January 1965), pp. 59–75.

[13] See *Convertibility of Space and Defense Resources to Civilian Needs: A Search for New Employment Potentials,* compiled for the Subcommittee on Employment and Manpower of the Committee on Labor and Public Welfare, Senate, 88th Cong., 2d Sess. (Washington, D.C.: U.S. Government Printing Office, 1964). Note especially Part III, "National Adjustments to Shifts in Defense Planning," and Part IV, "Studies in Regional Adjustment to Shifts in Defense Spending."

[14] W. W. Leontief *et al., Studies in the Structure of the American Economy* (New York: Oxford University Press, 1953).

[15] For example, See Walter Isard *et al., Methods of Regional Analysis: An Introduction to Regional Science* (Boston and New York: Technology Press of Massachusetts Institute of Technology and John Wiley & Sons, Inc., 1960).

book in several of the "case study" chapters—e.g., in the chapters on defense, natural resources, and education.

WHAT IS COST-UTILITY ANALYSIS?

Attempting to define cost-utility analysis poses somewhat of a semantics problem. Numerous terms in current use convey the same general meaning but have important different meanings to different people: "cost-benefit analysis," "cost-effectiveness analysis," "systems analysis," "operations research," "operations analysis," etc. Because of such terminological confusion, in this chapter all these terms are rejected and "cost-utility analysis" is employed instead.

Cost-utility analysis, as envisioned here, may be distinguished by the following major characteristics:

1. A fundamental characteristic is the systematic examination and comparison of alternative courses of action that might be taken to achieve specified objectives for some future time period. It is important not only to systematically examine all the relevant alternatives that can be identified initially but also to *design additional ones* if those examined are found wanting.[16] Finally, the analysis, particularly if thoroughly and imaginatively done, may at times result in modifications of the initially specified objectives.

2. Critical examination of alternatives typically involves numerous considerations, but the two main ones are: assessment of the cost (in the sense of economic resource cost) and the utility (the benefits or gains) pertaining to each of the alternatives being compared to attain the stipulated objectives.

3. The time context is the future—often the distant future (five, ten, or more years).

4. Because of the extended time horizon, the environment is one of uncertainty—very often great uncertainty. Since uncertainty is an important facet of the problem, it should be faced and treated explicitly in the analysis. This means, among other things, that wherever possible the analyst should avoid the use of simple expected value models.

[16] E. S. Quade, *Military Systems Analysis*, RM-3452-PR (Santa Monica, Calif.: The RAND Corporation, January 1963), p. 1.

5. Usually the context in which the analysis takes place is broad (often very broad) and the environment very complex, with numerous interactions among the key variables in the problem. This means that simple, straightforward solutions are the exception rather than the rule.

6. While quantitative methods of analysis should be used as much as possible because of items 4 and 5 above,[17] purely quantitative work must often be heavily supplemented by qualitative analysis. In fact, we stress the importance of *good* qualitative work and of using an appropriate combination of quantitative and qualitative methods.

7. Usually the focus is on research and development and/or investment-type decision problems, although operational decisions are sometimes encountered. This does not mean, of course, that operational considerations are ignored in dealing with R&D and investment-type problems.

8. Timeliness is important. A careful, thorough analysis that comes six months after the critical time of decision may be worth essentially zero, while a less thorough (but thoughtfully done) analysis completed on time may be worth a great deal.

THE PRIMARY PURPOSE OF COST-UTILITY ANALYSIS

In the context being considered in this chapter let us be very clear about what is the main purpose of analysis in general, and cost-utility analysis in particular. Contrary to what some of the more enthusiastic advocates of quantitative analysis may think, we visualize cost-utility analysis as playing a somewhat modest, though very significant, role in the overall decisionmaking process. In reality, most major long-range-planning decision problems must ultimately be resolved primarily on the basis of intuition and judgment. We suggest that the main role of analysis should be to try to *sharpen* this intuition and judgment. In practically no case should it be assumed that the results of the analysis will *make* the decision. The really interesting problems are just too difficult, and there are too many intangible (e.g., political, psychological, and sociological) considerations that cannot be taken into account in the analytical process, especially in a quantitative sense. In sum, the analytical

---

[17] Also because of inadequate data and information sources.

process should be directed toward assisting the decisionmaker in such a way that (hopefully!) his intuition and judgment are better than they would be without the results of the analysis.[18]

Viewing the objective of cost-utility analysis in this way is likely to put the analyst in a frame of mind that will permit him to be much more useful to the decisionmaker than if he takes a more hard-core view. There are two extremes here. On the one hand, it might be argued that the types of long-range-planning decision problems considered in this chapter are just too complex for the current state of analytical art to handle. Therefore, decisions must be made purely on the basis of intuition, judgment, and experience —i.e., the zero analysis position. At the other extreme are those who (naïvely) think that all problems should be tackled in a purely quantitative fashion, with a view essentially to making the decision. Such a view implies explicit (usually meaning quantitative) calculations of cost and utility for all the alternatives under consideration. This may be possible, at times, for very narrowly defined, low-level suboptimization problems; but even this is questionable.

More generally, in dealing with major decision problems of choice, if the analyst approaches his task in an inflexible hard-core frame of mind, he is likely to be in for trouble. For example, he may soon give up in complete frustration; or he may wind up with such a simplified model that the resulting calculations are essen-

---

[18] Apparently this view is held by Alain C. Enthoven, Deputy Assistant Secretary for Systems Analysis, Department of Defense. He writes: "Where does this leave us? What is operations research or systems analysis at the Defense policy level all about? I think that it can best be described as a continuing dialogue between the policy-maker and the systems analyst, in which the policy-maker asks for alternative solutions to his problems, makes decisions to exclude some, and makes value judgments and policy decisions, while the analyst attempts to clarify the conceptual framework in which decisions must be made, to define alternative possible objectives and criteria, and to explore in as clear terms as possible (and quantitatively) the cost and effectiveness of alternative courses of action.

"The analyst at this level is not computing optimum solutions or making decisions. In fact, computation is not his most important contribution. And he is helping some-one else to make decisions. His job is to ask and find answers to the questions: 'What are we trying to do?' 'What are the alternative ways of achieving it?' 'What would they cost, and how effective would they be?' 'What does the decisionmaker need to know in order to make a choice?' And to collect and organize this information for those who are responsible for deciding what the Defense program ought to be." See Alain C. Enthoven, "Decision Theory and Systems Analysis," *The Armed Forces Comptroller*, vol. IX, no. 1 (March 1964), p. 39.

tially meaningless; or his conclusions may not be ready for presentation until two years after the critical decision time and would therefore be useless to the decisionmaker.

The viewpoint taken here is that in most cases the relevant range is between the extremes mentioned above, and that in such a context there is a wide scope of analytical effort that can be useful. Furthermore, even when only a relatively incomplete set of quantitative calculations of cost and utility can be made (probably the general situation), much can be done to assist the decisionmaker in the sense that the term "assistance" is used in this chapter. To repeat: The objective is to *sharpen* intuition and judgment. It is conceivable that even a small amount of sharpening may on occasion have a high payoff.

One other point seems relevant. In that rare circumstance when a fairly complete set of calculations of cost and utility is possible and a resulting conclusion about a preferred alternative is reached, it may well be that the conclusion itself is not the most useful thing to the decisionmaker. For one thing, as pointed out earlier, the analysis usually cannot take everything into account—particularly some of the nebulous nonquantitative considerations. The decisionmaker has to allow for these himself. But more important, most high-level decisionmakers are very busy men who do not have time to structure a particular problem, think up the relevant alternatives (especially the *subtle* ones), trace out the key interactions among variables in the problem, etc. This the analyst, if he is competent, can do, and should do. And it is precisely this sort of contribution that may be most useful to the decisionmaker. The fact that the analysis reaches a firm conclusion about a preferred alternative may in many instances be of secondary importance.

SOME MAJOR CONSIDERATIONS INVOLVED IN COST-UTILITY ANALYSIS

At this point, one might logically expect the title to be "How To Do Cost-Utility Analysis"—a cookbook, so to speak. We avoid this for two main reasons: (1) If such a treatise were attempted it would take an entire book; and more important, (2) it is doubtful that even a book on the subject is possible. At the current stage of development of analytical methods, cost-utility analysis is an art rather than a science. The really significant problems to be tackled are each in a sense unique, with the result that it is not possible to give a definitive set of rules on how to do an appropriate analysis. All that can be done is to give some guidelines, principles, and illustrative examples. But books, or major parts of books, have been written on this subject.[19] Here the treatment must of necessity be more limited.

Some important guidelines to be followed in carrying out a cost-utility analysis (not necessarily in order of relative importance) are discussed in the following paragraphs.[20]

Proper Structuring of the Problem and Design of the Analysis

This is by far the most important of the guidelines. Given an incredibly complex environment, that which is relevant to the problem at hand must be included, and that which is irrelevant excluded. There are no formal rules to guide us. The experience, skill, imagination, and intuition of the analyst are paramount. It is at this point—the *design* of the analysis—that most cost-utility studies either flounder hopelessly or move ahead toward success. In sum, if we can structure the problem so that the *right questions* are being asked, we shall be well on the way toward a good analysis. This sounds trite, but it really is not. The author has seen all too many instances of large amounts of effort being expended on an analytical exercise addressed to the wrong questions.[21]

Another point is that typically the problem and the design of the analysis may well have to be *re*structured several times. Considerations that were initially thought to be important may, after some preliminary work, turn out to be relatively unimportant, and vice versa. Finally, in the process of doing some of the analytical work new questions and new alternatives may come to mind.

[19] For example, see Hitch and McKean, *The Economics of Defense,* especially Part II; and McKean, *Efficiency in Government.*

[20] Observance of these guidelines will not in itself produce a good analysis, but it will most surely help. Many of the points listed are based on Quade, *Military Systems Analysis,* pp. 8–24.

[21] Incredible as it may seem, there have been studies that started out by asking questions about which alternative would maximize gain and at the same time minimize cost—clearly an impossible situation.

The Conceptual Framework

In general there are two principal conceptual approaches:[22]

1. *Fixed utility approach.* For a specified level of utility to be attained in the accomplishment of some given objective, the analysis attempts to determine that alternative (or feasible combination of alternatives) likely to achieve the specified level of utility at the lowest economic cost.

2. *Fixed budget approach.* For a specified budget level to be used in the attainment of some given objective, the analysis attempts to determine that alternative (or feasible combination of alternatives) likely to produce the highest utility for the given budget level.

Either (or both) of these approaches may be used, depending on the context of the problem at hand. In any event, the objective is to permit *comparisons* to be made among alternatives, and for this purpose something has to be made fixed.

At this point a comment on the use of ratios (e.g., utility to cost ratios) seems in order. Very often such ratios are used to evaluate alternatives. The use of ratios usually poses no problem as long as the analysis is conducted in the framework outlined above (i.e., with the level of either utility or cost fixed). However, the author has on occasion seen studies where this was not done, with the result that the comparisons were essentially meaningless. For example, consider the following hypothetical illustration:

Alternatives	Utility (U)	Cost (C)	U/C
A	20	10	2
B	200	100	2

If the analyst is preoccupied with ratios, the implication of the above example is a state of indifference regarding the choice between A and B. But *should* the analyst be indifferent? Most probably not, because of the wide difference in scale between A

[22] The fixed level of utility or budget is usually specified by someone "outside the analysis"; i.e., it is usually a datum given to the analyst. Very often the analyst will use several levels (e.g., high, medium, and low) to investigate the sensitivity of the ranking of the alternatives to the utility or budget level.

and B. In fact, with such a great difference in scale, the analyst might not even be comparing relevant alternatives at all.[23]

Building the Model

Here the term "model" is used in a broad sense. Depending on the nature of the problem at hand, the model used in the analysis may be formal or informal, very mathematical or not so mathematical, heavily computerized or only moderately so, etc. However, the main point is that the model need not be highly formal and mathematical to be useful. In any event, the following are some important points to keep in mind:

1. Model building is an art, not a science. It is often an experimental process.

2. The main thing is to try to include and highlight those factors that are relevant to the problem at hand, and to suppress (judiciously!) those that are relatively unimportant. Unless the latter is done, the model is likely to be unmanageable.

3. The main purpose in designing the model is to develop a meaningful *set of relationships* among objectives, the relevant alternatives available for attaining the objectives, the estimated cost of the alternatives, and the estimated utility for each of the alternatives.

4. Provision must be made for explicit treatment of uncertainty. (There will be more on this later.)

5. Since by definition a model is an abstraction from reality, the model must be built on a set of assumptions. These assumptions must be made *explicit*. If they are not, this is to be regarded as a defect of the model design.

Treatment of Uncertainty

Because most really interesting and important decision problems involve major elements of uncertainty, a cost-utility analysis of such problems must provide for explicit treatment of uncertainty. This may be done in numerous ways.

For purposes of discussion, two main types of uncertainty may be distinguished:

[23] For a further discussion of the possible pitfalls of using ratios, see McKean, *Efficiency in Government*, pp. 34–37, 107–113.

1. Uncertainty about the state of the world in the future. In a national security context, major factors are technological uncertainty, strategic uncertainty,[24] and uncertainty about the enemy and his reactions.

2. Statistical uncertainty. This type of uncertainty stems from chance elements in the real world. It would exist even if uncertainties of the first type were zero.

Type 2 uncertainties are usually the least troublesome to handle in cost-utility studies. When necessary, Monte Carlo[25] and/or other techniques may be used to deal with statistical fluctuations; but these perturbations are usually swamped by Type 1 uncertainties, which are dominant in most long-range planning problems. The use of elaborate techniques to treat statistical uncertainties in such problems is likely to be expensive window dressing.[26]

Type 1 uncertainties are typically present in most long-range decision problems, and they are most difficult to take into account in a cost-utility analysis. Techniques that are often used are sensitivity analysis, contingency analysis, and a fortiori analysis.[27]

Sensitivity Analysis. Suppose in a given analysis there are a few key parameters about which the analyst is very uncertain. Instead of using "expected values" for these parameters, the analyst may use several values (say, high, medium, and low) in an attempt to see how sensitive the results (the ranking of the alternatives being considered) are to variations in the uncertain parameters.[28]

---

[24] For example: Will there be a war in the future? If so, when? General or local? With what political constraints? Who will be our enemies? Our allies? See C. J. Hitch, *An Appreciation of Systems Analysis*, P-699 (Santa Monica, Calif.: The RAND Corporation, August 18, 1955), p. 6.

[25] For a discussion of Monte Carlo techniques, see Herman Kahn and Irwin Mann, *Monte Carlo*, P-1165 (Santa Monica, Calif.: The RAND Corporation, July 30, 1957); and E. S. Quade, *Analysis for Military Decisions*, R-387-PR (Santa Monica, Calif.: The RAND Corporation, November 1964), pp. 407–414.

[26] Hitch, *Appreciation of Systems Analysis*, p. 7.

[27] Quade, *Military Systems Analysis*, pp. 23–24.

[28] Enthoven, in "Decision Theory and Systems Analysis," pp. 16–17, talks about sensitivity analysis in the following way: "If it is a question of uncertainties about quantitative matters such as operational factors, it is generally useful to examine the available evidence and determine the bounds of the uncertainty. In many of our analyses for the Secretary of Defense, we carry three estimates through the calculations: an "optimistic," a "pessimistic," and a "best" or single most likely estimate. Although it is usually sensible to design the defense posture primarily on the basis of the best estimates, the prudent decisionmaker will keep asking himself, "Would the outcome be acceptable if the worst possible happened, i.e., if all the pessimistic

Contingency Analysis. This type of analysis investigates how the ranking of the alternatives under consideration holds up when a relevant change in criteria for evaluating the alternatives is postulated, or a major change in the general environment is assumed. (For example, in a military context, the enemy is assumed to be countries A and B. We might then want to investigate what would happen if C joins the A and B coalition.)

A Fortiori Analysis. Suppose that in a particular planning decision problem the generally accepted intuitive judgment strongly favors alternative X. However, the analyst feels that X might be a poor choice and that alternative Y might be preferred. In performing an analysis of X versus Y, the analyst may choose deliberately to resolve the major uncertainties in favor of X and see how Y compares under these adverse conditions. If Y still looks good, the analyst has a very strong case in favor of Y.

Creation of a New Alternative. Although the three techniques listed above may be useful in a direct analytical sense, they may also contribute indirectly. For example, through sensitivity and contingency analyses the analyst may gain a good understanding of the really critical uncertainties in a given problem area. On the basis of this knowledge he might then be able to come up with a newly designed alternative that will provide a reasonably good hedge against a *range* of the more significant uncertainties. This is often difficult to do; but when it can be accomplished, it may offer one of the best ways to compensate for uncertainty.

Treatment of Problems Associated with Time

More likely than not, the particular problem at hand will be posed in a dynamic context; or at least the problem will have some dynamic aspects to it. While a "static"-type analysis can go a long way toward providing the decisionmaker with useful information, very often this has to be supplemented by analytical work that takes time into account explicitly.

---

estimates were borne out?" Carrying three numbers through all of the calculations can increase the workload greatly. For this reason, a certain amount of judgment has to be used as to when the best guesses are satisfactory and when the full range of uncertainty needs to be explored. If there are uncertainties about context, at least one can run the calculations on the basis of several alternative assumptions so that the decisionmaker can see how the outcome varies with the assumptions."

A case in point is with respect to the treatment of the estimated *costs* of the alternatives for a fixed level of utility.[29] The nature of the problem may be such that the costs have to be time-phased, resulting in cost streams through time for each of the alternatives. The question then arises whether the decisionmaker is or is not indifferent with respect to the time impact of the costs. If he is not indifferent concerning time preference, then the cost streams have to be "discounted" through time, using an appropriate rate of discount.[30] Determining specifically what rate to use can be a problem; but it is usually manageable.[31] If it is not, an upper bound rate and a lower bound rate may be used to see whether it really makes any difference in the final conclusions of the problem.

It should be pointed out that the analyst pays a price for introducing time explicitly into an analysis:[32]

1. It complicates the analysis by increasing the number of variables and hence the number of calculations. If we put time in, we may have to take something else out.

2. As implied above, it complicates the selection of a criterion for evaluating alternatives: solution X may be better for 1966 and worse for 1970; solution Y may be just the reverse.

Validity Checking

In the preceding paragraphs we have discussed building the analytical model, "exercising" the model (sensitivity and contingency analysis), etc. Another important consideration (often relatively neglected) is checking the validity of the model. Because the model is only a representation of reality, it is desirable to do

[29] Maintaining a fixed level of utility *through time* is often a tricky problem in itself. We cannot go into this matter in the present limited discussion.

[30] One may raise the question regarding under what conditions the decisionmaker *would* be indifferent. Economic theorists might argue that there probably should not be any such condition. However, in practice, decisionmakers often find themselves in an institutional setting (the Department of Defense, for example) where it is customary to be indifferent regarding time preference; hence, discounting of cost streams through time is not done. This is not to say that the decisionmakers are correct in principle.

It should be emphasized that the type of discounting under discussion here is purely to equalize cost streams through time with respect to time preference—not to compensate for risk.

[31] For example, see E. B. Berman, *The Normative Interest Rate,* P-1796 (Santa Monica, Calif.: The RAND Corporation, September 15, 1959).

[32] Hitch, *Appreciation of Systems Analysis,* pp. 11–12.

some sort of checking to see if the analytical procedure used is a reasonably good representation, within the context of the problem at hand. This is difficult to do, especially in dealing with problems having a time horizon five, ten, or more years into the future.

In general, we cannot test models of this type by methods of "controlled experiment." However, the analyst might try to answer the following question:[33]

1. Can the model describe known facts and situations reasonably well?

2. When the principal parameters involved are varied, do the results remain consistent and plausible?

3. Can it handle special cases in which we already have some indication as to what the outcome should be?

4. Can it assign causes to known effects?

Qualitative Supplementation

We have already stressed the importance of qualitative considerations in cost-utility analysis—particularly qualitative *supplementation* of the quantitative work. Introduction of qualitative considerations may take several forms:

1. Qualitative analysis per se as an integral part of the total analytical effort.

2. Interpretation of the quantitative work.

3. Discussion of relevant nonquantitative considerations that could not be taken into account in the "formal" analysis.

The latter item can be particularly important in presenting the results of a study to the decisionmaker. The idea is to present the results of the formal quantitative work, interpret these results, and then say that this is as far as the formal quantitative analysis per se will permit us to go. However, there are important *qualitative* considerations that you (the decisionmaker) should try to take into account; and here they are (list them). Finally, relevant questions about each of the qualitative items can be raised and important interrelations among them discussed.

SUMMARY COMMENTS

We stress again that the discussion above pertains to a long-range-planning context, with emphasis on specifying, clarifying,

[33] Quade, *Military Systems Analysis*, p. 20.

and comparing the relevant alternatives. Because comparative analysis is the prime focus, it is vitally important continually to emphasize *consistency* in the analytical concepts, methods, and techniques used. That is, instead of trying for a high degree of accuracy in an *absolute* sense (which is usually unattainable anyway), the analyst should stress development and use of procedures that will treat the alternatives being considered in an unbiased, consistent manner.

The main points presented in this chapter may be summarized as follows:

1. An analytical activity is an important part of the total program-budgeting process.

2. Cost-utility analysis pertains to the systematic examination and comparison of alternative courses of action that might be taken to achieve specified objectives for some future time period. Not only is it important to examine all relevant alternatives that can be identified initially but it is also important to design additional ones if those examined are found wanting.

3. The primary purpose of cost-utility analysis is usually not to *make* the decision but rather to *sharpen* the intuition and judgment of the decisionmakers. Identification of the relevant alternatives and clarification of their respective implications are of prime importance.

4. In a long-range-planning context, the following are some of the major considerations involved in doing a cost-utility analysis:

   (a) Proper structuring of the problem is all-important. The analysis must be addressed to the right questions.

   (b) In making comparisons, an appropriate analytical framework must be used. For example, for a specified level of utility to be attained in the accomplishment of some given objective, the alternatives may be compared on the basis of their estimated economic resource impact; or vice versa, for a given budget level the alternatives may be compared on the basis of their estimated utility.

   (c) It is usually necessary to construct a model (either formal or informal) to be used in the analytical process. Here the main purpose is to develop a set of relationships among objectives, the relevant alternatives available for attaining the objectives, the estimated cost of the alternatives, and the estimated utility for each of the alternatives.

(d) Uncertainty must be faced explicitly in the analysis. Sensitivity analysis, contingency analysis, and a fortiori analysis are three possible techniques that may be used in dealing with the problem of uncertainty.

(e) Although it complicates the analysis because of an increase in the number of variables, very often *time-phasing* of the impacts of the various alternatives is a requirement. If the decisionmakers are not indifferent with respect to time preference, the estimates of time-phased impacts must be "equalized" over time through the use of a "discounting" procedure.

(f) Since the model is only a representation of reality, it is desirable to do some validity checking of the analytical procedure; e.g., can the model describe known facts and situations reasonably well?

(g) Although cost-utility analysis stresses the use of quantitative methods, the analyst should not hesitate to supplement his quantitative work with appropriate *qualitative* analyses.

PART II

ACTUAL AND POTENTIAL APPLICATIONS OF
THE PROGRAM BUDGET IDEA

Chapter 4

THE DEPARTMENT OF DEFENSE

BY DAVID NOVICK

Until the end of World War II we managed our military affairs through two executive departments—War and Navy. The decision to re-examine our defense posture and our defense organization came about as a result of our experience with joint operations during the war, dissatisfaction with the handling of materiel and manpower problems, and the insistence of the Army Air Corps that it become a separate establishment.

At that time there were two schools of thought on how to organize the departments. Mr. Stimson and Secretary of War Patterson argued for a single unified department. But Secretary of the Navy Forrestal and Mr. Ferdinand Eberstadt[1] were in favor of creating a new top layer that would be a coordinating layer. In the conflict between Army and Navy views, Congress adopted the Navy position.

In the National Security Act of 1947, Congress set up a National Military Establishment headed by a Secretary of Defense with general authority over three executive departments—Army, Navy, and Air Force. Congress also recognized the World War II Joint Chiefs of Staff and gave them statutory authority as principal military advisers to the President, Secretary of Defense, and National Security Council.

Mr. Forrestal became the first Secretary of Defense and worked under this system for two years, by which time he was convinced that the view he had espoused just would not work. He recommended the establishment of a single executive department to President Truman, which the President proposed to Congress.

[1] Mr. Eberstadt, a New York investment banker, was a close friend and former business associate of Secretary Forrestal and had been chosen to represent the Secretary of the Navy on the drafting committee appointed to propose changes in the defense organizations. See *Unification of the War and Navy Departments and Postwar Organization for National Security, Report to Hon. James Forrestal, Secretary of the Navy,* Committee on Naval Affairs, Senate, 79th Cong., 1st Sess. (Washington, D.C.: U.S. Government Printing Office, 1945); referred to as the Eberstadt Report.

A major objective of the President's proposal was that "we should have integrated strategic plans and a unified military program and budget." The legislation, as enacted, fell far short of these goals. It authorized the Secretary to establish broad policies and programs but in no way moved to integrate the separate military departments. The 1949 amendment to the National Security Act asserted the role of the Secretary of Defense, and the Army, Navy, and Air Force lost their status as executive departments. In addition, a Title IV was added to the act creating a Comptroller at the Department of Defense level and in the offices of each of the service secretaries. The objective was to provide similar administrative integration at the resource or budget level to that sought for military activities.

By 1958 President Eisenhower recognized the need for expediting and strengthening the unification process. In his Defense Reorganization Message of 1958 he declared that "all doubts as to the authority of the Secretary of Defense" had to be settled once and for all. The further reorganization he initiated at that time created unified and specified commands, which were a formal recognition of the fact that the operations of each of the services were important, not so much as individual Army, Navy, or Air Force actions, but more properly as part of a combined effort responsible, through the Joint Chiefs, to the Secretary of Defense and the President. At that point the stage was set for full integration of our military activities, but fuller realization of these potentials was to await the appointment of Robert McNamara as secretary of Defense in January 1961.

Mr. McNamara's forceful personality combined with the recognition of a legal basis for action was to result in a major movement toward integrated action in defense planning. The reorganization of 1958 and the introduction of the new Secretary need not in themselves have provided the major change that we have now seen. In addition, a change was needed at the administrative level, which although recognized formally in the 1949 amendments creating the Office of Assistant Secretary of Defense (Comptroller), had not yet moved toward the kind of integration at the resource level that was now necessitated by the other moves.

Prior to 1961 despite many innovations and reforms in the financial management of the Department of Defense and the separate military departments, the Secretary of Defense did not integrate his military planning with his resource requirements or budget.[2] Although the Secretary presented an overall DOD budget to the Executive and Congress, it was a combination of the three separate departmental budgets rather than a completely integrated one. In addition, the requirements for resources (appropriation money) were organized in terms of activities or functions (such as "Construction") rather than that of major military or strategic objectives, as may be seen in Table 4.1. Consequently, the further detailed breakdowns were in terms of these same budget appropriation categories, and there was no device for transposing the conventional budget codes into a meaningful identification of resources required for major national security objectives. The budget, when stated in terms of procurement, construction, military personnel, operation and maintenance, etc., did not provide either the Secretary of Defense, the Executive, or Congress with any way of sorting out these major categories of resources and relating them to such major military objectives as defense of the continental United States or strategic offensive capability. The weaknesses of this method of financial planning have been summarized by Alain C. Enthoven as follows:

It (the pre-1961 system) had several important defects, perhaps the most important of which was the almost complete separation between planning and decision-making on weapon systems and forces, on the one hand, and budgeting on the other . . . In other words, the long-range plans for weapon systems, forces, and all of their supporting elements were made by the Services on the basis of their estimates of the forces required to assure our national security. Generally speaking, costs were not introduced systematically, either to test the feasibility of the whole program or for purposes of evaluating the efficiency of the allocation.

Budgeting, on the other hand, had as its point of departure the guideline dollar totals laid down by the Administration and based on estimates of the burden the economy could or should bear. The result was a gap. The "required forces" always cost much more than the Administration and the Congress were willing to pay. The process by which the conflict-

---

[2] A proposal for a new budget concept that would integrate the planning, programming, budgeting, and accounting activities of the Department of Defense was made by the writer in 1954 in *Efficiency and Economy in Government Through New Budgeting and Accounting Procedures*, R-254 (Santa Monica, Calif.: The RAND Corporation, February 1, 1954), and again in 1956 in *A New Approach to the Military Budget*, RM-1759 (Santa Monica, Calif.: The RAND Corporation, June 12, 1956).

TABLE 4.1 Summary of Budget Authorizations and Expenditures (in millions of dollars)

Title of appropriation groups	New obligational authority			Expenditures		
	1959 enacted	1960 estimate	1961 estimate	1959 actual	1960 estimate	1961 estimate
Military personnel: Total[a]	11,463	11,658	11,837	11,801	11,959	12,146
Active forces[a]	10,174	10,262	10,426	10,544	10,592	10,741
Reserve forces	649	681	612	616	667	611
Retired pay	640	715	799	641	700	794
Operation and maintenance	10,195	10,317	10,527	10,384	10,137	10,321
Procurement: Total	14,293	13,090	13,085	14,410	13,943	13,602
Aircraft	6,134	6,143	4,753	7,658	6,670	6,027
Missiles	4,107	3,244	3,825	3,339	3,500	3,479
Ships	1,947	1,139	2,035	1,493	1,651	1,644
Other	2,105	2,563	2,471	1,921	2,121	2,451
Research, development, test, and evaluation	3,775	4,189	3,910	2,859	3,680	3,917
Construction: Total	1,384	1,364	1,188	1,948	1,670	1,359
Active forces	1,358	1,291	1,153	1,862	1,608	1,302
Reserve forces	26	73	35	86	62	57
Revolving and management funds	57	30	30	−169	−444	−350
Total, military functions	41,168	40,647	40,577	41,233	40,945	40,995
Military assistance	1,515	1,300	2,000	2,340	1,800	1,750
Grand total, Department of Defense: Military	42,683	41,947	42,577	43,573	42,745	42,745

[a] Additional obligational authority available by transfer: $535 million in 1959, $430 million in 1960, $350 million in 1961.

ing interests were resolved was unsystematic and wasteful because it led to unbalanced programs.

Furthermore, the Secretary of Defense did not receive adequate cost data. The budgetary system identified cost by object classes—Procurement, Military Personnel, Installations, etc.—the *inputs* to the Defense Department, rather than by weapon systems and forces, such as B-52 wings and Army divisions, which are the tangible *outputs* of the Department . . . Moreover, cost data were presented and financial management was conducted at the Defense Department level on a year-at-a-time basis. The full time-phased costs of the proposed forces were not presented to the Secretary of Defense. Because the costs of most programs are small in their first years, this led to the starting of many programs that could not be completed at anything like existing levels. Although a certain amount of this is a desirable hedge against uncertainty, it is clear that there were a great many wasteful stretch-outs and cancellations of programs that would not have been started if the costs of all of the approved programs had been anticipated.[3]

Lacking management techniques for identifying resources to objectives, the Secretary of Defense did the budget and planning job by first bringing the overall defense budget into line with the fiscal policy of the administration. He then divided the total budget among the three military departments. The departments were then, for the most part, left alone to allocate their funds as they saw fit. As a result, each department tended to favor its area and special interests, often without concern for the total problem. Understandably they sought to guarantee larger shares in future budgets by concentrating on dramatic new weapons. The Navy concentrated on its newly developed nuclear capability, emphasizing attack and missile-carrying submarines and aircraft carriers. The Air Force centered its interest on strategic equipment—bombers and missiles. The Army focused on new defenses against aircraft and missiles. And probably more important, all these new developments were undertaken without much interest in, or information about, their resource requirements. There was some effort to determine development and procurement costs, but little attention was paid to the other resources (real estate, personnel, associated equipment, etc.) necessary for a weapon to become a usable weapon system.

The budget was projected for only one year into the future, and the Secretary of Defense and the Secretaries of the three depart-

[3] Address before the American Economic Association, Pittsburgh, Pa., December 29, 1962.

ments put all their emphasis on "next year's budget"—a budget that could not translate resources into objectives, could not project the future resource implications of proposed actions, and that did not distinguish between one-time investment outlays and recurring, or annual operating, expenses.

By January 1961 there had been quiet but long-standing recognition of this deficiency in relating military budgeting to planning. The RAND Corporation in 1954 had issued a report[4] suggesting a method for considering resource requirements in military planning, a method called "Program Budgeting." It proposed the identification of four major mission areas for the Air Force—strategic, defense, tactical, and transportation. It also proposed identifying to each of these mission areas not just equipments but the complete weapon system packages and support system packages necessary for their implementation. Finally, it proposed and demonstrated a new method for developing resource requirements in terms of weapon and support system packages so that they could in turn be related to the appropriate major mission area and this into a total Air Force posture. Perhaps more important, the RAND resource proposal was a part of a series of RAND developments in the field of weapon system analysis in which a major feature was the concept of evaluating alternatives and tradeoffs with a view to illuminating possible preferred solutions. Other requests for a "functional" or mission-oriented budget that had appeared by 1961 may have been motivated by a desire to use the information in seeking out preferred ways for applying resources to objectives, but no method for preparing such budgets was indicated.

There was then in 1961 a well-established legal basis for change and a recognition, at least in some quarters, of the need for major change. It was in this context that the new administration in 1961 embarked upon the planning for its military activities. One of the major features it introduced was the recognition of the need for a method for integrating resource programming and budgeting into military planning.

PROPOSAL FOR A PROGRAM BUDGET

The use of the term "program" in Washington had originated during World War II when it was used to describe a combination

[4] Novick, *Efficiency and Economy in Government.*

of activities to meet an end objective.[5] With the war's end, "program" was taken over by the Bureau of the Budget, but here it dealt with components such as personnel or the training of personnel rather than major end objectives. In the same way, "program" was used to lump together related administrative activities, such as procurement of equipment items. In none of these cases was the term "program" used to mean the output or ultimate goal of many interdependent activities (e.g., the combination of equipment, people, real estate, and related activities necessary for a military mission such as strategic bombardment or continental defense).

It was in this atmosphere that, in 1954, the new concept of program budgeting was projected for the Defense Department and the military services. Here "program" was to mean an integrated planning-programming-budgeting process that would bring together all of the resources to be applied to specific missions. The significant feature of this process is its effect on decisionmaking and control in the vital area of defense expenditures. This innovation is having a notable impact on financial management, but, as now administered, is leaving the traditional fiscal process relatively unchanged.

The new program-budget procedure has two primary aims: first, to permit analysis of total force structures for all of the services in terms of common missions or national objectives; second, to protect the resource impact (or financial requirements) of the proposed force structures over an extended period of years. To achieve the first objective we identify, for example, the Navy's Polaris weapon system as an element of the strategic retaliatory forces and have it compete for resources against other elements of the strategic forces such as Titan and Minuteman. This may be contrasted with the previous rationale, which put the Polaris in competition with other Navy programs having varying objectives, such as aircraft-carrier construction, antisubmarine warfare, etc. To accomplish the second objective, we project all of the development and procurement activities required to buy a new equipment; then add all the real estate, stocks, training, and other resources that are needed to put a new weapon system into the military inventory. To these investment outlays we add the recurring expenses that must be met each

[5] David Novick, *Which Program Do We Mean in "Program Budgeting"?* P-530 (Santa Monica, Calif.: The RAND Corporation, May 12, 1954). See also Don S. Burrows, "A Program Approach to Federal Budgeting," *Harvard Business Review,* May 1949, p. 272.

year we operate the equipment, and carry this process forward for a period of years that is either the expected life of the system or is administratively specified.

THE ROLE OF LONG-RANGE FINANCIAL PLANNING

Several major factors have in recent years created a new emphasis on unified longer range financial and nonfinancial planning for the entire military establishment. Such planning is in terms of missions, forces, and weapon systems, which are the actual products of defense expenditures, rather than in terms of the standard appropriation categories.

The strongest factor has been the diminishing relevance of the traditional military service boundaries in the implementation of the major missions or programs, such as continental defense or limited warfare. Today, responsibility for a major program is no longer within the exclusive province of an individual military service, but rather, in varying degrees, is shared by all of the services. Therefore, a budget organized in terms of the traditional services and the standard appropriation categories of procurement, construction, personnel, etc., is not readily adaptable for effective implementation of such interservice programs.

Beginning in the early 1950's weapon systems, because of their extreme technical complexity and increasing sophistication, have become enormously costly. This has made it more desirable, consequently, to be able to estimate in advance probable weapon system performance and cost and thus assist in the eventual choice between alternative weapons. Cost-effectiveness analysis[6] of alternative forces and weapon systems has therefore grown in importance. This technique stems basically from operations research in World War II.

The distinction between cost-effectiveness analysis and its predecessor, operations research, is very important. The emphasis of operations research, as the name implies, is on operations, while the emphasis in cost-effectiveness analysis is on forward planning. Freedom to allocate one's resources is usually severely limited in

[6] This term is the one usually employed in the Department of Defense. In the present study we use the term "cost-utility analysis." An illustrative example containing cost-utility analysis considerations in a military context is presented in the appendix to this chapter.

typical problems of operations research, whereas the purpose of cost-effectiveness analysis is to examine the effects of such alternative resource allocations.

Perhaps some mention should be made of how military planning has become the most important function in the military establishment. The swift nature of nuclear warfare with its requirement for response time measured in minutes, airborne alert, and so forth, resulting from the enormous speed of modern missiles carrying nuclear warheads, has shifted the emphasis in modern warfare from operations to planning. In the past, the relatively slow pace of military operations made it possible to deploy forces and weapons as the need arose, with a minimum of long-range advance planning. Today military planning has been cast in the central role not only because of the accelerated pace of nuclear war but also because of the long lead times necessary for weapons procurement, the enormous cost of weapons, and the wide choice of weapons through advanced technology.

The interest of Secretary of Defense McNamara in planning and management sciences has led him to seek out those who could help in this task. His interest has provided the needed impetus to effect a major change in the immense and complex Department of Defense. Equally important, the extraordinary capacity of the Secretary to master the complexities of vast programs has given vitality and stature to the new planning tools.

When Assistant Secretary of Defense (Comptroller) Charles J. Hitch first took office in 1961, he envisioned the introduction of the program-budgeting process over a period of several years. This span, however, was compressed by Mr. McNamara, who set as an initial objective the formulation of the FY 1963 defense budget in terms of major programs and weapon systems.

The new planning-programming-budgeting structure consists of five major elements:

1. A program structure in terms of missions, forces, and weapon and support systems.

2. The analytical comparisons of alternatives.

3. A continually updated five-year force structure and financial program.

4. Related year-round decisionmaking on new programs and changes.

5. Progress reporting to test the validity and administration of the plan.

The establishment of this system has considerably reduced the incidence of what Secretary McNamara has called "hectic and hurried"[7] decisions on major programs in the course of budget review. The annual budget now is essentially an increment of a longer range plan, although a substantial process is still involved in converting the program budget into the one used in the appropriation process.

The longer range plan, it should be made clear, is a unified Department of Defense plan rather than an aggregation of separate service plans. However, each service is still encouraged to assess competitive means for accomplishing a mission in which it has an interest. In this way service rivalries are maintained on a more productive basis. Service primacy has now become a less important issue than the relative importance of the missions and the potential contribution of each service to them. This may prove to be a primary advantage in the further implementation of a planning and programming framework in terms of missions, forces, and weapon systems.

With regard to possible implications of the new process for the organization of the services within the Defense Department, Secretary McNamara has disclaimed any intention to shift organizational responsibility from one service to another. He has, in fact, pointed out that the new process may serve as a substitute for such change. The actual execution of each mission is, after all, the responsibility of the interservice and functional commands. Thus, the continued organization of the services on a nonmission basis is no disclaimer of the importance of planning by mission.

The change of emphasis from annual budgeting in terms of appropriations to longer range planning in terms of missions, forces, and weapon systems has naturally had an impact on financial improvement programs. The emphasis on cost fostered by Public Law 863[8] is seen now as only part of the answer to the objective of

---

[7] "Annual Report of the Secretary of Defense, July 1, 1960, to June 30, 1961," Department of Defense, *Annual Report for Fiscal Year 1961* (Washington, D.C.: U.S. Government Printing Office, 1962), p. 27.

[8] "An Act To Improve Governmental Budgeting and Accounting Methods and Procedures," August 1, 1956, *United States Statutes at Large . . . 1956 and Proclamations*, Vol. 70, 84th Cong., 2d Sess. (Washington, D.C.: U.S. Government Printing Office, 1957), pp. 782–783.

achieving "cost-based" budgeting. Assistant Secretary Hitch in a speech to an accounting group explained the relationship of the new to the old:[9]

Cost-based budgeting and accrual accounting deal primarily with costs over shorter time periods and with the performance of all of the many tasks which go to make up an effective fighting machine. The program system is concerned with costs over a longer period of time and with performance in terms of acquiring and deploying the forces and equipment in accordance with program goals and plans. Both objectives are important, but we believe first attention must be given to the accounting needs of our programming system.

Much work remains to be done to derive the full benefits of the new process. The discussion to follow will highlight the more important remaining tasks.

PLANNING AND PROGRAMMING

Planning and programming, which are words that have been used often in this discussion, are really aspects of the same process; they differ only in emphasis. *Planning* is the production of the range of meaningful potentials for selection of courses of action through a systematic consideration of alternatives. *Programming* is the more specific determination of the manpower, materiel, and facilities necessary for accomplishing a program. In addition, except in the very short term where dollars are in effect "given," programming entails interest in the dollar requirements for meeting the manpower, materiel, and facility needs.

The new process results in improved planning through the designation of major "programs," and of "program elements" within them, as the units for planning and programming of forces, dollar costs, and manpower. Major programs represent the primary missions to be performed. The nine major programs currently identified in the Department of Defense program-budget structure are listed and described briefly on pages 92–93. Program elements are the forces, weapon (or support) systems, and similar types of integrated activities by means of which the missions are accomplished. As an example, the program elements that make up Program I: Strategic Retaliatory Forces are listed on page 93.

[9] Presented before the Federal Government Accountants Association of Washington, D.C., April 12, 1962.

Major Programs in the Department of Defense
Program-Budget Structure[a]

Program I

Strategic Retaliatory Forces: the forces that are designed to carry out the long-range strategic mission and to carry the main burden of battle in general. They include the long-range bombers, the air-to-ground and decoy missiles, and the refueling tankers; the land-based and submarine-based strategic missiles; and the systems for their command and control.

Program II

Continental Air and Missile Defense Forces: those weapon systems, warning and communications networks and ancillary equipment required to detect, identify, track, and destroy unfriendly forces approaching the North American continent.

Program III

General Purpose Forces: the forces relied upon to perform the entire range of combat operations short of general nuclear war. These include most of the Army's combat and combat support units, virtually all Navy units, all Marine Corps units, and the tactical units of the Air Force.

Program IV

Airlift and Sealift Forces: those airlift and sealift forces required to move troops and cargo promptly to wherever they might be needed. Included in the airlift forces are both the MATS transports and the Air Force Tactical Air Command troop carrier aircraft. The sealift forces include the troop ships, cargo ships, and tankers operated by MSTS and the "Forward Floating Bases."

Program V

Reserve and National Guard Forces: equipment, training, and administration of the Reserve and National Guard personnel of the several services.

Program VI

Research and Development: all research and development effort not directly identified with elements of other programs (i.e., where there has been no decision to produce for inventory).

[a] Excerpted from statement of Secretary of Defense Robert S. McNamara before the Committee on Armed Services on the Fiscal Year 1965–1969 Defense Program and 1965 Defense Budget, January 27, 1964, *Hearings on Military Posture and H.R. 9637*, House of Representatives, 88th Cong., 2d Sess. (Washington, D.C.: U.S. Government Printing Office, 1964).

Program VII

General Support: support activities of the several services and the agencies that serve the entire Department of Defense. It constitutes an "all-other" or residual category of activities or programs and includes all costs not capable of being directly or meaningfully allocated to the other major programs.

Program VIII

Military Assistance: equipment, training, and related services provided for armed forces of allied and friendly nations.

Program IX

Civil Defense: federal assistance for fallout shelters, warning and radiological monitoring systems, training and education for emergency preparedness, etc.

Program Elements Contained in Program I: Strategic Retaliatory Forces

Aircraft Forces
  B/EB–47
  RB–47
  B–52
  AGM–28A/B
  GAM–87
  B–58
  KC–97
  KC–135
  RC–135

Missile Forces, Land Based
  Atlas
  Titan
  Minuteman

Missile Forces, Sea Based
  Polaris System
  Regulus System

Command Control, Communications and Support
  SAC Control System (465L)
  PACCS (KC–135/B–47)
  UHF Emergency Rocket Communications System
  Base Operating Support
  Advanced Flying and Missile Training
  Headquarters and Command Support

The subdivision of the entire defense program into over 800 program elements could not have been accomplished in the limited time available without deferring many possible questions regarding the scope of each program element. Because the scope of many program elements was not necessarily matched to existing appropriation activities or organizations, it was initially somewhat indefinite. Further study in this area is still required.

Particularly troublesome has been the question of the proper distribution of the costs of supporting activities. Although such activities are not in themselves output-oriented in the same sense as a B-52 squadron, their costs must be allocated on some appropriate basis to the proper program elements. An installation or base, for example, may support two or more force units, and in some cases it is necessary to divide the support costs correctly between the units. More explicit rules must be developed to assure reliability in cost distribution methods. Without this reliability, comparison between one cost analysis and the next cannot be meaningful.

Within the program budget structure, planning decisions are made after comparing projected costs and effectiveness of feasible program choices. In such comparisons a methodical examination of alternatives is made in terms of quantitative estimates of cost (including manpower, equipment, facilities, etc.) and of the expected military benefits ("effectiveness") to be derived from the systems. A typical comparison might involve the merits of buying more Minuteman squadrons versus more Polaris submarines. Illustrative formats for presenting cost-effectiveness data to the Secretary, which were put into the *Congressional Record* by Assistant Secretary Hitch,[10] are shown in tables 4.2, 4.3, 4.4, and 4.5.

The programming aspect of the process consists of an eight-year force structure and a five-year financial program in terms of major forces, dollar costs, and manpower—all by program element within each of the major programs. This relates financial to nonfinancial planning in a way that is not possible with the standard appropriation structure. The Basic National Security Policy, the Joint Strategic Objective Plan, and the service plans can now be meshed with the Secretary's five-year plan.

[10] Statement of Assistant Secretary of Defense (Comptroller) C. J. Hitch before the Military Operations Subcommittee, July 25, 1962, *Systems Development and Management (Part 2)*, *Hearings before a Subcommittee of the Committee on Government Operations*, House of Representatives, 87th Cong., 2d Sess. (Washington, D.C.: U.S. Government Printing Office, 1962), pp. 513–547.

TABLE 4.2 Alternative Force Structures

This part of the summary would normally include:
(a) The currently approved program.
(b) The alternative (if any) proposed by the relevant service.
(c) The JCS recommended force structure.
(d) Other significant alternative possibilities.
The format for describing each alternative normally includes a projection of the relevant part of the force structure. For example:

Alternative I. Numbers of Aircraft End of Fiscal Year
(Figures and models are hypothetical)

Aircraft	1961	1962	1963	1964	1965	1966	1967
F–18	800	767	658	493	325	275	150
F–21	412	510	620	620	610	585	570
F–28	—	—	—	200	315	385	510

And similarly for each alternative.

Source: Statement of Assistant Secretary of Defense (Comptroller) C. J. Hitch, *Systems Development and Management (Part 2), Hearings before a Subcommittee of the Committee on Government Operations,* House of Representatives, 87th Cong., 2d Sess. (Washington, D.C.: U.S. Government Printing Office, 1962), App. IV (b), pp. 643–644.

TABLE 4.3 System Costs

For each alternative force structure, a summary of complete system costs is shown. For example:

Alternative I. Total Obligational Authority End of Fiscal Year
(in millions of dollars)

System	1961	1962	1963	1964	1965	1966	1967
F–18							
R&D							
Initial investment							
Annual operating							
Subtotal							
F–21							
R&D							
Initial investment							
Annual operating							
Subtotal							
F–28							
R&D							
Initial investment							
Annual operating							
Subtotal							
Grand total							

Source: See Table 4.2.

TABLE 4.4 Evaluation of Effectiveness

This section will, of course, vary with the weapon systems and forces in question, with the objectives, mission, etc. Moreover, various areas are more or less amenable to quantitative analysis. The following two examples are illustrative of evaluations of alternative strategic retaliatory forces and tactical attack air forces.

Strategic Retaliatory Forces

	Alternative Forces, FY 1967			
	I	II	III	IV
Population and floor space destroyed:				
United States				
Population				
Floor space				
Allied				
Population				
Floor space				
Sino-Soviet				
Population				
Floor space				
Expected number of targets destroyed:				
Category I				
Category II				
Category III				
Category IV				
Category V				
Category VI				
Others				

Tactical Air Forces
(Attack Mission)

	Alternative Forces, FY 1966			
	1	II	III	IV
Per day:				
Tons of ordnance delivered				
Aircraft hours on station				
Sorties				
Expected number of targets				
destroyed:				
Category I				
Category II				
Category III				
Category IV				
Others				

Source: See Table 4.2.

TABLE 4.5 Summary of Comments or Recommendations

(a)	By Services.
(b)	By Joint Chiefs of Staff.
(c)	By Director of Defense Research and Engineering, Comptroller, and others.

Source: See Table 4.2.

Funding considerations no longer need be the overriding factor to which plans are adjusted. Former Deputy Secretary Roswell L. Gilpatric contrasted this earlier type of planning process with the present one in the following words:[11]

In the past, the Defense Department has often developed its force structure by starting with a budget and sending it off in search of a program. Our new system of program packaging has reversed this procedure, by first determining our over-all strategy, then fitting the hardware and the manpower to those objectives.

This does not mean that the overall defense cost level is of no concern. It certainly is, but arbitrary ceilings are no longer used.

Financial planning for a period longer than a year must always carry the qualification that the actual provision of adequate resources cannot be guaranteed. If resource levels are changed, however, a financial plan that is more directly translatable to program output simplifies the revision of nonfinancial goals.

Financial planning in terms of major programs and program elements, and budgeting in terms of appropriations, are linked by use of the same measure of cost—total obligational authority. They are also linked by the use of planning and programming cost categories that can be related by appropriations. The principal cost categories are research and development, investment, and operations. These highlight the key decision points in the life of a weapon system. Each of the cost categories is related to several of the appropriation categories, and in time it may be possible to achieve an even closer coordination between the two classifications.

Translation of financial planning in terms of major programs and program elements to budget activities can be made somewhat

[11] "Defense—How Much Will It Cost?" *California Management Review,* vol. V, no. 2, Winter 1962, p. 53.

easier by further analysis and revision of the program element structure. Effective work of this kind has already been accomplished for the Research and Development and General Support programs. The frequent costings now required on a program element basis have brought increasing attention to programming-budgeting consistency and understanding of relationships.

One of Secretary McNamara's objectives is to have at all times an up-to-date Five-Year Force Structure and Financial Program. Obviously such a goal can be achieved only by the use of some type of continuous review process rather than by the traditional comprehensive annual requirements review. Consequently, a new program change proposal system was developed to help attain this objective.

PROGRAM CHANGE PROPOSAL SYSTEM

A major motivation in establishing the Program Change Proposal (PCP) system was that the cost of approved programs be kept within the approved limits. Program decisionmaking would be limited in validity if, in fact, actual costs exceeded the levels on which approvals had been based, as had happened frequently in the past. Advance authorization for any cost variances from the approved levels would now be required. This would make it clear that, in the Secretary's words, "a reliable cost estimate is an important factor and that those sponsoring the system are expected to personally assume responsibility for the accuracy of that cost estimate."[12]

The PCP system represents the first effort by the Department of Defense to establish a general mechanism other than the annual budget for programming, decisionmaking, and control.[13] Its adoption provided the DOD with a more methodical and systematic procedure for making major program decisions and has proven to be a significant contribution in the management of the DOD. The system occupies a key position in program budgeting in the DOD.

[12] *Department of Defense Appropriations for 1963, Hearings before a Subcommittee on Appropriations,* House of Representatives, 87th Cong., 2d Sess. (Washington, D.C.: U.S. Government Printing Office, 1962), Part 2, p. 38.
[13] "DOD Programming System," U.S. Department of Defense, Directive No. 7045.1, October 30, 1964.

Through it, additions, deletions, or modifications to the approved five-year program can be introduced and acted on at any time.

The PCP system contains a number of important features in addition to providing a means for continuously revised programming and budgeting. It assists in maintaining at all times an approved force and financial plan projected over a span of five years. Where previously the traditional budget cycle had the effect of holding up programming decisions until periodic budget reviews, it is now possible for a service's major program proposals to be prepared and submitted for Secretary of Defense approval without regard to the annual budget cycle. Through the PCP system and the Five-Year Force Structure and Financial Program, a mechanism is provided for freeing program decisions from the annual budget cycles.

The submission of a PCP by a service usually comes as the culmination of a major study. Such a study is practically essential in view of the requirement that the proposal include estimates of cost and effectiveness over the long term, and consider alternatives and tradeoffs. For example, a proposal for a particular R&D effort must be accompanied by cost estimates, not only for the R&D itself but also for the procurement and operation of the resulting military system. This provides a picture of the total cost implications of proposed measures.

Costs, through the PCP system, are continuously related to missions and military effectiveness. Such statements of costs and effectiveness serve management in its critical planning objective to weigh the costs and benefits of alternative courses of action for the purpose of allocating available resources in a manner that either maximizes total effectiveness for a given budget level or minimizes total cost for a given level of effectiveness.

The PCP system enhances the services' ability to present the Secretary of Defense with carefully worked out program proposals and pertinent data to support them. Such proposals are received by the Office of the Secretary of Defense staff agencies for review and by the Office of Systems Analysis for evaluation. The service data accompanying the PCP permit a review and evaluation by OSD agencies in the light of the total defense program. At the OSD level, competing systems' cost and effectiveness can be evaluated without regard to questions of service jurisdiction. For example, Navy close-support manned aircraft systems can be compared with similar Air Force systems.

Staff review of PCP's by the OSD is accelerated by the designation for each proposal of a coordinating office responsible for "spearheading" and integrating the review and proposing the response of the Secretary of Defense. Comments by the Joint Chiefs of Staff are furnished directly to the Secretary, with a copy to the coordinating office. The Secretary is not shielded from controversy because the coordinating office is required to inform him of differences of opinion.

Expeditious submission and handling of changes is essential to the effectiveness of the PCP system. The importance of the annual budget process in decisionmaking has been due, at least in part, to the fact that in the budget process decisions *must* be made, and this element of immediacy is worth retaining and encouraging.

In practice, the PCP system has not worked as smoothly as the foregoing description would indicate. Both the services and OSD have found it difficult to treat major decisions on an individual basis. As a result, the majority of change proposals are now scheduled for mid-calendar submissions to provide the OSD with a comprehensive review prior to the development of the budget. In addition, in FY 1965 comprehensive force reviews were made early in the year using the Joint Strategic Objective Plan submitted by the Joint Chiefs of Staff as the force proposals. The Secretary of Defense then issued tentative force guidance based on an evaluation of the JSOP, and the services submitted PCP's to obtain approval of the specific manpower and dollars to support the forces and to balance out the remainder of their programs.

THE PROGRAM AND THE BUDGET

As indicated earlier, the new program-budget procedure leaves the traditional fiscal process relatively unchanged. After the Secretary has made his decisions in program terms, these are then, in October of each year, reconstructed into the conventional budget, as shown in Table 4.1. At this point there is a melding of the post-1961 and pre-1961 procedures.

The Secretary of Defense communicates to the services and defense agencies his tentative decisions on matters raised by the joint OSD and Budget Bureau review of the budget estimates. This is done by the Subject/Issue (S/I) process, more popularly known as "Operation Snowflake." An individual service Secretary or a defense agency may request reconsideration when the service Secretary or defense agency believes it is in order. These requests are then the subject for *reclama*.

PCP's received after August 1 are not processed as PCP's but are incorporated in the budget review process. Thus a few PCP's may still be pending by October 1, and these may or may not be so processed depending on their substance. PCP's that are incorporated in the budget review are resolved through S/I procedures. Naturally, any decisions made outside of the budget review, but subsequent to the submission of budget estimates, must be reflected in an amendment to the budget estimate.

The format used by OSD for S/I submission provides for a tabulation of the costs involved in the request and the costs of the alternatives submitted by OSD, a description of the subject under discussion, and an evaluation of all points that should be considered in deciding the issue. The last paragraph sets forth briefly the alternatives available to the Secretary of Defense. The final statement on the paper is the Secretary's decision, together with a financial adjustment sheet setting forth the detailed budgetary effect of the decision.

Although the PCP system permits decisionmaking on an individual program basis, it does not rule out a simultaneous consideration of competing programs. It does not imply that each program is reviewed without any regard to the relative importance of all defense programs and to the total resource requirement level. This is why continuous analysis of the entire defense program is necessary.

It was originally thought that only summary-type data would be required in the initial submission of a change proposal. However, Mr. McNamara's requirement has been for rather full justification of the proposal and as complete detail (forces, costs, manpower, procurement schedules, financing, etc.) as is appropriate to the evaluation.

In order to secure current data on changes of lesser magnitude than those that have been discussed thus far and to reflect various

costing and pricing changes, all data in the five-year plan are updated monthly. The major update takes place early in January to
bring the program into complete agreement with the Department
of Defense budget submitted to Congress. This base is then updated at the end of each month to reflect all decisions and changes
made during the month. Thus the program is always current. Development of computer procedures for the Five-Year Force Structure and Financial Program has made this possible.

The need for progress reporting on a program basis has been
graphically stated by Secretary McNamara:[14]

The effective management of approved programs also requires a reporting system that keeps top officials constantly informed of the progress being made in achieving established objectives—in both physical
and financial terms on the basis of program entities and not merely in
terms of the bits and pieces of programs financed in various appropriation accounts.

The whole concept of progress reporting as a part of the programming system has been the subject of much discussion and
consideration. However, at the beginning of 1965 the progress-
reporting procedures for about two hundred of the most important
materiel items had not yet been implemented.

Progress reporting is also required for programs of an operating
nature. Actual performance should be reported in relation to
planned levels, using specific performance and workload indicators
pertinent to the program element.

There is a vast amount of information associated with five-year
planning. Effective use of these data by the Secretary of Defense
and his principal advisers is dependent to some extent on imaginative staff analysis of important trends and issues and the corrective
actions required.

An important need exists for a systematic projection into the
future of program costs resulting from partial program approvals.
For major weapon systems, such as the Nike-X or F-111, it is
customary for Department of Defense management to approve first
only the research and development phase of the program. Approval
of investment is then contingent on success in the R & D phase. For
realistic five-year planning it is necessary to anticipate possible
changes in the official program.

[14] "Annual Report of the Secretary of Defense," *op. cit.*, p. 27.

The Department of Defense is now equipped with a comprehensive system for the continual programming of forces, manpower, and dollars—a remarkable achievement for a $50-billion-a-year organization, which since its inception has operated on a markedly different basis. However, regardless of how sophisticated a tool the programming system is in translating plans into programs, it cannot of itself ensure a high quality of planning. Here, one must recall the previous distinction between planning and programming.

In planning, one seeks a continual review of objectives and the means for their attainment. The preferred alternative remains preferred only as long as no additional knowledge of program prospects in relation to other competitive systems dictates another choice. The concern is with weighing and evaluating, and applying all of one's knowledge in the process. In the cost-effectiveness analyses used in planning, detailed cost estimates (which are characteristic of operating budgets) are not required.

In programming, one moves closer to actuality and acquires a greater respect for stability. Objectives are not challenged as frequently as in planning; instead, attention is concentrated on translating preferred alternatives to reality. More precise costing is now in order, because one must be able to anticipate the budgetary consequences of approved programs.

Planning is of necessity a more informal process than programming, more a matter of attitude than of procedure. One must be sure that as much attention and zeal go into the development and use of planning tools as into the development of a programming system.

One must face up to the inherent limitations in planning for the acquisition of enormously complex weapon systems involving advanced technology. Such systems take years to progress from inception to operational status—in an environment in which strategic needs may change rapidly. Accelerated development and production of a desired weapon of designated capabilities require early decisions that are inevitably subject to varying degrees of uncertainty. The effects of these uncertainties on cost estimates must be determined because they will be important factors in decision-making.

A particular uncertainty affecting cost estimates stems from the advanced performance characteristics specified for new weapon

systems. Tests of developmental hardware may disclose performance shortcomings from design objectives, the correction of which
results in additional effort and cost. Another important uncertainty
stems from the present lack of knowledge in regard to the detailed
composition, deployment, and employment of future systems. Some
assumptions may later prove to have been invalid, which would
affect the validity of the estimates. Cost factors and relationships
may not have been realistic, perhaps because of a scarcity of data
on similar hardware. It is not difficult to become somewhat dis-
trustful of all weapon system cost estimates made at the crucial
stages for decisionmaking—i.e., during development and at the
inception of production.

With so many uncertainties facing the military cost analyst, a
premium is placed on experience and judgment. The proportion
of experienced cost analysts to the growing workload is diminishing, partly because of the rapidly increasing demands engendered
by the new planning-programming-budgeting process. The importance of increasing the overall supply of military cost analysts has
been recognized by the Air Force, which is considering the establishment of a separate cost analysis career specialty, supported by
a special training program.

Other steps can be taken to improve cost analysis. Contractors'
methods of reporting costs to the various elements of the Department of Defense might warrant re-examination, particularly in
view of the introduction of PERT Cost. A need exists for a review
of the specialized costing capability in the advanced equipment
areas, covering the activities in these areas of the government,
industrial contractors, and nonprofit organizations. Also needed
is more systematic comparison of actual cost experience with newer
weapon systems against the earlier estimates.

In spite of the difficulties involved, cost-effectiveness analysis
of alternative systems still remains one of the best methods to assist
in selecting the preferred means of accomplishing national security
objectives. The new programming system will foster interest in
such studies as well as support them by bringing together programs
and costs by major program and program element.

The increased emphasis in the Department of Defense on systematic planning and programming will undoubtedly have a profound effect on industry. There will be an increased demand for

contractor studies and longer range projections both from the military department and the OSD. More emphasis will be placed on the quality of the cost estimates.

KEEPING TO BUDGETS

The concern of the Secretary that overall costs of approved programs must not be exceeded without prior review and approval has been a primary motivation in the adoption of the PCP system. It will compel an earlier recognition by the services and their contractors of possible cost overruns for the entire life of a program. Continuous cost estimating by industry will be required in the course of the program, not only for control, but also for testing the validity of the original decision.

The new defense planning-programming-budgeting process has aroused considerable interest both in Congress and throughout the executive branch of the government. The preparation and presentation of the 1963, 1964, and 1965 Department of Defense budgets as the outcome of the new method of planning and programming brought the subject to the close attention of the Armed Services and Appropriation Committees. Committee members were impressed with the Secretary's overall grasp of the defense program, and because of this were favorably inclined toward the process contributing to his understanding.

Though accepting the new process as an essential tool of planning, and even claiming some credit for its adoption, the House Appropriations Committee still wanted the budget format left unchanged. It is, of course, a virtue of the new process that it does not require a change in budget format. Planning and programming are simply superimposed on the budget and govern its substance, although not its form. The relationship is explicitly stated in the House Appropriations Committee report:[15] "Basically, each annual appropriations bill is simply an additional annual increment to the longer range Defense program."

The need for an extended budgetary time horizon was recognized in a study of the federal budget by the staff of the Subcom-

[15] *Department of Defense Appropriation Bill, 1963*, House of Representatives Report No. 1607, 87th Cong., 2d Sess. (Washington, D.C.: U.S. Government Printing Office, 1962), p. 7.

mittee on Economic Statistics of the Joint Economic Committee. The generalized use of cost-benefit relationships was advocated as a means of achieving better budgets.[16]

In the executive establishment, the Bureau of the Budget is encouraging the departments and agencies to plan, program, and budget on a longer range basis. The Bureau of the Budget, the Department of the Treasury, and the Council of Economic Advisers are cooperating in preparing longer term economic projections.

The Department of Defense example, congressional interest, and Bureau of the Budget sponsorship of longer range planning should help to accelerate interest elsewhere within the government in the kind of planning-programming-budgeting process used in the Department of Defense. Such possible application is the subject of the following five chapters of Part II.

Appendix to Chapter 4

ILLUSTRATIVE EXAMPLE OF COST-UTILITY CONSIDERATIONS IN A MILITARY CONTEXT

BY GENE H. FISHER

As indicated in Chapter 3, there are people who believe that any analytical effort of value to a decisionmaker dealing with major problems may prove exceptionally difficult, perhaps impossible. Two reasons in support of this belief are (1) an extremely complex environment, along with a host of nonquantifiable variables; and (2) a short deadline to complete a study.

No doubt there are such instances. However, we have taken the position that even in rather severe cases *something* can be done, and that this something may often be very useful in spite of the lack of extensive calculations of utility and cost. In this appendix, an example having the above characteristics is selected deliberately

16 *The Federal Budget as an Economic Document,* prepared for the Subcommittee on Economic Statistics of the Joint Economic Committee, 87th Cong., 2d Sess. (Washington, D.C.: U.S. Government Printing Office, 1962).

to illustrate the kind of analysis that might be done.[1] The example is a military one, extracted from an actual study conducted at The RAND Corporation some time ago. To avoid a security-classified discussion, much of the substantive material has had to be suppressed. However, it is hoped that enough of the essential content of the problem is preserved so that a few of the more important points can be illustrated.

GENERAL STATEMENT OF THE PROBLEM

Basically, the problem may be stated as follows:

1. Investigate the possible role of long-endurance aircraft (LEA)[2] for use in new weapon (or support) systems to perform a variety of Air Force missions in the 1970–1975 time period.

2. In each mission area compare LEA-type systems with alternative possibilities, including missile as well as aircraft systems.

3. Investigate the possibilities for *multipurpose* use of the LEA; i.e., of developing a basic aircraft and adapting it to several mission areas. What are the cost savings? What degradations, if any, in utility (system effectiveness) might be incurred in a given mission area by using a multipurpose vehicle rather than one "optimized" to that particular mission?

4. Assess the implications for possible new development programs to be initiated in the near future, with a view to initial operational capability in the early 1970's.

5. Consider the time to do the study: about *six weeks.*[3]

FURTHER CONSIDERATION OF THE PROBLEM

The statement of the problem as outlined above appears fairly straightforward, although the short time period for doing the study

[1] Some years ago such an example might have been regarded as atypical. In today's environment, however, it is probably most typical.

[2] A long-endurance aircraft is one designed specifically to remain airborne in unrefueled flight for a prolonged period of time (in some cases several days). Usually the emphasis on long endurance involves compromises in certain of the other performance characteristics, especially speed and cruise altitude.

[3] In all fairness it should be pointed out that The RAND Corporation had in previous years done a considerable amount of work on the technical and design aspects of LEA. However, work on *system* applications of LEA was somewhat more

imposes a significant constraint. However, even preliminary thinking about the problem soon leads to a set of considerations, which
in turn rapidly lead to the conclusion that the problem is a difficult
one. Some of the more important considerations are outlined in the
following paragraphs.

A wide range of possible mission area applications might be
considered; for example: strategic bombardment, limited war,
defense against submarine-launched ballistic-missile attack, air
defense of North America (against the air-breathing threat), command and control, satellite launching platform, antisatellite-missile
launching platform, air transport, and intelligence and/or reconnaissance patrol applications.

The future environment (1970–1975) in practically all the
mission areas is very uncertain. In limited war, for instance, what
kinds of limited-war scenarios[4] should we consider? Obviously, we
cannot single out one that is "most probable." A range of scenarios
must be considered. This range should not necessarily be chosen on
the basis of likelihood, but rather to illustrate possible roles for the
LEA.

Within most of the mission areas, there is a wide range of alternative systems to be considered—even including the Navy's proposals for an advanced Fleet Ballistic Missile (Polaris) system in
the strategic area. (Some of the more relevant alternatives are discussed later.)

After only slight initial examination, it becomes obvious that the
most critical considerations do not concern the LEA vehicle itself,
but rather the *payload subsystems* that have to be developed and
procured to give an LEA system its capability in a given mission
area. There are exceptions: probably command and control, for
example. But, in general, the payload subsystems have the more
interesting and difficult technical problems; and preliminary cost
analysis indicated that the development cost for a subsystem in a

---

limited. In any event, six weeks was a short time to do a study of this type, at least
by RAND standards. But time to do a study is relative. In a military staff environment in the Pentagon six weeks would no doubt be considered a relatively long time.

[4] Here "scenario" essentially means the context or setting within which the particular type of war is assumed to take place: for example, the geographic area, the
political environment at the beginning of the conflict, the political objectives to be
attained, the constraints on weapons (nuclear weapons or not?), the sanctuaries, if
any, etc.

given area (such as strategic bombardment) would be considerably greater than for the total development program for the LEA itself. In short, what initially is specified as mainly an aircraft problem rapidly turns primarily into a subsystem type of problem.

The main characteristics of an LEA are extended airborne capability (endurance), large payload, and long range.[5] These are so-called positive characteristics. The main negative ones are low speed and possibly constraints on altitude capability. Therefore the analyst should think immediately about mission applications where the positive characteristics are desired and where low speed is not a handicap or perhaps is even desirable (e.g., in certain types of intelligence/reconnaissance operations). One example is a mission area in which airborne patrol operations are important. Another is a situation where vulnerability on the ground to an initial enemy attack is a problem, and an alternative basing scheme is required. The LEA used as an airborne platform provides such a scheme. But there are still other possibile alternative basing schemes: ground mobility, water-based platforms (surface), water-based platforms (submersible), etc. These alternatives would have to be taken into account in the analysis.

From this partial list of considerations it is clear that the problem at hand is indeed a complex one. The real question is what can be done with it in the short period of time available for analytical effort. For illustrative purposes, let us take one mission area—strategic bombardment—and consider some of the more relevant factors.

SOME CONSIDERATIONS IN THE STRATEGIC BOMBARDMENT AREA

In considering whether currently planned strategic systems for the early 1970's should be supplemented, two major intelligence-type uncertainties are paramount:

1. Whether the enemy is likely to achieve technological advances such that his offensive capabilities will render U.S. fixed base (hardened) missile systems vulnerable on the ground to a first strike.

[5] There are tradeoffs among these, of course.

2. Whether the enemy is likely to achieve a reasonably effective defense against intercontinental ballistic missiles (an AICBM capability) during the early 1970 time period.

Although the analyst cannot *resolve* these uncertainties, he can and should trace out their implications, enumerate the relevant alternatives that might be used to meet them, and possibly suggest ways to hedge against them.

With respect to the first uncertainty (item 1), it is clear that the LEA would be of interest if the problem is one of seeking alternative basing schemes to avoid or reduce vulnerability on the ground. The LEA could be used as a standoff missile launching platform in a system having a substantial part of the force on continuous airborne alert. With respect to the second uncertainty (item 2), the LEA offers no *unique* features; but it could be used as an airborne platform from which low-altitude penetrating missiles (to avoid AICBM defenses) could be launched. When items 1 and 2 are combined, however, it could be that an LEA system (with low-altitude penetrating missiles) might be attractive. But such a system would have to be compared with the alternatives.

What are some of the relevant alternatives? The following is an illustrative list.

For the case in which the prime objective is to reduce initial vulnerability to a surprise attack, the alternatives are:

1. LEA used as a standoff platform for launching airborne ballistic missiles (ALBM's) in a system having a substantial part of of the force on continuous airborne alert.

2. Land mobile (truck and/or rail) ballistic-missile systems.

3. Water mobile (barge) ballistic-missile systems.

4. Incremental fleet ballistic-missile (Polaris) force. (Incremental to the currently planned Polaris force.)

5. *More* Minuteman missiles to try to compensate for their ground vulnerability by having a bigger force. (Incremental to the currently planned Minuteman force.)

For the case in which the main purpose is to have a system that can penetrate enemy ICBM defenses, the alternatives are:

1. Low-altitude penetrating missiles launched from an airborne platform—an LEA or some other aircraft.

2. Land-based (fixed) ballistic-missile systems with low-altitude penetrating re-entry devices.

3. Land-based (fixed) ballistic-missile systems with multiple warhead (possibly including decoys) re-entry devices to confuse the enemy ICBM defense.

4. Sea-based ballistic-missile systems with low-altitude penetrating re-entry bodies or with multiple warhead capability.

For a combination of the above two cases, i.e., where the main concern is about the initial vulnerability of U.S. strategic systems and about the enemy having an AICBM capability, the alternatives are:

1. LEA used as a standoff platform for launching low-altitude penetrating missiles in a system having a substantial fraction of the force on continuous airborne alert.

2. Land mobile (truck or rail) ballistic-missile systems with low-altitude penetrating re-entry devices or with multiple warhead re-entry bodies.

3. Water mobile (surface) ballistic-missile systems with low-altitude penetrating re-entry devices or with multiple warhead rc-cntry bodies.

4. Same as item 3 except *below* the surface platform (e.g., submarines or submersible barges).

The main problem is to conduct an analysis to compare the above alternatives on a cost-utility basis, with a view to determining preferred alternatives under certain assumed scenarios. Ideally, this would proceed somewhat as described below. (We assume a fixed utility conceptual framework; a fixed budget context could be used instead.)

An enemy target system is specified to be destroyed with some probability of success (say, 90 per cent). Campaign analyses are conducted to determine the force size that would be required for each alternative to do the specified task. This involves determining the number of U.S. weapons surviving the initial enemy attack, determining the force that is successfully launched to make the responding strike on the specified enemy target system, assessing losses to the enemy defenses, calculating target destruction, and the like.[6] Given the resulting force-size calculations, we then proceed with a resource analysis to determine the *total system cost* (research and development, investment and operating cost) for

---

[6] It should be emphasized that these campaign analyses are very *difficult and time-consuming.*

each of the alternatives required to do the job specified initially. These system costs can then be compared, to try to determine which alternative is likely to accomplish the given task at the lowest cost. Finally, the analyst might repeat the analysis for varying levels of initial enemy attack and varying types of U.S. responses, and then conduct a qualitative analysis to supplement the quantitative work.

The preceding discussion is in the realm of a "hard core" cost-utility analysis, one that is not easy to do and is certainly very time consuming. Because only six weeks were available on this particular problem for the entire study, the analysis was far from complete. The real question is what *can* be done, if anything, within these limitations. We maintain that a great deal can be done far short of a type of analysis involving a relatively complete set of calculations of utility and cost.[7] For one thing, a mere *enumeration* of all the relevant alternatives may be very helpful; better yet would be to furnish data and information bearing on utility and cost of these alternatives.

Summary Analyses of Cost and Utility

One thing that can be done is to develop summary analyses of cost and utility and present them along with a qualitative statement of some of the key implications. Examples are contained in Fig. 1 and Table 4.6.

Fig. 1 shows total system cost (research and development, investment and operating cost[8]) versus force size for several alternative systems. In this example force size means number of missiles in position ready to go. In the case of a system like Minuteman, it means number of missiles in silos ready to fire. In the case of an LEA system carrying airborne air-to-surface missiles, it means number of missiles continuously airborne on station ready to go. Used in conjunction with data pertaining to utility (as in Table 4.6), system cost versus force size curves can be useful.

For example, suppose that alternatives A and C are in the same "ball park" with respect to certain key utility variables (say, pen-

---

[7] Recall that our objective in analytical work is *not* to "make the decision" but rather to try to *sharpen* the decisionmaker's intuition and judgment.

[8] Operating cost is usually computed for a fixed period of years, say, five or seven.

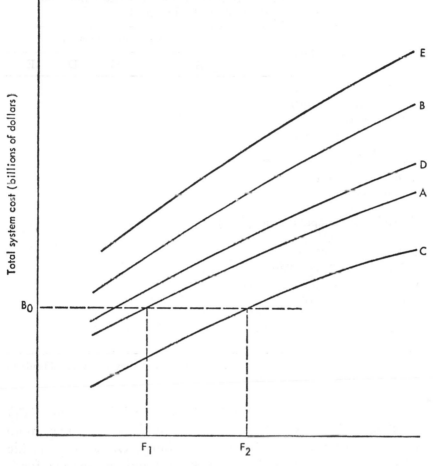

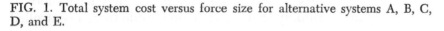

Force size (number of ready missiles)

FIG. 1. Total system cost versus force size for alternative systems A, B, C, D, and E.

etration capability and single-shot kill probability) but that C is clearly more vulnerable to an initial enemy strike than is A. The difference in the system cost curves for A and C in Fig. 1, then, essentially represents what we pay for getting reduced vulnerability. But there are other ways to play this game. Suppose the decisionmaker has a given budget (B_0 in Fig. 1) to spend for supplementation of the already planned strategic forces. For B_0 he can

TABLE 4.6 Selected Data Bearing on Utility Considerations for Alternative Systems A, B, C, D, and E

Description	Alternative System				
	A	B	C	D	E
Quantitative information					
Effective range (n mi)					
Cruise speed (kn)					
Penetration speed (kn)					
Warhead yield (MT)					
Circular error probability (CEP)					
Single shot kill probability					
Against soft targets					
Against hard targets					
Extended strike option time (days)					
(etc.)					
Qualitative information[a]					
"Show of force" capability					
Multidirectional attack capability					
Ground vulnerability					
In-flight vulnerability					
Controlled response capability					
(etc.)					

[a] Some of these items have quantitative aspects, but they are very difficult to assess in a study with a short time deadline.

get a force size of F_1 for alternative A, or a much larger force (F_2) of system C. He may judge that the larger force of C may more than compensate for its higher vulnerability. Or he may decide that F_2 of C is roughly equivalent to F_1 of A and decide to go for C for other (qualitative) reasons: for example, C may have more of a show of force capibility than A, or be preferable from a controlled response point of view.

In any event, *the decisionmaker is clearly in a better position to sharpen his intuition and judgment with the benefit of Fig. 1 and Table 4.6.*[9] This is an illustrative example of what was meant earlier in this appendix when we indicated that there are numerous things that can be done between the extremes of no analysis whatever and

[9] It is assumed, of course, that a textual discussion goes along with the figure and the table, so that the decisionmaker can profit from any interpretive comments that the analyst may make.

"hard core" cost-utility analysis. The above example is certainly far short of the detailed analysis, but it nevertheless may be useful.

A Purely Qualitative Analysis

Quite often a purely qualitative comparison can be very useful, especially when used as a supplement to the kind of analysis presented above. An illustrative example is contained in Table 4.7.

Here, the various alternatives are listed in the stub of the table, and in the body various qualitative comments are made regarding certain key capability characteristics for each of the alternative systems. In cases where a large number of alternatives are under consideration, such information can be useful in "weeding out" those cases that are likely to be of little interest and in selecting those items for further and more detailed deliberation.

A Subsystem Illustrative Example

Subsystem considerations are often of paramount importance in a given decision problem, particularly when uncertainties are present. In our present illustrative example, assume that one of the alternatives under consideration is an LEA system using a chemically fueled low-altitude penetrating missile (LAPM) launched from the LEA airborne platform located in a standoff position outside enemy territory. Assume further that we are somewhat uncertain about the gross weight versus low-altitude range relationship for this new LAPM, which is not yet developed and which, if developed, would not be operational until some six years from now. Upon examination, suppose that the analyst finds that LAPM gross weight is very sensitive to low-altitude range, and that this relationship can be graphed for two cases: an "optimistic" curve and a "conservative" relation between weight and range. See Fig. 2. We note that a rather severe weight penalty is incurred in moving from a range permitting coverage of 70 per cent of the enemy target system (R_0) to one permitting a 95 per cent coverage (R_1).

It may be instructive to explore the consequences of the relationships portrayed in Fig. 2. As an illustrative example, let us consider a sensitivity analysis of total system cost as a function of the key variables in Fig. 2 and two additional variables: force size (defined as total number of missiles in the system that are continuously

TABLE 4.7 System Comparison (Illustrative Example)

Alternative system	Invulnerable to			Useful for			Time on station (days)	Alert capability[a]
	Improved enemy ICBM's	AICBM defense	Air defense	Hitting known hard targets	Penetrating for recce-strike	"Show of force"		
A	No	No	Yes	No[b]	No	No	Unlimited	No
B	No	Somewhat	Yes	Possibly	No	No	Unlimited	No
C	Yes	Yes	Somewhat	Yes	No	Yes	2–3[c]	Yes
D	Yes	No	Yes	No	No	Yes	2–3[c]	Yes
E	Yes	Yes	Yes[d]	Yes	Yes	Yes	2–3[c]	Yes
F	Yes	Yes	Somewhat	Yes	No	Yes	2–3[c]	Yes
G	Yes	No	Yes	No	No	No	90	Yes
H	Yes	Yes	Yes[d]	Yes	No	No	90	Yes
I	No	Yes	Yes	Yes	No	No	Unlimited	No

a Number of missiles on station can be increased in times of tension.
b Poor CEP and low yield.
c Assuming no refueling on station.
d With existing Soviet Union defenses.

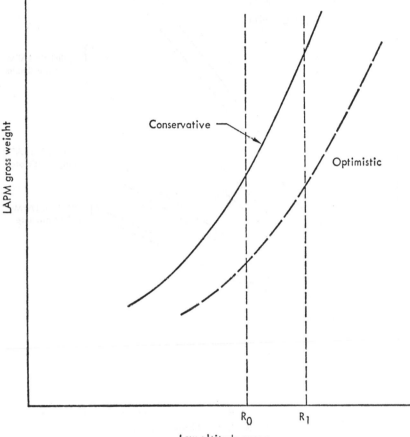

R_0 = LAPM range permitting coverage of 70% of the enemy target system

R_1 = LAPM range permitting coverage of 95% of the enemy target system

LAPM gross weight

Conservative

Optimistic

R_0 R_1

Low altitude range

FIG. 2. LAPM gross weight versus low-altitude range.

airborne on station), and the average fly-out distance from base to station.[10] The results may look something like Fig. 3.

From Fig. 3 it is clear that we have examples of both sensitivity and relative *insensitivity*. Total system cost is *very* sensitive to LAPM range (and hence gross weight), and it is fairly sensitive to

[10] The importance of average fly-out distance from base to station (U.S. bases are assumed) depends on the strategic scenario being considered. If a quick response to an initial enemy first strike is desired, a long fly-out distance would be required. If not, a short fly-out distance might suffice.

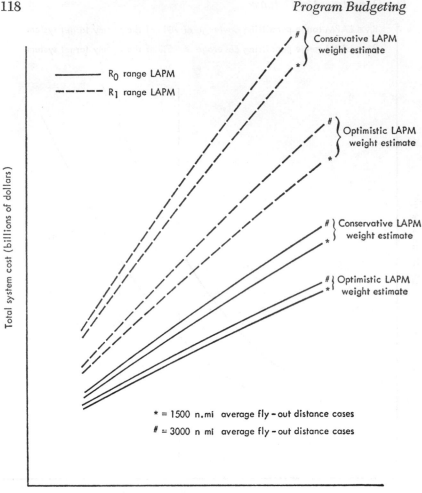

FIG. 3. Total system cost versus force size for various cases.

whether the optimistic or conservative estimate of the weight versus range curve is used. Also, these sensitivities seem to increase as total force size increases. On the other hand, total system cost is relatively insensitive to average fly-out distance from base to station.[11]

The marked sensitivity to low-altitude range (and hence missile gross weight) is not surprising. As missile weight increases, the

---

[11] This is not always the case. Here we are assuming a relatively efficient LEA platform from the standpoint of endurance. For less efficient LEA's, total system cost can be relatively more sensitive to average fly-out distance from base to station.

number of missiles that can be carried per LEA decreases. This means that to obtain a given total force of missiles continuously airborne on station, a larger number of LEA's must be procured. The total system cost spirals upward not only because of increased aircraft and missile procurement but also because of increased number of personnel, facilities, supplies, etc.

Here we have an example of how a relatively simple analysis of subsytem characteristics can contribute toward sharpening intuition and judgment about the impact on the total system. In this case it might suggest certain component research and development programs that would result in a more favorable relationship between LAPM gross weight and low-altitude range (e.g., research in propulsion components for LAPM-type missiles).

Research and development in component areas may be significant. In cases where major uncertainties (or other reasons) make it difficult to make a compelling argument for immediate initiation of development for the *total* system, the analysis may suggest relatively inexpensive *component* development programs that will in effect provide somewhat of a hedge against some of the major uncertainties in the problem.

Chapter 5

THE SPACE PROGRAM

BY MILTON A. MARGOLIS and STEPHEN M. BARRO

SCOPE AND ORGANIZATION OF THE SPACE PROGRAM

Since passage of the National Aeronautics and Space Act in 1958 the U.S. space program has grown in scope and size with extraordinary rapidity. Total military and civilian space expenditures, which were on the order of $100 million per year in the immediate post-Sputnik period, are now approaching a plateau of more than $7 billion annually.

Responsibility for nonmilitary space exploration, scientific investigation, technological development, and utilization of space capabilities is vested in the National Aeronautics and Space Administration (NASA). The agency, which employed 33,000 in 1964, currently spends approximately $5 billion annually on space flight missions and support functions.[1] Table 5.1 shows how NASA spending has grown since the agency was founded.

Since 1961, when President Kennedy proclaimed the national goal of "a manned lunar landing within this decade," manned space flight has become NASA's primary mission. It accounts for approximately 70 per cent of the agency's current (FY 1965) budget. Project Apollo, the lunar landing project, expends most of this money —$3.6 billion in the current year and an estimated $20 billion total before the lunar landing is achieved. Major Apollo tasks include development of a three-man spacecraft (the Apollo Command and Service Modules) for earth-orbital and earth-to-moon flights, a lunar landing vehicle (Lunar Excursion Module), and the Saturn family of launch vehicles, which according to current NASA practice are funded under the manned flight program. Apollo also requires construction of major launch and support installations at Kennedy Space Center, production and test facilities at locations throughout the country, a new mission control center at Houston, and an augmented worldwide tracking network.

[1] The requested 1965 NASA appropriation was $5.2 billion. All but $73 million, explicitly designated for aircraft technology, is to be spent on the space program.

TABLE 5.1 NASA Space Expenditures, 1958–1966 (in millions of dollars)

Fiscal year	Total expenditures
1958	89
1959	146
1960	401
1961	694
1962	1229
1963	2515
1964	4355[a]
1965	4939[a]
1966	5032[a]

[a] Estimates.

The other current manned flight project, Project Gemini, is intended to extend space flight experience obtained with the 1961–1962 Mercury manned flights and to develop capabilities and techniques required for Apollo. Two-man Gemini flights, scheduled to begin during 1965, will test new spacecraft systems, demonstrate endurance in orbit of up to two weeks, and develop rendezvous and other orbital maneuver techniques.

The emphasis on manned space flight is likely to be maintained in future years as efforts are initiated to apply and extend Apollo capabilities. New projects will include earth-orbital manned space stations and systems for long-duration lunar exploration, both with logistics support systems. They will be based at first on Apollo equipment and technology; later, on more advanced developments. At some future date the decision may be made to extend further the region of manned space flight by preparing for manned expeditions to the planets.

NASA pursues a broad program in the space sciences. Scientific flight activities include the Explorer series of instrumented satellites, orbiting geophysical and astronomical observatories, biological experiments in space, deep space and solar probes, and atmospheric and extra-atmospheric sounding rockets. Lunar exploration activities include television reconnaissance of the lunar surface by Ranger spacecraft, an effort (Project Surveyor) to soft-land scientific payloads on the lunar surface, and a project to place a survey vehicle in lunar orbit. In the field of planetary exploration, the Mariner series of Venus and Mars flyby flights will be followed by larger, more advanced planetary probes, including planetary orbiters and landers.

The space agency also supports continuing projects to apply space capabilities in the fields of satellite communication and meteorological forecasting. The present tendency is to transfer responsibility for these activities to other agencies as the systems become reliable and operational.

Advanced research in space sciences and development of new space flight technology is carried out on a wide front. Major effort is concentrated in the fields of chemical, nuclear, and nuclear-electric propulsion, space power supplies, electronics, advanced structures, and space vehicle subsystems, biology, and space medicine. NASA supports basic research in many scientific disciplines at its own centers, under contract with outside research organizations, and by means of grants under its Sustaining University Program. NASA also operates tracking networks for manned and unmanned satellites and deep space flights.

Table 5.2 summarizes the allocation of funds by program activity in NASA's FY 1965 budget.

The Department of Defense undertakes certain space activities that contribute to national defense or that may provide future military capabilities. DOD projects include satellite surveillance and warning systems, development of the Titan III booster, a military space communications system, antisatellite system development, and navigational satellite systems. DOD also operates the Atlantic and Pacific Coast test ranges and elements of the space detection and tracking network. In 1966 the Air Force will begin development of a military Manned Orbiting Laboratory (MOL), which is to conduct scientific investigations in space relevant to potential military capabilities. In addition, defense agencies sponsor research and development (some involving flight projects) in many areas of science and technology that are basic to space flight. These activities—in propulsion, electronics, structures, space medicine, etc.—are valuable to the civilian space effort as well as to purely military missions. Table 5.3 provides a summary of the DOD's space spending broken out by major program area.

Other program participants include the Atomic Energy Commission, which conducts joint research with NASA on nuclear propulsion and space power supply systems; the Weather Bureau

TABLE 5.2 NASA FY 1965 Budget Estimates (new obligational
authority in thousands of dollars)

Research and development budget		
Budget activities and programs		FY 1965
Manned space flight		$3,011,900
Gemini	$ 308,400	
Apollo	2,677,500	
Advanced missions	26,000	
Completed missions	—	
Space applications		86,100
Meteorology	37,500	
Communications	12,600	
Other applications	36,000	
Advanced technological satellites	$ 31,000	
Technological utilization	5,000	
Unmanned investigations in space		649,800
Spacecraft development and operations	521,600	
Geophysics and astronomy	190,200	
Lunar and planetary exploration	300,400	
Bioscience	31,000	
Launch vehicle development	128,200	
Space research and technology		283,300
Launch vehicles and spacecraft	104,400	
Space vehicle systems	38,800	
Electronic systems	28,400	
Human factor systems	16,200	
Basic research	21,000	
Propulsion and space power	178,900	
Nuclear-electric systems	48,100	
Nuclear rockets	58,000	
Chemical propulsion	59,800	
Space power	13,000	
Aircraft technology		37,000
Supporting operations		313,900
Tracking and data acquisition	267,900	
Sustaining University Program	46,000	
Total		$4,382,000

Construction of facilities	
Budget activity	FY 1965
Manned space flight	$234,330
Space applications	—
Unmanned investigations in space	7,018
Space research and technology	26,620
Aircraft technology	4,001
Supporting operations	9,031
Total	$281,000

TABLE 5.2 (*Continued*)

Administrative operations		
Installation		FY 1965
Manned space flight		$304,570
John F. Kennedy Space Center, NASA	$ 47,877	
Manned Spacecraft Center	98,104	
Marshall Space Flight Center	158,589	
Space science and applications		93,949
Goddard Space Flight Center	83,156	
Pacific Launch Operations Office	883	
Wallops Station	9,910	
Advanced research and technology		167,138
Ames Research Center	31,806	
Electronics Research Center	2,561	
Flight Research Center	10,402	
Langley Research Center	55,270	
Lewis Research Center	65,617	
Space Nuclear Propulsion Office	1,482	
Supporting operations		75,343
Northwestern Office	595	
Western Operations Office	5,398	
NASA Headquarters	69,350	
Total		$641,000

Source: National Aeronautics and Space Administration, *Budget Estimates, Fiscal Year 1965, Vol. I, Summary Data.*

(Department of Commerce), which participates in development and operation of meteorological observation satellites; and several other federal agencies, which make minor contributions. Table 5.4 summarizes the contributions to the space program by each participant agency in terms of new obligational authority and budget expenditures.

The space program is relatively free of complications that arise in other fields of government activity out of interactions among federal, state and local, and private efforts. Nonfederal space activity is confined, thus far, to the space communications projects of American Telephone and Telegraph Company and Communications Satellite Corporation and to privately financed studies and research projects carried out in anticipation of government contracts.[2] The space program is also relatively free of difficulties

[2] This refers to sponsorship and financing of space activity. Most of the actual development and production work is, of course, carried out by private industry.

TABLE 5.3 DOD Space and Space-Related Programs[a] (new
obligational authority in millions of dollars)

Item	1961	1962	1963	1964	1965
Manned space flight	58.0	100.0	133.2	93.6	81.0
Communications	55.2	104.6	59.6	78.8	49.3
Navigation	23.6	22.0	42.1	27.9	24.8
Detection and early warning	122.5	180.8	102.5	61.9	34.6
Space defense	8.2	33.0	45.9	62.7	24.9
Vehicle and engine development	3.7	68.3	308.2	384.5	282.0
Space ground support[b]	57.8	102.6	166.3	168.1	196.8
Supporting research/development[c]	74.2	155.7	147.3	159.6	158.0
General support[d]	420.7	531.2	574.2	578.7	622.7
Total	823.9	1298.2	1579.3	1615.8	1474.1

[a] All program totals are as contained in the President's budget for FY 1965.

[b] Includes range support, instrumentation, and satellite detection, tracking, and control.

[c] Includes basic and applied research and component development.

[d] Includes laboratory and research center in-house programs, development support organizations, general operational support, and space-related military construction not otherwise charged to specific space projects.

arising out of fragmentation of responsibility among federal departments and agencies. The problem of divided responsibility, which creates serious obstacles to program budgeting in many fields of government activity, is essentially limited to the area of competition and complementarity between NASA and the Department of Defense. Interactions between these agencies that affect the budgetary process will be discussed later in some detail.

IMPLICATIONS OF SPACE PROGRAM CHARACTERISTICS FOR PROGRAM BUDGETING

System and Project Orientation

It is fortunate from the point of view of program budgeting that space activities are system-oriented and that the program is organized into a manageable number of projects. System orientation means that it is possible to associate most space expenditures, and most of the effort expended on space activities, with specific physical systems; that is, the space program consists mainly of a number of efforts to develop, test, manufacture, and operate aggre-

TABLE 5.4 New Obligational Authority and Expenditures for Federal Space Programs (in millions of dollars)

Federal space program	New obligational authority			Expenditures		
	FY 1963 (actual)	FY 1964 (estimate)	FY 1965 (estimate)	FY 1963 (actual)	FY 1964 (estimate)	FY 1965 (estimate)
National Aeronautics and Space Administration[a]	3626.0	5189.5	5230.8	2515.3	4354.8	4939.1
Department of Defense	1579.3	1615.8	1474.1	1367.5	1583.0	1548.0
Atomic Energy Commission	213.9	227.6	212.7	181.0	217.7	220.4
Department of Commerce (Weather Bureau)	43.2	2.7	20.8	12.2	19.0	21.7
National Science Foundation	1.5	2.4	2.9	1.1	1.5	1.8
Total	5463.9	7038.0	6941.3	4077.1	6176.0	6731.0

Source: NASA, 1965 Budget Estimates, Special Analysis H.
[a] Excludes aircraft technology.

gations of physical equipment that perform clearly defined functions. Further, each space project, which encompasses all activities
required to achieve a specific objective in space, requires a particular combination of equipment items ("hardware") and a particular set of associated service functions. Therefore, a "natural"
basis for a program element breakout is available: Expenditures
may be classified according to the physical system with which they
are associated; systems may be arrayed according to the project
in which they are used; and projects with similar objectives may
be collected under mission headings.

The situation is similar to that encountered in connection with
the Strategic Retaliatory and Continental Air Defense programs of
the defense program budget, where boundaries between program
elements are established according to the physical characteristics
of weapon systems, and "program elements" embrace weapon
systems that perform a particular kind of mission. This contrasts
with the General Purpose Forces category of the defense program
budget, in which elements are defined primarily on the basis of
military organization rather than according to function, and the
entire aggregation, as indicated by the "general-purpose" appella-
tion, is not related to any specific military mission. Activities carried
on within the space program generally correspond to defense activities of the former type, to which the concepts of program budgeting
have most successfully been applied. In principle, because expenditures can be associated with systems, systems with projects, and
projects with missions, it should be relatively easy to develop a
set of mission-oriented budget categories that reflect the various
objectives of the space program. This would accomplish one of the
main purposes of program budgeting. However, other program
characteristics, notably the characteristic of interdependence,
which is discussed below, create obstacles that impede and complicate this conceptually simple enterprise.

Time Horizon

A second program characteristic that is favorable to program
budgeting is that many of the development and production tasks
carried out as parts of space flight projects are intrinsically of long
duration. Certain major hardware items, such as launch vehicles
and rocket engines, take five to eight years to develop. Long lead

times are associated with the manufacture of these and other systems and with construction of launch, test, and tracking facilities. A long-range outlook is dictated in some instances by purely astronomical considerations, e.g., the "launch windows" for Mars exploration that occur roughly every two and one-half years. In order to exercise direction over contractors' efforts and to maintain coordination among them, space program officials must prepare detailed technical and financial plans extending several years into the future. NASA, in fact, already prepares five-year overall budget projections. However, unlike the military Five-Year Force and Financial Plans, they are not available outside the agency headquarters. In many areas of government activity one of the major tasks of the program budgeteer would be to convert from single-year budget and program planning to planning over a meaningful time horizon. This has largely been accomplished by the agencies that participate in the space program and needs only to be formalized for inclusion in a program budget.

Interdependence

The program characteristic that most complicates what would otherwise be a straightforward exercise in program budget organization is interdependence among different space activities. Within the space program, more than in other areas of government activity, interactions among systems, projects, and missions are pervasive to the point that it is often difficult to identify the activities that should constitute a single program item or to delimit genuine program alternatives. The problem of interdependence, which has its most severe impact in the space field, raises conceptual difficulties that may affect fundamental program budgeting principles. Among other things, interdependence makes it difficult to present a total space program budget broken down by end objective or end product, and it complicates the analytical process of making tradeoff analyses. Therefore, the more important forms of interaction that arise in the course of program planning and methods for dealing with them will be discussed here at some length.

Major space vehicle systems and ground installations are often used in many different flight projects. Items that are most likely to have multiple uses, such as boosters, propulsion systems, launch facilities, and tracking networks, have tended to be expensive relative to items that are peculiar to individual projects. The nonrecurring costs incurred to create these systems—costs of performing R & D and constructing facilities—have been particularly significant. They constitute a substantial fraction of total national expenditures for space. Obviously, an inconsistent or arbitrary method of allocating their costs among the different space flight projects can distort the program budget presentation and make interproject cost comparisons meaningless.

Because of interdependence, it is often difficult to compute the true incremental cost of carrying out a project. This is a serious difficulty that must be overcome. The ability to generate incremental costs is an essential planning function, for these costs must be known if one is to compare alternative sets of projects or study the financial implications of program perturbations. Systematic, rapid measurement of incremental costs depends on (1) a financial format that permits recurring and nonrecurring costs to be easily separated; and (2) an economically meaningful, uniform method of handling the recurring and nonrecurring costs of commonly used systems.

Allocation of recurring costs, e.g., the costs of manufacturing and testing operational space vehicles (both launch vehicles and spacecraft) and conducting flight operations, is a relatively simple problem. Aerospace industry experience shows that the unit cost of an item of flight hardware tends to decline as additional units are produced according to a relationship known as the "learning curve."[3] It follows from the learning curve principle that the cost of hardware items procured for a particular flight project depends not only on the number of units required by that project but also on the number required by all user projects. If a project is eliminated and, as a result, the demand for a particular hardware item is reduced, then the unit cost of the item increases to all other projects that require it concurrently or at a later date. It is impos-

[3] One form of the learning curve principle states that the unit cost of producing an item of hardware declines by a constant percentage each time the quantity produced doubles. For example, if a production process follows a 90 per cent learning curve, then the cost of the twentieth unit produced will be 90 per cent of the cost of the tenth unit; the cost of the fortieth unit will be 90 per cent of the cost of the twentieth, and so forth. For a full exposition of the theory, see Harold Asher, *Cost-quantity Relationships in the Airframe Industry*, R-291 (Santa Monica, Calif.: The RAND Corporation, July 1, 1956).

sible, therefore, to compute the hardware procurement cost incurred by an individual project unless the project is placed within the context of an overall program. When program changes affect the number of vehicle launches or their relative timing, it becomes necessary to recompute procurement costs throughout the entire program to determine all the separate system financial implications. No special conceptual difficulty arises, but the amount of computation required in the program budgeting process is significantly increased.

The problem of handling nonrecurring costs—costs of system development and facilities construction—is much more fundamental. To illustrate the difficulties that arise, consider the problem of treating the development cost of a launch vehicle that is to be used by many different projects to carry out a variety of missions in space. Three alternative methods for distributing the development cost are apparent:

1. Each flight project that is to use the launch vehicle is charged with a portion of the development cost. The amount that a project is charged is based on the number of vehicles that it is planned to consume during the time period covered by the program plan.

2. The total development cost is borne by the project that is to use the launch vehicle first.

3. No attempt is made to allocate the cost. Instead, launch vehicle development is treated as an independent project that produces an intermediate product.

The first method has little to recommend it, except for deceptive neatness and simplicity from the accounting point of view. The number of user projects against which development costs are charged and the amounts charged to them are determined arbitrarily by the selection of a planning time horizon. Development cost to each project varies with the number of vehicle launches, and even with the launch rate, although development cost is, in reality, fixed and nonrecurring. Total project cost, including allocated development cost, need not measure or approximate the true incremental cost of carrying out the project. In many cases, where vehicle development cost is large compared with other costs associated with the individual flight projects, the results will be heavily biased. It would be difficult to distinguish the costs of development from other costs incurred by the using projects or to reconstruct the total resource implications of the development effort itself. Further, the timing of the resource impact of launch vehicle development will be confused with the timing of the resource impact of other requirements of the using projects. The evaluation of both the using projects and the launch vehicle development effort is hampered by this allocative procedure.

The second method (allocation of development cost to the first user) has actually been employed by NASA in connection with the Saturn launch vehicle development effort. Saturn development cost appears in current NASA budgets as an entry under Project Apollo, within the Manned Space Flight mission category. In the context of Apollo, this may appear to be a rational procedure, because there is no other firmly programmed flight project that will use the Saturn vehicles.[4] Saturn-using projects that may be added later will treat launch vehicle development cost as a "free good"—correctly so, because no decisions concerning those projects will affect the Saturn development cost.[5]

But does the Saturn-Apollo procedure provide a valid model for budgetary treatment of future launch vehicle developments? Even if we assume that the decision to develop the Saturn vehicles was justified solely by Project Apollo—which is unlikely, because planners undoubtedly considered long-run needs for booster capability, even though specific post-Apollo flight missions were not defined—it does not follow that similar circumstances will exist in the future. A future decision to undertake development of a launch vehicle may be justified by requirements from a number of flight projects, not a single project as in the Apollo-Saturn case. If so, it would be proper to allocate development costs among all the projects that were used to justify the development decision, and to allow only those user projects that were added subsequent to the decision to treat development as a free good. This introduces two difficulties. First, it raises the problem of allocating development costs among the first group of user projects. Second, and more important, it requires a knowledge of what missions and projects the decisionmakers had in mind when they approved development of the new launch vehicle. The first difficulty leaves

[4] The first follow-on projects to Apollo that will use Saturn IB and Saturn V launch vehicles may be initiated in FY 1966.

[5] It is necessary, however, to separate carefully costs incurred to modify launch vehicles for a subsequent user project from initial vehicle development cost.

us with a slightly reduced version of the original cost allocation problem; the second means that the program budget structure will depend on interpretations of the decisionmakers' thought processes. Thus, the second proposed method of cost allocation does not provide a complete solution to the problem, and it introduces a new form of arbitrariness.

The main advantages of the third method (setting up major common items as separate projects) are that the cost of each major activity is shown separately, without the bias that results from arbitrary cost allocation, and that true incremental cost is shown for each element. Launch vehicle development cost is correctly treated as a "joint cost" and is isolated from the "separable" costs associated with individual final projects.[6] Consequently, the content of budget elements is unambiguous and project boundaries remain constant as the program evolves. The resulting program budget format is useful for program administration as well as for planning and decisionmaking. However, even when this preferred method is used, the program budget is not freed of all the problems caused by interdependence. Two difficulties remain. First, the budget format is complicated by the introduction of intermediate mission and project categories alongside the final mission categories (e.g., launch vehicle development becomes a separate mission, multipurpose facilities construction is added to the support mission, etc.). Second, because certain flight projects and intermediate projects are interdependent, it becomes necessary to have more information about the program than is conveyed by the program budget format to determine what items or groups of items are alternatives, what intermediate projects are prerequisites of final projects, and what tradeoffs among projects are possible.

On the grounds of clarity and consistency, it is necessary to prefer the third method, i.e., to treat financially significant, nonrecurring activities whose outputs are required by more than one flight project as separate program elements and to treat their costs as nonseparable joint costs. However, consistency and clarity are obtained at a price: the goal of arranging program activities and

---

[6] See Roland N. McKean, *Efficiency in Government Through Systems Analysis* (New York: John Wiley & Sons, Inc., 1958), pp. 44–46.

expenditures according to their ultimate functions is compromised. Each attempt to compare program alternatives when certain classes of expenditures are placed in intermediate categories requires a review of all program elements—not only those that explicitly differ from one alternative to the other—to make sure that all interdependencies have been taken into account.

STRUCTURE OF THE SPACE PROGRAM BUDGET

The current NASA budget resembles a program budget format in several important respects. It is organized around projects, which are essentially equivalent to program elements, and it is projected several years into the future. In addition, the existing NASA mission categories are suitable for use in a program budget, except for changes needed to handle the kinds of interdependent activities that were discussed above and to extend the budget's scope to encompass the military space program.

Mission Headings

Ideally, it would be desirable to formulate a set of mission categories that correspond to the ultimate objectives of the space program. We find, however, that identifying these objectives is no simple matter. The whole question of "space program goals" has been discussed at too vague and abstract a level to be relevant to the program budgeting process, and it has been obscured by public controversies over the wisdom of undertaking particular space missions. Among the goals that have been suggested are:
1. Advancement of scientific knowledge.
2. Contribution to national security.
3. Economic benefits.
4. Enhancement of national pride and prestige.
5. Satisfaction of human curiosity and the urge to explore.
In an ideal program budget format, projects that are directed at increasing scientific knowledge would be grouped under one mission category, projects aimed at military application of space capabilities would be collected under another, projects that are undertaken for the purpose of enhancing national prestige would comprise a third, and so forth. Expenditure entries under the mis-

sion headings would then represent amounts of money allocated to the space program to further distinct national purposes.

In reality, of course, no such classification of projects is possible. A typical space flight project contributes simultaneously to several objectives, some of which, such as scientific investigation and military application, are relatively concrete, while others, such as national prestige, are extremely vague. There is no way to assign a value to the contribution of a project to each objective or to associate definite portions of a project's cost with particular goals. In addition, as has been shown in the previous section, it is necessary to supplement the set of projects that contribute directly to final program objectives with additional projects that accomplish intermediate functions.

A set of mission categories that is useful in practice must be based on well-defined characteristics of projects at a lower level of abstraction than "ultimate objectives" or "national goals." An "end-product" rather than an "end-objective" type of categorization is called for. The categories should have the following characteristics:

1. They should group projects that are functionally related in an operationally well-defined sense (e.g., according to type of payload, region of space in which they operate, etc.).

2. They should separate projects that serve distinct *concrete* objectives (e.g., projects that provide economic benefits or military capabilities should be separated from purely scientific efforts).

3. They should reflect the space program as currently constituted and projected but should be flexible enough to allow for growth in program scope and variety of subjects.

At the present stage of development of the space program we believe that it is appropriate to classify final projects according to:

1. Whether they involve manned or unmanned flight.
2. If unmanned, whether they are conducted for the purpose of:
   (a) Scientific investigation and exploration;
   (b) Application of space capabilities to purposes outside the space program;
   (c) Advancement of space technology.
3. The region of space in which flights are carried out, i.e., earth-orbital, lunar, or planetary.

Projects in the scientific investigation and exploration category may be further classified according to the field of knowledge with which they are concerned, e.g., astronomy, geophysics, biology; applications projects may be classified, first, as either military or civilian and then according to the specific field to which they contribute, e.g., communications, weather forecasting, navigation, surveillance.

A suggested set of final mission categories applicable to the current and near future U.S. space program is as follows:

1. Manned Space Flight
   Earth-orbital
   Lunar   } Manned Missions
   Planetary

2. Scientific Investigations and Exploration
   Earth-orbital:
      Investigation of the Earth's environment
      Astronomy, solar physics, and astrophysics
      Biological investigations
   Lunar exploration
   Planetary exploration

3. Civilian Applications
   Communications
   Meteorological forecasting

4. Military Applications
   Surveillance and warning
   Communications
   Weapon systems

5. Advanced Technological Development

} Unmanned Missions

This classification scheme is essentially identical with the one now followed by NASA. To complete the set of categories, as discussed above, it is necessary to add certain intermediate functions. At least two are required: one that comprises launch vehicle development projects and other activities that contribute to space launch capability; another to accommodate tracking and data acquisition, range operations, and other functions performed in support of flight operations. Finally, certain program-wide support functions may be aggregated into an additional category. Details of the suggested format are discussed later in the chapter.

Manned Space Flight

The above scheme of classification corresponds closely, within the unmanned flight area, with a breakout of the flight program by end objective. However, such objectives as enhancement of national prestige, satisfaction of the human urge to explore, etc., are ignored. The question then arises of why the same scheme may not be extended to the manned flight area. Why is a sharp distinction made between manned and unmanned flight projects and why are the manned projects not classified as scientific, applications, or development activities? The answer depends on an assessment of the main purposes of past, present, and near future manned flight projects.

The manned flight program to date consists of Projects Mercury, Gemini, and Apollo. Project Mercury in a series of one-man orbital flights during 1961–1962 demonstrated a capability to launch a man into space, support him there, and recover him; it also showed that man could be useful in space to perform flight control functions, make observations, and carry out experiments. Gemini, a series of two-man flights started in 1965, will demonstrate long-duration, multimanned space flight, develop and practice rendezvous techniques and other space maneuvers, and carry out a set of experiments. Project Apollo is intended to carry out a series of three-man, long-duration orbital flights and, ultimately, to place astronauts in an orbit around the moon from which they will undertake an excursion to the lunar surface.

In terms of the classification scheme given above, what objectives are served by these projects? Certain objectives are clearly not relevant: There are no readily discernible economic benefits or other "civilian applications"; nor are there *direct* military applications, although the general development of manned space flight capability may eventually contribute to important military missions. Are the manned flight projects primarily intended to advance scientific knowledge? The answer is clearly No for Projects Mercury and Gemini, for they include scientific experimentation as a minor, subsidiary activity. Although these projects represent major technical accomplishments with respect to man's ability to survive and function in space, they are not scientific accomplishments in the sense that they do not make substantial contributions to human understanding of the physical universe. For Apollo, there is more of a question. The lunar landing will undoubtedly provide some very valuable scientific information, including some that might not easily be obtained by unmanned landing vehicles. However, the dominant feeling among scientists seems to be that Apollo cannot be justified as a scientific project and that projects aimed primarily at obtaining scientific information on the moon would be very different from those associated with Apollo as well as considerably lower in cost. Science may be immensely benefited by Project Apollo, but, as is clear from NASA and administration statements on the subject, it is not the dominant or controlling objective of the program.

Having eliminated the "applications" objectives from consideration and having relegated the scientific and military objectives to secondary positions, we are left with essentially two kinds of purposes for the manned flight program:

1. The contribution that manned flight makes to the nation's or the government's prestige, political objectives, and international relations, including its contribution to competition with the Soviet Union. This purpose is usually discussed under such headings as "establishing American leadership in space" and "winning the space race." It is directly responsible for the commitment to land a man on the moon by 1970. This type of objective is often closely associated with discussions of space contribution, of unspecified form, to national security.

2. Mercury, Gemini, and Apollo as projects primarily intended to develop certain basic manned flight capabilities that will, in time, provide the technical foundation for manned flight projects serving a variety of specific purposes—scientific, military, economic, etc. The present manned program may be conceived of as a long-term investment that is expected to have substantial future payoffs in terms of projects with concrete objectives but which are presently of uncertain nature.

We conclude from the foregoing that current manned flight projects have multiple objectives; that the least tangible objectives may be the most important; and that a primary purpose of the current effort is the general one of developing and demonstrating capabilities in the field of manned flight as an investment in the future. Consequently, it is not feasible to attempt to separate or classify manned projects by end objective. Under present circumstances manned space flight may legitimately be considered an end in itself. It is the most expensive space mission and it should be clearly identified in the program budget.

What about future manned missions? The post-Apollo generation of manned missions, which may include such things as DOD's Manned Orbiting Laboratory, extended earth-orbital and lunar Apollo, and other small manned space stations, will have objectives that are quantitatively but not qualitatively different from those of Mercury-Gemini-Apollo. They will still be essentially "general-purpose" systems designed to extend operational capabilities in space rather than to provide specific benefits to fields external to the space program. Later on, as the mechanics of manned flight become routine, scientific laboratories may be established in space or there may be manned space-borne military systems or other space facilities with civilian applications. Then it will be appropriate to list manned projects under a variety of mission headings according to their differentiated functions. However, for a period that should extend at least ten to fifteen years into the future, it appears that the manned program will be so general-purpose in nature—both as an investment in future space flight and as a valuable end item in itself—that it will not be fruitful to try to distribute its costs among other end objectives. For the present, a separate manned flight mission seems to be the preferred solution.

CONVERSION FROM THE PRESENT BUDGET TO A PROGRAM BUDGET FORMAT

The current NASA budget is composed of Research and Development, Administrative Operations, and Construction of Facilities subbudgets. Each subbudget is organized according to the following program areas:[7]
  A. Manned Space Flight
  B. Space Applications
  C. Unmanned Investigations in Space

[7] National Aeronautics and Space Administration, *Budget Estimates, Fiscal Year 1965.*

D. Space Research and Technology

E. Aircraft Technology

F. Supporting Operations

This breakout corresponds to the NASA administrative structure, which organizes agency activities under four offices: Office of Manned Space Flight (OMSF), Office of Space Science and Applications (OSSA), Office of Advanced Research and Technology (OART), and the Office of Tracking and Data Acquisition (OTDA).[8] Research and Development expenditures are further divided among individual projects and sets of projects. Administrative Operations and Construction of Facilities funds are not distributed by project but by NASA center (geographic location).

Merger of Subbudgets

An obvious first step in converting to a program budget format is elimination of the tripartite division of expenditures among Research and Development, Administrative Operations, and Construction of Facilities. Activities budgeted under Administrative Operations include not only administrative functions but substantial amounts of in-house research and development, hardware test and evaluation, and technical project direction. These items should be identified with specific projects or missions whenever it can be done without arbitrariness so that it will be easier to measure the total resources consumed by a given project. Construction of Facilities items should be carried under project or mission headings where possible. For example, the cost of constructing a launch pad or assembly building for a particular launch vehicle should appear under the same heading as other nonrecurring costs associated with that vehicle; the cost of constructing a test stand for a rocket engine or booster stage should be treated in the same manner. The cost of the manned mission control center at Houston should appear under the Manned Space Flight mission heading as a supporting project because it can be allocated to the manned space flight function but not to any individual manned flight project.

[8] OMSF administers the Manned Space Flight program area; Space Applications and Unmanned Investigations in Space are under the jurisdiction of OSSA; Space Research and Technology and Aircraft Technology are under OART; and the activities of OTDA plus NASA's Sustaining University Program are lumped under the Supporting Operations heading.

Amalgamation of NASA and DOD Space Budgets

Space projects of the Department of Defense may be usefully divided into two groups. One comprises projects that are related to specific weapons or support systems or that otherwise contribute to specific military missions. It includes surveillance and missile warning satellite systems, military communication satellite development, navigational satellite systems, and projects for satellite inspection and interception. Expenditures for this group of projects may be incorporated into a national space program budget under a new Military Space Applications mission heading, which may be treated as an addition to the present set of NASA space missions, parallel to the existing civilian applications category. The second group comprises projects that do not contribute directly to military space applications and that are not otherwise of strictly military significance. Many of these projects are similar in purpose and technology to projects administered by NASA. They include activities in manned space flight, scientific investigation of the space environment, launch vehicle and propulsion development, and advanced space research and technological development, all of which have counterparts within the civilian program. In the interest of facilitating comparisons among activities that have similar objectives, regardless of the auspices under which they are administered, expenditures for projects in this group should be shown under the same mission headings as technically related NASA projects. Thus, DOD's MOL should be listed under the manned space flight category, together with NASA's Gemini and Apollo; Titan III, Agena, and other booster development efforts should appear under the same heading as corresponding NASA projects; range support functions should be placed in a support mission category together with NASA's data acquisition and tracking activity; and projects to develop advanced spacecraft subsystems, materials and techniques, and other space science research should be appropriately listed under the Advanced Research and Technology heading.

Amalgamation of NASA and DOD programs in this manner may seem to be a mechanical exercise in accounting organization, but it can have a significant impact on decisionmaking. Consider, for example, the two major areas in which the agencies have parallel activities: manned space flight and launch vehicle development.

In these areas the DOD's MOL and Titan III projects are currently in competition, respectively, with NASA's Extended Apollo space station and its Saturn IB launch vehicle. Decisions about these projects involve the very substantial issue of what is to be the military role in space, and they may significantly influence the content of the nation's space program for many years. The main points at issue are the precise nature of current military objectives in space, the degree to which they may be achieved by each set of proposed projects, the extent to which the projects supplement or duplicate each other, and the cost and time that each requires. It is noteworthy as well as predictable that in the context of interagency rivalry, with no unifying frame of reference or analytical consideration of the problem, extraordinary methods of decisionmaking—special panels, studies, etc.—have supplanted ordinary bureaucratic techniques. Such methods are not necessarily bad, but they do increase the likelihood that the resolution of the issue will hinge on factors other than project effectiveness and cost. Broad cost-utility analysis, operating in a program budget framework, is intended to cope with exactly this type of problem. If a program budget were in operation, we do not say that a solution would be readily forthcoming or that the result would be free from extraneous influence. The latter depends, for one thing, on the extent to which decisionmaking authority over the space program is centralized in conjunction with the budgeting function. There is little doubt, however, that the controversy would be illuminated and the main points at issue brought more clearly into focus if the alternatives were presented and analyzed in a consistent manner within an overall program context. This is the kind of task that program budgeting is intended to facilitate.

Military activities in space are subject to special security restrictions, which make it very difficult in practice to perform the indicated program manipulations. Some projects in the military space field are classified; others are not even explicitly identified in the Department of Defense Five-Year Force and Financial Plan. Therefore, some numbers for the program budget display are not available and others are not available in as much detail as would be desirable.

A problem also arises out of interaction between military space projects and other DOD activities. Some major systems, such as boosters and launch facilities, are used in the guided missile program as well as for space launches. The Atlantic and Pacific test ranges, whose operating costs are paid for mainly out of the DOD budget, also serve both guided missile and space programs. In addition, many areas of advanced research and development (R&D on propulsion, guidance systems, power supplies, etc.) apply both to the space program and to nonspace weapon system technology. Thus, considerable arbitrariness is unavoidable in delimiting those DOD expenditures that may be regarded as elements of the national space program. This determination is made more difficult than might otherwise be the case by the security restrictions mentioned above, which prevent full analysis of the content and purpose of individual projects and estimation of the amount of spending that is in the borderline area.

Revision of Mission Headings

Certain revisions of the mission categories have been outlined in the foregoing discussion of space program characteristics and objectives. They should be carried out as part of the process of conversion from the current NASA budget to a unified program budget that covers the entire space effort. The suggested changes are as follows:

1. *Eliminate the Aircraft Technology category.* NASA has jurisdiction over certain aircraft research and development largely for historical reasons. Although there are certain interactions between the aircraft work and other parts of the NASA program (e.g., between the X-15 aircraft project and the manned space flight mission), the aeronautics expenditures cannot properly be treated as an element of a national space exploration budget.

2. *Define a new Launch Capability mission.* As discussed earlier, the problem of interdependence among different program areas that arise out of common usage of launch vehicles by many different projects can best be resolved by explicitly recognizing launch capability development as a distinct, intermediate mission. The reason for establishing a separate budget category is not that launch vehicle development is technically unique or otherwise intrinsically different from other space program tasks but that it requires very large nonrecurring expenditures and has a considerable number of users among whom the costs of development cannot be readily allocated. For example, development costs of the Saturn launch vehicles, which will be used in a great variety

of future space missions, amount to more than $1.5 billion in FY 1965, out of a total NASA R&D budget of $4.382 billion. These costs should not be allocated to the Apollo project, as is done at present, or to any combination of final projects. Rather, it is suggested that these expenditures be treated as if an independent launch vehicle organization were providing a service to the final users by developing hardware and providing fixed launch facilities. Variable costs of launches, i.e., the incremental costs of manufacturing operational vehicles and performing launch operations, would still be charged to the individual users.

Introduction of the new Launch Capability category is the most important budgetary change that we suggest. The new mission currently accounts for a larger share of space program expenditures than any other item in the budget. The major activities that it includes are as follows:

(a) Saturn vehicle development, including engine development (now listed under Manned Space Flight as part of Project Apollo).

(b) Development of small- and medium-size launch vehicles, including Centaur, Scout, Delta, etc. (now funded under Unmanned Investigations in Space).

(c) Propulsion projects, now carried under Space Research and Technology, that have reached the system development stage.

(d) Titan III, Agena, large solid engines, and other booster and propulsion projects now funded by the Department of Defense.

(e) Construction of launching pads, prelaunch and checkout facilities, and booster and engine test stands.

(f) Parts of the Administrative Operations budgets of Marshall Space Flight Center, Kennedy Space Center, and other development centers.

Some expenditures associated with launch vehicle development but that involve special vehicle modifications for individual projects may appropriately be retained under the final project headings (e.g., the cost of modifying Titan II and Agena for Project Gemini). The cost of flight hardware procured for development tests of the launch vehicle would be included in the Launch Capability mission, while costs of operational vehicles would be charged to the final users.

3. *Define a new Flight Support mission.* This is another intermediate mission that includes tracking and data acquisition activities, now listed under NASA Supporting Operations, and certain support items, including range operations, now listed under and presently paid for out of the military budget. The category is intended to include activities that are carried out in support of the space flight program as a whole but that cannot be readily allocated to individual flight projects.

4. *Define an Administrative, General Support, and Miscellaneous mission.* This category comprises items in the current Administrative Operations budget that cannot be assigned to individual projects or other missions, including headquarters and center administration, certain Construction of Facilities items for general-purpose facilities, and miscellaneous items, such as the Sustaining University Program.

Detailed Program Budget Structure and Cost Analysis

The program budget can become a useful framework for comparing alternative rates of activity within the individual program element, as well as for comparing program elements with one another. Its ability to contribute to detailed project analysis depends to a considerable extent on the way in which expenditures are disaggregated below the project level. The subproject breakout should provide a clear separation between nonrecurring and recurring costs and a set of recurring cost elements that can easily be related to indices of activity (number of launches, pounds in orbit or on the lunar surface, etc.).

There is no difficulty in deciding what cost elements are appropriate. Space projects adhere closely to a standard pattern: the essential elements of a typical project are development and production of a spacecraft, procurement of launch vehicles, and performance of prelaunch, launch, and flight operations. Sometimes there are additional elements, such as launch vehicle modification, construction of special facilities, or in the case of manned flight projects, crew training and recovery operations. NASA budget presentations generally identify these elements. Their main fault is that they fail to separate spacecraft development and production cost or to separate the cost of developmental flight hardware (both spacecraft and launch vehicles) from other system development costs.

This deficiency, which must be remedied if there is to be a complete separation of nonrecurring and recurring costs, reflects a difficult practical problem in cost analysis. A typical spacecraft contract provides for development of the vehicle and delivery of a specified number of test and operational units. The number of deliverable units is generally quite small—on the order of 10 or 20. There is no chronological separation of development and production processes; during much of the project the two go on simultaneously. Typically, a large part of the contractor's effort is devoted to designing, testing, and integration of spacecraft subsystems that are supplied by subcontractors. The subcontractor's own efforts, like the prime's, are carried on in a way that makes it difficult to separate recurring hardware costs from other elements of the subsystem contract. As a result, the accounts of spacecraft producers do not segregate items that can readily be identified as parts of recurring production cost. Estimates of the incremental cost of additional delivered units have to be derived by analytical techniques applied by persons not directly involved with the contractor's operation. They must work with limited data, making a series of somewhat arbitrary decisions as to what elements of current and past programs have been recurring and what have been nonrecurring charges. Thus, to produce useful detail below the program element level, a cost-analysis activity must operate in conjunction with other components of the program budgeting apparatus.

An integrated cost-analysis and budgeting capability can be a very valuable long-range planning tool. It can, for example, permit rapid comparisons to be made of the financial implications of complete alternative space programs, which need only be specified in the form of launch schedules. Analyses can be carried out on the year-by-year incremental financial effects of the following kinds of program variations:

1. Addition or deletion of a project or substitution of one project for another.

2. A change in the number of planned launches within a project.

3. Speedup or stretchout of a development program, or of a schedule of operational launches.

4. A major change in the method of carrying out a project (e.g., a shift from earth-orbital to lunar-orbital rendezvous on a lunar mission).

Chapter 6

TRANSPORTATION IN THE PROGRAM BUDGET

BY JOHN R. MEYER

The development of transportation is generally a major concern of government in planned and market economies alike. Furthermore, the legitimacy of this concern, for better or worse, is almost universally conceded. Thus approximately 5 per cent of the federal administrative budget in the United States can be accounted for by expenditures to develop and operate transportation facilities. Important additional federal expenditures are financed from trust funds, particularly for highways. Transport expenditures are even greater, relatively, for state governments, which, to a rough approximation, would seem to spend about one-quarter of their total budgets on transportation. In other industrialized countries the relative importance of transportation expenditures as a proportion of governmental budgets would seem to be of the same or greater magnitude.

There is, however, one major difference in the governmental approach to transportation expenditures, particularly at the federal or national level, between the United States and other western countries. Transport development in the United States is a function of many agencies, bureaus, and departments and, in particular, there is no one bureau, department, or ministry of transportation. This lack of a major center of responsibility is almost unique to the United States; no other major western industrialized country follows this practice to the same degree. Without a central ministry for directing the transportation activities of the national government, the application of program-budgeting techniques is, of course, complicated. Also complicated is the problem of accurately estimating government transport expenditures, particularly as they relate to different functional objectives.

The fragmentation of transport expenditures by the federal government in the United States is not, however, quite total. Over half is concentrated in the transportation section of the Department of Commerce, as headed by the Under Secretary of Commerce for Transportation. Similarly, another 20 per cent, almost exclusively associated with the development of capacity required for emergency defense needs, is accounted for by the Department of Defense. Other significant amounts are attributable to the Federal Aviation Agency, the Department of Agriculture, the Department of the Interior, the National Aeronautics and Space Administration, the Civil Aeronautics Board, the Housing and Home Finance Agency, and the Department of the Treasury.

It should be noted that the federal government in the United States is an important consumer as well as developer or promoter of transportation activities. This chapter is exclusively concerned with the development or promotional aspects. Although the distinction is sometimes a fine one, the government as a consumer of transportation usually undertakes such consumption incidental to the achievement of other governmental objectives, and it is transportation development as an *objective* of government activity that is of concern here. Therefore, only "consumer payments" by the government that clearly exceed any rational estimate of costs or normal market prices are included.

FEDERAL TRANSPORTATION PROGRAMS BY FUNCTION

Five reasonably distinct objectives of federal government expenditures on transportation development can be identified:

1. General development of freight and passenger transportation between major cities and points of commerce within the United States.

2. Provision of better accesss to rural areas and more remote small towns and cities.

3. Relief of urban traffic congestion problems associated with commuter work trips.

4. Creation of standby transportation capacity possibly needed in times of war mobilization or other national emergency.

5. Promotion of national prestige or international trade.

Congress seemingly has these five objectives in mind, implicitly or explicitly, when it appropriates money for transportation development. This is not to deny that other schemes of categorizing by congressional purpose might not be equally as useful. Admittedly, too, there is some overlapping in these categories. Furthermore, many specific programs or expenditures may serve more than one of the five objectives. These particular categories, though, seem to be reasonably comprehensive and to provide a useful framework for interpreting the federal budget as it relates to transport development.

One caveat should be immediately entered about this or any other categorization scheme that might be offered for organizing transport development expenditures of the federal government. Patriotism being the rightfully popular quality that it is, it is not surprising that most government expenditures on transportation have been implicitly or explicitly justified at one time or another as being related to the national defense. This propensity for classifying transportation expenditures as latently useful for defense is perhaps a carryover from a time when mobility and transportation were obviously quite essential to proper defense. Such essentiality is not, however, quite so obvious in this day and age of intercontinental ballistic missiles and nuclear explosives; the transportation requirements in modern war seem to be much more highly specialized and little related to the normal transportation requirements of daily life. Nevertheless, the old ways do persist, with the result that national defense is invoked as a justification for virtually any or all types of government transportation expenditures, no matter how remote the real emergency need might be.

In the functional classifications of the budget that follow, defense justifications of transport expenditures have been somewhat skeptically viewed. Only expenditures that are quite clearly and almost exclusively related to the development of standby transport capacity in excess of normal civilian needs, and that might be useful for emergency defense purposes, have been classified as "defense standby" expenditures. Furthermore, transport developments that clearly have a full justification or seem to be nearly utilized to their full capacity by conventional civilian needs have *not* been classified as defense standby, even though they quite obviously might have considerable value in time of national emergency or mobilization. To take a particular example, the highways built under the Interstate Highway Program of the Bureau of Public Roads are formally known as interstate and national defense highways, but *none* of these costs have been allocated to defense standby because these highways are clearly quite heavily used by civilian transportation alone. (Interstate highways, however, may have been built to somewhat higher design standards in some cases than were otherwise needed because of defense considerations.) In essence, almost any industry that produces a service or product that is widely used as an input into industrial processes, or is required for the convenient fulfillment of normal daily human tasks, would almost certainly have a considerable value or need in a circumstance of defense mobilization; it does not seem particularly relevant, therefore, to emphasize this one aspect of transportation expenditures in evaluating the relative amounts and qualities of different federal outlays for these activities. Similarly, on the grounds that they are acts of consumption more than of development, transport undertakings related to military training have not been included, e.g., the Federal Aviation Agency's military support operations. Also, research and development related almost exclusively, at least in the first instance, to military hardware has been excluded.

FEDERAL TRANSPORT EXPENDITURES FOR FY 1965 BUDGETED BY FUNCTION

The federal government's expenditures on transport development, rearranged by the five functions or objectives as just defined, are shown in Tables 6.1 through 6.5. These tables are for the most part self-explanatory. A perusal will indicate the general character of the different types of expenditures considered to be related to achievement of the five basic objectives, each table pertaining to one objective. The figures reported are for FY 1965 as *budgeted*. FY 1965 was chosen as the most recent year for which good information is available. Budgeted figures were used even though in certain cases deviations from the budget have been legislated, a major reason being that budget figures are readily available and the exact character of many legislative changes is not fully determined. Also, budget estimates seemed to be legitimate forms for a discussion of program budgeting. The reported figures largely pertain to new appropriations requests; actual expenditures for FY 1965 may exceed the reported figures because of funds carried over from previous years for which no new appropriation or authorization was required. Figures re-

TABLE 6.1 Federal Budget for General Intercity Domestic Transport Development, FY 1965 (in millions of dollars)

Type of program	Annual budget level
Interstate Highway Program, nonurban-commuter portion of capital outlays[a]	2,352.0
Grants-in-aid to primary system highways	434.0
Estimated share (70%) of Bureau of Public Roads general and administration expenses	34.3
Domestic navigation aids in Rivers and Harbors Program of Army Corps of Engineers	
Operating expenses (including 50% of protection of navigation expenses)[b]	93.0
Capital outlays; navigation projects[c]	198.7
Alteration of bridges over navigable waters	2.4
Capital outlays; multiple-purpose projects having navigational features at 10% of total value	17.5
Rehabilitation of navigation projects of use to domestic operators	7.0
Estimated share of general investigation expenses	3.0
Estimated share of advanced engineering and design expenses	4.0
Estimated share of general expenses	2.0
TVA navigation facilities operating cost (net and inclusive of depreciation)	4.6
Net loss of Saint Lawrence Seaway Development Corporation	3.3
Federal Aviation Agency	
Operation of Traffic Control and Airport Program (total of $549 million less $140 million military)	409.0
Facilities and equipment (total of $75 million less $5 million military related)	70.0
Grants-in-aid for airports (total of $75 million of which $25 million was arbitrarily allocated to rural access)[d]	50.0
Research and development (total of $42 million less $9 million related to military)	33.0
Net profit on operation of Washington National Airport	−0.1
Net loss on operation of Dulles International Airport (net of revenues and inclusive of depreciation)	6.5
NASA Aircraft Technology Program (approximately 50% of total program; the remainder allocated to military)	35.9
Administrative costs of regulatory agencies	
Civil Aeronautics Board	10.8
Federal Power Commission (natural gas regulation)	7.0
Interstate Commerce Commission	25.9
Total annual budget level	3,803.8
Totals by mode	
Highways (inclusive of 45% of ICC costs and 50% of bridge alteration over navigable waters expense)	2,833.2
Railroads (45% of ICC administration costs)	11.7
Air	615.1

TABLE 6.1 (*Continued*)

Type of program	Annual budget level
Water (including 5% of ICC costs and 50% of bridge alteration over navigable waters expense)	335.6
Pipelines (including 5% of ICC costs)	8.3
Possible supplementals	
Eastern Seaboard high-speed railroad	—

[a] This was estimated on the basis that the nonurban and noncommuter portions of the Interstate Highway Program represent 85 per cent of the total Interstate Program. Specifically, about 60 per cent of the total Interstate Program is nonurban. Of the remaining 40 per cent in urban areas, it was estimated that about 40 per cent represented expenditures to serve urban peak-hour commuters only. Because of scale economies and other considerations explained more fully elsewhere, this estimate is probably somewhat high. Still, the figure reported above for strictly intercity connecting operations would appear to be not too unreasonable an allocation.

[b] This figure represents a somewhat arbitrary but, hopefully, not too inaccurate allocation between domestic and overseas waterborne commerce. The overseas allocation is shown in Table 6.5. This allocation is in rough agreement with that made by G. Murray of the Bureau of the Budget.

[c] This figure represents the total of $234.3 million of navigation projects budgeted for FY 1965 that were considered by the American Waterways operators to be "of particular interest to navigational interests" less $35.6 million in projects that were largely or exclusively of a deep channel character. These $35.6 million are reported in Table 6.5 for overseas water carriage. Not reported in any of these tables is approximately $30 million budgeted for primarily recreational navigational facilities.

[d] Testimony by Federal Aviation Agency Administrator Halaby before the Subcommittee on Independent Offices Appropriations indicated that about 25 per cent of the program was for new airports, which was increased in this table by an additional 8 per cent to allow for additional improvements for existing smaller airports.

lated to certain types of trust-fund or government-enterprise activities have been netted where specific tolls, tariffs, or other charges are made for rendering the services; an attempt has been made to indicate the exact character of these netting procedures wherever performed.

The estimates shown in Tables 6.1 through 6.5 should be interpreted as only rough approximations in most cases. As noted, the present organization of transportation expenditures in the federal government is such that the functional objectives often are served by many different departments and projects. Also, several objectives, transport and nontransport alike, are likely to be embodied within one particular project. Perhaps the most striking example of this problem is represented by the multiple-purpose (flood control, irrigation, and navigation) projects of the Corps of Engineers. As

TABLE 6.2 Federal Budget for Transport to Improve Rural Access, FY
1965 (in millions of dollars)

Type of program	Annual budget level
Grants-in-aid to secondary system roads	289.2
Estimated share (10%) of Bureau of Public Roads general and administration expenses	4.9
Forest, public lands, and Indian reservation highways	143.4
National Park roads, parkways, trails, etc. (including new construction and maintenance)	43.5
Alaska Railroad profit	−0.2
Civil Aeronautics Board subsidies of local service air carriers (including subsidy of local services of N.E. Airlines)	71.5
Civil Aeronautics Board subsidies of Alaskan and Hawaiian air services	9.5
Federal Aviation Agency aid to smaller airports[a]	25.0
Total	586.8
Totals by mode	
Highways	481.0
Railroads	−0.2
Air	106.0
Possible supplementals	
DC-3 Replacement Program	—
Highway Program for Appalachia	—

[a] Some allowance also might be made for Federal Aviation Agency expenditures
on operations, facilities, equipment, etc., but no very meaningful basis was readily
available for making such allocations. Such allocations here would reduce similar
items in Table 6.1 correspondingly.

shown in Table 6.1 and explained more fully in the footnotes,
the navigation benefits from these projects were very arbitrarily
estimated. Similarly, the Interstate Highway Program has been
distributed rather arbitrarily between expenditures aimed at development of better intercity freight and passenger transport and
outlays for the improvement of peak-hour commuter capability in
urban areas (as shown in Tables 6.1 and 6.3, respectively). The
allocation in this case is a bit less arbitrary than with multiple-
purpose water projects, being based on some considerable analysis
of the cost characteristics of urban highway facilities,[1] but it is
still subject to challenge. Similarly, the arbitrary allocation of 50
per cent of the National Aeronautics and Space Administration
aircraft technology program to civilian development and 50 per

[1] John R. Meyer, John F. Kain, and Martin Wohl, *The Urban Transportation
Problem* (Cambridge, Mass.: Harvard University Press, 1965), particularly chaps. 4
and 9.

TABLE 6.3 Federal Budget for Urban Commuter Transportation, FY 1965 (in millions of dollars)

Type of program	Annual budget level
Commuter-related portion of Interstate Highway Program	414.7
Grants-in-aid to urban highway systems[a]	241.0
Estimated share (20%) of Bureau of Public Roads general and administration expenses	9.8
Grants-in-aid for urban transit systems (Housing and Home Finance Agency)[b]	85.2
Civil Aeronautics Board subsidies of helicopter services	3.0
National Capital Transportation Agency	1.8
Total	755.5
Totals by mode	
Highways	665.5
Public transit	90.0

[a] These funds tend to be spent on important access arterials in urban areas. Inclusion here under the heading "commuter" is justified on the grounds that these arterials mainly represent additional capacity needed for peak-hour commuter travel.

[b] Inclusive of $10 million in public facility loans for urban transportation.

TABLE 6.4 Federal Budget for Military Standby Transport and Related Capability, FY 1965 (in millions of dollars)

Type of program	Annual budget level
Maritime Administration	
Construction differential subsidy	124.9
Reserve Fleet and Reserve Shipyard Program	6.1
Training programs	5.7
Estimated share (50%) of general and administration expenses	4.8
Military airlift and sealift	
Air Force	1,330.5
Navy	65.0
Army	29.3
Federal Aviation Agency military-related expenditures[a]	154.0
Total	1,720.3
Totals by mode	
Water	206.5
Air	1,484.5

[a] It might be argued that only a fraction of these costs should be allocated to military standby because some are almost certainly assignable to normal military training and other operations. On the other hand, the Federal Aviation Agency is in some regards almost entirely subject to military take-over in time of war and therefore might be construed as almost a military-standby operation *in toto*.

TABLE 6.5 Federal Transportation Budget for Promotion of National Prestige and International Trade, FY 1965 (in millions of dollars)

Type of program	Annual budget level
Maritime Administration	
Operating-differential subsidies	190.0
Research and development	10.1
Net income of Federal Ship Mortgage Insurance Fund	−3.5
Net income of Vessel Operations Revolving Fund (exclusive of NS *Savannah*)	−0.1
Proceeds of War Risk Insurance Revolving Fund	−0.1
NS *Savannah* experimental ship operations net loss (joint AEC-Maritime Administration venture)	5.8
Harbor navigational aids, Corps of Engineers	
Operating expenses (including 50% of protection of navigation expenses)	27.3
Capital outlays: deepwater navigation projects	35.6
Rehabilitation of deepwater navigation projects	5.0
Estimated share of general investigation expenses	0.5
Estimated share of advance engineering and design expenses	0.5
Estimated share of general expenses	0.3
Coast Guard: estimated civilian expenses	322.7
Panama Canal supporting operations (less operating profit of Panama Canal Company	32.0
Federal Maritime Commission	3.3
Inter-American Highway	4.0
General transportation research (including census of transportation)	2.5
United States Travel Service	4.0
International airmail subsidy[a]	10.4
Excess freight payments for shipping government-aid cargoes[b]	80.0
Total	730.3
Totals by mode	
Water	709.4
Highway	4.0
Air	10.4
General	6.5
Possible supplementals	
Supersonic Transport Development	—
Panama Canal "Replacement"	—

[a] Estimated on basis of foreign rates paid by Post Office Department being equal on a ton-mile basis to domestic rates.

[b] As stated by Nicholas Johnson, Administrator of the Maritime Administration, in a speech at Long Beach, Calif., September 16, 1964.

cent to military development is strictly a guess. The breakdown of Federal Aviation Agency expenditures between military and civilian operations is based on testimony of Najeeb Halaby (then Administrator of the FAA) before congressional committees and should not represent quite as arbitrary an allocation as the NASA separation. In general, it should be emphasized that the numbers reported are an attempt to construct some first approximations to the kind of numbers that might be useful in adopting a program-budgeting approach to federal transport expenditures. For the purposes of this book it is as much the organization as the implementation of the estimates that is considered important. It would indeed be hoped that personnel in the relevant governmental agencies might find this organization of the material sufficiently provocative to stimulate an effort to obtain more refined estimates.

The conceptual rationale underlying the allocations reported in the various tables is quite simple. In Table 6.1, dealing with federal expenditures for general intercity domestic transportation development, four basic types of government expenditures are reported:

1. Federal expenditures on major interstate highways made in the form of grants by the Bureau of Public Roads for Primary System Highways (roughy approximated by what formerly was known as the Federal-State Highway System) and the Interstate Highway Program.

2. Expenditures made for improving rivers, harbors, canals, and intercoastal waterways useful in domestic intercity water carriage, the major portion of which is embodied in the program of the Corps of Engineers.

3. Expenditures for development of airways, airports, and aviation in general as these are incorporated in the programs of the Federal Aviation Agency and the National Aeronautics and Space Administration.

4. Administrative costs incurred by federal regulatory agencies that have been constituted over the years for controlling or channeling the activities of private transportation companies.

The totals at the bottom of the tables constitute simple summations of the figures reported in the body of the tables grouped by different modal characteristics. The "Possible supplementals" reported in Tables 6.1, 6.2, and 6.5 represent citations of transport programs now under consideration within the federal government and with seeming potential for adoption at some future and reasonably early date. These citations represent a partial and preliminary attempt to implement the longer planning horizons sought in program budgeting. No specific numerical estimates have been attached to these supplemental programs because in many cases only very crude estimates of total cost are available, and these total estimates would be difficult to translate into annual fiscal year equivalents at this time. For example, it might be guessed that a high-speed railroad between Boston and Washington might cost upward of $1 billion, but this figure would be a very rudimentary guess and could not be placed on an annual basis without details on a feasible planning and construction schedule for such an undertaking.

Federal expenditures for transportation to improve rural access, as reported in Table 6.2, follow much the same pattern as those for general intercity transport development. Again, there are important highway programs in which the Bureau of Public Roads is the dominant element; however, some very significant expenditures on rural highways are to be found in the budgets of the Department of Agriculture's Forest Service and the Department of the Interior's Indian and National Park Services. The Federal Aviation Agency again plays a very large role in the development of air transport, but the Civil Aeronautics Board enters significantly through its subsidies to local service air carriers (as differentiated from the large trunk airlines primarily serving the 250 or so largest commercial airports in the United States). This subsidy program is administered according to a complex formula designed to induce the provision of air service to localities that could not commercially sustain such service. Hope exists, as repeatedly expressed by Congress, that these local service air carriers could eventually become self-sustaining, though most of the evidence to date has been to the contrary, because the subsidies have tended to increase over time rather than decrease.[2]

The very large role of the Bureau of Public Roads in federal transportation is also demonstrated by the figures of Table 6.3,

----

[2] Most instructive in this regard are the annual Hearings of the Subcommittee on Independent Offices Appropriations of the Committee on Appropriations of the House of Representatives. In essence, these local service air subsidies have drifted from a little over $50 million per year five or six years ago to approximately $80 million per year today. This has occurred in spite of reasonably vigorous efforts at several levels of government to reduce these outlays.

pertaining to federal expenditures for urban commuter transportation. Of particular importance is the portion of the Interstate Highway Program estimated to be primarily commuter related and therefore deleted from the Interstate Highway estimates shown in Table 6.1. Also shown are the grants-in-aid that long have been made by the Bureau of Public Roads to aid urban highway system development, especially as these urban highways are needed to tie together important portions of the federal highway system. Incidentally, the totals of these grants-in-aid to urban highways are reported as being commuter related in Table 6.3 on the grounds that they are used to develop large urban arterials whose capacity is rarely taxed fully except during the peak commuter periods. Of a somewhat different character are the grants-in-aid recently authorized by Congress for urban transit systems to be administered by the Housing and Home Finance Agency. This program calls for loans or direct grants, usually on some sort of matching basis, to be made to urban transit systems to improve equipment and general performance capability. The Civil Aeronautics Board subsidies of helicopter services are reported as a commuter aid in Table 6.3, rather than as expenditures for general intercity transport development, on the grounds that much of the appeal of helicopter services is their ability to move more quickly from urban downtown areas to suburban airports and that this speed advantage is particularly great during the commuter hours.

Shown in Table 6.4 are federal transport development expenditures for defense-standby purposes. As noted previously, only what might be called hard-core defense transportation expenditures have been reported in this category. By far the largest single item in FY 1965 budget is the Military Air Transport Service expenditure as represented by the airlift capability of the Department of Defense. The Federal Aviation Agency's expenditure on defense-related undertakings is also quite large. The Military Sea Transportation Service, taken together with what might be construed as the defense portion of the Maritime Administration Program, also represents a considerable expenditure on sea transport maintained as a defense standby. The standby characteristics of the defense airlift and sealift capabilities, incidentally, should not be construed too rigidly, i.e., to apply only to extreme national emergencies or war situations. Without much question the Military Air Transport Service, the Military Sea Transportation Service, and to a lesser extent the ship mothball program of the Maritime Administration have proven to be very useful in recent lesser war emergencies, such as Korea, Suez, and Vietnam. In short, MATS and MSTS essentially represent investments in the creation of greater mobility for modern military situations in lieu of possibly or necessarily maintaining larger military establishments at many points about the globe. Coast Guard expenditures of approximately $100 million annually on reserve training and other programs having to do with military preparedness were not included on the grounds that they were aimed not at the creation of reserve transport capability as such but rather at meeting general military needs.

The final objective category established for the analysis of federal transportation expenditures—that concerned with national prestige and promotion of international trade—is somewhat heterogeneous in character, as illustrated by Table 6.5. The national prestige and trade promotion expenditures tend to be of three types:

1. Expenditures to develop particularly dramatic or technologically advanced types of transportation facilities, such as the supersonic transport airliner, the atomic ship *Savannah,* the Inter-American Highway, or the Panama Canal.

2. More or less direct subsidies to particular types of private economic activity that tend to result in a "showing of the U.S. flag" in more remote parts of the world or at least to acquaint those other parts of the world with the characteristics of the United States; for example, the United States Travel Service and Maritime Administration undertakings.

3. Facilitation of international trade by providing necessary facilities and services required to perform such carriage reasonably efficiently and safely; for example, harbor developments and the Coast Guard.

One rather remarkable aspect of the different programs reported in Table 6.5 is the extent to which the seemingly separate, or even possibly disparate, ends of promoting national prestige and international trade tend to blend into one another when formulated as specific transport undertakings. This fortuitous circumstance is well illustrated by the Supersonic Transport Program reported as a possible supplement in Table 6.5. Seemingly, the best justification for the SST program would be that it would maintain U.S. leadership in the development of commercial airliners and possibly help our international balance of payments by reducing the purchases of foreign-made supersonic airliners by U.S. commercial airlines or by increasing the sales of such airliners we in turn might make to foreigners.[3]

It should be noted that international airmail subsidies were estimated on a most conservative basis. Specifically, the subsidy was considered to be equal to the difference in the average rates paid domestic airlines for carrying domestic mail and the higher rates paid for international airmail carriage. There are many who believe, particularly the all-cargo air carriers, that domestic airmail rates are entirely too high and result in an implicit subsidy of domestic trunk airlines.

Federal government expenditures on transportation by the five different functional categories are summarized in Table 6.6. Perhaps the most interesting single figure in the table is the grand total of $7.5 billion. The predominance of expenditures for the

TABLE 6.6 Federal Transport Development Budget Summarized by Function, FY 1965 (in millions of dollars)

Function	Budget
General intercity domestic development	3,803.9
Improvement of rural access	586.8
Urban commutation	755.5
Defense standby	1,720.3
National prestige and trade promotion	730.3
Total	7,596.8

[3] Some expenditures reported under national prestige and trade promotion obviously represent quite arbitrary classifications. For example, it might be argued that if expenditures for the development of the Inter-American Highway are counted, then those made by the Agency for International Development to promote more rapid economic development in less industrialized countries of the world might also be properly included. It would seem, though, that expenditures for the Inter-American Highway are at least potentially more directly related to American trade and prestige considerations than are general expenditures made for transportation improvements within underdeveloped countries. Similarly, the Travel Service might be construed as being no more legitimate an expenditure on transportation promotion than expenditures made by the Department of Commerce to promote export trade in general. The only defense is that the Travel Service expenditures are reasonably directly oriented to stimulating the sale of U.S. transportation services, while general stimulus of export trade is more aimed at promoting the sale of American manufactures or goods.

general improvement of intercity domestic transportation is also quite clear; expenditures in this category account for almost exactly one-half of the total. Somewhat surprising, perhaps, is the extent of expenditures for defense standby—in spite of the fact that they were quite narrowly defined. The three other categories of expenditures are not insignificant, however, since each represents well over a half-billion dollars annually. Furthermore, there are good reasons for expecting each of these three smaller categories, particularly urban commutation and national prestige, to be expanded considerably in the near future.

RATIONALITY AND THE FEDERAL BUDGET FOR TRANSPORTATION DEVELOPMENT

The achievement of more rational, or at least economically more rational, policy decision is, of course, the ultimate objective of program budgeting. One obvious approach to evaluating the rationality of federal expenditure programs in transportation would be to consider their consistency with formally announced goals of the federal government in the transportation sector. The most definitive recent announcement of such goals was President Kennedy's Message on Transportation of April 5, 1962.[4] In this message President Kennedy asserted four primary objectives:

1. Attempt to recoup to as large an extent as practicable and consistent with broader national objectives the cost of different federal transportation investments from the users of these investments, the objective being to make the federal government's treatment of different modes more nearly uniform and therefore less distortive of market choices in transportation.

2. Rely on the free market to a greater extent than in the past as a means of allocating traffic between different modes, and accordingly, reduce reliance on formal regulatory procedures; together with the more equal user tax treatment, this greater competitive freedom would be expected to improve overall transport efficiency.

---

[4] *The Transportation System of Our Nation, Message from the President of the United States,* April 5, 1962, House of Representatives Document No. 384, 87th Cong., 2d Sess. (Washington, D.C.: U.S. Government Printing Office, 1962).

3. Attempt to coordinate urban land-use planning and urban transportation planning more closely and to improve the attractiveness of public commuter transportation relative to private transportation.

4. Make the international transportation activities of U.S. carriers more self-sufficient or self-reliant so as to reduce federal subsidies of these activities.

Some indication of the relationship between excise and user tax receipts from the different transport modes and federal government expenditures on these modes can be obtained from Table 6.7. It is quite clear that a closer balance between expenditures and user-related excise receipts is achieved with domestic transportation than with international. In keeping with the 1962 Presidential Message, at least some effort is being made to recover part of the costs of federal development of domestic transportation facilities in almost every instance. This is especially true with respect to the three domestic modes—highway, water, and air—that are particularly heavy beneficiaries of federal expenditures. The federal expenditures involved in domestic rail and pipeline operations are so relatively small that discrepancies might not be viewed too adversely. Furthermore, rail and pipeline expenditures are either administrative costs associated with the government's own regulatory efforts or attempts to perpetuate certain unprofitable services, mainly rail commuter operations.

Perhaps one of the more surprising aspects of Table 6.7 is the extent to which federal tax receipts from highway vehicles, gasoline, diesel fuels, and other similar excises tend to exceed the total expenditures made by the federal government on domestic highway development. This excess is almost entirely due to automobile excises, which presently are charged to the general fund rather than to the highway trust fund and might be construed as a payment for the general overhead of government assessable to highway programs. Ironically, although U.S. railroads would seem to have a reasonably legitimate case when they assert that competitive modes tend to be more generously helped by the federal government than they themselves are, the common railroad assertion that highway modes are particularly privileged beneficiaries of federal aid would seem to be unsubstantiated. Of course, it is entirely possible that some of the federal "overcollection" from highways is offset by

TABLE 6.7 Federal Transport Development Budget and Related
Excise Receipts by Mode, FY 1965[a] (in millions of dollars)

Transport modes	Budget (1)	Related excise receipts (2)	Difference: (1) minus (2)
Domestic highway	4,022.3[b]	5,780.0	−1,757.7
Domestic rail	54.3[b]	10.0[c]	44.3
Domestic water	335.6	35.0[c]	300.6
Pipelines	8.3	—	8.3
Domestic airlines (net of military)	724.1	178.0[d]	546.1
International water	709.4	—	709.4
International air	10.4	—	10.4
Unassigned	12.3	—	12.3
Total	5,876.7	6,003.0	−126.3

[a] Exclusive of all defense-standby expenditures.

[b] Including one-half of the $85.2 million of Housing and Home Finance Agency grants-in-aid for urban transit systems.

[c] One-half of the remaining excise taxes collected on passenger travel other than by air. The other one-half was credited to highways.

[d] Including $8 million of new excise taxes not enacted at the time of compilation and $27 million of revenues from tax on gasoline used in motorboats. In this connection, it should be noted that approximately $30 million of capital outlays on new navigational facilities with almost exclusive recreational use has been excluded from the expenditures reported.

contrary tendencies at the level of local and state government, though the evidence available would tend to suggest that any such contrary tendencies are insufficient to offset the federal collections.[5]

In general, hasty inferences should not be drawn from the aggregate comparisons presented in Table 6.7. While certain aggregates may be very imbalanced, particular component activities within each could display tendencies entirely at deviation with the aggregates. For example, there is at least some evidence that users of rural portions of federal and interstate highway systems pay less in excise taxes than the total federal costs of the services they consume. Diversion to urban highway needs of all or part of the $290 million now spent by the federal government on secondary roads has, in fact, been seriously advocated; however, the increased importance of urban, as against rural, voters may be as important

[5] For evidence on this point, see Meyer, Kain, and Wohl, *Urban Transportation*, chap. 4; and Philip H. Burch, Jr., *Highway Revenue and Expenditure Policy* (New Brunswick, N.J.: Rutgers University Press, 1962). It should be noted in passing that a very strong probability exists that railroads often are somewhat heavily, or even very unfairly, taxed on their property holdings at the local and state level.

as economics in explaining this advocacy. Similarly, users of very-high-performance interstate and federal highway facilities in urban areas during peak hours seem to pay less than the costs of the facilities they use.[6] Also, it is at least conceivable, if not reasonably probable, that much of the discrepancy between total expenditures and the total excise receipts on domestic airways is accounted for by private general aviation and is not attributable to commercial operations. In the same vein, although it is quite clear that domestic water operations in the aggregate are clearly in bad imbalance between receipts and expenditures, much of this discrepancy is probably due to operations in upstream areas where more locks and other special facilities are required and not at all to more efficient downstream operations. Furthermore, navigation development expenditures are often dictated as much by considerations of local pride or political needs as by legitimate commercial requirements registered by the private water operators themselves.

The reported discrepancy between total expenditures for development of domestic water transport and excise returns from these activities would be somewhat less if a marginal cost approach to the pricing of these services was adopted. Specifically, a reasonably valid argument could be made that the present users of waterways should not be burdened with the fixed costs of previous investments made in the development of the waterways, particularly since such investments seem to have a reasonably long economic and physical life and were often motivated as much by political as by commercial considerations. If this view is adopted, then only the operating and maintenance costs of these navigational aids and facilities should be sought in the form of user charges. A rough estimate of these costs would be approximately $100 million per year, which would reduce the relevant discrepancy on water operations considerably, particularly if proposed new excise taxes on fuel used on inland waterways are eventually enacted.

[6] The user tax receipts realized from private automobile commutation tend to run at a level of about 11 mills per vehicle mile; the costs of providing high-performance limited-access highways for commuters (computed on an appropriate incremental cost basis by which all the costs of the additional capacity are charged to the peak-hour users as well as an appropriate proportion of the costs of providing the basic facility) seem to lie generally in the range of 15 to 25 mills per vehicle mile. The exact level will depend on the particular circumstances in which the urban highway is placed, its ramp, other structural requirements, etc. See Meyer, Kain, and Wohl, *Urban Transportation*, chaps. 4 and 9.

In short, more detail is needed before asserting with great accuracy that the federal government favors certain domestic *commercial* modes of transportation significantly more than others. A good prima facie case would seem to exist, though, for asserting that commercial barge operations are at least somewhat favored.

Achievement of the second Presidential objective of 1962, greater reliance on market forces to determine traffic allocations between different modes, would seem to be highly inconsistent with several aspects of the federal transport development programs as now designed. For example, one specific recommendation of the Presidential Message was that minimum-rate regulation of bulk commodities be abolished. The probable consequence of any such action would be a considerable intensification of competition between rail and barge for such traffic, particularly in upstream areas where the cost advantages for barge transport might be expected to be minimal or even nonexistent and where the need for, or reliance on, federal expenditures to keep costs low would be greatest. In essence, continued expenditure to improve the performance of barge operators in upstream areas could be expected to offset at least partially the probable competitive impact of eliminating minimum-rate regulations from railroad bulk carriage. On the other hand, subsidization of barge operations is one way of stimulating competitive checks to the railroads, possibly a desirable goal if there is to be less government regulation.

The relationship between the local service air carrier subsidies and achievement of the Presidential goal of less regulation is quite complex. The 1962 Presidential Message recommended virtually complete elimination of regulation over minimum passenger tariffs for the airlines, railroads, and buses. Earlier there was strong federal endorsement of the notion that railroads in particular should be allowed much greater freedom to abandon uneconomic passenger services wherever these were identified. The Civil Aeronautics Board subsidies of local service air carriers might be viewed, on the one hand, as the source of an alternative first-class passenger service that would minimize community objections to railroad abandonment of uneconomic passenger services to smaller cities; on the other hand, the subsidies would tend to mitigate the development of more effective bus service to such communities and would make it more difficult for bus lines to charge rates that would make such services compensatory. However, federal aid given to the development of secondary road systems and other rural highways probably exceeds the excise tax receipts from operations over such highways, and to this extent bus lines also may be recipients of a local service subsidy. There is always the question, of course, of whether it makes good sense to have the government engaging in the provision of "offsetting" subsidies to at least nominally competitive services.

The relationship between the budgeted programs and the achievement of "more balance" or "better planning" in the urban context is also not entirely clear. In reality, the consistency or inconsistency of these relationships depends a great deal on the particular procedures used to administer the funds for aiding urban commuters. One interesting aspect of the grants-in-aid for urban transit systems to be made by the Housing and Home Finance Agency is that these grants will be bestowed by a *different* agency than that controlling federal highway grants, the Bureau of Public Roads. Such a separation of responsibilities at the federal level might be justified by the need for providing "competitive checks" on the inherent propensities of the two agencies involved. Still, it would seem to pose at least some possibility of uncoordinated or inconsistent development of federal aid to commuters. The separation could cause the urban transit grants-in-aid administered by the Housing and Home Finance Agency to be more oriented to *rail* commuter needs and intensify the conventional orientation of the Bureau of Public Roads, so that it would be concerned almost exclusively with providing sufficient highway capacity to carry virtually all commuter traffic reasonably expeditiously in private automobiles. There is considerable evidence to the effect that a less costly and perhaps even higher quality of service could be provided for urban commuters by a better coordinated or disciplined use of highway capacity.

Given the nature of "rural bias" evidenced in the allocation of state funds between city and rural areas in many states and the limited tax base available to many urban jurisdictions, it seems entirely possible that the federal government may be the only practical source of financial aid to sustain needed transit facilities. The reliance upon undifferentiated or completely uniform excise taxes as a primary source of highway financing also complicates the problem of financing local transit services. These uniform highway charges make it very difficult for transit operators to increase revenues by charging higher rates during peak periods, even if they might be very much cost-justified. Lack of more sophisticated pricing methods for measuring the strength of demand for different urban transportation facilities also complicates the problem of attempting to establish benefit cost comparisons for different types of commuter transportation.

Achievement of self-sufficiency (i.e., lower subsidy requirements) in international transportation operations also would not seem to be particularly well served by the present federal budget. Particularly in conflict with this goal is the operating differential subsidy for U.S. ships as it is now administered by the Maritime Administration. There is considerable evidence that these operating differential subsidies tend to be internally inconsistent and to induce behavior that is quite incompatible with the American maritime industry's capitalizing on its comparative advantages.[7] Experimental undertakings such as the nuclear ship *Savannah* or the development of a supersonic transport would seem to be at least potentially more consistent with the self-sufficiency objectives; however, there are some who believe that these particular experimental developments may have been chosen more from the standpoint of maximizing national prestige than of improving the competitive position of U.S. international carriers.

Still another test of the rationality of federal transportation programs might be their consistency with broader objectives, either implicitly or explicitly accepted as a social consensus. For example, considerable agreement long seems to have existed that the federal government should undertake to tie the more remote parts of the country to the more populous ones; it is generally felt that such ties provide better for the national defense and even perhaps broaden the basis of communication and interdependency on which the federal union or even the national democracy may be based. Certainly many of the expenditures listed in Table 6.2 for improving "rural access" probably would be considered desirable by a large number of citizens on this basis.

[7] Allen R. Ferguson *et al.*, *The Economic Value of the United States Merchant Marine* (Evanston, Ill.: Northwestern University Press, 1962). Nicholas Johnson, Administrator of the Maritime Administration, said much the same in a speech delivered in Long Beach, Calif., September 16, 1964.

Similarly, an appealing political argument for support of inland waterway development is contained in the view that government should promote competition in transportation by making available a wide range of alternatives to consumers wherever the costs of doing so are not excessive. Thus one might speculate that much of the expenditure on domestic navigation aids is "justified" or "rationalized" on the premise that this program promoted the development of a "competitive check" to potentially excessive railroad economic power. Such an argument seems to have had a particularly powerful appeal twenty, thirty, or forty years ago when the number of economic alternatives or challenges to railroad monopoly positions were obviously fewer than they are today, or at least not so widely recognized. If in the future greater reliance is to be placed on competition in lieu of transport regulation, then promotion of these competitive checks may have renewed justification.

Another question that might be posed about the relationship between federal transportation programs and more broadly accepted or defined social objectives is the effect of present programs on income distribution. It is particularly interesting to consider the question of whether federal transportation programs are basically regressive or progressive in their incidence of benefits to different income classes. For example, a limited argument could be made that the Interstate Highway Program and domestic navigation aids tend to be slightly regressive in character, since it might be expected that the wealthy are more likely to own automobiles or pleasure boats than the poor. However, the regressive effects are probably not marked because these same programs also should tend (within the limits allowed by government regulation) to lower the general level of cost for moving freight, an action that is likely to bestow benefits on virtually all segments of society. Somewhat similar remarks might be applied to the other highway programs, those aimed at rural access and urban commuters. In both cases the diffusion of benefits across society could be quite wide—and in any case tracing incidence would be very complex. Similarly, the Maritime Administration's program seemingly benefits domestic shipowners, probably a reasonably wealthy class, and working seamen, who are probably not so wealthy, with the overall effect on income distribution negligible.

Certain of the federal transportation programs, though, are almost certainly regressive in their income effects. Particularly vulnerable to this charge are the aviation programs. For example, if, as
is often argued, most of the discrepancy between civilian payments
for airport and airway development is accounted for by a deficit on
private plane operations, this would suggest that a reasonably
wealthy class of society—those who use, own, or operate private
planes, corporate or otherwise—are the main beneficiaries of the
subsidized portion of the Federal Aviation Agency's activities. Even
if some of the Federal Aviation Agency's deficit is attributable to
commercial aviation, the conclusion still would be much the same;
it is estimated that business travelers and those with family incomes
over $10,000 per year account for a very high percentage (over 60
per cent) of total commercial airline travel.[8] The same arguments
apply to the Civil Aeronautics Board's subsidies to local service air
carriers and helicopter services.

The grants-in-aid for urban transit systems to be administered by
the Housing and Home Finance Agency also could prove regressive. Much will depend on exactly how the grants are administered.
If they are used primarily to aid long-distance rail commuters from
city centers to more remote suburbs, the effect will be potentially
or almost certainly regressive, while if used to improve downtown
and central city systems, the benefit incidence might be progressive.

In sum, the transportation programs of the federal government
would seem to range from neutral or only slightly regressive to
substantially regressive in their income distribution characteristics.
The net effect of the overall program is probably regressive, but to
establish such an assertion definitely would require considerably
more research. Furthermore, even if regressive at the moment,
greater use of transport investments to help economically retarded
regions (e.g., the highway program for Appalachia) could redress
the balance. Again, however, caution seems wise, because it is not
clear that transport developments in "depressed areas" will necessarily aid the poor of those regions.

[8] These figures are based on results of the most recent travel survey conducted by
the Survey Research Center of the University of Michigan.

IMPLEMENTATION OF PROGRAM BUDGETING FOR FEDERAL TRANSPORTATION EXPENDITURES

The essential features of program budgeting have been defined in previous chapters, particularly in Chapters 1, 2, and 3. Program budgeting is oriented to a structuring of government decision processes in which economic rationality is emphasized. As will be noted in Chapter 10, program budgeting, if fully implemented, could embody all the following elements:

1. Restructuring budgetary exhibits so as to make them more useful or relevant to decisionmaking.

2. Adopting a longer time horizon so that the future budgetary implications of programs adopted today are better understood.

3. The adoption of more rigorous procedures for evaluating government programs, usually in the form of a cost-utility or cost-effectiveness analysis.

4. Adopting administrative or institutional reorganizations required to enforce or implement the major allocative decisions resulting from program budgeting.

Restructuring of the budgetary exhibits has been the major preoccupation of this chapter. A very preliminary effort has also been made to extend the time horizon for transport evaluations by listing possible supplementals and indicating some of the potential implications of certain recently initiated programs.

More and better cost-utility (or cost-effectiveness) analyses for evaluation of federal transportation programs would almost certainly be an advance. Almost as surely, though, such analyses are likely to have a fairly limited role in determining the actual decisions with respect to federal expenditures on transport development. In the first place, some very good political reasons work toward this outcome. Federal government expenditures on transportation embody some of the most sacrosanct and well-established portions of the pork barrel, and experience strongly suggests that a reluctance exists to forgo these expenditures, as important as they often are to the election ambitions or needs of incumbents. Furthermore, historically and at present, government transportation expenditures have been aimed at serving other than narrow economic efficiency objectives. Clearly of interest in many transport investment decisions by government are such considerations as regional development, income redistribution, creating yardsticks or controls for inhibiting monopoly power (real or imagined), providing for more mobile and effective national defense, and national unity. Given this multiplicity of objectives, it is perhaps not surprising that efficiency considerations have hardly dominated many public transportation investment decisions in the past.

Investment decisions in public transportation can take, moreover, several different forms. Some involve a complex balancing of many political and economic considerations to achieve at least a modicum of consistency in the comprehensive development of a particular transport system. A splendid example is the Federal Highway Program. It was obviously highly desirable, if not imperative, that the Interstate Highway Program be planned at the federal level in cooperation with local and state governments to ensure that the individual state programs were consistent with one another and created a comprehensive highway system that served interstate and national interests as well as local or intrastate objectives. The legislation creating the Interstate Highway Program, enacted in 1954, contained relatively precise specifications of how and where the system was to be constructed. For this particular transport investment decision, it is difficult to see how cost-utility analyses would have made a major contribution, though more extensive application of such analyses during the preliminary design stages could have been quite productive. Given the complexity of the political and economic decisions involved, and the emphasis on designing a geographically consistent system, it probably would be difficult to improve on the congressional process as a means of developing such a program in an orderly and systematic fashion.

A second type of public transport investment decision is akin to the traditional capital budgeting problem of a private business firm evaluating an investment for the development of a new product. The fundamental question is whether a government investment in the development of a new transport facility is likely to be justified by the benefits realizable or, even more precisely, recoupable through taxation or licensing. A splendid example is evaluation of supersonic transport. The rationality of developing a 2,000-mile-per-hour airplane depends primarily on an assessment of what the expected market for such high-speed air travel might be over the next few decades. While the SST is interchangeable to a limited extent as an investment project with the development of lower-cost subsonic air travel (by means, say, of very large subsonic jets derived from military heavy logistic airplanes), there are many good reasons to suspect that the two airplanes might serve entirely different markets and therefore are not basically alternatives to one another. Specifically, it is at least conceptually possible that the demands for tourist air travel may grow sufficiently to justify development of a large subsonic jet at the same time that the development of a supersonic transport is justified by expansion of demands for long-distance business travel.

Choices between competitive alternatives for achieving the same transportation objectives do, of course, occur, and in such instances cost-utility analyses usually will be appropriate. A contemporary example of a true confrontation of transport alternatives for achieving the same objective is the problem, now under consideration, of providing better intercity transportation for the Eastern Seaboard corridor between Boston and Washington. Among the alternatives worthy of consideration are: (1) increasing airport capacity through, for example, the creation of more airports in the corridor or by increasing the capacity of existing airports through such means as installation of all-weather landing facilities and better airway controls; (2) institution of better use of *existing* airport and airway capacity (e.g., by stricter regulation of general aviation use particularly during the rush hours) combined with improvement of air service by, for example, substituting Electra or small jet airplanes (DC-9, Boeing 737, or BAC 111's) for the smaller and slower propeller-driven aircraft now used in the corridor; (3) the improvement of the all-weather and economic capabilities of vertical or nearly vertical takeoff planes of the helicopter or VSTOL types; (4) the development of higher performance and, possibly, automated highway turnpikes (automation being the elimination of the requirement of constant driver control); and (5) institution of higher speed rail transport. These different modal possibilities, moreover, might be used in different combinations within the corridor, especially since the transportation situation between New York and Washington is very different from that between New York and Boston with respect to volume and other important characteristics. One of the more interesting facets of government investigation of possibilities for improving transport in the Northeast corridor is the fact that although it started off as a reasonably comprehensive survey of all possibilities and modes, press reports suggest retrogression into a survey of the specific possibilities for high-speed rail transport, even though there was little evidence in the preliminary studies to suggest that high-speed railroading had any presumptively obvious advantage over other modes. In short, the Northeast corridor investigation seems to be a case in which cost-utility analyses in different alternatives would be quite appropriate but where such an approach may not be used. The project, however, is still in progress and a more comprehensive and analytical approach may yet prevail.

It is worth noting that when formal benefit-cost analyses have been used to evaluate transport investments of the federal government, the results have not been universally attractive from either the standpoint of conceptual accuracy or what was indicated about the quality of the investments made. Specifically, despite the use of extremely low interest rates, often in the 2 or 3 per cent range (justified on the grounds of borrowing rather than opportunity costs), exaggeration of the economic life of some of the facilities used (100 years being not too uncommon), extremely generous counting of benefits, and extremely conservative estimates of cost, the reported benefit-to-cost ratios often have been barely above one, a presumed cutoff level.

One of the more interesting and potentially misleading procedures used to compute benefits for transport investments is that adopted sometimes for navigation installations on inland rivers or waterways. The practice often has been to compute benefits on the basis of the differences between the rates *charged* by railroads and prospective barge operators rather than differences in the actual *costs* of performing the services by the different modes. Because of the nature of railroad value-of-service rate-making, the rate discrepancy is usually much larger than the cost differential. Of course, to the extent that the institution of barge competition would be required to eliminate the implicit monopoly profits involved in value-of-service railroad rates, it might be argued that the present procedures are quite legitimate. On the other hand, it should be at least legally and conceptually possible to eliminate these monopoly profits by less expensive means in a regulated industry such as railroading. Actually, the main barrier to reduction of railroad rates on certain types of traffic, particularly bulk traffic that is water competitive, is regulation itself.[9] Regulatory agencies tend to worry about the competitive effect of rail rate reductions on other modes. Also, regulators often require railroads to maintain certain "socially" necessary services that can only be operated at a loss, and the regulatory agencies therefore consider it appropriate to permit the railroads considerable monopoly profits elsewhere to cover such losses. This whole sequence of interactions between regulatory decisions and investment decisions by government agencies illustrates, of course, the extent to which these policies may be quite inconsistent or even contradictory.

One could also question on somewhat more specific technical grounds the potential usefulness of cost-utility analyses in evaluating transportation investments. Transport investments by their very nature tend to be highly interdependent, one with another and with locational choices made by consumers and other industries. In essence, evaluation of transportation investments almost demands some form of general equilibrium approach. Cost-utility analyses by their very nature tend to be more partial in character and, indeed, derive much of their empirical attractiveness from their partial analytical characteristics. Furthermore, because the choice between different transport alternatives is likely to be as contingent on regional income distribution, employment, and competitive effects as on efficiency measured in a narrow or partial equilibrium context, this suggests that evaluation of transportation investments should measure the impact of a change in the transportation system on these other variables as well. To do so, it may be necessary to couple a model of the transport sector to a general macroaggregative model of the economy, perhaps implemented by fairly complex interregional-interindustry models or through some combination of these appropriately blended to suit particular decision needs or requirements.[10]

[9] A recent and most relevant example was the protracted hearing before the Interstate Commerce Commission on the Southern Railway's proposal to cut its rates for carrying grain in large-volume hopper cars. The rate reduction was vigorously opposed not only by competing barge lines but also by the Tennessee Valley Authority—on the grounds that the rate reduction would reduce the benefits attributable to their installed navigation aids!

[10] A very interesting effort to construct a model of this type for one specific application is to be found in Brian Martin, *A Model for Evaluating Transportation Investments in Underdeveloped Countries*, Transportation and Economic Development Seminar Discussion Paper No. 1 (Cambridge, Mass.: Harvard University, 1964) (mimeo.).

Cost-utility analyses, however, still may be extremely useful in evaluating alternative transportation investments in particular circumstances. At a minimum, such analyses can be useful in choosing between mutually exclusive alternatives for achieving specific goals, particularly if these goals are subcomponents of an overall transport system design. In general, cost-utility or related analyses may be extremely helpful in determining which particular components should be combined in alternative transportation systems for further evaluation and study. The final choice between alternative systems, though, is probably best reserved to a broader analysis in which aggregate income, employment, and regional effects are all at least crudely measured. In short, something akin to cost-utility analyses will almost certainly be needed for what might be called "initial design" exercises but is not likely to be overwhelmingly important in choosing between different basic transportation systems designed to serve roughly similar ends. This is not particularly inconsistent, moreover, with the applications now made of program budgeting in the defense sector, where the program objectives are usually specified by broad considerations of military strategy and the final choice of system involves considerations broader than cost-utility alone.

Enforcing major program-budgeting decisions in the context of transportation is likely to be somewhat difficult. Almost immediately involved is consideration of the time-honored proposal to create a new Department of Transportation with Cabinet-level status. Perhaps the best argument for creating such a new department is that it could not possibly result in worse coordination of different federal transportation activities than now occurs. Furthermore, it might lead to some improvement by creating a center of decisionmaking in which the tradeoffs between different transport means for achieving roughly similar objectives would be more carefully and intelligently scrutinized. If some of the regulatory function were also placed within this new agency, a possibility also might exist for better coordination between federal investment decisions in transportation and the regulation of private transportation enterprises.

A major argument against creating a new Department of Transportation is that it would tend to reduce certain healthy competitive checks that are now operative. At present, different independent bureaucracies compete with one another in certain activities and through this competition provide an informal audit on each other's performance. For example, it was felt necessary by many to place the new federal urban transit grants-in-aid in the Housing and Home Finance Agency rather than in the Bureau of Public Roads (or close by within the Department of Commerce) because of a need to approach urban transit problems with a fresh and different outlook from that historically evinced by the Bureau.

The potential effectiveness that might be gained by the consolidation of federal transportation activities within one department would depend very much on exactly how any reorganization took place. If, for example, the reorganization were to be merely a superficial one in which largely autonomous agencies were to be transferred under a new administrator but were not to lose much of their autonomy, probably little would be gained. That is, if the reorganization merely took the form of transferring the Bureau of Public Roads, the Federal Aviation Agency, and similar transport-oriented agencies into some new department with little modification of present operating procedures, the net gain would be minuscule. On the other hand, it is also reasonably clear that little would be lost by such a reorganization, even including most of the presently existing "competitive checks." Thus, if there was even some little hope that consolidation of these various federal transportation activities would improve coordination, the effort might be worth hazarding.

Similar remarks might be applied to a possible reorganization of regulatory activities, including a transfer of some of them into any Department of Transportation that might be newly created. It has been argued by some, in fact, that the net effect of most Interstate Commerce Commission and Civil Aeronautics Board activities is now so negative that any reorganization that tended to diminish or eliminate their influence would probably be an improvement. Again, there also is much to be said for an effort to coordinate regulatory decisions with investment decisions at the federal level. If there was a major transfer of regulatory activities away from their present location in largely autonomous agencies (which, strictly speaking, are the creatures of the legislature and not the executive) to an executive department, a need almost surely would exist to reconsider the role of courts and court appeals in transportation regulatory matters. Such a transfer would seem to be usefully considered only if there is a basic policy decision to reduce greatly government regulation of transportation—a step, of course, that would be very much in keeping with the recommendations of the 1962 Presidential Message.

Several other schemes of administrative reorganization also might facilitate enforcement of program budgeting in transportation. For example, one potentially effective way to achieve some of the goals of program budgeting might be creation of an investment review board for federal transportation investments. Such a review board logically would represent an extension of the activities of this kind now performed by the Bureau of the Budget. As such, the board would almost certainly be best located somewhere in the Presidential Office (and would, therefore, not necessarily be inconsistent with the creation of a new Department of Transportation). If such a board were created, it would seem wise to exclude from its consideration expenditures on military-standby activity; in general, a strong argument could be made that all expenditures of this kind could be controlled within the Department of Defense, where the bulk of such undertakings is already housed. Obviously, the effectiveness of any investment review board for transportation would depend on how it was constituted; probably the worst possible way to proceed would be to have its membership comprised of representatives of the various operating agencies with responsibilities for specific transportation programs.

Administrative reorganization of government regulatory activities might also advance the implementation of program-budgeting decisions. For example, it might make a good deal of sense for regulatory as well as program-budgeting purposes to reconstitute the Civil Aeronautics Board as a general regulatory agency for passenger undertakings, transferring to the new agency all passenger regulatory activities of the Interstate Commerce Commission. Similarly, the Interstate Commerce Commission might be reorganized as an agency exclusively concerned with freight regulation, transferring to it those activities of the Civil Aeronautics Board and the Federal Power Commission that pertain to freight regulation. Such a reorganization should be helpful in reducing specific industry identifications of regulatory agencies and could lead to somewhat better recognition of the interrelationships between different promotional activities and subsidies of the federal government.

In sum, it is reasonably evident that program budgeting as developed and refined in the Department of Defense probably would need considerable alteration to adapt it to the specific needs of transportation. Such adaptations would not seem to be impossible—only quite difficult to effectuate. Furthermore, the use of cost-utility analyses to evaluate alternative transportation investments, and more specifically to help design better overall transport systems, would seem to be potentially useful. At the moment, however, the problem may not be so much that of making detailed cost-utility comparisons as simply having the notion recognized that efficiency is at least one criterion that should be considered when evaluating federal government transportation investments. Furthermore, and perhaps more immediately, a program-budgeting approach, even without detailed cost-utility analyses or centralized control, would perhaps lead to a more orderly approach to the evaluation of how different transportation programs are likely to serve the multifarious, often conflicting, and often something less than efficiency-oriented, objectives of the federal government's programs for transportation development.

Chapter 7

EDUCATION IN THE PROGRAM BUDGET

BY WERNER Z. HIRSCH

Education is provided in the United States by a very large number
of administrative units. For example, in late 1962 there were about
36,000 school districts (and many private and parochial schools).
In addition, there were more than 2000 institutions of higher
learning, about 700 public and 1300 private.

At that time 3.3 million men and women were gainfully
employed in the provision of formal education. Education expenditures in FY 1963 amounted to about $31 billion: public educa-
tion accounted for about $25 billion, and private and parochial
education accounted for about $6 billion. The trend from the
preceding decade of about four-fifths of all expenditures for education coming from public funds continued in FY 1963. Of total
education expenditures, almost 15 per cent went for construction,
with the percentage figure somewhat higher in the public than
in the private sector. Public school expenditures of $25 billion in
FY 1963 were financed jointly by federal, state, and local governments. The federal government's contributions were relatively
small: they amounted to about $3.6 billion, or about 10 per cent.

Of the $31 billion total expenditures for education, about $22
billion were for primary and secondary education, and $9 billion
for higher education. Of the first amount, 88 per cent was spent by
public institutions, while the corresponding percentage figure for
higher education was 60.

The federal government's participation in the financing of education has been aimed primarily at higher education, and much of
the federal financial contribution has been indirect, i.e., through
the support of university research. In recent years most of the
direct support has been in the form of training grants and fellow-
ships. Federal financial support of primary and secondary education is given mainly under Public Laws 815[1] and 874[2]. In FY

---

[1] "An Act Relating to the Construction of School Facilities in Areas Affected by
Federal Activities," September 23, 1950, *United States Statutes at Large . . . 1950–*

1963 it amounted to about $332 million or 1.5 per cent of all primary and secondary school expenditure. A further important federal contribution has been the school lunch program, which in 1963 amounted to $379 million. These are mainly indirect supports, and financially they are much more important than the direct federal support to primary and secondary schools. The federal government has also been financing adult education and international education programs, as well as such related activities as library services and research and development.

Almost no one in or outside the government appears to have a clear view of the nature, scope, and mix of the federal education budget. In 1963 the House Committee on Education and Labor pointed out that "while the Federal Government is involved in many parts of the educational system, and a major partner in the higher education system, there is little evidence of a well-coordinated program." A great many committees and agencies take part in funding and administering education in the United States. The report of the House Committee concluded that we suffer from "the inadequacy and misleading nature of available educational statistics" and that "inconsistencies and even contradictions have arisen in our education activities."[3]

Forty-two federal departments, agencies, and bureaus have funds for education in their budgets. Major participants in the financing of education are the Department of Health, Education, and Welfare; the National Science Foundation; the Veterans Administration; the Department of Agriculture; the Department of Defense; the Atomic Energy Commission; and the National Aeronautics and Space Administration. In the Department of Health, Education, and Welfare, education activities are concentrated in the Office of Education, the Office of Vocational Rehabilitation, and the Public Health Service, especially in the National Institutes of Health. Agencies with less interest in education are the Departments of Commerce, Interior, Justice, Treasury, and the Housing and Home Finance Agency.

1951, vol. 64, 81st Cong., 2d Sess. (Washington, D.C.: U.S. Government Printing Office, 1952), pp. 967–978.

2 "An Act to Provide Financial Assistance for Local Educational Agencies in Areas Affected by Federal Activities," September 30, 1950, in *ibid.*, pp. 1100–1109.

3 U.S. House Committee on Education and Labor, *The Federal Government and Education* (Washington, D.C.: U.S. Government Printing Office, 1963), pp. iii, iv.

Many of these agencies also participate in international education, although in this area the major responsibility rests with the Department of State, the Agency for International Development, the Peace Corps, and the U.S. Information Agency. Only two agencies, the Office of Education and the National Science Foundation, have education as their primary concern. The latter was established as an independent agency as recently as 1950; its mandate is to develop and encourage basic research and education in the sciences.[4]

Over the years federal funds for education have been on the increase, and sources of support have been subject to marked change. Thus in FY 1951, as in the years immediately following World War II, the Veterans Administration Budget for the provision of assistance for the education of servicemen under the Servicemen's Readjustment Act of 1944 constituted almost 90 per cent of the federal education budget, while today it is less than 5 per cent.

Education budget requests originate in dozens of federal agencies, and their authorization and appropriation is dispersed among numerous committees of both houses of Congress. Nearly every committee of Congress has jurisdiction over some type of education legislation.[5] For example, in the House of Representatives the Committee on Education and Labor has jurisdiction over the Office of Education, the Science and Astronautics Committee over the National Science Foundation, the Interstate and Foreign Commerce Committee over the Public Health Service and the National Institutes of Health, and the Committee on Veterans' Affairs over veterans' education, etc.

KEY EDUCATION OBJECTIVES AND DECISIONS

The basic education questions calling for decisions by government officials (and citizens) are as follows: What knowledge and skills should be developed; when, where, how, by whom, and for whom? That is to say, in a given year what kind of education should be offered for how many students, by how many teachers

[4] *Ibid.*, p. 2.
[5] *Ibid.*, p. 4.

(and support personnel), with what background and training, and in what facilities? In addition, there is the issue of who should pay for the education. A proper answer to this last problem requires tax incidence considerations.

In clarifying these questions, it is important to be aware of this nation's traditional heritage. First, in the United States we make free primary and secondary education available to every American, and free higher education to most of those who have the ability to benefit from it. Second, the United States operates under a federated political and fiscal system. Both issues reflect our basic philosophy of life and at the same time provide a setting within which education decisions must be made.

We must now take a look at the nation's main educational objectives. Clearly, the creation of human capital is of great national concern. In this respect, education is an investment designed to produce an enterprising and skilled labor force that can be counted on to contribute to economic growth, prosperity, technological advances, and national security. Education enables people to hold rewarding jobs and in turn provides the nation with economic and military strength. Another important objective is to provide students (and perhaps indirectly their parents) with the joy and satisfaction of learning (current benefits associated with the consumption portion of education). A further objective is to preserve and enlarge the cultural heritage of the country and to strengthen its democratic institutions.

For a theoretical approach, let us consider a hypothetical country with a monolithic government, in which the education ministry can take far-reaching steps affecting education. Although the head of state together with the legislature must decide on the overall investment level of the country, the education ministry makes recommendations about the level of investment in education. Priorities must be established and decisions made about how much money and skilled manpower of different types is to be allocated to primary, secondary, higher, and adult education, respectively. The education industry disseminates accumulated knowledge for the use of individuals, and this knowledge pool must constantly be enlarged with additional knowledge. This is done through fundamental and applied research, which competes with education for personnel and funds. Although the allocation of scarce resources among education and research calls for difficult decisions, further priorities might have to be established among knowledge areas. Under a centralized fiscal system, the major funding issue relates only to the allocation of financial burdens to the various income levels of the population.

In our own federated fiscal system it should be clear that we, too, face all these decisions as well as others. For example, the launching of the first Sputnik persuaded the U.S. government to offer financial support to education in science and engineering, and to this day a hot debate is in progress about the wisdom of the step. The federal government plays only a minor role in directly financing education. Nevertheless, it is in its power to be a catalyst and bring about adjustments. Federal funds not only must support education but also must induce state and local governments to exert greater efforts and possibly bring about improvements in their teaching methods and curricula as well as in financing methods. Major decisions must be made about the local, state, and federal role in financing different education programs, and criteria are necessary to facilitate these decisions. Before purposeful changes can be discussed, an understanding of educational activities and the existing budget is needed.

THE EXISTING FEDERAL EDUCATION BUDGET

To review the existing federal education budget, we must examine not only the budget of the U.S. Office of Education but also the budgets of the other agencies that receive education funds. This summary will be followed by examples showing how the existing budget format and budgeting process fail to elucidate key education decisions.

In *The Budget of the United States for the Fiscal Year Ending June 30, 1965,*[6] funds for education are dispersed through more than forty agencies. The administrative education budget in this document is reproduced in Table 7.1. It suffers from serious shortcomings, which will be discussed below in detail.

Although Section VI of the *1965 Budget* contains special analyses of certain programs (e.g., health, research and development), no

[6] Published in Washington, D.C.: U.S. Government Printing Office, 1964.

TABLE 7.1 Administrative Federal Education Budget: Fiscal Years 1963, 1964, and 1965 (in millions of dollars)

Program or agency	Payments to the public			Recommended new obligational authority for 1965
	1963 Actual	1964 Estimate	1965 Estimate	
Administrative budget funds				
Assistance for elementary and secondary education:				
Schools in federally impacted areas	343	350	395	418
Defense education: science, mathematics, foreign language instruction, guidance and testing	49	61	76	84
Assistance for higher education:				
Construction of academic facilities	—	3	38	464
College housing loans	284	223	208	300
Defense education: student loans, fellowships, language and area centers	116	149	162	165
Land-grant colleges, Howard University, Gallaudet College	28	30	33	28
Assistance to National Science Foundation:				
Basic research and specialized research facilities	106	132	148	224
Grants for institutional science programs	31	37	58	98
Science education	51	70	74	137
Other science activities	18	21	22	29
Other aids to education:				
Vocational education	55	73	127	205
Other defense education assistance	20	24	23	23
Indian education services	78	84	92	97
Library of Congress and Smithsonian Institution	38	48	51	45
Other	27	41	65	79
Proposed education legislation	—	3	118	718
Subtotal, administrative budget	1,244	1,348	1,691	3,115[a]
Trust funds	2	2	2	2[a]
Intragovernmental transactions and other adjustments (deduct)	33	48	52	
Total	1,214	1,302	1,641	

Source: The Budget of the United States Government for the Fiscal Year Ending June 30, 1965 (Washington, D.C.: U.S. Government Printing Office, 1964), p. 120.

[a] Compares with new obligational authority for 1963 and 1964 as follows: Administrative budget funds: 1963, $1,420 million; 1964, $1,888 million; Trust funds: 1963, $2 million; 1964, $2 million.

such effort has been made in connection with education. Therefore, we are forced to undertake a separate examination of each
agency.

First let us consider the U.S. Office of Education. Its 1963 expenditure budget is summarized in Table 7.2. However, it should be
realized that this office's expenditures of $624 million are only
about one-fifth of the total federal education budget.

The Vocational Rehabilitation Administration of the Department
of Health, Education, and Welfare spent in FY 1963 $98 million,
of which $71 million was given for grants to states, $24 million for
research and training in the United States, $2 million for research
and training abroad under a special foreign currency program, and
$2.5 million for salaries and expenses.

The 1165-page *1965 Budget Appendix*[7] provides nine pages of
detail on the Office of Education and the Vocational Rehabilitation
Administration. For example, Tables 7.3 and 7.4 are given in support of item 4 in Table 7.2, "Payments to school districts." Payments
to school districts for the maintenance and operation of schools
are made under the Act of September 30, 1950. They are to assist
in the maintenance and operation of schools in areas where enroll-
ments are affected by federal activities. Such payments are made
principally to school districts; however, where such districts cannot
assume responsibility for educating children of parents connected
with the federal government, payments are made to other federal
agencies for the provision of such education under federal auspices.
Also, under certain circumstances the Commissioner of Education
can make arrangements for the provision of free public education
for children of members of the Armed Forces on active duty who
are not residing on federal property.

Payments are made to more than 4000 eligible school districts
and federal agencies on account of the attendance of approximately
2 million children of parents connected with the federal government in all states, Puerto Rico, Virgin Islands, Guam, and Wake
Island.

Table 7.3 summarizes payments to school districts by programs
(as the term is used in *1965 Budget*) and their financing, and Table
7.4 presents the data by object classification.

---

[7] *Appendix: The Budget of the United States Government for the Fiscal Year
Ending June 30, 1965* (Washington, D.C.: U.S. Government Printing Office, 1964).

TABLE 7.2 FY 1963 Expenditure Budget of the U.S. Office of Education (in thousands of dollars)

Category	Amount
General and special funds	
Expansion and improvement of vocational education	34,330
Further endowment of colleges of agriculture and the mechanic arts	11,950
Grants for library services	7,257
Payments to school districts	276,869
Assistance for school construction	66,242
Defense educational activities:	
Assistance for elementary and secondary education	48,690
Assistance for higher education	116,476
Other aids to education	33,169
Expansion of teaching in education of mentally retarded children	960
Expansion of teaching in education of the deaf	1,383
Cooperative research	5,015
Educational research (special foreign currency program)	20
Salaries and expenses	12,041
Colleges of agriculture and the mechanic arts (permanent)	2,550
Promotion of vocational education, Education Act of February 23, 1917	7,144
Intragovernmental funds	−392
Total	623,705

Source: 1965 Budget, pp. 218–221.

TABLE 7.3 Payments to School Districts by Programs and Financing (in thousands of dollars)

Payments	1963 Actual	1964 Estimate	1965 Estimate
Program by activities			
Payments to local educational agencies	200,477	86,966	339,950
Payments to other federal agencies	13,793	17,500	19,500
Total program costs funded— obligations	274,270	104,466	359,450
Financing			
Unobligated balance brought forward	−367	−217	—
Recovery of prior year obligations	−7,749	—	—
Unobligated balance carried forward	217	—	—
Unobligated balance lapsing	15,951	217	—
New obligational authority (appropriation)	282,322	104,466	359,450

Source: Appendix: The Budget of the United States Government for the Fiscal Year Ending June 30, 1965 (Washington, D.C.: U.S. Government Printing Office, 1964), p. 385.

TABLE 7.4 Payments to School Districts by Object Classification

Object classification	1963 Actual	1964 Estimate	1965 Estimate
Personnel summary			
Allocation accounts			
Total number of permanent positions	10	11	11
Full-time equivalent of other positions	4	5	5
Average number of all employees	12	15	15
Employees in permanent positions, end of year	9	10	10
Employees in other positions, end of year	5	5	5
Average GS grade	9.0	9.0	9.0
Average GS Salary	7,007	7,184	7,307
Program and Financing			
Program by activities			
Payments to local educational agencies (costs—obligations)	—	216,204	—
Financing			
New obligational authority (proposed supplemental appropriation)	—	216,204	—

Source: *1965 Budget Appendix*, p. 386.

A careful analysis of the rest of the budget of the Department of Health, Education, and Welfare reveals further major education funds in the National Institutes of Health and the Public Health Service. The former agency supports faculty directly through research career awards and indirectly through research grants and facility and equipment grants. It supports students through pre- and post-doctoral fellowships and training grants. The education support of this agency was in excess of a quarter of a billion dollars in FY 1963, while that of the rest of the Public Health Service was about $20 million.

The Department of Defense spent more than $100 million to provide education for military personnel in Defense Department schools. More than $160 million was spent on education in civilian institutions, e.g., Army, Navy, and Air Force ROTC. A further $200 million was granted to universities for the support of research.

The National Science Foundation had a $200 million budget, most of it devoted to the support of education. The Veterans

Administration had an education budget of about $150 million for readjustment training, vocational rehabilitation, and war orphan scholarships. Many other federal departments supported education in various forms from a few million dollars to around $60 million a year. The latter figure pertains to the Department of Agriculture and the Department of the Interior.

SOME SHORTCOMINGS OF THE EXISTING BUDGET

The existing budget, which incorporates financial support for education in forty-two departments and agencies, makes it difficult to appraise the place of education in the federal government and the role of the government in providing and financing education. In more general terms, the budget neither facilitates the development and implementation of a policy for education nor the examination of the role of education in pursuance of a national education policy. These shortcomings of budget format are perhaps best discussed under the following headings:

1. Intermingling of grant and loan funds.
2. Lack of identification of relevant information, which prevents:
   (a) Coordination of interrelated decisions;
   (b) Consideration of full-cost implications of decisions;
   (c) Consideration of alternatives and their tradeoffs.

Intermingling of Grant and Loan Funds

Until quite recently federal funds for education were made available solely on a grant or contract basis. However, a new development has taken place; loans are made both to students to tide them over the costly years of their training and to colleges to help finance their building programs. In FY 1963 the loans reached the half-billion-dollar level—almost the size of the 1963 expenditures of the U.S. Office of Education. The administrative education budget, reproduced in Table 7.1, intermingles grant and loan funds. In the absence of a careful separation between these two funds, we face problems that are somewhat similar to those encountered by adding tax receipts of school districts to funds raised by them through the sale of bonds.

Lack of Information Preventing Coordination of Interrelated Decisions

Quite a few education activities require budgetary decisions by more than one level of government. In other cases, education activities of different types supplement one another. Therefore, gains can often accrue from presenting information in an orderly, internally consistent manner to facilitate the joint consideration of these activities and their possible coordination.

For example, all three levels of government participate actively in the financing of higher education. Local school districts have assumed major responsibility for the financing of junior colleges, with state governments providing subsidies. The main financial responsibility for colleges and universities rests with the state, while the federal government is providing increasing amounts of direct and indirect financial aid. This aid is made available by numerous federal agencies. For example, student fellowships are offered, among others, by the Office of Education, the National Science Foundation, the National Institutes of Health and other parts of the Public Health Service, the National Aeronautics and Space Administration, the Atomic Energy Commission, and the Department of the Interior. Many more federal agencies make indirect support available.

1965 Budget includes a special analysis of federal aid to state and local governments.[8] This information could be presented in a more useful form. The data follow department lines and much information is concealed, which makes it virtually impossible to take a comprehensive look at the federal support for college students and to integrate it effectively with the financial efforts of the states.

Well-organized information can improve decisions about education activities that supplement one another. In recent years the federal government has provided loan funds for the construction of student housing facilities. Some federal agencies, including the National Science Foundation, the National Aeronautics and Space Administration, and the National Institutes of Health under differing conditions, have offered grants for research facilities. State and

[8] *1965 Budget*, pp. 427–435.

private funds have also been used to finance the construction of college plants and equipment. These construction projects could be better evaluated and integrated if the budgetary information were more readily available in an explicit and internally consistent end-product oriented form.

Lack of Information Preventing Consideration of Full-Cost Implications

A discussion on the full-cost aspects of a decision should include two somewhat different issues. First, there is the time horizon issue. This full-cost issue is important mainly with regard to financing research and building activities in support of education. Were the federal government to contemplate financing national educational television, for instance, it should consider not only the first-year costs but also the long-term cost implications, perhaps over the next five years.

The second issue related to a full-cost discussion is the need to consider as many of the costs as possible, not just the obvious elements. For example, the cost of instituting a universal junior college system should include not only the junior college expenditures associated with such a proposal but also the implications of further unbalancing of very precarious demand and supply situations for instructional staff in high schools and colleges. One result could be an across-the-board increase in teachers' salaries.

Lack of Information Preventing Consideration of Alternatives and Their Tradeoffs

Our increasing investment in education and in such complementary activities as basic and applied research, both so essential for our future economic and military health, necessitates a systematic consideration of tradeoffs to enable us to make judicious choices. The present budget does not provide organized information that can help estimate the implications, for example, of trading off an additional billion dollars to be spent on higher education for the same amount to obtain more basic research, or applied research. Or should the money be spent to retrain obsolete manpower and help win the war against poverty?

The federal dollar invested in education should do extra duty. It can induce local and state governments to invest more heavily in education, and it can induce them to invest in especially advantageous educational activities. It can have desirable and disadvantageous side effects in terms of economic growth, economic stability, income distribution, etc. These points should be in the minds of those who make education decisions, yet the present budget is of little help to them.

APPLICABILITY OF PROGRAM CONCEPT TO EDUCATION

Let us examine a schematic presentation of the lifetime flow of students through the formal education system (see Fig. 1). Virtually all individuals attend primary grades and some years of high school. Most high school education is college preparatory, while some is explicitly vocational. From the vocational programs students mainly progress either into the labor force (and the nonworking population) or into a junior college system. From the college preparatory courses students enter either regular colleges —including the service academies—or undergraduate divisions of universities, or junior colleges. Part of the junior college students enter four-year colleges to work toward their bachelor's degree; part of the college population continues in graduate and professional schools of universities.

Regardless of whether they have a college education, Americans can participate in a variety of adult education activities, from extension programs to retraining courses. Some federally financed activities are mainly designed to help veterans, others are for government employees, and still others are for farmers.

In short, the educational system assumes a vertical structure, with lower levels of education facilitating and leading into higher levels, and special adult training and retraining programs offering some shortcuts and flexibility.

What are some of the key characteristics of a useful program category in the field of education? Tentatively, an education program should:

1. Directly and effectively relate to the nation's major education objectives, and in this sense it should be end-product-oriented.

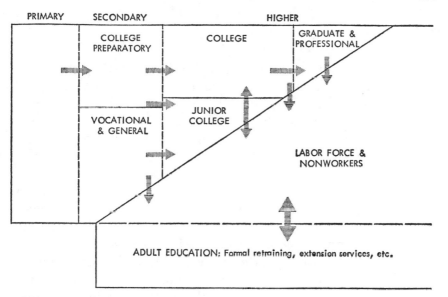

FIG. 1. Lifetime flow of students through the education system. (Prepared by Morton Marcus of The Institute of Government and Public Affairs, University of California at Los Angeles; reproduced here with permission.)

2. Lend itself to a meaningful breakdown into program elements that can readily be related to each other.

3. Have administrative relevance and provide for administrative effectiveness.

4. Directly relate to sources of funds and facilitate viable inter-governmental fiscal relations.

With these characteristics in mind, we will next identify the major education programs, remembering that program budgets should have a reasonably long time horizon (e.g., five years) and permit full-cost pricing.

As was pointed out, the education system has a number of components, many of which are vertically related to one another. Thus primary education produces an intermediary output, much of which is preparatory to secondary education, which in turn is preparatory to college attendance.

The identification of key education programs is difficult, partly because of our inability to separate investment and consumption aspects of education, on the one hand, and its research aspects, on the other. Nonetheless, one might recommend the subdivision of the federal education budget into the following main programs: (1) primary education, (2) secondary education, (3) higher education, and (4) adult education.

Each of these four main programs can have significant program elements. For example, in terms of its mission and educational activities, secondary education can be separated into college preparatory and vocational. Except in small rural high schools and private preparatory schools, the two types of education can take place in the same district, which makes expenditure separation into the two groups very difficult, if not impossible.

Similarly, in line with the California experience, it appears desirable to divide higher education into junior college, college, graduate, and postgraduate education. Again, adult education can have a number of program elements. In the abstract we might want to distinguish between continued education and retraining, the first group being further subdivided into general and vocational (or professional) education. Federal participation in these programs stems from a variety of concerns. The most obvious is the desire to educate government employees so that they can better and more efficiently fulfill their responsibilities. Furthermore, we have long-standing training commitments to farmers and veterans and, more recently, to residents of depressed areas in this country.

In addition to these four main programs, it appears useful to single out three further programs: library services, research (and development) in educational institutions and research centers, and international education. The seven programs are summarized in Table 7.5. Library services provide important support for our categories of higher and adult education as well as research and development. Not unlike library services, research supplements and supports our major educational efforts in that it creates new knowledge that is disseminated by our schools, colleges, and universities. International education falls into a slightly different category in that it enters all levels of education, with the direct beneficiaries being foreigners.

THE EDUCATION PROGRAM BUDGET FOR FY 1963

An effort will now be made to provide data for the main programs of Table 7.5 in FY 1963. Because no separate data exist, it

TABLE 7.5 Education Programs in an Idealized Federal Budget

Program	1963	1964	1965	1966	1967
Primary education					
Secondary education					
College preparatory					
Vocational					
Higher education					
Junior college					
College					
Graduate					
Postgraduate					
Adult education					
Continued general (liberal)					
Continued vocational					
(professional)					
Government employees					
Nongovernment employees					
Retraining					
Library services					
Research (and development)					
International education					

appears necessary to combine primary with secondary education. We will distinguish between federal grants and federal loans. The FY 1963 data that will be presented are estimates of federal education funds and are not strictly comparable with U.S. education expenditure data.[9]

In Table 7.6 federal funds for major education programs are presented in terms of their administrative purposes and sources of support. The funds are arranged by the nature of their support in Table 7.7.[10]

For example, federal support for primary and secondary education is given both directly and indirectly. The indirect support consists mainly of financing such auxiliary school services as lunch

[9] The "funds" data are prepared on an obligation rather than an expenditure basis. Federal funds data include the following types of items (for FY 1963) that are not included in the U.S. education expenditure figures: (1) student stipends under federal fellowship and training program (about $200 million); (2) education of military dependents overseas (about $45 million); (3) value of commodities distributed under the school lunch program (about $180 million); and (4) surplus property donations (about $110 million).

[10] In Table 7.7 funds that appeared in Table 7.6 as "Other" under primary and secondary education and higher education are grouped together with across-the-board direct support.

TABLE 7.6 Federal Education Program Budget Arranged by Sources of Support FY 1963 (Obligations in thousands of dollars)

Source of support	Amount
I. Grants, etc.—Total	3,620,220
A. Primary and secondary education—Total	991,858
1. Federally impacted area support (Public Laws 815 and 874)	332,200
2. Military dependents, schools	45,289
3. Military dependents, bus transportation	550
4. National Defense Education Act	62,622
5. Public lands revenue for schools	44,549
6. Teaching grants (Educational Exchange Program)	6,800
7. Course content improvement group (National Science Foundation)	3,637
8. Science education (National Science Foundation)	3,901
9. Vocational education	26,323
10. Indian education	60,876
11. School aid to District of Columbia and territories	18,021
12. School lunch program	379,258
13. Job placement services for high school seniors	6,900
14. Other	932
B. Higher education—Total	1,242,397
1. Training grants	255,988
2. Fellowships	108,389
3. Institutional grants	38,695
4. Traineeships	23,423
5. Special training programs	9,784
6. Veterans' education	68,446
7. Military academies	51,493
8. Training state and local personnel	5,765
9. Basic research and research facilities in U.S. educational institutions proper	551,376
10. Other, including surplus property transfers	129,038
C. Adult education—Total	209,945
1. Vocational and technical training	67,551
2. Veterans' education	29,007
3. Training federal personnel in nonfederal facilities	31,869
4. Training state and local personnel	3,589
5. Apprenticeship and training programs	4,458
6. Education in federal correctional institutions	2,518
7. Indian education	6,165
8. Cooperative agricultural extension service	63,008
9. Mine safety training	1,400
10. Other	380

TABLE 7.6 (*Continued*)

D. Library services—Total	23,896
1. Library of Congress	12,073
2. Library Services Act grants	7,406
3. National Library of Medicine	3,321
4. National Agricultural Library	1,096
E. Research (and development)—Total	1,089,124
1. Applied R&D in educational institutions and research centers	1,089,124
F. International education—Total	63,000
1. AID cooperative projects	54,000
2. Grants for observation and advisory service under the Educational Exchange Program	9,000
II. Loans—Total	481,851
A. Primary and secondary education—Total	616
1. Loans to private schools	616
B. Higher education—Total	481,235
1. Student loan program	90,692
2. College housing loans	390,543

Source: Department of Health, Education, and Welfare, Office of Education, *Annual Survey, Federal Funds for Education and Related Activities,* and records.

and job placement programs. The direct support is mainly across the board, with all schools eligible to apply for it. In 1963 most of the support was for veterans and war orphans. However, there are some funds earmarked for the support of such special groups as American Indians and residents of the District of Columbia and U.S. territories. In addition, there are funds earmarked for special types of education, e.g., science education and vocational education.

Federal support under Public Laws 815[11] and 874[12] is somewhat different in character from most other support. In many respects it is made available in lieu of taxes to local and state government, and for certain purposes it may not be combined with other federal aid to education. However, we can also take a different view of payments to federally impacted areas. Because a sizable portion

[11] *U.S. Statutes . . . 1950–1951,* pp. 967–978.
[12] *Ibid.,* pp. 1100–1109.

TABLE 7.7 Federal Education Program Budget Arranged by Nature of Support FY 1963[a] (Obligations in thousands of dollars)

Nature of support	Amount
I. Grants, etc.—Total	3,620,220
A. Primary and secondary education—Total	991,858
1. Across-the-board direct support (4–7, 14)	118,540
2. Support in lieu of taxes[b] (1–3)	378,039
3. Support for special groups (10, 11)	78,897
4. Support for special education (8, 9)	30,224
5. Indirect support (12, 13)	386,158
B. Higher education—Total	1,242,397
1. Across-the-board direct support (1–5, 10)	565,317
2. Support for special groups (6–8)	125,704
3. Indirect support through R&D (9)	551,376
C. Adult education—Total	209,945
1. Support for special groups (1–10)	209,945
D. Library services—Total	23,896
1. Across-the-board (1, 2)	19,479
2. Support for special groups (3, 4)	4,417
E. Research (and development)—Total	1,089,124
F. International education—Total	63,000
II. Loans—Total	481,851
A. Primary and secondary education—Total	616
B. Higher education—Total	481,235

Source: Table 7.6.

[a] Numbers in parentheses refer to items in Table 7.6.

[b] For some purposes support in lieu of tax payments may be deducted from federal support of education.

of the federal grants are made on behalf of children whose parents work on federal property located outside the school district, parts of the funds can become available without strings and controls. The relevant portion of these funds could then be included in the across-the-board direct support.

Regardless of which view we take of funds made available under Public Laws 815 and 874, it is revealing that relatively little money is given to schools in terms of across-the-board support, i.e., some-where between $150 and $350 million in FY 1963.

Federal funds to higher education entail, on the one hand, support on an across-the-board basis and, on the other hand, support for special groups (e.g., veterans, military academies, state and local personnel). During FY 1962 federal grants provided direct support to 182,000 students, full and part time, at all academic levels at a cost of more than a quarter of a billion dollars. Nearly 60 per cent of these funds went to veterans under the readjustment training and rehabilitation programs (both of which are being reduced at a rate of nearly 50 per cent each year) and to war orphans. Eighty-seven per cent of the funds for graduate student support went to students in the sciences and engineering. These figures exclude the military academies.[13] Most of the direct support is directed toward predoctoral work and takes the form of fellow-ships given directly to the student or the institution or research assistantships as parts of research grants and contracts.

Although some of the federal funds are for direct support of higher education, other funds provide support indirectly through research and development. Support for basic research and research facilities has been increasing rapidly in recent years, from $210 million in FY 1959 to $550 million in FY 1963. About one-third of this total amount comes from the National Institutes of Health and the Department of Defense, respectively. Next in importance are the National Science Foundation, the Atomic Energy Commission, the Department of Agriculture, and the National Aeronautics and Space Administration.

The very fact that major research and training funds are included in the administrative budgets of the agencies mentioned above raises the intriguing question of whether education produces an intermediate or a final output. In terms of legislative intent, many research and training funds are awarded to help specific agencies accomplish their missions. However, the classification in Tables 7.6 and 7.7 treats research in educational institutions and research centers and training efforts as purely educational activities. It would be very proper indeed to have a different viewpoint and exclude from the education program budget those research

---

[13] *Federal Government and Education*, p. 14.

and training funds that directly relate to specific government missions other than education. The excluded items could then be grouped into the program budgets of other departments. Clearly this view would result in a substantially smaller total education budget figure than the $3.6 billion given in Tables 7.6 and 7.7— possibly somewhere between $2.6 and $3.0 billion.

APPLYING PROGRAM BUDGETING TO ELUCIDATE EDUCATION DECISIONS

The philosophy underlying this chapter has been that the education budget of the federal government should give expression to the nation's position toward education, and should facilitate long-range projections even though the education demand and supply picture involves major uncertainties. Although different types of education and their output cannot be measured in simple quantitative terms, the program budget, if properly designed, can provide partial quantitative information that elucidates some of the consequences of spending funds of different programs. Fewer difficulties need to be overcome on the input side, where it is often possible to stipulate the requirements for manpower (by types), material, and supplies to support specified activities. These requirements can readily be expressed in money terms. However, it must be kept in mind that much of the nation's investment in education is designed to create human capital. It follows that education decisions relate heavily to the future, and if they turn out to be wrong, they cannot be readily reversed. Thus it is of paramount importance to be aware that today's action or inaction with regard to education can constitute sins of omission or sins of commission whose burdens will fall mainly on future generations.

As was pointed out in Chapter 2, program budgeting can facilitate the making of decisions on three different levels. For education this means that on the highest level program budgeting can be employed to help select the proper budget size on the basis of information about the preferred mix between education, defense, space, natural resources, etc., and the private sector. On the second level, program budgeting can help in the determination of the best mix of different education programs, often involving judgments about vaguely defined objectives. Finally, there is the relatively low-level decision, which relies on factors for cost and output to determine the most effective way of attaining a given program objective.

It must be remembered that education decisions, unlike defense decisions that are in the hands of a monolithic federal agency, are made by literally tens of thousands of administrative units. Furthermore, three levels of government share in the responsibility to raise education funds, all in competition with private educational institutions. As was pointed out earlier in this chapter, in terms of funds the federal government is the smallest of the four partners and in recent years provided only slightly more than 10 per cent of the money. Although federal funds are relatively small, they have been increasing and, more important, they can be made available in a way that local and state school officials consider them costless. Local school officials tend to look at state subsidies in a similar way.

Thus the executive branch and Congress ponder not only the question of how much federal aid to education should be made available but also the form it should take. Crucial questions are: Who should benefit; who should pay; what strings, if any, should be attached; and what are the objectives to be obtained? Elucidation of these questions calls for a benefit-burden analysis that explicitly allows for spatial benefits and cost spillovers. A conceptual framework, developed and implemented in relation to a case study, has been published by the author.[14]

The dispersion of education decisionmaking and complicated intergovernmental fiscal relations must be kept in mind in the preparation of program budgets and in devising applications for them. This admonition holds no less for federal education than for the local school district decisionmaker.

A few samples will next be explored to illustrate possible applications of education program budgets. Only two of the three types of decisions mentioned earlier in this section deal primarily with program budgeting by the federal government. The relatively low-level decision concerned with finding the most effective way of

[14] Werner Z. Hirsch, Elbert W. Segelhorst, and Morton J. Marcus, *Spillover of Public Education Costs and Benefits* (Los Angeles: Institute of Government and Public Affairs, University of California, 1964), p. 465; see also Hirsch, "Regional Accounts for Public School Decisions," paper presented at the Third Regional Accounts Conference, Miami Beach, Fla., November 20, 1964.

attaining a given subprogram objective basically involves the local school district and therefore will not be considered.

We shall concentrate first on a decision facing the President and his budget advisers. To the extent that the education budget, as well as the budgets of other major federal activities, is end- (or intermediate-) product-oriented, and at least some outputs are in quantitative terms, the tradeoff discussions about an additional billion dollars for education, defense, resources development, or space exploration become sharper and more meaningful. More specifically, on the basis of the 1963 program budget figures the following questions suggest themselves: In the light of a 1963 GNP of about $585 billion, a $93 billion federal budget, and a $25 billion public education budget, is a $3.6 billion federal education budget of optimum size?[15] Or would, for example, an additional billion dollars for education prove more beneficial to the nation than adding $1 billion to NASA's 1963 budget of $3.7 billion for space exploration, or to DOD's 1963 budget of $57.8 billion for defense? Are we putting too much into our defense program and not enough into education? Or vice versa?

Partial answers to these questions would require not only our estimate of contributions that can be expected from a marginal dollar invested in defense space exploration or education, but also the multiplier effects of such contributions. Thus, for example, unlike an additional federal defense or space exploration dollar, an increment of federal contributions to education, depending on the form it takes, could lead to further state and local education funding. In this sense, the additional federal education dollar will carry extra duty, and this increment needs to be estimated and considered in a discussion of whether we would not be better off if the federal government were to increase its education budget.

Another consideration of the desirability of further federal contributions to the financing of education centers around the issue of distributional equity. This issue has a bearing on the allocation of financing responsibilty to the three levels of government. If we agree that the federal government is mainly responsible for income redistribution and that large-scale spatial cost and benefit spill-

[15] *Economic Report to the President, Transmitted to the Congress January 1964,* House Document No. 278, 88th Cong., 2d Sess. (Washington, D.C.: U.S. Government Printing Office, 1964), pp. 207, 274.

overs exist, as well as that they should be either neutralized or made consistent with some norm of distributional equity, greater federal financial participation might be appropriate. Increased federal funds provided through grants (aid), for example, change the distribution of education costs and benefits to different geographic areas and income groups. Because the federal income tax is progressive, larger federal subsidies are likely to improve distributional equity.

Let us turn to another type of decision and ask the question: If the federal education budget is $3.6 billion (or $3.3 billion if we exclude the $0.3 billion aid to federally impacted areas), is a mix of $1 billion (or $0.7 billion if the $0.3 billion is excluded) for primary and secondary education, $1.1 billion for higher education, $0.2 billion for adult education, $0.02 billion for library services, $1.1 billion for research (and development), and $0.06 billion for international education the preferred mix? What is the relative merit of spending an additional given amount of money for each of these programs?

Answers are not easy to come by, but a few simple yardsticks suggest themselves. For example, although the federal budget for primary and secondary education is smaller than that for higher education, many more students attend schools than colleges and universities. The ratio is about 9 to 1.[16] At the same time, adequate higher education per student is not that much more expensive than primary and secondary education. Because education has a vertical structure, another consideration is that good college education is likely to be much more effective when it is accorded to students with a solid primary and secondary education. Therefore, if there is no immediate crisis that requires a mammoth increase in the supply of scientists and engineers, an orderly long-run program, well balanced on all levels of education, appears to be in order.

On the surface it would appear that since across-the-board direct federal support for primary and secondary education is so small (for example, in FY 1963 it was only slightly more than $100 million), the marginal dollar would yield the highest return. Before we could be confident, however, that primary and secondary educa-

16 *Statistical Abstract of the United States, 1963,* Bureau of the Census, U.S. Department of Commerce (Washington, D.C.: U.S. Government Printing Office, 1963), pp. 127, 136.

tion can use additional federal funds better than any other education program, a number of important issues must be investigated. By how much will an additional federal dollar for primary and secondary education increase funds provided for education in general compared with an additional federal dollar for another education program? By how much will an additional dollar for primary and secondary education increase education benefits compared with other education programs?

Although the economist can have only partial answers at best to these resource allocation questions, policy-makers would want to consider them in conjunction with some political "facts of life." For example, the issue of separation of school and church appears to have stymied all congressional efforts to increase the support for public schools. This particular impediment to legislation exists only to a lesser extent in connection with higher education, and it plays almost no role in relation to the other programs. Therefore, major increases in federal support for education may have to be selected from among such programs as adult education, library services, research (and development), and international education.

The question can also be raised whether a 1963 expenditure of $26 million for vocational high school education constitutes an optimum level. In the light of projected demand increases for skilled workers, it may be highly desirable to offer more students schooling in technical high schools, and federal grants for vocational training may be able to induce local governments to take appropriate steps. As a result, marginal returns from such an investment may be high.

Similarly, the question can be raised concerning the heavy emphasis on science. Direct and indirect federal support of institutions of higher learning has no doubt further unbalanced the relative position of the natural sciences, social sciences, and humanities. Although we do not have readily available national statistics, data can be found for specific universities. This leads to the question of whether, for example, $50 million could not be more effectively used if channeled into the humanities rather than into the social or natural sciences.

There is also the issue of adult education, only one aspect of which will be considered here. On June 20, 1964, President Johnson called for an Urban Extension Service in dedicating a new University of California campus at Irvine. No doubt this interest stems, in part, from the exceptional success of our Agricultural Extension Service. With the rural population rapidly declining and urban America growing by leaps and bounds, the President's call appears at first logical and perhaps overdue. Yet much careful work is needed before one can be sure that federal funds for urban extension could be well spent in comparison with other opportunities. For example, the objectives of agricultural extension were clear and almost universally agreed on: make two blades grow where one was growing, and do so efficiently. Also, these objectives were to be achieved with the aid of mechanical and chemical means whose effectiveness had been established in advance, e.g., better ways to cultivate, fertilize, fight diseases, and irrigate crops. However, on the urban scene we have neither agreement on objectives nor tested knowledge to improve urban life and form. Therefore, perhaps we should invest more heavily in urban research before we use federal funds for an urban extension effort.

Application of benefit-cost analysis can elucidate a higher education decision, although it may involve the federal government only indirectly. Early in 1964 the Education Policies Commission proposed universal junior college education, and some suggestions will be made as to how the relative merits of this proposal can be analyzed with the aid of a benefit-cost analysis.[17] There are 908,000 "potential" college students who, according to the proposal at hand, would enter colleges to be educated for a two-year period. For simplicity's sake, it will be assumed that:

1. These 908,000 youngsters will be in college on a full-time basis.

2. Costs will be the same as those of college students presently enrolled in various institutions. (Because junior colleges are less expensive to operate during the freshman and sophomore years, than regular liberal arts colleges or universities, this assumption produces an upward cost bias.)

3. Benefits will be the same as those of college students presently enrolled in various institutions. (Because junior colleges are likely to offer education inferior to that of other institutions of higher learning and, more important, because the caliber of those pres-

[17] The Education Policies Commission, *Universal Opportunity for Education Beyond the High School* (Washington, D.C.: National Education Association, 1964).

ently not in college is on the average inferior to that of those attending college, this assumption produces an upward benefit bias.)

4. Marginal cost equals average cost.

Under these assumptions, additional operating costs of $2.8 billion, capital costs of $0.7 billion, foregone earnings of $0.4 billion, and miscellaneous private costs of $0.2 billion, or a total of $4.0 billion a year can be expected. Incremental annual student income benefits (in present-value terms) total $2.5 billion. The resulting benefit-cost ratio would be about 0.63.

Although this ratio does not reflect all the items that are germane to the proposal at hand (a good example is the employment impact of the proposal), it appears to indicate that investment in universal junior college education is likely to produce negative returns. At the same time, under similar assumptions, adding eight-week sessions for five summers following the 7th through the 11th grades would produce a benefit-cost ratio of 2.2. The social cost of the additional sessions would tend to be much smaller than costs associated with the junior college proposal—perhaps only one-third in amount. However, if we are concerned that about 3.5 million teenagers are in the work force today and that of this total 2 million are out of work, placing teenagers in junior colleges is a very attractive way of reducing unemployment in the immediate future.

ARRANGEMENTS FOR EFFECTIVE USE OF PROGRAM BUDGETING

Even if promising program budgets can be designed and an agreement reached to apply benefit-cost analysis whenever possible, there remains the task of providing an institutional arrangement that will ensure effective use of these tools in negotiating and implementing major allocative decisions in the education field. The importance of such a step becomes especially clear if we remember that although the federal education budget in FY 1963 amounted to $3.6 billion, the U.S. Office of Education budget was a mere $0.6 billion. Furthermore, in that year state and local government raised more than $22 billion for education.

Opposition to major changes in the budgeting procedure and evaluation capability with regard to education could be forthcoming not only from federal departments but also from the fifty state departments of education and the tens of thousands of local school districts and their organized spokesmen. Also, the official position of the National Education Association, the Council for Higher Education, etc., will have to be considered.

Part of the opposition is likely to stem from a general uneasiness regarding change. The existing budget and budgeting procedures are so patently uninformative that they effectively conceal most of the needed insight. Many old-timers are quite comfortable in such a situation, which makes it difficult for any operation to be judged and evaluated seriously.

There are other more basic objections to be expected. Effective program budgeting by the U.S. Office of Education could strengthen the hand of this agency not only in relation to other parts of the federal government concerned with education but also in relation to state and local governments. Program budgeting might force the latter to move in a similar direction, especially if federal aid would include such a direct or indirect requirement.

Another serious objection is based on the view held by many educators that education is unique and that its achievements defy measurement. They are likely to be appalled by the mere thought that outputs of education would be discussed and compared and that a benefit-cost framework would be applied. In addition, there are the other potential general difficulties that are discussed in Chapter 11.

These potential difficulties need to be remembered in our attempt to design a set of arrangements that will ensure the effective use of program budgeting for major allocative decisions by the White House and Congress.[18] To facilitate the successful institution of program budgeting, it would be most important to create an environment in which the various federal departments with education funds, as well as state education departments, would be induced to adopt comparable program budget and benefit-cost analysis procedures and use them effectively when resource allocation decisions are made. Beyond this, the system should be such as to stimulate states to have local school districts adopt reasonably uniform program budgets and benefit-cost analyses, all closely integrated with the state and federal procedures.

[18] See Chapter 5.

Achieving this objective does not necessarily require the creation of a new department of education with cabinet level status. This might even prove undesirable because many budget items included in Table 7.7 are of great concern to officials in one or more other policy areas, as well as to education officials. A good example is federal support for medical research in universities. These funds concern decisionmakers in the education, health, and research fields.

What then is needed is a recasting of the present budget to replace the uninformative administrative education budget reproduced as Table 7.1. Hand in hand with such an education program budget exhibit, the budget exhibit of the U.S. Office of Education and other agencies with major education funds should also be modified. In addition, the Bureau of the Budget might develop more detailed program budget information in cooperation with the Office of Science and Technology, to facilitate its review of federal science (and education) programs.

Furthermore, the U.S. Commissioner of Education could be given broader powers and responsibilities and a more attractive "carrot," which would help to bring about more effective horizontal and vertical communication between education decisionmakers. Such communication and dialogue could take place using an integrated, internally consistent program budget and benefit-cost framework, leading hopefully in future years to more closely integrated resource allocation decisions. It would be naive to assume that such a step would be easy. As a matter of fact, in many instances federal and local school officials will have opposing interests, which program budgeting and benefit-cost analysis will not reconcile. However, these methods of analysis can guide federal officials in the responsibility of bringing local education decisions into closer harmony with national objectives. They can also aid state and local officials to adjust themselves better to federal education policies by helping them understand their trade-off positions.

If we are optimistic and assume that program budgeting will be instituted in the near future, the old administrative budget will have to be continued in the short run side by side with the new program budget. Budget categories should be such that cross-classification is facilitated. As was discussed earlier, there are many forces that will work in a direction favoring retaining the existing administrative budget. To bring about wider acceptance of program budgeting, it would be important for the Bureau of the Budget, as well as the Council of Economic Advisors, to move generally to this approach. The budget conferences between the various federal departments or units within the departments and the Bureau of the Budget can now be carried out within a program budget framework. But in the major education areas the institution of a program budget by the U.S. Office of Education, including all federal education financing, could induce other departments to follow suit. Furthermore, if the discussion of federal grant proposals would take place within a program budget framework, state and local governments might be induced to make their proposals and evaluate the impact of federal proposals on their operations and finances in a similar framework.

Chapter 8

FEDERAL HEALTH EXPENDITURES IN A PROGRAM BUDGET

BY MARVIN FRANKEL

The nature and scale of federal activity in the health field, as in a number of other fields, have undergone great long-term changes. During the early years of the Republic and for an extended period thereafter the scale of expenditures was modest and the outlays were associated largely with the health care of merchant seamen, the armed forces, and veterans. Other health functions of wider social consequences remained of nominal proportions until quite recent times. Certain programs of broad sweep have emerged only within the past fifteen to twenty years. They are primarily under the aegis of the Department of Health, Education, and Welfare, which authorizes grants to nonfederal agencies, organizations, and individuals for the support of a range of health activities that today claim a large share of federal health outlays.

The shift from modest participation to major involvement in the health field by the federal government appears to have taken firm hold during and shortly after World War II. From 1935 to 1963 expenditures for health purposes by all public agencies—federal, state, and local—rose from 20 per cent of combined public and private outlays to only 25 per cent; but the federal share of all public outlays increased from about 17 per cent in 1935 to around 40 per cent by 1950 and to approximately 50 per cent by the early 1960s. The trend in federal monies used for health research is even more marked. Between 1953 and 1963 these outlays advanced more than tenfold, and in the latter year they were nearing the $1 billion level.[1]

The changes have meant a marked rise in federal health dollars in relation to gross national product and a sharp increase, from about 1 per cent in 1935 to 5 per cent in 1965, in the share such

[1] The figures are estimates based on data in *Health, Education, and Welfare Trends*, U.S. Department of Health, Education, and Welfare (Washington, D.C.: U.S. Government Printing Office, 1963), pp. 26, 108.

outlays claim of the federal budget. The trends give justification, if any is required, for the need for better information about federal health activities, and they suggest that the benefits accruing from the use of a tool such as program budgeting might be large.

The forces underlying these trends are mixed and in certain respects paradoxical. The element of paradox comes from the fact that certain of the forces have contributed strongly to better health and reduced demands for health services. Aspects of this contribution include a substantial long-term decline in the hazards of nature (storm, fire, flood, and famine), a falling incidence over the decades in a host of diseases and illnesses of both major and minor nature, and a significant fall since the mid-thirties in the death rate from accidents. We now possess a much improved understanding of the forces causing illness and, compared with an earlier period, much more powerful methods of treatment. When illness does strike, it tends to be of shorter duration, with lesser aftereffects. Perhaps indicative of these latter facts is the two-fifths reduction over the last thirty years in the average length of hospital stay.[2] The upshot of such trends is a healthier population, the chief mark of which is a comparatively longer and still rising average life-span.

The paradox of rising federal health outlays in the face of these trends is explainable by two circumstances. First, and quite simply, the trends are in part attributable to federal efforts in the health field. Rising federal outlays have helped to make the trends possible, and their continuance will in part depend on continued federal support. Because future gains in health improvement may be more difficult than earlier ones, inasmuch as the easier problems tend to be overcome first, further increases in the federal contribution may be necessary to the achievement of new and higher health goals.

Second, social, economic, demographic, and related changes have generated counterforces to health-improving trends that have prompted growing federal involvement. The growth of urban and suburban complexes has intensified environmental and com-

---

[2] *Trends*, p. 29. This statistic doubtless reflects a growing tendency by physicians to hospitalize patients for various lesser illnesses, which in earlier periods would have been treated at home. This practice is associated with both rising patient incomes and health insurance claim requirements. The tendency to remove patients to convalescent homes or to their residences also contributes to shorter stays in the hospitals.

munity health problems—or brought them more obtrusively to attention—and has encouraged higher expenditures in the fields of hospital construction, sanitation, and air pollution. The increasing geographic mobility of Americans and the weakening of family ties, both byproducts of urbanization, may signify rising personal independence and responsibility, but they have also made the disadvantaged and less fortunate, including those in ill health, more dependent on the government. Less frequently than in the past does the family provide needed recovery and nursing care, with the result that greater reliance is placed on community and federal support.

Of importance also is the increase in the so-called dependent age groups of the population to whose health needs the government contributes in various direct and indirect ways. Over the past four decades the percentage of the population represented by the 65-and-over group has doubled and currently stands at about 9.3 per cent. Of more recent vintage is the upward drift in the 19-and-under group, from about 33.5 per cent in 1950 to 40 per cent today. For both groups the absolute increase in numbers is yet more impressive.[3]

By no means least important in explaining advancing federal and public involvement in health activities is the factor of rising per capita income and with it rising health standards. More is demanded and expected from government in such fields as community and environmental health, health education, and research. Expectations are heightened by the development of new, complex procedures and methods, many of which are expensive. The consequences for expenditures are compounded by a lagging productivity in many segments of this predominantly service area, causing a relative rise in costs. Hospital care, research, and facilities construction are all relatively more costly than in past years.

Also deserving mention is the changing sentiment during this century, especially since the thirties, as to the proper dividing line between the domains of public and private responsibility and the appropriate scope for federal action in meeting the citizenry's needs. The provision of certain medical services that not too many

[3] Since 1925 the 65-and-over group has increased from 5.8 to 18.2 million persons. Since 1950 the 19-and-under group has risen from 51.4 to 78.4 million. Data are from *Trends*, p. 3.

years ago would have been considered a wholly private responsibility has come to be viewed as a proper object of federal support. Popular attitudes on this subject have tended increasingly to resemble those on education. That is, such services as are needed to maintain basic health, like those needed to ensure basic education, are due each individual as a matter of right. Or at least in the case of health they ought not to be foregone because of inability to pay.

The scale of participation already reached by the federal government in the health field underscores the need to make budget formats and reporting in this area more informative. The potential value of such improvements is raised further by the outlook for federal expenditures in health. The dominant prospect is for continued expansion over the near future in the federal role. Forces already cited that underlay expansion in the past still operate: population continues to rise; urban areas continue to grow, decay, and change; standards continue to move up; and the growing complexity and scale of some health problems, like water and air pollution, heighten the sense of need for larger federal contributions. Technological advances have been and will continue to be a large factor. As new but often costly ways for saving and prolonging lives become possibilities, we can expect pressure, through public action, for their exploitation for the benefit of all.

The breadth of many health programs and their almost indefinitely expansible character will also contribute to future growth. For example, among the program objectives of the Division of Community Health Services of the Public Health Service are the following:

1. To improve, strengthen, and extend community and personal health services.

2. To develop solutions to special problems inherent in migrant labor and school populations and in multijurisdictional metropolitan areas.

3. To propose legislation, regulation, and policy in grants-in-aid and to manage such grants.

The purposes of the National Institutes of Health include:

1. Conduct of both fundamental and clinical research aimed at the conquest of disease and the improvement of human health, and the support of similar research at universities, etc.

2. Support for the development of research training and for applicants in all fields essential to the advancement of health through research.

3. Aid in the construction of research facilities.

4. Acceleration of the application of new health knowledge.[4]

These program statements, which also indicate congressional intent, suggest that the goals being pursued are of an ever-retreating kind. There is no clear standard of fulfillment, but rather each success sets the stage for a renewed effort toward a higher objective. Inherent in the problem situations to which the programs are directed is an enormous "backlog of need," successive portions of which will in time and with rising standards come to be recognized and given priority rankings for action. Such backlogs of need are common to many health areas receiving federal assistance, including mental illness, medical care of the aged, and care of the chronically ill and disabled.

The point is well illustrated by the report in 1962 of President Kennedy's Panel on Mental Retardation. The panel made a large number of recommendations in each of several specific fields within its subject of study, implementation of which would necessitate substantial additional federal financing.[5] The problems and needs emphasized by the panel are in the main of long standing and represent but a portion of the lengthy backlogs of problems in the various health fields that in any year, whether past or future, await formal recognition and recommendation. Their existence underscores the potential value of an approach such as program budgeting for understanding and evaluating a major category of federal outlays.

EXISTING BUDGET STRUCTURE AND DISPLAY

Like federal expenditures of other major types, outlays related to health are distributed among many departments and agencies. In the Administrative Budget some twelve such agencies plus six

[4] *Handbook on Programs of the U.S. Department of Health, Education, and Welfare,* U.S. Department of Health, Education, and Welfare (Washington, D.C.: Government Printing Office, 1962), pp. 58, 80.

[5] For a brief account of the panel's report, see *New Directions in Health, Education, and Welfare,* U.S. Department of Health, Education, and Welfare (Washington, D.C.: U.S. Government Printing Office, 1963).

cabinet departments, in addition to the Department of Health, Education, and Welfare, are involved. The Trust Funds bring in one new agency, for a total of twenty.[6] Of the estimated $5.4 billion allotted to these agencies in 1965 for health-related purposes, close to $2.5 billion is accounted for by the Department of Health, Education, and Welfare, which is usually thought of as housing the nation's major health programs. Of this department's contribution, about a third is allocable to the Welfare Administration, whose main activity is the making of public assistance grants for hospitals and health care; another third is allocable to the several National Institutes of Health, whose central concerns are research and training. The Veterans Administration and the Department of Defense are, respectively, responsible for roughly $1.2 billion and $1.1 billion, the bulk of these sums being given in each case to the direct support of medical and hospital care for past and present service personnel and their families. The remaining $500 million is widely dispersed, being shared among such units as the Housing and Home Finance Agency, the Agency for International Development, the National Science Foundation, and the Small Business Administration. The extent of involvement of agencies and departments in health activities is summarized in Table 8.1.[7]

The Budget of the United States Government for the Fiscal Year Ending June 30, 1965[8] offers four principal types of breakdown that yield information on federal outlays and activities in health as well as in other fields. One type is based on a classification by administering agency; another is based on type of expenditure, with at times a strong program-orientation; a third is based on broad purpose or function; and the fourth is in terms of distinctions among investment, development, and operating outlays. Not infrequently a particular breakdown will combine two or more of these approaches.

[6] This tally is limited to agencies that finance health outlays by means other than employee benefit contributions. All federal agencies contribute to a health benefits fund for employees.

[7] The entries in this table and the figures just cited above should not be compared with those in Table 8.5 below, which is presented in connection with a suggested program budget for health. The tables use somewhat different ground rules to determine when an expenditure should be included in a particular health category, and Table 8.5 is based on quite limited information sources in which the health-related aspect of outlays could not always be identified.

[8] Published in Washington, D.C.: U.S. Government Printing Office, 1964.

TABLE 8.1 Federal Health Expenditures by Agency, FY 1965 (in
millions of dollars)

Agency	Estimated amount
Administrative budget	
Department of Health, Education, and Welfare	2,469.3
Veterans Administration	1,245.5
Department of Defense	1,097.0
Agency for International Development	107.5
Atomic Energy Commission	93.1
Department of Agriculture	59.7
National Aeronautics and Space Administration	54.0
National Science Foundation	35.0
Housing and Home Finance Agency	29.2
Civil Service Commission	25.5
Department of State	17.2
Department of Labor	16.8
Department of Justice	12.4
Panama Canal	6.5
Department of the Interior	5.4
Peace Corps	4.8
Small Business Administration	2.8
General Services Administration	2.0
United States Information Agency	0.1
Contributions by federal agencies to federal employees' health benefits fund not included above	124.5
Total net budget expenditure for health	5,408.3
Trust funds	
Civil Service Commission	−2.9
United States Soldiers' Home	6.9
Total trust fund expenditures for health	4.0
Total budget and trust fund expenditures for health	5,412.3

Source: The Budget of the United States Government for the *Fiscal Year Ending June 30, 1965* (Washington, D.C.: U.S. Government Printing Office, 1964), Table G–1, p. 399.

The use of the agency classification as an approach for understanding the content and purpose of activities in a particular area is obviously limited. Except to the extent that administrative structure and activities are uniquely related, one cannot get information on the latter. In the health area one finds a correspondence of sorts in the Department of Health, Education, and Welfare, but it is much too rough to permit even a superficial analysis of activities.

Thus, the Food and Drug Administration performs functions directed toward consumer and household protection and the control and prevention of disease. So also does the Public Health Service. Again, within the Public Health Service research on chronic diseases is supported both within the National Institutes of Health and outside them. Outside the Department of Health, Education, and Welfare the problems are compounded. Similar types of health-related functions are widely dispersed and, being usually subsidiary to the primary function of the department or agency, are often difficult to identify.

The classification by type of expenditure is more helpful. The extensive and relatively detailed table "Analysis of New Obligational Authority and Expenditures by Agency"[9] provides such a classification subordinate to the major breakdown by agency. Here it is possible to identify many kinds of health expenditures both outside and within the Department of Health, Education, and Welfare and to gain some notion of differences and overlap among them. Thus, one finds lines for medical care, research, and administration among entries for the Veterans Administration; a line for health and safety among entries for the Bureau of Mines, Department of the Interior; a line for environmental health outlays for the District of Columbia. Yet for the entire Department of Defense only two lines possibly connected with health are to be found—one for the U.S. Soldiers' Home and another for cemeterial expenses. For many other agencies significantly involved in health activities no instructive lines are to be found. One reason, not unjustified, is simply that such health activities as are undertaken are regarded as inputs to, or aspects of, categories bearing nonhealth labels.

Another handicap is that the classification is not consistent in terms of the types of categories of which it makes use. In some instances these categories are of the familiar object type—personnel, construction, operation, and maintenance. In others they have an evident program character. In still others, the source of funds or type of financing appears to be the dominant principle of organization. Such circumstances, along with the use of agency as a primary basis of breakdown, make it impossible to achieve any meaningful consolidation along the lines of health programs or other major kinds of outlays.

[9] *1965 Budget,* pp. 150–286.

The breakdown by broad purpose or function, such as is found in Part 4 of *1965 Budget,* is explicitly program-oriented. It cuts across agency lines and in measure reassembles, wherever found, outlays having a like purpose. Expenditures and new obligational authority are pulled together under such rubrics as National Defense, International Affairs and Finance, Commerce and Transportation, Housing and Community Development, and others. Troubles arise, however, in trying to follow the breakdowns much below the highest levels of aggregation. Both asymmetries in classification and the consolidation of dissimilar activities arise to plague analysis.[10] More relevant for this discussion is the failure to treat health as one of the major functions. Health appears in the subcategory Health Services and Research, under the broader label Health, Labor, and Welfare. Some but not all the health outlays of the Department of Health, Education, and Welfare are entered here. The remainder, along with the health outlays of other agencies, are subsumed under other major functions, generally without identification as to their health content. Thus, under National Defense, all Department of Defense health acivities have, in effect, been handled as inputs to other entries, and no reference to such activities is to be found. The upshot is that of the estimated expenditure of $5.4 billion for health for 1965, less than $3 billion can be located, and then only in a comparatively gross form.

Little need be said about the classification in terms of investment, development, and operating outlays.[11] A number of health-related entries are to be found, but none for agencies other than the Veterans Administration and the Department of Health, Education, and Welfare. Entries for these two agencies are scattered, with health activities again treated as subordinate to, or inputs into, other major categories and subcategories. To the extent that identification can be made, the descriptive labels are too broad to communicate much information.

[10] Under the major function Education are the subcategories Assistance for Elementary and Secondary Education and Assistance for Higher Education. These are followed by Assistance to Science Education and Basic Research, which contains all the National Science Foundation outlays; a substantial fraction of these outlays represent contributions to higher and secondary education. In another place, all National Institutes of Health are lumped together in a single entry.

[11] *1965 Budget,* Table D–2, "Investment, Operating, and Other Expenditures," pp. 356–370.

The comparatively sparse information on federal health activities made available through these four approaches is, however, greatly supplemented by a special analysis of health programs that appears for the first time in *1965 Budget*.[12] All agencies and departments involved in the health field are listed, and their dollar contributions are indicated. (See Table 8.1) A summary table of all outlays, classifying them into six major categories, also is presented.[13] Yet another breakdown, much more detailed, is developed in terms of the broad purposes or functions previously discussed. That is, the total health outlay is distributed among such major categories as national defense, international affairs and finance, natural resources, education, and so on. This presentation, a truncated version of which is offered here as Table 8.2, is by far the most informative on health activities of all the budget breakdowns. One can gain from it a meaningful, if general, notion of the content of these activities and of their range and diversity. One can also observe the extent to which they contribute to, or are aspects of programs such as national defense or natural resource development.

This latter characteristic is at the same time a disadvantage. Because the central emphasis is on the broad functional categories rather than on health as such, one is not readily able to see the various health entries in relation to one another. It is not just that many essentially similar health activities are classified as belonging to different major functions. It is also that the method of classification and the degree of detail presented are more or less unique within each major function. To illustrate, under the major function Health, Labor, and Welfare there are twenty-one entries. Under the major function National Defense there are seven. Under Veterans Benefits and Services there is one. It is not possible to select with any confidence from among the Health, Labor, and Welfare entries any that would be comparable with one or more of the

---

[12] Special Analysis G, pp. 397–406.
[13] The categories, with expenditure estimates (in millions) for 1965, are:

Hospital and medical care in federal facilities	$2,006
Federal grants and payments for hospital and health care in nonfederal facilities	1,029
Medical research	1,125
Training, including training research	333
Preventive and community services	390
Construction of hospitals and health facilities	528

See Table G–2, p. 400.

TABLE 8.2 Federal Health Expenditures by Function, FY 1965 (in millions of dollars)

Function and agency	Amount[a]
National defense	
Department of Defense:	
Hospital and medical care of military personnel and others	911.0
Research in preventive medicine, etc.	125.1
Department of Health, Education, and Welfare: Stockpiling of medical supplies	15.0
Atomic Energy Commission: Research on radiation effects	93.1
Total	1,205.1
Agriculture and agricultural resources	
Department of Agriculture:	
Plant and animal research; meat and poultry inspections	103.2
Total	59.7
Commerce and transportation	
Small Business Administration: Loans for construction and operation of nursing homes and other health-related facilities	2.8
Health, labor, and welfare	
Department of Health, Education, and Welfare:	
Operation of Freedmen's Hospital	3.8
Health services for Indians	67.8
Quarantine activities	6.0
Education and training for public health	28.8
Grants for maternal and child welfare	85.0
Public assistance grants for hospital and health care	715.0
Enforcement of pure food and drug laws	42.8
Total	2,449.7
Education	
Department of Health, Education, and Welfare:	
Practical nurse training	5.0
National Science Foundation: Support of basic health research	35.0
Total	42.1
General government	
Department of Justice: Medical care of prisoners	12.4
General Services Administration: Matching grant for hospital in Washington, D.C.	2.0
Total	61.1
Grand total of health expenditures	5,412.3

[a] The totals in this abridged table include items that have been omitted by the author for brevity. For complete data, see *1965 Budget,* Table G–4, pp. 404–406. Other major functional categories are International Affairs and Finance, Space Research and Technology, Natural Resources, Housing and Community Development, and Veterans Benefits and Services.

National Defense entries; and such an exercise with respect to the Veterans Benefits and Services category obviously would be pointless.

One also finds certain anomalies in the approach that are less than fully satisfying, though perhaps of small importance under the circumstances. The category Health, Labor, and Welfare, unlike certain of the others, is diffuse in meaning and lacks an explicit purposive or program orientation. The entries under it suggest the rather puzzling notion of health outlays in support of health, of labor, and of welfare. The major category Education contains entries relating to nurse training and health research. But should these activities be thought of as inputs into education? Or should they be thought of as a form of education that contributes to health? The latter interpretaion is in fact the one adopted for educational elements found elsewhere in the table.[14]

To summarize, in the present budget each of the methods used to organize information on federal health outlays is subject to some or all the following limitations:

1. Incomplete identification of health activities.

2. Lack of a systematic, integrated classification of these activities.

3. Absence of, or insufficient activity orientation in, the classification used.

4. Insufficient consolidation of activities.

As a result, one can obtain from the budget only a rough and uneven understanding of the main components and the pattern. The potential for analyzing and evaluating them is therefore greatly restricted.

ADVANTAGES AND LIMITATIONS OF A HEALTH PROGRAM BUDGET

A first question one might ask is whether, given their nature, health activities merit a separate, independent status in a program budget. The question arises because these activities often are constituents of, or inputs into, other activities whose purpose or goal orientation is the dominating one. Outlays by the Department

[14] For example, Education and Training for Public Health and National Institutes of Health (Research) are entries under Health, Labor, and Welfare rather than under Education.

of Defense for hospital care, for example, though they assist in maintaining the health of one segment of the population, are undertaken on behalf of national defense, and the latter is their justification. Similarly, grants by the Agency for International Development for the construction of health facilities in foreign countries, although they contribute to the health of particular groups of foreign citizens, have a different main purpose—support of the international position and broad international interests of the United States. Might it not be best to handle these kinds of health outlays in the manner suggested by Table 8.2, i.e., classify them along with various other nonhealth outlays according to the main activity of which they are supportive?

The dual character of some kinds of health activities, or overlap with nonhealth activities, raises a similar question. Here the problem is not the subordination of a particular activity to another, but the fact that the activity can reasonably be classified in more than one way. Thus, training grants by the National Institutes of Health, which are intended to increase the number and quality of trained personnel in various health fields, represent support for a particular type of education as well as contributing to the nation's health. Hence they can properly be included in either area. Again, research on the effects of pesticides on fish and wildlife contribute to the health of the citizenry and also to the conservation of our natural resources. In both examples either of the two purposes served provides a legitimate basis for classification. Where healthlike activities have a multiple-purpose character, ought they to be included in a separate health budget, along with activities more or less exclusively health-oriented?

Obviously, no one approach need be relied on to the exclusion of others. Specific decision needs, as well as a more general need for understanding patterns, relationships, and trends in activities, suggest that each of several distinct classifications carries benefits and may deserve separate recognition. Consider the decision aspect of the matter, and in particular that aspect in which a health activity or outlay is undertaken for some larger purpose—say, national defense. The worth of the health activity will in the first instance be judged in terms of its contribution to defense, and this contribution will be weighed against the contributions of other input activities for which, in measure, health may be a substitute.

One will seek in principle to use such an amount of the health input (or any other input) as will under diminishing returns bring its marginal contribution to exact equality with the marginal contribution of other inputs. For this type of decision it is necessary to have information of the sort contained in Table 8.2, which tells us something of the relation between inputs and output.

But this type of information will not alone suffice if, as often happens, an input contributes also to other purposes besides defense. Health outlays by the military, for example, whatever their immediate intent, contribute importantly to the physical well-being of a large group of citizens. They thereby complement nondefense health outlays, and by relieving the nondefense sector of some of the health burdens it must carry, they also represent a substitute for them. One possibility is that the nondefense benefits of defense-sponsored health outlays are large and deserve to be expanded, perhaps at the expense of other federal health outlays, even though their additional contribution to defense is slight or negligible. Another possibility is that the defense-sponsored health outlays, or some of them, are inefficient substitutes for similar outlays by other agencies. They might, that is, contribute significantly less than would the latter to the citizenry's health and perhaps even to the nation's defense.

The assessment of these possibilities calls for a first step of assembling, in some suitable format(s), information on health activities as such, no matter which agencies perform them and what immediate goals they may be thought to serve. The case for this kind of consolidation is equally strong where concern is not so much with input-output relationships as with the dual character of an activity that permits it to be included in more than one area. Federal support of graduate and professional training in the medical sciences, for example, will for some purposes be better understood if it is placed within a context of all federal programs for education. This approach will facilitate its assessment vis-à-vis other educational programs. For other purposes a framework embracing health programs will be desirable. Both approaches are in order if a fuller assessment is to be made.

Within the field of health, as in other fields, there exists a hierarchy, or series of complementary hierarchies, of potentially useful decision (a better word might be evaluation) contexts. Toward the top of the hierarchy, interest centers on whole classes of activities, accompanied by a corresponding need for information. Federally financed medical care might be thought of as one such class of activity. Given the usual budget constraint, it competes for available funds against other classes of health activities of a comparably high order. A competitor class of activity might be research on communicable, chronic, neurological, and other diseases or, collectively, programs in support of environmental health.[15] Toward the bottom of the hierarchy concern is more localized and specific. Particular programs, such as control of tuberculosis, support of graduate training for microbiologists, or provision of health services to migrant agricultural workers, are the candidates for consideration. Each represents an element in the class of programs immediately above it and competes with other programs in this same class. Between the extremes of the hierarchy, intermediate stages usually can be distinguished, which are also often the focus of deliberations.

A simple sketch of this kind of hierarchy is given in Fig. 1. We can think of major programs, designated by Roman numerals, as competing with one another for funds, and within II, for example, of subordinate programs A, B, and C competing with one another. We can also think of the latter programs as competing individually with the subordinate programs A and B under IV. This type of competition is implied in the direct comparison of II and IV.

One can visualize a program budget whose structure conforms to this hierarchy. The obvious virtue of such a budget would be its ability to supply information in response to decision or other needs on any activity or class of activities at any stage in the hierarchy. "Horizontal" analysis of competing elements within a class of activities, and of competing classes of activity at a given stage, would be facilitated. So also would analysis of the "vertical" relation between subordinate and superordinate classes of activities.

Needless to say, this model represents an ideal whose practical implementation to any large degree in the field of health faces serious obstacles. Two difficulties can be distinguished, though in practice the line between them tends to be blurred. First, some categories of health activities do not lend themselves well to any

[15] For example, programs concerned with air pollution, sanitation, water supply, and radiological hazards.

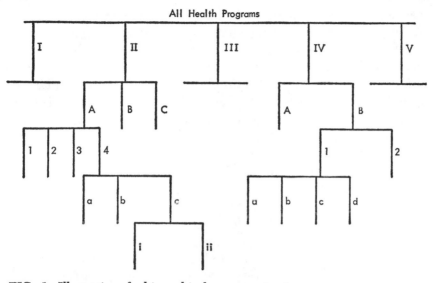

FIG. 1. Illustration of a hierarchical program structure.

great amount of horizontal and/or vertical structuring. Research grants by the National Institutes of Health to universities and other institutions have as their overriding objective the support of designated kinds of biological and medical research. But they also make an important byproduct contribution to the development of trained manpower in the biological sciences. Similarly, community hospitals, financed in part by grants and loans from the Public Health Service, serve primarily in treating the sick and injured. But they also offer substantial benefits through their training of technical and professional personnel and the provision of ancillary medical services to the community. In these cases, because of the close and subtle interweaving of primary and secondary activities, there is no easy way to measure the relative importance of each. One must, therefore, employ grosser program categories than one would like and in the process sacrifice horizontal or vertical detail. The ultimate result is less adequate information for program assessment purposes than would otherwise be available.

The second difficulty, insufficient information, leads to much the same consequences. Although certain activities may be entirely distinguishable, not only in principle but as a practical matter, an insufficiency of information may prevent a distinction from being made. The insufficiency may in turn simply reflect incomplete re-porting by the administering agency. Or it may indicate deficiencies in data-collection procedures. An entry frequently used in reporting on Public Health Service programs, such as the control of tubercu-losis or of accident hazards, is simply Research, Training, and Tech-nical Services.[16] One suspects that summary reporting of this type, which is disturbingly frequent, is an aspect of the information problem rather than of the more basic first difficulty cited in the preceding paragraph.

Judicious design of the program classification system, although not a solution to difficulties of the first type, will sometimes minimize their effects. Acceptable conventions or rules of thumb can sometimes be found for separating interlaced activities and allocating their costs to the appropriate accounts. The second type of difficulty can be much mitigated if not remedied by the design of better data-collection systems and improved reporting proce-dures, though admittedly it is often easier to imagine them than to implement them in workaday situations. Where solutions to both difficulties can be found, they take time to discover and apply; this fact limits sharply for the near future, the extent to which pro-gram budgeting can be carried in the health field.

A PROGRAM BUDGET FOR HEALTH

The Development of a Program Structure

The intent of this and the following sections is to identify and assemble in an activity-oriented way the health outlays of the federal government. Unlike the type of consolidation illustrated in Table 8.2, in which health outlays are consolidated in terms of nonhealth functions, our procedure accords separate status to health and seeks to structure the outlays in an internally consistent way. Necessarily, for reasons already set forth, the approach is highly aggregative.

Presumably there is no single "correct" classification scheme to be discovered. Rather it is probable that there are at least a few,

[16] *Appendix: The Budget of the United States Government for the Fiscal Year Ending June 30, 1965* (Washington, D.C.: U.S. Government Printing Office, 1964), pp. 398, 403.

and possibly several, alternatives that might be found equally promising. The one chosen will undoubtedly need to be developed and refined through successive steps in trial and experiment with the data. At best it will represent a compromise between what is desirable in an ideal sense and what in light of the data is feasible. Nothing more is claimed for the classification offered here (and quite imperfectly implemented) than that it is a tentative first step. Hopefully, it will add a bit to our understanding of federal health activities and suggest directions for further effort.

We may think of federal health activities as being directed toward five main goals or categories. One is the prevention and control of disease and other health hazards. In this category fall, for example, regulatory actions by the Food and Drug Administration, activities by the Public Health Service in connection with radiological hazards, and research in preventive medicine by the Department of Defense. A second category involves the treatment of illness and injury to restore health. This category would include a substantial fraction of the hospital services rendered by the Veterans Administration, a major fraction of the loans and grants by the Public Health Service for the construction of hospitals, and the medical care provided prisoners by the Department of Justice. A third category is the provision of long-term care, both inpatient and outpatient, for the chronically ill, the disabled, and the aged. Certain formula grants by the Public Health Service to the states for the development of special programs and services should be included here. So also should be included the outlays for domiciliary care made by the Veterans Administration. The distinction between this third category and the second is straightforward. The emphasis of the latter is on restoring the health of the temporarily ill, while the former stresses the care and maintenance of those with disabilities lasting over an extended or indefinite period.

Much graduate, professional, and technical training in health fields is supported by the federal government. Some of these outlays can be classified as belonging to one or another of the foregoing categories, and it seems appropriate to follow this procedure when possible. Thus, outlays in support of training in the public health field would be placed in the control and prevention category. Other training outlays, such as those supporting the graduate education of biochemists or social workers, are not specific to a single goal. Our fourth category, therefore, embraces training activities not allocable to the first three. A similar allocation problem exists with respect to federal support of health research. Some types of research can be identified sufficiently closely with control or treatment or long-term care to be included within one of these categories. But much research, by its very nature, defies structuring in these terms. Other research cannot be allocated because it is reported in a general and aggregative way. Hence our fifth category is research.

To summarize, we have:

1. Control and Prevention.
2. Treatment and Restoration.
3. Long-term Care and Domiciliary Maintenance.
4. Training (not classifiable to items 1, 2, or 3).
5. Research (not classifiable to items 1, 2, or 3).

To these five categories must be added a sixth, Other, to contain outlays that for whatever reason, cannot reasonably be allocated to the other five. For some purposes one might wish to add also two supplementary categories, paralleling four and five, which would serve to consolidate all training and all research.

This program format can be extended through secondary classifications, subordinate to each of the primary categories. A promising approach at this level is by type of disease or illness to which the primary activity is directed. Under Control and Prevention might be:

(a) Communicable diseases.
(b) Neurologic, metabolic, and degenerative diseases.
(c) Mental diseases.
(d) Chronic diseases and disabilities of age.
(e) Occupational hazards.
(f) Environmental and other hazards.
(g) Unallocable.

This breakdown might in principle be duplicated under Treatment and Restoration, for the same all-inclusive list of illnesses whose prevention is sought is also that for which treatment is necessary. However, the circumstances under which treatment, whether in the form of hospital or outpatient care, is administered and reported, and the rubrics under which federal support in this category is provided, suggest that implementation of such a breakdown would be extraordinarily difficult. The following breakdown is perhaps a more practicable alternative:

(a) Chronic diseases.
(b) Mental illnesses.
(c) General illnesses.
(d) Rehabilitation and development.[17]
(e) Unallocable.

Further modest variation appears desirable for the Long-term care and Domiciliary Maintenance category. From the breakdown immediately above, entries (c) and (d) might be eliminated and replaced with those of Physical and Congenital Disabilities and Care of the Aged. These entries, unlike the ones they replace, are pertinent to the provision of long-term care.

For both Training and Research the same secondary breakdown as is given under Control and Prevention is attempted. Neither this breakdown nor any modification that approximates it is well-suited to Training, because some important types of training span two or more of the entries in it; it is continued here provisionally simply for the sake of symmetry.

Other secondary-level breakdowns for some of our primary categories, to be thought of as supplements to rather than alternatives for the secondary breakdowns just described, are of potential interest. Under Control and Prevention we might have the following:

(a) Certification, regulation, and enforcement.
(b) Care, quarantine, and detention.
(c) Technical services.
(d) Research.
(e) Training.
(f) Unallocable.

For Treatment and Restoration, secondary breakdowns might be:

(a) Hospital care.
(b) Outpatient care.
(c) Other care.
(d) Research.
(e) Training.
(f) Unallocable.

---

[17] This would include, for example, vocational rehabilitation associated with illness, treatment of narcotics addiction, development of self-sufficiency and abilities in the handicapped.

With the addition of another entry, Nursing Homes, and perhaps the deletion of Other Care, this same classification would also serve under the category Long-Term Care and Domiciliary Maintenance. For Training, an occupation-oriented breakdown would be informative. Logical entries would include Technicians, Nurses, Physicians, Scientists, and Administrators.

The structuring of activities might well be extended beyond the secondary level to third, fourth, and perhaps even fifth levels, though allocation problems could be expected to become increasingly acute as one descended the ladder of detail. No attempt along these lines is made in this chapter. Difficulties relating to the multipurpose nature of many activities, to information needs, and to taxonomy would tend to compromise such efforts. Other more traditional types of structuring, like the familiar object classification, and classification by agency, might be provided at virtually any level. A classification by agency almost certainly should parallel and be regarded as a complement to an activities budget. This is perhaps also true of classification by type of financing, i.e., direct, grants and contracts, loans. To a certain extent this type of structuring was employed in the data discussed below.

Application of a Program Budget to Health

In this section an effort is made to employ classifications such as those discussed above to structure federal health outlays. As noted previously, the effort is quite preliminary, reliance for information having been placed chiefly on *1965 Budget,* its *Appendix,* Congressional *Hearings,* and standard publications of the Department of Health, Education, and Welfare.

Table 8.3 presents data for the major program categories, with a subordinate breakdown by type of disease, ailment, or hazard. The figures cover all health-related outlays except those of the Department of Defense[18] and those associated with foreign-aid programs. The sheer size of the overall total, $4.8 billion, as well as the magnitudes of the major program categories, are impressive. Treatment

---

[18] *1965 Budget Appendix* and other sources cited in the text give very little information on the health component of defense outlays and far less than is needed to arrange this component in program-budget terms. Although information on the health component of the nondefense sectors was generally much better, estimates and guesswork were often necessary, and incomplete coverage was sometimes unavoidable.

TABLE 8.3 Estimated Federal Expenditures for Health and Related
Purposes, FY 1965[a] (in thousands of dollars)

Category	Amount
Control and prevention	
Infectious and allergic diseases	94,814
Neurologic and degenerative diseases	3,450
Chronic diseases and those of age	19,773
Accidents and occupational hazards	20,831
Food and drug hazards	153,918
Child health and nutrition	211,262
Other (including Environmental Health)	231,687
Total	735,735
Treatment and restoration	
Rehabilitation and development	230,333
Chronic diseases	44,290
General illnesses	1,049,662
Other (including unallocable facilities costs)	328,174
Total	1,652,459
Long-term care and domiciliary maintenance	
Chronic diseases	4,721
Care of aged	249,400
Mental illness	411,933
Unallocable[b] and other	105,716
Total	771,770
Training (n.a.)[c]	
Infections and allergic diseases	11,215
Neurologic and degenerative diseases	16,776
Mental illness	83,193
Chronic diseases and those of age	32,242
Unallocable[b] and other	177,628
(Allocable[d])	(49,540)
Total	328,054
Research (n.a.)[c]	
Infectious and allergic diseases	58,871
Neurologic and degenerative diseases	69,600
Mental illness	92,262
Chronic diseases and those of age	325,364
Occupational and other hazards	3,759
Unallocable[b] and other	563,138
(Allocable[d])	(89,938)
Total	1,112,994

TABLE 8.3 (*Continued*)

Category	Amount
Other	
Training and research combined[e]	28,581
Unallocable[b]	193,050
Total	221,631
Grand total	4,822,643

Source: The chief source of information for developing the data was *Appendix: The Budget of the United States Government for the Fiscal Year Ending June 30, 1965* (Washington, D.C.: U.S. Government Printing Office, 1964). Use also was made of the Congressional *Hearings* and standard publications of the Department of Health, Education, and Welfare.

[a] Figures are based on total program costs, funded, as estimated for 1965. Health outlays by the Department of Defense and outlays under international programs are excluded.

[b] Refers to outlays that overlap two or more of the other categories.

[c] The abbreviation "n.a." denotes outlays not allocated or classified to other categories. Where training and research outlays can be identified as inputs to other program categories, they have been so allocated.

[d] Denotes the total of training or research outlays that have been allocated as inputs to other major categories.

[e] Refers to research and training outlays that cannot be separately identified.

and Restoration is the largest single claimant, receiving one-third of all health outlays, with the broadly defined entry, General Illnesses, accounting for over 60 per cent of this sum. These results are not unexpected because return of the ill to health is a continuous, immediate, and ubiquitous problem.

The massive support given to Research, reflecting a trend in this direction of the past ten to twelve years, makes it the second largest category. The content of this category is obscured by the size of the unallocable component. That chronic diseases and diseases of age should be the largest identifiable research element is perhaps surprising because within the other major program categories this is an important cost element only for Long-Term Care and Domiciliary Maintenance. The explanation probably lies in the age trends of the population and in the fact that chronic diseases, if not presently the most costly to the federal government, are among the most costly to the nation and take the greatest toll of life. Other large expenditure categories include Rehabilitation and Development, whose content embraces occupational training and retraining associated with illness and physical handicaps, Child Health and Nutrition, and Mental Illness.

If the cost of some individual elements is impressive, so also by contrast is the distribution of the grand total among a variety of programs. Federal participation covers a wide spectrum and, one might guess, will not lend itself to shrinkage in the years ahead.[19]

Many health goals are attainable by two or more means, and a choice must be made or a balance struck among them. By helping us to see the relations among expenditure categories, a program budget assists in delineating the choice possibilities. The structure of Table 8.3 suggests some of these possibilities. For example, the development through research of a better means of treating industrial wastes may lessen the efforts that must be made for control and prevention in this area at the community level, and it may also lessen the need for federal assistance to states and communities. Similarly, research that extends our ability to immunize against communicable diseases will permit lower outlays for control and prevention or treatment and restoration. The more thoroughgoing our efforts toward the control and prevention of chronic diseases, the less necessary will be expenditures for the treatment and restoration of these diseases.

Training outlays may also substitute for outlays (or re-enforce benefits) in the other categories. Thus, the training of physicians to a higher level of capability may expedite diagnoses and patient recovery, which would reduce the need for federal support in the domain of treatment and restoration.

In certain instances it should be noted that an increase in one type of outlay may lead to an increase rather than a reduction in another. As examples, research sometimes culminates in new, expensive medical procedures where none previously existed, and it sometimes yields methods that prolong life without curing illness. Because of the nature of the demand for health services or pressure on the government to supply them, the new procedures and methods will tend to be used and health outlays will rise. These are simply cases, replete in medical history and observable in other fields, in which new products or services bring with them their own markets.

Besides the substitution or re-enforcing possibilities of these types in which different means, or expenditure categories, serve the same goal, there are the more common ones in which a choice between means is also a choice between goals. To spend more for the

[19] On this point, see above, pp. 210–212.

long-term care of the aged may, under the ordinary budget constraint, require spending less on similar care for the mentally ill or less on control and prevention of the diseases of age or of allergic diseases.

Many of these possibilities of choice contain an evident problem of intertemporal coordination or time-phasing. Research and training in particular are lead-time items in terms of their contributions. Outlays for research on mental illness, however efficacious they may ultimately prove, will not yield benefits this year and so are not a practical substitute for current treatment and restoration outlays for this malady. Rather, the meaningful substitution is that between this year's research outlays and treatment and restoration outlays three, five, or ten years hence. Similarly, stepped-up research or training expenditures for chronic diseases will not reduce this year's need for the long-term care of those afflicted with these ailments, but they may do so two or more years hence. As noted above, the opposite outcome, when an increase now in one type of expenditure leads to an increase in another type at some future date, is also a possibility.

To handle such intertemporal relations calls for the preparation of a series of health budgets covering several successive years. The period to be covered might be five years, the same as that used at present in the Department of Defense. This figure, plainly a compromise, commends itself as being sufficiently near at hand to permit meaningful projections, yet far enough in the future to permit expenditure estimates to reflect those intertemporal relations that can be reasonably well identified. The resulting budget format might resemble that shown in Table 8.3 but would contain columns in which estimates could be entered not only for next year but for the four subsequent years. In projections for years beyond the present, one would seek to recognize the many determinants of expenditures, including especially the impact of current expenditures on future outlays.

A health budget that was organized in this way and continuously updated would offer a coherent framework, now totally absent, in which current decisions could be made and future ones planned. Besides providing a vast amount of integrated information, such a framework would give focus to problems of choice and facilitate inquiry and analysis.

Specific Decision Needs and Opportunities for Choice

Notwithstanding the fact that the figures in Table 8.3 are statistically quite rough and cover but a single year, they can be used to give concreteness to some of the large-choice problems that are, or should be, of concern in the health field. One notes the quantitative ordering of the major entries, with Treatment and Restoration at the top, followed by Research. Control and Prevention and Long-Term Care and Domiciliary Maintenance come next, very close together, with Training well down on the list. Is this a desirable and rational ordering? The high aggregate cost of treatment and restoration reflects both the scale of this activity and its high unit costs. The scale is a consequence of the extent of need and also of the extent to which the federal government has come to recognize this need. The high unit cost results from the expensiveness of the resources consumed by the activity, such as hospital space, drugs, and physicians' services. The question arises: Are there ways of reducing either the need or the unit cost? In terms of our program budget, there are two: more or better control and prevention, and more or better research. The first can reduce the scale of treatment and restoration activity; the second can reduce both the scale and the unit costs. The benefits of research may in part come indirectly, being initially realized in the form of improved control and prevention. Since the largest claimant within the Treatment and Restoration category is General Illnesses, which covers in the main illnesses susceptible to cure or prevention by known means, rather than the chronic and less tractable maladies, there may be lines of effort in the domains of research and of control and prevention whose expansion or initiation would reduce significantly both scale and unit costs. That is, such types of effort might bring high marginal returns.

Aggregate outlays for health research, as shown in Table 8.3, exceed $1 billion. Is this sum excessive, or is there room for further expansion? This type of expenditure is strategic in predicting future cost and product benefits. It is the stream of these future benefits, discounted to the present, that must be considered. What are the expected payoffs year by year? Will the major impact of $1 billion of research expenditures this year come three years hence? Five? Eight? In a time-phased health budget, what recognition should be given to research outlays in year 1 in projecting treatment and restoration outlays in year 5? What period will be needed for this year's investment in research to be amortized by its benefits? How would the time pattern of expected benefits be affected if current research outlays were selectively raised by $100 million? $200 million?

These questions are inherently difficult, and even the best of efforts at data gathering and analyses are unlikely to yield better than blunt insights and notional answers. But such insights and answers, quite lacking now, are essential if we are to sense where our health expenditures are taking us and what means are best suited for altering the pattern and rates of benefit flows. Through its structuring and related groupings a program budget helps us to see the questions to be asked and the lines of investigation to be pursued.

Questions similar to, but more specific than, those mentioned above arise when one studies the major categories. Research expenditures on chronic diseases and on diseases of age are more than three times as great as those on mental illness and comprise better than one-fourth of total health research expenditures. Yet over 50 per cent of the expenditures on long-term care are allocated to mental illness, and less than one-third go for chronic diseases and diseases of age. In the light of these relatively long-term care burdens, is the research balance a good one? Might it not be advantageous to shift it more toward mental illness? What are the anticipated future long-term care burdens in these areas? How would they appear in a projected time-phased health budget? Does that prospect justify the apparent lopsidedness in the prevailing allocation of research funds? If so, perhaps we need to take a closer look at the distribution of outlays under Training, which is also a lead-time item. Over twice as much is being spent on training in the mental illness field as in the area of chronic diseases and diseases of age, presumably on the supposition that the need for trained personnel in the former field will be correspondingly greater.

Attempts to answer questions such as these, important in themselves, may lead to the discovery of weak points in a program budget. In the format of Table 8.3 one such weakness is the asymmetry of breakdowns under the major entries.[20] This characteristic can sometimes frustrate a line of inquiry by rendering impossible a comparison of subcategories across the major entries. For example, there is no entry under Long-Term Care and Domiciliary Maintenance that can be directly compared with the entry Neurologic and Degenerative Diseases under Training. A related weakness lies in the breadth of a subcategory such as General Illnesses (under Treatment and Restoration). The label conceals a great deal, and meaningful comparisons with other subcategories are difficult. The size of the category (over 60 per cent of the total of the major entry) makes this circumstance the more serious.

If the data permitted, it might also be advantageous to distinguish between long-term care involving domiciliary maintenance and that not involving it, and to identify distinguishable types of domiciliary maintenance. The additional detail thus provided would be useful in the consideration of various allocation problems.[21]

These weaknesses should not be taken as representative of the limitations inherent in a program budget, but rather as problems meriting study and remedial effort. They are problems that may well be surmountable through changes in the program format, in the underlying information system on which implementation of the system depends, or in both. Or they may lend themselves to substantial mitigation through the use of special backup analyses that probe beneath the more visible information flows.

OTHER APPLICATIONS WITHIN A PROGRAM-BUDGET FRAMEWORK

Types of Service

The main program categories of Table 8.3 are repeated in Table 8.4, but with a subordinate classification in terms of type of service or method by which the outlays make their contribution. The

[20] The reasons for this asymmetry were given on pages 226–228.

[21] For example, it might be helpful to know, by type of illness, expenditures on domiciliary maintenance as distinct from other kinds of long-term care, and to know to what extent domiciliary maintenance was provided by general, multipurpose, and special-purpose hospitals and nursing homes.

comparatively large size of the unallocable categories limits what can be discovered. We can, however, observe the importance of hospital care, which dominates both the Treatment and Restoration category and the Long-Term Care and Domiciliary Maintenance category. The amount shown for Training and Research is of approximately equal importance to that given for hospital care, and the two together account for over three-fifths of total health expenditures.

The information offered in Table 8.4 supplements that in Table 8.3 and throws into relief a few rather different substitution possibilities. For example, might heavy outlays for Hospital Care, under Treatment and Restoration, be reduced over time by exploiting more effectively the possibilities for less costly outpatient care? Might Long-Term Care and Domiciliary Maintenance costs be cut or, with a given budget, the services in this category increased, by developing more fully the potential for nursing homes and placing less emphasis on hospital facilities and services? Substitution opportunities of this sort are no less worthy of attention than the kind suggested by Table 8.3.

Agency Responsibilities

The essential content of Table 8.5 differs from the kind ordinarily found in a program budget, even though the same major-program entries are used. The table is concerned with the organizational arrangements for supplying health services and shows, for the major-entry levels only, expenditures by department or agency. Each program category is dominated by one or two agencies: the Department of Health, Education, and Welfare and the Department of Agriculture dominate Control and Prevention; the HEW and the Veterans Administration dominate Treatment and Restoration; the HEW and specifically the National Institutes of Health dominate Research. This feature is less conspicuous, however, if one regards the Department of Health, Education, and Welfare not as a monolithic unit but as a conglomerate of many separate agencies. Perhaps more noteworthy is the presence in each category of a number of different agencies and the presence of some agencies in several categories.

This very extensive overlapping of agency responsibilities, together with the multiple responsibilities of some agencies, leads to

TABLE 8.4 Estimated Federal Health Expenditures Classified by Type of Service, FY 1965[a] (in thousands of dollars)

Type of service	Amount
Control and prevention	
Certification, regulation, and enforcement	140,171
Care, quarantine, and detention	7,101
Technical services	57,521
Training	15,105
Research	56,025
Unallocable[b] and other	459,812
Total	735,735
Treatment and restoration	
Hospital care	1,107,956
Outpatient care	153,803
Training	34,435
Research	27,641
Unallocable[b] and other	328,624
Total	1,652,459
Long-term care and domiciliary maintenance	
Hospitals	418,556
Nursing homes	81,677
Research	7,000
Unallocable[b] and other	264,537
Total	771,770
Training and research[c] (n.a.)	1,469,629
Unallocable[b] and other	193,050
Grand Total	4,822,643

Source: See Table 8.3.

[a] Figures are based on total program costs, funded, as estimated for 1965. Health outlays by the Department of Defense and outlays under international programs are excluded.

[b] Refers to outlays that overlap two or more of the other categories.

[c] Represents the total of the categories Training, Research, and Training and Research Combined (under Other) in Table 8.3. As denoted by n.a., these are training or research outlays not allocated to other categories (see Table 8.3, Note c).

concern over the possible adverse effects of competing interests and jurisdictional claims on the planning and implementation of programs. It also causes one to doubt whether there can exist in the administrative echelons the kind of overall perspective that would seem indispensable if federal health resources are to be rationally allocated. Certainly, one would not expect that the many health functions would or could be handled optimally under these conditions.

TABLE 8.5 Estimated Federal Health Expenditures Classified by Agency, FY 1965[a] (in thousands of dollars)

Agency		Amount
Control and prevention		
Department of Health, Education and Welfare		400,761
Food and Drug Administration	51,017	
Welfare Administration	47,228	
Public Health Service	302,516	
Department of Agriculture		252,620
Department of Labor		2,361
Department of the Interior		15,680
Department of State		113
Housing and Home Finance Agency		29,200
Public Works Acceleration (Presidential Funds)		35,000
Total		735,735
Treatment and restoration		
Department of Health, Education, and Welfare		696,297
Office of Education	16,500	
Vocational Rehabilitation Administration	146,978	
Welfare Administration	40,160	
Special Institutions	9,727	
Public Health Service:		
General	478,966	
National Institutes of Health	3,966	
Veterans Administration		860,878
Civil Service Commission		26,655
Department of Labor		14,660
Department of the Interior		100
Department of State		871
Department of Justice		2,898
United States Information Service		100
Public Works Acceleration (Presidential Funds)		50,000
Total		1,652,459
Long-term care and domiciliary maintenance		
Department of Health, Education, and Welfare		399,585
Welfare Administration	249,400	
Public Health Service	117,688	
Saint Elizabeths Hospital and Special Institutions	32,497	
Veterans Administration		360,490
Department of Justice		8,895
Small Business Administration		2,800
Total		771,770

TABLE 8.5 (*Continued*)

Agency		Amount
Training (n.a.)[b]		
Department of Health, Education, and Welfare		326,429
Saint Elizabeths and Freedman's Hospitals	1,704	
Public Health Service:		
General	110,538	
National Institutes of Health	214,187	
Veterans Administration		1,625
Total		328,054
Research (n.a.)[b]		
Department of Health, Education, and Welfare		889,536
Welfare Administration	3,110	
Saint Elizabeths Hospital	383	
Public Health Service:		
General	68,622	
National Institutes of Health	817,421	
Veterans Administration		41,358
Atomic Energy Commission		93,100
National Aeronautics and Space Administration		54,000
National Science Foundation		35,000
Total		1,112,994
Other		
Training and Research Combined:[c]		
Department of Health, Education, and Welfare		28,581
Special Institutions	570	
National Institutes of Health	28,011	
Unallocable:[d]		
Department of Health, Education, and Welfare		126,732
Welfare Administration	1,060	
Public Health Service:		
General	69,460	
National Institutes of Health	56,212	
Veterans Administration		62,280
Public Works Acceleration (Presidential Funds)		2,000
General Services Administration		2,038
Total		221,631
Grand Total		4,822,643

Source: See Table 8.3.

[a] Figures are based on total program costs, funded, as estimated for 1965. Health outlays by the Department of Defense and outlays under international programs are excluded.

[b] See Note c, Table 8.3.

[c] Refers to training and research outlays that cannot be separately identified.

[d] Refers to outlays that overlap two or more of the other categories.

It does not necessarily follow, however, that results in the health field fall below an acceptable norm. The possibility that they might, as suggested by the results of Table 8.5, may in measure derive from the program format, or activity structure, in terms of which agency outlays have been classified. It is conceivable that there are other program formats under which the grouping of agencies would appear more logical—i.e., under which there would be a closer identity between agency and function. If so, one must deal with the question, Which type of program structure is to be preferred for planning, review, decision, and implementation purposes? A more fundamental consideration is that a format that is valuable for planning programs and understanding their interrelations may not be an equally good format in terms of which to organize for their administration and implementation. For example, although two programs might have very different goals, problems encountered in their continuing operation may be much alike, and their administration may require similar resources and professional talents. It might then make a good deal of sense to house both programs under the same administrative roof. Or again, two programs with similar goals and appearing under the same major entry in a program budget may be administered best by separate agencies because they require different resources and face different problems.

It should be remembered also that great strength may lie in administrative arrangements, such as the prevailing ones, that have grown gradually over time in response to exigencies of various kinds. Although these arrangements may not seem wholly rational, they often possess a pragmatic viability that would be lacking in alternatives ostensibly more orderly but designed apart from the environment in which they are to function.

A compilation such as that of Table 8.5 is nonetheless a step toward a better understanding of the relations between activities and the agencies carrying them out. The questions it raises deserve study and offer an initial basis on which inquiry might take place.

Major Types of Financing

The decision to support a particular activity calls for a corollary decision on ways of financing it, and the latter in turn has a bearing on the method by which the activity is actually carried out. The relative importance of major types of financing for each of the major program entries is indicated in Table 8.6. All of those activities whose conduct and operation involve the federal government as the principal—i.e., as the equivalent of owner and manager—are classified as Direct. The construction by private contractors of facilities to be operated by the government, as well as materials and supplies purchased by the government for its own use, are allocated to this category. In contrast, the term Grants is used when funds are allocated by the government, without obligation of repayment, to support activities managed and conducted by non-federal recipient agencies or individuals. Arrangements having this character, even though they may be formally labeled as contracts, are classified as grants. The federal portion of matching grants, as well as outright grants, is included in this category.

TABLE 8.6 Estimated Federal Health Expenditures Classified by Type of Financing, FY 1965[a] (in thousands of dollars)

Type of financing	Amount
Control and prevention	
Direct[b]	328,898
Grants[b]	356,743
Loans	29,200
User Charges[c]	20,894
Total	735,735
Treatment and restoration	
Direct	995,393
Grants	651,636
Loans	210
User Charges	5,220
Total	1,652,459
Long-term care and domiciliary maintenance	
Direct	398,907
Grants	351,850
Loans	2,800
User Charges	18,213
Total	771,770
Training[d]	
Direct	9,041
Grants	352,593
Loans	11,200
User Charges	557
Total	373,391

TABLE 8.6 (*Continued*)

Type of financing	Amount
Research[d]	
Direct	370,448
Grants	806,442
Loans	—
User Charges	12,051
Total	1,188,941
Other	
Direct	101,989
Grants	65,967
Loans	—
User Charges	53,675
Total	221,631
Grand total	
Direct	2,204,676
Grants	2,585,231
Loans	43,410
User Charges	110,610
Total	4,943,927

Source: See Table 8.3.

[a] Figures are based on total program costs, funded, as estimated for 1965. Health outlays by the Department of Defense and outlays under international programs are excluded.

[b] Defined and discussed on pp. 241–242.

[c] Denotes financing through charges for services and includes public-enterprise charges.

[d] Covers all training or research, including that which has been allocated to other categories. Hence, the total includes duplicate expenditures.

Grants are seen to be somewhat more important than direct financing, comprising over half the total. The relative importance of the grant is especially high in both the Training and Research categories, though it is by no means minor in any of the others. Much of the rapid rise in federal health outlays over the past decade and a half has taken place through the grant mechanism, which has served as the strategic instrument for federal promotion, support, and regulation with a minimum of actual federal participation.

The central issue raised by a breakdown of this sort is whether certain types of activities are best carried out by certain kinds of financing and whether existing balances in this regard are satis-factory. One might suppose that the emphasis on grants (including contracts) in the Research and Training categories was appropriate, for there are extensive facilities and large staffs for these purposes outside the government, in foundations and universities. Similarly, one might feel that direct financing should, as it does, occupy a dominant place under Treatment and Restoration, for it is often only through direct federal involvement that eligible individuals, geographically dispersed over many states, can be brought together in a limited number of specialized hospital facilities.

But is the present blend of financing methods even approxi-mately optimal? Would it be desirable, for example, to make greater use of grants to state and local governments, relying on them for administration and implementation? If so, in what activity areas? What sorts of health activities might be made self-financing, and is this approach being used as fully as is warranted? Are there programs for which changes in the method of financing would achieve greater effectiveness or lower costs? Might, for example, a shift from the direct financing of some of these programs to match-ing grants provide the leverage needed for greater state and local efforts?

It is admittedly difficult to focus on the questions in this area by reference to such highly aggregative data as are found in Table 8.6. In principle, however, the table could be disaggregated, and with this would come a better understanding of the financing alterna-tives and their implication.

Major Beneficiary Groups

Table 8.7, like the previous two tables differs in its essential content from the ordinary program budget. (It also employs the major program entries as subcategories, though that is incidental.) It provides, in summary, a picture of the health assistance rendered to major, identifiable special groups. The picture is not complete, for only a little over one-third of all health outlays could be classi-fied in this way. As expected, veterans are the major beneficiary group, receiving two-thirds of the $1.8 billion total. The substan-tial sum going to the aged also would be expected. But perhaps somewhat surprising is the large amount allocated to children. The major underlying factor here can be gleaned from the entry in Table 8.3, Child Health and Nutrition. Medical payments under

TABLE 8.7 Estimated Federal Health Expenditures Classifiable to
Special Groups, FY 1965[a] (in thousands of dollars)

Special group	Amount
Children:	
Control and prevention of disease	219,262
Treatment and restoration	55,000
Total	274,262
Aged: Long-term care and domiciliary maintenance	249,400
Workers: Control and prevention of disease	19,656
Federal employees: Treatment and restoration	50,819
Veterans:	
Treatment and restoration	861,985
Long-term care and domiciliary maintenance	353,602
Total	1,215,587
Grand total	1,809,724

Source: See Table 8.3.

[a] Figures are based on total program costs, funded, as estimated for 1965. Health
outlays by the Department of Defense and outlays under international programs are
excluded.

maternal and child welfare provisions, together with those parts of
the school lunch and milk programs that can reasonably be regarded as health related, explain this outcome.

The groupings in Table 8.3 help us to understand how the
benefits of federal health programs are distributed and how they
might be measured. It is of some significance, for example, that
veterans are beneficiaries of half of all outlays for Treatment and
Restoration and of about 45 per cent of those for Long-Term Care
and Domiciliary Maintenance. One's judgment of the welfare contribution of these activities might well differ if their benefits were
more widely dispersed or if a group such as the aged were seen to
share more fully in them. The table is not sufficiently detailed or
complete to help much in probing these issues. Greater disaggrega-
tion of the program entries and a fuller and more logical identification of the beneficiary groups is obviously needed.

The roughness of the results and the evident gaps in the five
tables ought not to be regarded as a measure of the limits of what
can be done, even in the near future, to classify and display federal
health outlays. They are, however, indicative of the handicaps

currently faced by those outside the spending agencies, and doubt-less many within them, in seeking to understand the extensive and complex participation of the federal government in the health field. They also are indicative of some of the directions in which we might seek to move in developing a program budget for health.

FEDERAL HEALTH OUTLAYS IN WIDER PERSPECTIVE

Decisions about federal health expenditures inevitably take place against a backdrop of similar kinds of expenditures by state and local governments and by households and businesses. If these latter expenditures were nominal as compared with federal outlays, they might safely be neglected in federal decisions. In fact, however, they comprise the bulk of all health outlays. Federal health expen-ditures of roughly $4.1 billion in 1962 represented only one-eighth of a total of all such expenditures of nearly $33 billion. The com-bined state and local share of the total was approximately the same. By contrast, private outlays of over $24 billion were by far the largest of the three components and three times as great as all public expenditures.[22]

The federal contribution, it appears, is critical in at least a few health areas. Of the $1.5 billion spent by the nation on health research in 1963, about $1 billion came from federal sources, and those sources were clearly important though far from dominant in financing the construction of medical facilities and the provision of hospital care.[23] But beyond reciting a few gross facts such as these, it is extraordinarily difficult, on the basis of published infor-

[22] The federal figure of $4,157 million and the combined state and local figure of $4,159 million are from Table 7, p. 11, of the *Social Security Bulletin*, vol. 26, no. 11, November 1963. The private-sector figure of $24,650 million is from Table 5, p. 10, of the *Bulletin*. These figures, while entirely adequate for the discussion in the text, are not directly comparable with those in the program budget tables. The years of reporting differ, and there are differences also in underlying sources of information and in definition and scope.

[23] The research figures are as follows: federal, $973 million; state and local, $45 million; private, $532 million. The figures for medical-facilities construction are: federal, $240 million; state and local, $393 million; private, $850 million. For hospital care, private expenditures were $6,407 million and total public expendi-tures, $4,620 million. No figure is available for the federal component, but its im-portance might be guessed from our program budget entries in Table 8.4. The data are drawn from, or are estimates based on, information in the following sources: *Social Security Bulletin*, vol. 26, no. 11, November 1963, Table 6, p. 11, and Table 5, p. 10; *ibid.*, July 1963, Table 2, p. 24; and *Trends*, p. 35.

mation, to compare expenditures by the various sectors in each of the major health areas. It is apparent that the federal government spends large sums for such purposes as vocational rehabilitation, medical assistance for the aged, the training of professional personnel in health fields, the treatment of mental illness, and environmental health; but one cannot readily determine how these outlays compare with those for similar purposes by other sectors. As a result, it is not possible to give meaningful consideration to a range of issues central to the making of judgments and decisions on federal programs. We know a good deal less than we should about issues such as the following:

1. The re-enforcing, or perhaps offsetting, effects that arise through the interaction of federal and nonfederal efforts.

2. Duplication and overlap of programs between the three sectors.

3. Whether a new or augmented federal effort in a particular health area might best be implemented directly or by working through established state and local programs.

4. Opportunities that might exist for coordinating efforts and sharing costs with the nonfederal sectors.

With regard to the last two points, it should be noted that the federal government has at its disposal a powerful and much-used instrument—the matching grant—for prompting and directing others to contribute toward certain goals. But this instrument cannot be used to best advantage by federal policymakers and administrators unless they know reasonably well the character and severity of the health burdens that others already carry. More generally, gaps in our knowledge, such as those just noted, make it difficult to determine the form and scale a new program should take or even, in some cases, whether it should be undertaken at all.

Among the approaches that might be taken to reduce or close these gaps in our knowledge, an obvious one is to extend the program budget to the nonfederal sectors. This would, in principle, be quite logical. In practice, the problems encountered would probably be less formidable than one might at first suppose. Within the federal government the need is for a program budget structured in considerable detail on an annual basis. For the state- and local-government and private sectors one would want to follow the same program format, but not in as much detail or with such regularity. The intent is not to provide guidelines for program development and budgeting within these sectors but rather to outline the setting in which federal action takes place. This goal might be accomplished through a comparatively rough and brief initial effort, much less intensive and less formal than that required to prepare a federal program budget, followed by occasional updating and supplemented as needed by *ad hoc* special studies. It is a fair presumption that an approach such as this, by delineating the broad context in which federal health outlays have their impact and by helping to bring into focus the relations between federal and nonfederal burdens and contributions, would make a federal program budget for health a sharper, more precise, and more effective tool.

Chapter 9

PROGRAM BUDGET FOR NATURAL RESOURCES ACTIVITIES

BY WERNER Z. HIRSCH

Natural resources in the United States are developed and managed by federal, state, and local governments as well as by numerous private firms. The federal government has a long-standing interest in the nation's resources, and in FY 1963 it allocated about $3.1 billion for this purpose. More important than the size of the investment is the fact that in the field of water resources, for example, federal programs control the development pattern along major streams and their tributaries.

Federal and Indian lands comprise nearly a fourth of the total area of the United States. They contain major resources of timber, minerals, wildlife, and grazing lands, and they are the source of a large part of the nation's water supply. The federal government not only spends nearly 20 per cent of the national income, it is also the nation's single largest user of raw materials. To carry out its responsibilities for national security, the government is concerned with the availability of adequate supplies of essential raw materials. Efforts to accomplish this objective include stockpiling and support for the development of substitutes. Finally, the federal government must play a creative role to resolve conflicts in resource uses and misuses and to arbitrate between interests of different government units as well as of private groups.

There are many demands made on federal funds, and since we have limited natural resources that must be put to a variety of uses, the federal government faces some difficult choices. Improved tools are needed to articulate these choices and to facilitate judicious decisions. This need is widely recognized. One example will be given here. When Jerome B. Wiesner transmitted to President Kennedy the report of the Federal Council for Science and Technology on *Research and Development on Natural Resources*, he stressed "the need for improved planning and management techniques . . . for resources analysis."[1] Benefit cost analysis and program budgeting are examples of such techniques.

Judicious development and management of our natural resources require a carefully defined national resources policy. However, no clear policy statement can be readily found. Further difficulty results from the fact that in the United States natural resources activities are carried out by many separate private and public bodies. Government budgets are still partly structured in terms of items of expenditure rather than in terms of intermediate or final outputs. This fragmentation and the budget format are conducive to the neglect of tradeoffs between parts (i.e., Should less be devoted to A, more to B?). It is conducive to a lack of coordination and the neglect of interrelationships among the parts. At the same time, with major attention focused on the annual budget, insufficient attention tends to be given to "intertemporal coordination," that is, to the impacts of alternative actions on future cost and benefit streams.

In this chapter we shall first examine some assumptions and objectives of our natural resources policy. Then we shall review how natural resources activities are treated in the existing budget and consider steps that would bring it closer to becoming a program budget. Next we shall present examples of how program budgeting can elucidate allocation decisions. Finally, we shall consider certain administrative and institutional arrangements needed to implement allocation decisions in the natural resources field.

OBJECTIVES AND ASSUMPTIONS

Basically, natural resources activities are designed to improve the economic performance of the country in the present and future. However, it has been difficult either to find or to develop precise statements on the goals and objectives of our natural resources policy. A rather vague position is taken in a Department of Agriculture *Policy Guide,* which states: "National programs, through planning and coordination, should be directed at the conservation,

---

[1] Office of Science and Technology, Executive Office of the President, *Research and Development on Natural Resources* (Washington, D.C.: U.S. Government Printing Office, 1963), p. iv.

development, and management of these resources to support a balanced and strong economy."[2]

Some of the dimensions of a national natural resources policy are indicated in President Kennedy's 1962 Message relative to our conservation program, in which he called for a water policy that would provide "sufficient water sufficiently clean in the right place at the right time to serve the range of human and industrial needs."[3] One key aspect—cost—was left out. Because there are many competing demands for our limited funds, cost considerations clearly must play an important role in the formulation of a natural resources policy.

Much of the writing on our natural resources policy follows the premise that the natural resource base of the U.S. economy is the essential ingredient in our industrial and military power, and that our natural resources are becoming increasingly scarce. This view was forcefully expressed by President Kennedy in his 1961 Message on Natural Resources to Congress:

From the beginning of civilization, every nation's basic wealth and progress has stemmed in large measure from its natural resources. This Nation has been, and is now, especially fortunate in the blessings we have inherited. Our entire society rests upon—and is dependent upon—our water, our land, our forests, and our minerals. How we use these resources influences our health, security, and well-being.

But if we fail to chart a proper course of conservation and development—if we fail to use these blessings prudently—we will be in trouble within a short time. In the resource field, predictions of future use have been consistently understated. But even under conservative projections, we face a future of critical shortages and handicaps.[4]

The scarcity view is based on rather pessimistic assumptions about the substitutibility of other forms of capital for natural resources. Being somewhat more optimistic about beneficial

---

[2] *Land Water Resources—A Policy Guide,* U.S. Department of Agriculture (Washington, D.C.: U.S. Government Printing Office, 1962), p. 49.

[3] *President Kennedy's Message on Conservation to the Congress of the United States,* U.S. Department of the Interior (Washington, D.C.: U.S. Government Printing Office, March 1, 1962), p. 10.

[4] *Message from the President of the United States Relative to Our Natural Resources,* House of Representatives Document No. 94, 87th Cong., 1st Sess., February 23, 1961 (Washington, D.C.: U.S. Government Printing Office, 1961), p. 1.

changes in technology, Resources for the Future, Inc., takes "a position of qualified optimism regarding the adequacy of resources to support economic growth during the balance of the century."[5]

Let us now turn to a more detailed examination of ingredients and considerations of a natural resources policy. A natural resources policy can be regarded as a set of general guidelines concerning natural resources activities, e.g., research, resources development, resources management and conservation, and regulation to resolve conflict. Presumably we would like to have specific decisions regarding natural resources activities consistent with such a set of general guidelines. For example, maintaining a broad menu of research on new water sources to cover all interesting "bets" might be one general guideline. We should keep asking: Is the allocation of our natural resources effort related to water reuse, desalinization, long-distance water transportation, etc., consistent with this guideline, or are we putting too many eggs in too few baskets?

Because the time horizon is usually long, there are few instances in which we can expect definitive answers. Also we should recognize that close coordination of our choices involving consistency of specific decisions with an appropriate set of guidelines is basically beyond our reach. The best we can do is to proceed from an existing state of affairs by means of "incrementalism," hoping to make marginal adjustments consistent with our policy objectives.

Basic choices appear to lie between natural resources activities, which to differing degrees develop and/or conserve natural resources. These resources must be defined in the broadest possible terms to include all such nonhuman assets as fresh air, aesthetically beautiful sites, etc. The choice problem is further complicated by the regional aspects of natural resources, which call for many decisions to be delegated to regional and local offices.

Let us next explore the environment in which natural resources goals are pursued. What is to be assumed about society's goals? Most of us feel a stake in the quality of the environment, in the development of other individuals, in the maintenance of a high

---

[5] Hans Landsberg, "Situation and Outlook for Resources in the United States," *Natural Resources: Trends, Policies and Administration*, J. L. Fisher, ed. (Chicago, Ill.: American Association for Public Administration, 1963), p. 3.

degree of freedom despite the growing interdependencies that tend to limit it, in progress toward greater equality of opportunity, and in a gradually rising standard of living.

What is to be assumed about the future environment? Many aspects are uncertain, indeed dependent on our policies (and projections of uncertainty are just as significant as projections of other aspects of the environment). At the same time we believe there is likely to be a population expansion, further urbanization, automation and increased leisure, rising levels of income, more education, greater variety of choice, continued international disagreement and cold wars, and so on. We are likely to retain our historic attitude toward "plentiful resources" and waste them.

What is to be assumed about the behavior of institutions in various circumstances? Faced with various institutional arrangements and benefit cost structures, how will federal, state, and local agencies, private firms, research institutions, etc., behave? Answers to these questions are difficult to come by, although we cannot detect forces that would check the continuous growth of the importance of the federal government.

Assumptions must be made about all of these issues so that we can begin to project the demand for and supply of natural resources in years to come. For example, key specific factors likely to affect the demand for natural resources, and about which assumptions must be made, include the following:[6]

1. The rate of growth of United States and world population.

2. The rate of economic growth in the United States and other countries.

3. The rate and character of technological change.

4. Changes in special needs for military security and defense technology.

5. The balance of trade and exchange between nations.

6. Our national economic, political, and social objectives.

7. The tides of migration among different regions in the United States, and between urban and rural areas.

8. Changes in working and leisure times and habits.

---

[6] Office of Science and Technology, *Natural Resources*, pp. 4–5.

THE EXISTING NATURAL RESOURCES ACTIVITIES BUDGET

In *The Budget of the United States Government for the Fiscal Year Ending June 30, 1965* and *Appendix,*[7] natural resources activities appear in about a dozen federal agencies. Matters are further complicated by the legislative branch of the federal government. For example, while the Forest Service is in the Department of Agriculture and is so shown in its budget, the service's budget is considered by a House Appropriations Subcommittee concerned with the Department of the Interior. On the other hand, the Bureau of Reclamation, which is in the Department of the Interior, has its budget included in a Public Works Appropriations bill, which includes, among others, the Atomic Energy Commission budget.

Some of the problems associated with the present budget have been recognized by the executive branch of the government, which provides a summary of the natural resources activities budget. For example, *1965 Budget* includes a modified administrative natural resources budget, which pulls together items from eleven federal agencies. It is reproduced in Table 9.1. Expenditures for FY 1963 approximated $2.5 billion. They are broken down into five major programs: $1.7 billion were spent to finance land and water resources; $300 million for forest resources; and $100 million each for recreational resources, fish and wildlife resources, and mineral resources.

The FY 1963 natural resources budget has serious shortcomings, which become especially clear when we keep in mind some key considerations on resource allocation decisionmaking. Decisions about natural resources activities should, whenever possible, be based on information that indicates their effects on major related activities and in future years. Decisionmakers should be able to consider tradeoffs and interrelationships more effectively, and they should be given the opportunity to take the full cost implications of their choices into account instead of looking merely at the down payment implications.

Specific criticisms of the existing natural resources budget fall into four main categories. The first concerns the breakdown of the

[7] Published in Washington, D.C.: U.S. Government Printing Office, 1964.

TABLE 9.1 Natural Resources Activities Budget: Fiscal Years 1963, 1964, 1965 (in millions of dollars)

Program or agency	Payments to the public			Recommended new obligational authority for 1965
	1963 Actual	1964 Estimate	1965 Estimate	
Administration budget funds				
Land and water resources:				
Corps of Engineers	1,072	1,075	1,133	1,152
Department of the Interior:				
Bureau of Reclamation	344	335	324	324
Power marketing agencies	37	50	60	69
Bureau of Indian Affairs	109	109	110	116
Bureau of Land Management	50	55	56	61
Office of Saline Water	9	11	12	13
Tennessee Valley Authority	53	57	68	51
Federal Power Commission	11	12	13	13
International Boundary and Water Commission and other	15	17	32	18
Subtotal	1,699	1,720	1,808	1,817
Forest resources:				
Forest Service	287	338	321	338
Bureau of Land Management	16	15	18	19
Recreational resources:				
Present programs	112	122	123	118
Proposed legislation	—	—	15	40
Fish and wildlife resources	94	104	110	114
Mineral resources:				
Bureau of Land Management	47	48	49	49
Bureau of Mines and other	24	60	64	60
General resource surveys and administration	73	76	80	82
Total, administrative budget	2,352	2,483	2,588	2,637[a]
Trust funds				
Indian tribal funds	67	69	54	44
Other	55	69	53	55
Total, trust funds	122	138	107	100[a]
Intragovernmental transactions and other adjustments (deduct)	18	10	6	
Grand Total	2,456	2,611	2,688	

Source: The Budget of the United States Government for the Fiscal Year Ending June 30, 1965 (Washington, D.C.: U.S. Government Printing Office, 1964), p. 97.

[a] Compares with new obligational authority for 1963 and 1964 as follows: Administrative Budget Funds: 1963, $2,447 million; 1964, $2,588 million. Trust Funds: 1963, $134 million; 1964, $109 million.

budget into programs and program elements. Second, the time horizon of the existing budget is too short. Longer budget projections are needed so that intertemporal effects can be estimated and closer intertemporal coordination can be achieved. Third, budget figures should reflect *full* costs, in place of merely down payments. Fourth, some of the budget figures require refinement.

The need for an extended time horizon has been recognized by the Bureau of the Budget.[8] For example, the latter has requested executive departments and establishments to submit estimates for federal public works programs covering a five-year period, i.e., the budget year and four succeeding years. In the late spring of 1964 the first tabulations became available, mainly related, unfortunately, to administrative responsibilities rather than programs. Furthermore, it appears that this exercise was not too well conceived and induced every agency to project expenditures slightly increased over the present year. In short, everybody more or less wanted to do more of what he was already doing.

Although many natural resources activities have different requirements over the life cycle of the activity, this cycle tends to have four phases that can overlap: research, development (or investment), resources management and conservation, and regulation. Appropriations for research, for example in the field of water desalting, should be made with the full realization that if useful results are obtained, major investments for resources development will be needed, which in turn will be followed by a later need for funds to manage, conserve, and sometimes regulate the resources. In connection with the last three issues, consideration can be given to imposing user charges to cover all government outlays. However, it is desirable to reach an early decision, even on the user charge, so that possible full cost implications of the research decision or the development decision are understood from the outset. Even the timing of these future outlays could and should be anticipated.

Many natural resources activities require investment in capital goods that have a 30-, 50-, or even 100-year life span. Clearly under these circumstances uncertainty is all-pervasive. Although we may have clues to the costs and benefits and must make judgment about

[8] U.S. Bureau of the Budget, *Circular*, No. A-35 revised, November 7, 1963; and Summary Tables from Advance Federal Public Works Programs, 1964–68, April 25, 1964.

them, we cannot have a high confidence in our empirical estimates.

Nevertheless, we must attempt to obtain the best possible estimates of full cost and benefit streams from alternative natural resources policies. The cost streams must include the full costs of research, resources development, resources management and conservation, and regulation. They must be compared with corresponding benefit streams. One such example would be a desalinization proposal which, as is well known, involves large uncertainties. However, in addition to attempting an estimate of potential value of desalinization, if it proves successful, we must also consider the chances that the process will be a success. Clearly both of these estimates are surrounded with great uncertainty, which is only part of the uncertainty that surrounds such an investment.

Because natural resources decisions often are made in an uncertain atmosphere, officials must turn to imprecise guidelines, as noted before, and must rely on their judgments to no small extent. Insofar as research about natural resources development and conservation is concerned, one very general guideline in the face of all-pervasive uncertainty is to stimulate research along a broad front, including the encouragement, up to a point, of parallel or multiple approaches to the solution of important problems.

Furthermore, attention should be paid to the possibility of making decisions sequentially and avoiding premature final commitments to the "best" solution of a particular problem. Also, in the light of great demand and technological uncertainties, effort should be made to retain flexibility of action. Steps to attain greater flexibility could include using general purpose rather than highly specialized design and using less durable structures in some natural resources development projects.

Finally, a few words will be said about the quality of budget figures as given in the consolidated natural resources budget. We shall use the Forest Service's resources budget as an example. *1965 Budget* shows 1963 actual payments by the Forest Service for forest service activities to amount to $287 million. An examination of the *1965 Budget Appendix* reveals that $28 million, or about 10 per cent, are disbursements of fees and earmarked funds and are not used for forest resources activities.[9] The bulk is in the form of payments to states from the national forest fund. For example,

[9] *1965 Budget Appendix*, p. 175.

25 per cent of the money received from the national forests is paid to the states for public schools and roads in the county where such forests are situated.

A PROGRAM BUDGET FOR NATURAL RESOURCES ACTIVITIES

Natural resources activities decisions have many dimensions that must be kept in mind when we select a natural resources budget format. Matters are complicated by the longevity of many resources, by the high uncertainty attached to future demand and supply conditions, and by the many interrelated purposes to which various natural resources can be put.

One way of looking at natural resources leads to the functional breakdown already noted:

1. Resources research.
2. Resources development.
3. Resources management and conservation.
4. Regulation to resolve conflict.

On the other hand, if we emphasize the conservation aspects of natural resources, we can visualize the following useful grouping:

1. Air, water, and land.
2. Fuels, energy, and minerals.
3. Soils, forests, and forage.
4. Fish and wildlife.

This breakdown leaves us with some bothersome overlapping. For example, it is often hard to separate the conservation of land, soils, forests, forage, and minerals.

Finally, emphasis on the intermediate products and/or end products of natural resources activities could result in the following eight major programs:

1. Land (mainly agricultural) resources.
2. Water resources.
3. Forest resources.
4. Recreational resources.
5. Nonoceanic fish and wildlife.
6. Oceanic resources.
7. Mineral resources.
8. Air resources.

As in so many cases, there is no single best way of grouping expenditures. For example, it should be quite clear that certain expenditures that we place under natural resources activities in this chapter could readily be transferred to the health activities of the federal government. The most obvious are related to water and air pollution control. Furthermore, a case could be made for considering expenditures on recreational resources as designed to improve the nation's health.

Admittedly, our eight resources activities also involve some overlapping. More important, funds are often spent on two or more programs in such a way that we cannot allocate them with any precision. In spite of these shortcomings, this categorization appears to offer some merit. It is not very different from that given in Table 9.1, except that it separates land and water resources and adds air resources and oceanic resources categories. Furthermore, the present budget does not include agricultural resources in the natural resources budget; instead, they are placed into the Agriculture and Agricultural Resources Budget. While most items included in the latter category affect agricultural land resources indirectly, only a few have a direct effect. The latter activities come under the heading of Soil Conservation Service, agricultural conservation, etc.

The addition of oceanic resources and air resources programs stems less from the fact that important expenditures are presently made than from our expectation that both will be increasingly important in the future. Exploration of the oceans is one of the last frontiers of mankind. The heavy investment needed, great uncertainty of results, and major spatial benefit spillovers to be expected will probably require federal financing or regulation if we are to succeed. Air pollution control has many similar characteristics that will call for federal financing and/or regulation, and the magnitude of the air pollution danger is being recognized only now.

Clearly, activities in relation to the eight resources differ. For example, our basic concern in the case of air relates to quality, i.e., air pollution control, while our concern with mineral resources is primarily one of quantity. In most other instances, the nation is interested in both the quantity and quality of the resource, although in recent years the emphasis on quality aspects has gained in importance. These considerations have a bearing on the selection of appropriate program elements and subprograms.

Ideally we could follow the functional breakdown of research, development, etc., and have the eight natural resources as subcategories (Table 9.2). Or, we could start out with the eight natural resources and for each attempt to gain information on the four different functions (Table 9.3). There is little hope at this time of developing comprehensive data that could follow the first approach. Most of the available data are related to a specific natural resource, and a breakdown into research, development, conservation, and regulation is virtually impossible.

We propose, therefore, to structure the natural resources program budget by types of resources activities as programs (and subprograms), and whenever possible to identify expenditures for research, development, management and conservation, and regulation, respectively. Hopefully, over the years we shall gain further insight and succeed in identifying more and more expenditures in functional terms.

With this object in mind, let us next examine some natural resources programs with a view to identifying meaningful components, i.e., subprograms. The land resources program can be readily subdivided into two major subprograms: agricultural land conservation and urban greenbelt development. Of the two, the first is by far the more venerable and more important at present. Since the early thirties, federal agricultural land conservation legislation has had a dual purpose: conservation and price (and income) support for farmers. Thus, agricultural conservation payments are made to farmers with a view to having a beneficial effect not only on agricultural land but also, and this is perhaps more important, on farm prices and therefore farm income through reduced output. The expenditures of the Department of Agriculture in this area have to be considered from both points of view. In very recent years some serious interest has been shown in preserving urban open space, and within the federal government this task has been assigned to the Housing and Home Finance Agency. It is a new program, and the first funds were expended in FY 1964, but it is growing. For FY 1966 the President has requested new obligational authority to the amount of $29 million, twice that of 1965. Each of these land resources subprograms could require

TABLE 9.2 Federal Natural Resources Activities Program Budget, Arranged by Major Functions (in millions of dollars)

Function	1963	1964	1965	1966	1967
Natural resources research:					
Land resources					
Water resources					
Forest resources					
Recreational resources					
Nonoceanic fish and wildlife					
Oceanic resources					
Mineral resources					
Air resources					
Natural resources development:					
Land resources					
Water resources					
Forest resources					
Recreational resources					
Nonoceanic fish and wildlife					
Oceanic resources					
Mineral resources					
Air resources					
Natural resources management and conservation:					
Land resources					
Water resources					
Forest resources					
Recreational resources					
Nonoceanic fish and wildlife					
Oceanic resources					
Mineral resources					
Air resources					
Natural resources regulation to resolve conflict:					
Land resources					
Water resources					
Forest resources					
Recreational resources					
Nonoceanic fish and wildlife					
Oceanic resources					
Mineral resources					
Air resources					

TABLE 9.3 Federal Natural Resources Activities Program Budget, Arranged by Resources (in millions of dollars)

Resource	1963	1964	1965	1966	1967
Land resources:					
Research					
Development					
Management and conservation					
Regulation to resolve conflict					
Water resources:					
Research					
Development					
Management and conservation					
Regulation to resolve conflict					
Forest resources:					
Research					
Development					
Management and conservation					
Regulation to resolve conflict					
Recreational resources:					
Research					
Development					
Management and conservation					
Regulation to resolve conflict					
Nonoceanic fish and wildlife:					
Research					
Development					
Management and conservation					
Regulation to resolve conflict					
Oceanic resources:					
Research					
Development					
Management and conservation					
Regulation to resolve conflict					
Mineral resources:					
Research					
Development					
Management and conservation					
Regulation to resolve conflict					
Air resources:					
Research					
Development					
Management and conservation					
Regulation to resolve conflict					

research, resources development (investment), resources management and conservation, and regulation to resolve conflicts.

Next we shall turn to some subprograms on water resources activities. First, there is the demand by cities and farms for fresh water. This water must have certain quantity characteristics over time; it also must have quality dimensions, which will differ depending on whether the water is for drinking or industrial use or irrigation. In addition to the need for enough water, there is the danger of temporary excess. Thus, another subprogram is flood prevention. At least three other subprograms can be identified: electric power generation, navigation improvement, and water-based recreation opportunities. Clearly, as happens so often, some of the subprograms can be put together with other programs—navigation improvement with transportation, water-based recreation opportunities with recreation. In Table 9.4 we do indeed group the latter with recreation resources.

A few words will be said about recreational resources activities and their relation to other recreation activities. It appears useful to divide all outdoor recreation into:

1. User-oriented outdoor recreation.
2. Intermediate outdoor recreation.
3. Resource-based outdoor recreation.

The first type is usually the responsibility of municipal and county governments, while intermediate outdoor recreation—parks or lakes of several hundred acres that require about a five-hour drive to be reached from major population centers—are usually administered by state and county governments. At the moment, the federal government's main direct interest is in resource-based recreation available in National Parks, National Forests, and National Wildlife Refuges. These recreation facilities can be distinguished because they usually encompass several thousand acres, are a considerable distance from major population centers, and involve overnight stays. They tend to include scenic and/or historical sites, hiking trails, camping areas, lakes, etc.

Although there are numerous ways to categorize mineral resources activities, a particularly useful dichotomy is based on whether or not they are energy sources.

The natural resources program budget suggested here has been summarized in Table 9.4. In Table 9.5 we have attempted to present FY 1963 expenditure figures for programs and subprograms

TABLE 9.4 A Suggested Federal Natural Resources Activities Program Budget[a] (in millions of dollars)

Natural resource	1963	1964	1965	1966	1967
Land resources:					
Agricultural land conservation					
Urban greenbelt development					
Water resources:					
Water supply					
Flood prevention and control					
Navigation improvement					
Electric power generation					
Forest resources					
Recreational resources:					
User-oriented outdoor recreation					
Intermediate outdoor recreation					
Resource-based outdoor recreation					
Nonoceanic fish and wildlife					
Oceanic resources					
Mineral resources:					
Energy sources					
Nonenergy source resources (metallic minerals)					
Air resources					

[a] Wherever possible, expenditures of programs will be presented separately for research, development, management and conservation, and regulation to resolve conflict.

presented in Table 9.4. At the outset it should be said that it is very difficult, if not impossible, to separate natural resources expenditures for research, development, management and conservation, and regulation. In some cases, the difficulties are more than empirical. Thus, for example, there can be some conceptual disagreement as to whether funds expended by the Department of Agriculture under its Soil Conservation Service activities are development or operation expenditures. For this reason, in most cases, we have not separated expenditures into these functional categories. The exception relates to water resources activity. Here it seems possible to separate expenditures to some extent into development, operation, and regulation. We hasten to add that this separation is at best rough and partial. We also are aware of the fact that not all of the $11 million expenditures of the Federal Power Commission were spent on regulating water resources. Parts were spent on regulating energy sources.

TABLE 9.5 A Federal Natural Resources Activities Program Budget, FY 1963 (in millions of dollars)

Natural resources	1963 expenditures
Land resources	
Agricultural land conservation:	
Soil Conservation Service—conservation operations and Great Plains program	118
Agricultural conservation program (including CCC loan)	219
Emergency conservation measures	3
Conservation reserve and cropland conversion	309
Bureau of Land Management	50
Urban greenbelt development:	
Open-space land grants of Housing and Home Finance Agency	—a
Total	699
Water resources	
Development:	
Water supply:	
Irrigation and water conservation:	
Bureau of Reclamation	86
Soil Conservation Service	4
Bureau of Indian Affairs	4
Water supply and water pollution control (PHS)	23
Waste treatment facilities (PHS grants)	52
Office of Saline Water	9
Flood prevention and control:	
Corps of Engineers	368
Bureau of Reclamation	1
Soil Conservation Service	54
International Boundary and Water Commission	1
Tennessee Valley Authority	3
Navigation improvement:	
Corps of Engineers	227
Saint Lawrence Seaway Development Corporation	1
Tennessee Valley Authority	8
Multiple-purpose dams and reservoirs with hydroelectric power facilities:	
Bureau of Reclamation	150
Corps of Engineers	273
International Boundary and Water Commission	10
Tennessee Valley Authority	13
Steam-electric powerplants—TVA	75
Power transmission facilities:	
Tennessee Valley Authority	30
Bureau of Reclamation	47
Bonneville Power Administration	15
Southwestern Power Administration	1
Operation and maintenance, general investigations, river basin planning	225

TABLE 9.5 (*Continued*)

Natural resources	1963 expenditures
Regulation—Federal Power Commission	11
Total	1,691
Forest resources	
Forest Service	287
Bureau of Land Management	16
Total	303
Recreational resources	
Resource-based recreation:	
Bureau of Outdoor Recreation	1
National Park Service	111
Water—included in water resources	—
Forests—included in forest resources	—
Total	112
Nonoceanic fish and wildlife	
Bureau of Sport Fisheries and Wildlife	66
Oceanic resources	
Bureau of Commercial Fisheries (except oceanographic program)	10
National Oceanographic Program (obligations):	
Department of Commerce	24
Department of Defense	56
Department of Health, Education, and Welfare	4
Department of the Interior	16
Department of the Treasury	1
Atomic Energy Commission	4
National Science Foundation	20
Smithsonian Institution	1
Total	136
Mineral resources	
Bureau of Land Management (mineral lease payments to states)	47
Bureau of Mines:	
Conservation and development of mineral resources	29
Helium fund	− 10
Office of Coal Research	1
Office of Minerals Exploration	2
Office of Oil and Gas	1
Total	80
Air resources	
Public Health Service—air pollution	10
Grand total	3,087

ᵃ Less than $500,000.

A review of Table 9.5 reveals that of the $3.1 billion federal expenditures for natural resources activities in FY 1963, more than half involved water resources. Of the $1.69 billion expenditures for water resources, $225 million were for operation and maintenance, $11 million (or actually somewhat less) were for regulation, and the rest were development expenditures. Second in magnitude were expenditures for land resources. In FY 1963 almost $700 million were spent in connection with agricultural land conservation. As mentioned earlier, most of these expenditures had a dual purpose: bona fide land conservation, on the one hand, and price and income maintenance of farmers, on the other. Expenditures on urban greenbelt developments started only after FY 1963.

Third in order of expenditures were those for forest resources, amounting in FY 1963 to about $300 million. Parts of these expenditures should be allocated to recreational resources, which amounted to about $112 million, while oceanic resources expenditures amounted to $136 million. Expenditures on the other three programs were quite small: $80 million on mineral resources, $66 million on nonoceanic fish and wildlife resources, and $10 million on air resources. The latter activity has been rapidly increasing in recent years, the FY 1966 estimate being $24 million.

NATURAL RESOURCES DECISIONS REQUIRING ELUCIDATION

The nation continually faces a variety of important natural resources decisions, many of which are assigned to the federal government—some *in toto,* some in part. These decisions must usually be made while the future demand for and supply of resources are highly uncertain. What are some of these decision areas and how can program budgeting help articulate the choices? In the following pages no attempt will be made to be inclusive in coverage. We cannot even be sure to cover the most significant resources decisions. We are hopeful, however, that some of the issues that will be raised can serve as informative examples.

Before going further, we would like to remind the reader that whereas this volume is concerned with federal budgetary decisions, they seldom can be made without due regard to the numerous state, local, and private decisionmakers who are also engaged in natural resources activities. In many resources areas private entrepreneurs are major, if not dominating, factors; and except for resource-based outdoor recreation, state and local governments overwhelmingly dominate the recreation scene. Keeping these complicated relations in mind, we shall first attempt to sketch the present status and expected changes in the demand for and supply of natural resources, and then to indicate how program budgeting can facilitate some of the choices. The following discussion will proceed along the eight-program lines that were identified earlier.

The United States has been blessed with an ample supply of land, and no national shortages for either agricultural or urban land are in the offing. Even the rapid encroachment of urban land uses on agricultural land is not expected to bring about national shortages of agricultural land. However, in recent years people and governments have started to show concern about the rapidly deteriorating quality of the landscape in and around our cities. Financial inducements to cities, designed to persuade them to acquire land for local parks and greenbelts, have become a distinct interest of the Housing and Home Finance Agency.

Quite a different concern about land resources exists in the Department of Agriculture. It continues to finance farmers to practice soil conservation, with the additional purpose of implementing certain farm-income stabilizing policies. Funds spent on these activities are not negligible, and continued attention should be given to ascertaining the benefits associated with this investment and comparing them with alternatives.

Next, let us consider water resources. The Office of Science and Technology in the Executive Office of the President foresees: "The United States, on the average, will not be short of water in the next fifty years; that is, we will not be short of water for the country as a whole, on the one hand, and for years of average precipitation, on the other. But (by the year 2000) regional shortages could arise in large areas, in the upper Missouri Basin, in the Southern Pacific region, in the Gulf Coastal States, and even in the eastern Great Lakes."[10] Even if we accept this optimistic outlook, expected regional water shortages call for certain national, as well as regional, efforts. For example, a variety of steps could be taken to increase the supply of usable water, be it through further progress in de-

10 Office of Science and Technology, *Natural Resources*, p. 6.

salinization, weather modification, water reuse, or development of new water sources through improved methods for transporting water long distances. Such steps involve research, development, and operating funds, and the relative merits of these alternatives should be explored. Research funds for either of these steps should be considered in comparison with funds that could improve the quantity, quality, and time availability of water through a better understanding of the interactions between vegetation, soils, and water, and how to influence these interactions to improve water resources. The question is whether an additional dollar spent on improving water desalinization, water reuse, or long-distance water transportation, etc., is likely to produce larger benefits. Even if the decision favors more dams, the federal government faces a variety of capital investment decisions. In the case of the arid Southwest, for example, it appears that among the alternatives are the building of further dams to supply water in a single state; a kind of Southwest Regional Plan that will supply jointly parts of California, Arizona, and Nevada; and an International Water Plan for the western part of the continent to include parts of the United States and Canada.

Program budgeting in conjunction with benefit cost analysis in the water resources field can be especially helpful in identifying decisions that are not consistent with the national welfare. Irving K. Fox and Orris C. Herfindahl present an interesting example. They point out that the peculiar "structure of interest group relationships which generates decisions on water investment by federal agencies . . . fosters optimistic estimates of benefits and costs . . . [and] generates a powerful joint effort to secure favorable congressional action on the projects decided upon."[11] The interest groups that combine forces are, on the one hand, contractors, landowners, shippers, construction material firms, and local merchants —beneficiaries who bear only a small fraction of the cost of the project—and, on the other hand, the Corps of Engineers, whose interest is served by an expanding program.

Aspects of this phenomenon can be detected among key California decisionmakers who have continuously sought to increase California's water supply. Federal participation in the financing of

[11] "Attainment of Efficiency in Satisfying Demand for Water Resources," *American Economic Review*, vol. 54, no. 2, May 1964, pp. 199–200.

many western water plans has placed the marginal cost of water to California below that to the nation. This differential can induce California to seek more water than can be used efficiently. The fact that water pricing in California discriminates in favor of irrigation uses (where there are powerful pressure groups) has further stimulated the drive for large-scale investments to bring more water into California in general and Southern California in particular.

As a result, some important choices beneficial to the nation at large might be neglected. For example, we might make major premature commitments to invest in capital facilities with a 50- to 100-year life expectancy at a time when no urgent need for such an investment exists. In fact, such facilities could become obsolete in short order because great strides through desalinization using atomic energy might take place during the next five to ten years. If there is no immediate need for additional water, if we are willing to use the pricing mechanism more effectively, and more important, if far-reaching technological advances—possibly making some conventional water sources obsolete—are likely to come about shortly, wisdom demands that new major capital investments be postponed for a little while.

At the moment the federal government spends very small amounts of money on water desalinization research—about $12 million in FY 1965. Program budgeting should aid in making useful comparisons and in deciding whether of a $1.2 billion Department of the Interior budget more should perhaps be spent on water de-salting research.

Of all the major natural resources, only forest products appear to have become relatively scarce in the United States. For example, the relative price of lumber has risen by 300 per cent since 1870; and the Forest Service has warned that the projected rate of cutting trees of saw timber grade over the next forty years considerably exceeds anticipated growth.[12] Thus the federal government faces some serious decisions and must choose between further forest product imports and the encouragement of a better balance between domestic timber growth and cutting. In all of these

[12] *Timber Resources for America's Future,* Forest Service, U.S. Department of Agriculture, Forest Resource Report No. 14 (Washington, D.C.: U.S. Government Printing Office, January 1958), p. 96.

deliberations it must keep in mind that private industry can adjust itself and seek substitutes.

Let us turn next to recreational resources. The total acreage of the State Parks, National Park Service, and Forest Service in 1950 was 210 million acres; in 1960 it was 218 million acres.[13] Demand for outdoor recreation has been sharply increasing and promises to continue. Thus, the Outdoor Recreation Resources Review Commission estimated that participation in outdoor recreation during a summer will increase from 4.4 billion separate outdoor recreation activity occasions (participation by an individual in a single recreation activity during a day) in 1960 to 6.9 billion activity occasions in 1976. By the year 2000 this total could rise to over 12.4 billion occasions, almost three times the 1960 figures.[14]

The expected increases in recreation demand will further add to the pressure on existing recreational resources, including forests and fish and wildlife resources. Consideration must be given to increasing the number of National Parks, National Forests, and National Wildlife Refuges, as well as improving and conserving existing parks, forests, ranges, wildlife refuges, and wetlands for migrating waterfowl. In part, the latter objectives can be attained by more effective measures to reduce forest damage resulting from fire, insects, and disease. Program budgeting in conjunction with benefit cost analysis can help in making wise choices about both investing more in the acquisition of additional wilderness areas and/or park lands and spendng additional funds on effectively fighting natural phenomena that can endanger our forests, ranges, and parks.

For many purposes it is useful to lump together nonoceanic fish and wildlife resources with recreational resources. The former indirectly benefit sport fishermen and hunters. Sport fishermen also benefit from certain investments in oceanic resources, which have additional objectives, however. They include military concerns, purely scientific inquiries, fishing industry problems, and exploitation of raw materials on the bottom of the ocean. Having witnessed in recent years the phenomenal increase in efforts to explore space, we can visualize a sudden large-scale concern with the exploration of the oceans.

---

[13] Outdoor Recreation Resources Review Commission, *Outdoor Recreation for America* (Washington, D.C.: U.S. Government Printing Office, 1962), p. 50.
[14] *Ibid.*, p. 32.

Next we shall take a look at our metallic minerals and energy resources. Great increases in demand have occurred. For certain minerals we have become increasingly dependent on imports. On the other hand, a report by the Federal Council for Science and Technology concludes that "resources of fossil fuels should be adequate for the next few decades."[15] However, the report also sees a need for the development of further energy sources. Decisions will have to be made about investing in the development of low-grade fossil fuels, electric power generation, and nuclear energy. The Geological Survey is reported to have estimated potential uranium resources in this country, comparable in quality to ore now being mined, to be more than twice the energy equivalent of all coal, oil, and gas resources now believed to exist in this country.[16] However, this estimate assumes that breeder reactors will make it possible to convert relatively abundant uranium 238 into fissionable plutonium.

If it becomes possible to convert thorium into a fissionable material, or if an atomic fusion process is developed to a practical stage, abundant energy sources will become available. Either alternative will need federal encouragement and funds, and program budgeting can help elucidate decisions. It can also help articulate choices designed to reduce regional inequalities in the availability of low-cost energy.

Finally, a few words need to be said about the rapid deterioration of the air over most of our cities. Particularly during the last twenty-five years air pollution has become a major problem, and hardly any steps have been taken to cope with it. There is need for more research on the effects of atmospheric pollutants and perturbations on people, animals, plants, and buildings. Also needed is research on the prevention and control of natural and man-made emissions to the atmosphere. In FY 1963 about $10 million was spent by the federal government in the air resources field. Because air pollution involves large-scale spatial benefit spillovers, local and even state governments are unlikely to take the necessary steps to control and mitigate its damage.

Another decision area that needs to be elucidated relates to the pricing of certain natural resources uses. Pricing decisions are complicated by the fact that many resources activities have joint

[15] Office of Science and Technology, *Natural Resources*, p. 6. See also Joseph L. Fisher and Neal Potter, *World Prospects for Natural Resources* (Baltimore, Md.: The Johns Hopkins Press, 1964), pp. 60–61.
[16] *Ibid.*, p. 59.

costs, and some of them fulfill social wants, while others fulfill merit wants. To bring about a more efficient development and use of our natural resources, careful consideration must be given to applying user charges more often and to bring these charges into closer harmony with costs and/or benefits.

Charging more realistic user fees for irrigation water is especially important in the western United States, where water for irrigation purposes is priced from 2 to 12 cents per 1,000 gallons, while the average price of residential and industry water runs about 35 cents per 1,000 gallons. The establishment of realistic user charges is also needed in the recreation field. Not only are the user charges of National Parks very low, but until recently use of National Forests and other recreation areas run by such agencies as the Corps of Engineers and the Tennessee Valley Authority was entirely free. As a result, great distortions in uses are likely to occur. The vast upsurge in demand for recreational facilities might be coped with in the short run through more appropriate pricing.

To illustrate possible applications of natural resources program budgeting, let us next explore an example relating to decisions facing the President and his budget advisers, since at present there is no single body responsible for natural resources problems. The issue might be stated in the following way: If in FY 1963 the federal government spent about $3.1 billion for natural resources activities, did it spend the right amount for land resources, water resources, forest resources, etc., and was the research, development, management, and regulation mix appropriate? Specifically, was it wise to spend almost half of our natural resources budget to invest in developing further water resources? This figure is especially large in relation to the $10 million spent on desalinization research, which, if successful, can revolutionize the water supply. In 1964 a task force under Roger Revelle, set up by the White House to examine desalting of the sea, stated: "We have confirmed the essential validity of the Oak Ridge National Laboratory conclusion—that relatively low-cost fresh water can be obtained with very large-scale dual purpose operations where there is a sufficiently large market for electric power, and that nuclear energy plants appear to have better economic potential in those very large sizes than fossil fuel plants."[17] In the light of these optimistic conclusions the President appears to have decided to invest more heavily in the

[17] Quoted in *Saturday Review*, February 6, 1965, p. 56.

research and development of desalinization processes. He might even decide to use the $1.5 billion and $10 million figures to slow down pork-barreling of further river basin development legislation.

Next, the question can be asked whether an expenditure of about $75 million for water pollution control and of $10 million for air pollution control in FY 1963 constitutes an optimum level. The universal increase in population density and the effluents associated with it make water and air pollution more and more important dangers to urban society.

These are issues that can be readily articulated within the program budget, but such a budget can also lend itself to elucidating relatively new concerns. For example, in early 1965 President Johnson expressed an interest in natural beauty. To preserve and improve the nation's natural beauty, the President proposed new activities that can be funded jointly by three separate agencies— the Land and Water Recreation Fund of the Bureau of Outdoor Recreation, open space land grants of the Housing and Home Finance Agency, and the Highway Trust Fund of the Bureau of Public Roads. In a sense, these activities can be looked upon as a new subprogram.

Finally, we will present an example that applies benefit cost analysis to specific water resources projects and helps compare their relative merits. Our example is the so-called Santa Maria Project,[18] a proposal to provide water for irrigation and protection from floods in the Santa Maria Valley of California. This project involves many complex considerations, only a few of which can be touched upon here. Readers who are interested in more detail should turn to the reference cited below.

The contemplated direct benefits from the Santa Maria Project come from the effect of the water reservoir on the underground water supply, the effect of the reservoir on net farm incomes, and the effect of the project on limiting flood damage. The Vaquero Reservoir portion of the Santa Maria Project was estimated to make it possible, on the average, to replenish the underground water supply of the Santa Maria Valley with an additional 18,500 acre feet per year. The principal effect of replenishing the underground water supply is the irrigation of more acres of land in the valley

[18] The material presented in the following paragraphs was taken from a case study of the Santa Maria Project proposal presented and discussed in detail in Roland N. McKean, *Efficiency in Government Through Systems Analysis* (New York: John Wiley & Sons, Inc., 1958), chap. 12, pp. 214–244.

area. It was estimated that some ten to twelve thousand additional acres could be irrigated if the project were undertaken. This in turn was translated into an estimate of the increase in net farm incomes that might result from having the additional acres of land under irrigation. In terms of 1949 dollars these annual "irrigation benefits" were estimated to be about $1.2 to $1.4 million.

Another expected benefit from the project is a decrease in probable annual flood damage in the valley. Part of the damage-limiting effect would be attributable to the reservoir itself, and part to the channel-levee works. Estimated annual average savings from limiting property damage in the future were estimated to be about $600,000 (1949 dollars).

In addition to the direct benefits outlined above, certain indirect or secondary benefits might be associated with the project. The Bureau of Reclamation defined these as representing the "increased net income from processing, transporting, and merchandising products of the area and from the projected increase in the sale of consumers' goods and services to local farmers."[19] The amount of secondary benefits estimated to be attributable to the project was about $600,000 annually.

The estimated cost of the total Santa Maria Project proposal was prepared in terms of two main categories: (1) the initial investment (primarily construction), assumed to occur over a four-year period,[20] and (2) the annual operating cost, assumed to occur over a fifty-year period. Most of the initial investment cost was assumed to be financed by federal funds, and most of the operating cost was assumed to be met by local governments. The estimated total costs of the project, undiscounted and in terms of 1949 dollars, may be summarized as follows:

Initial Investment (over a 4-year period)	$27 million
Total Operating Cost (for a 50-year period)	36 million
Total	$63 million[21]

[19] *Ibid.*, p. 229.

[20] Initial investment costs include: dam and appurtenant works; camp construction; land, easements, and rights-of-way; clearing the reservoir area; relocation of railroads, highways, and utilities; levee and channel construction; clearing the floodway; contingencies, engineering, and overhead.

[21] The federal portion was estimated to be:

Initial Investment	$26 million
Operating Cost	13 million
Total	$39 million

As indicated earlier, because of the limited space available here all the relevant benefit cost considerations pertaining to the Santa Maria Project cannot be discussed in detail. However, an attempt is made to highlight some of the more important ones.

A brief summary of several of the quantitative benefit-cost calculations for the Santa Maria Project is presented in Table 9.6. Although these data are enlightening, we stress again that they represent only part of the total story and that they should be viewed only as an aid in sharpening the decisionmaker's intuition and judgment. In most water resource project proposals, nonquantitative considerations are usually very important. The Santa Maria Project is no exception.

From the viewpoint of this chapter, Table 9.6 contains some very interesting information, particularly because the question of uncertainty is explicitly recognized. Some highlights of the table may be summarized as follows:

1. The present worth (present value of project outputs minus present value of project total cost) is a positive number, except for very high rates of discount. From this standpoint the project would certainly seem worthy of *consideration* for inclusion in a total water resource program. (However, the fact that the present worth is positive does not in itself *justify* including the project in the total program.)

2. Uncertainty is allowed for in several of the items: the discount rate is varied over a relevant range in items 1 and 2; ranges for present worth are given in item 4.

3. Rough measures of "secondary benefits" are given (items 5 and 6). Whereas these items should not be included among the benefits to the *whole* economy, the induced income effect in the areas adjacent to the project may be a significant consideration.

4. The benefit cost ratio is *not* included in the table. Although such a ratio is popular in water resource circles for ranking various projects, we have cautioned against using ratios for this purpose. So does R. N. McKean, who suggests that if some measure is to be used for ranking projects, the "internal rate of return" (item 7 in Table 9.6) is preferable to the benefit cost ratio.[22] However, even here he injects a note of caution: "attention should not be focused on the

[22] The internal rate of return is defined as the rate of discount that reduces the present worth of the project to zero. For a discussion of the argument in favor of using this concept to rank projects, see McKean, *Efficiency in Government*, pp. 89–92.

TABLE 9.6 Suggested form of cost benefit exhibit, Santa Maria
Project as illustration (in 1949 dollars)

1. Present worth[a] (present value of outputs minus present value of costs)

2½%,	50-year horizon	$24 million
5%,	50-year horizon	4 million
8%,	50-year horizon	−6.5 million

2. Cost that would have to be covered by a national water-resources budget:
Present value of the nation's investment stream:[b]

2½% discount rate	$25	million
5% discount rate	24	million
8% discount rate	23	million

3. Time paths of undiscounted benefits and costs

Streams	Construction (4 years)	1–5	6–10	11–15	16–20	21–25	26–30	31–35	36–40	41–45	46–50
Total benefits	—	8.9	9.0	10.0	10.0	9.9	9.8	9.8	9.7	9.6	9.5
Total costs	26.7	.3	.4	.4	.3	.4	.4	.3	.4	.4	.3
Installation costs	26.7	—	—	—	—	—	—	—	—	—	—
Federal costs	25.5	.1	.1	.2	.1	.1	.2	.1	.1	.2	.1

4. Variability of outcome
Present worth "not likely" to fall outside this range   −$2 to +$4 million[c]
Present worth "extremely unlikely" to fall outside this range
   −$6 to +$10 million[c]

5. Effect on personal wealth distribution[d]
Number of land ownerships (farms, not city lots)   458
Average value of land and buildings per farm-owner in watershed (1950)
   $100,000[e]
Average net benefit to farmers (as distinct from nation) per farm-owner
   $8,000[f]

6. Effect on regional wealth distribution
Average income per family in Basin (assumed to be same as entire county)
   $3,500
Percentage increase of income in Basin due to project   3%[g]

7. Basis for ranking, if required, to facilitate allocation of national water-resources budget[h]
Internal rate of return (rate of discount which reduces present worth
to zero)   6%

Source: Roland N. McKean, *Efficiency in Government Through Systems Analysis* (New York: John Wiley & Sons, Inc., 1958), Table 25, pp. 240–241.

[a] If the exhibits are to be used for the comparison of this project with private investment, property and income taxes paid on private ventures should be allowed for; in this illustration, a rough allowance could be made by reducing the positive present-worth estimates by 45%.

In the estimation of this figure, the venture is looked upon as though it were a large corporation. The corporate income tax, on the average, has been about 45% of net profits in recent years. An allowance for higher property taxes after the project has been allowed for in the estimation of net farm income after the project. No further allowance for property tax on the project is suggested in this case.

[b] The nation's investment stream is the net excesses, in the periods in which they

internal rate of return to such an extent that its limitations or the other items in the table are ignored."[23]

So far, we have focused on *intra*project analysis. Although this is important, the decisionmakers in charge of the total national water resources program eventually have to face up to the question of comparison of, or ranking of, projects. Ideally, one would like to be able to proceed somewhat as follows. Assume that a given budget level is made available for a total national water-resources program, and that a menu of project proposals exists for consideration as an inclusion in the program. Assume further that through an analytical effort a single unique ranking system is devised so that the various projects in the menu can be listed in order of their overall desirability, along with their respective estimated costs.[24] If this were the case, it would be a simple matter for the decisionmakers to proceed down the list of projects and go as far as the given budget level would permit. In fact, however, the real world is quite different. Things are much more complicated, and in particular it is not possible to devise a single unique system for ranking projects. This is not to say that quantitative measures are not useful. They can be,

---

occur, of costs over benefits. In this case, these excesses occur only during the construction period, i.e., during years 1 through 4. It is not clear just what budget is to be allocated, or what costs must therefore be covered by the budget; here it is assumed to be these investment costs from the nation's standpoint.

c Such ranges are believed to be useful supplements to "best estimates" even though precise "probabilities" cannot be associated with them. If one insists on precision the first range might be defined as that in which results would fall 75% of the time (if we could imagine repeated trial runs), the second range as that in which results would fall 90% of the time. These ranges are solely for illustrative purposes; the writer has not dealt with the project enough to have much "feel" for the variability of possible outcomes.

d These indicators of wealth distribution and effects of project on wealth distribution are merely illustrative. Present worth of benefits at 5% was used in estimating these subsidy effects.

e Assumed to be the same in watershed as in entire county; figure (rounded) taken from *County and City Data Book 1952*, p. 112.

f This amount is positive, even if net benefits to the nation are negative, chiefly because farmers do not pay costs that are allocated to flood control.

g Increase in local income assumed to be 1.2 × gross benefits attributed to project.

h The internal rate should not be used as a basis for ranking interdependent projects, such as several possible sizes of a proposal. This figure (6%) was derived by plotting present worth as a function of the discount rate and then by interpolating to find the rate at which present worth appeared to become zero.

23 *Ibid.*, p. 243. McKean also emphasizes that the internal rate of return should *not* be used as a basis for ranking *interdependent* projects or for ranking several possible sizes of a given project.

24 Particularly in the water resources field some people apparently think that using benefit cost ratios (or some other measure) can approximate this ideal state of affairs. As noted previously, we caution against taking such a view.

but they must be studied with care and used along with qualitative information and judgment in reaching final conclusions.

To illustrate some of these points, we turn to McKean's discussion of the Santa Maria Project versus another proposal, the Green River Watershed Program.[25] Pertinent summary data on the latter project are contained in Table 9.7. Regarding comparison of the two projects, McKean writes as follows:

The analyses of the two projects produce exhibits that differ from each other greatly. If the estimates were taken at face value, the Green River project would be an attractive candidate under most water-resource budgets. For a relatively small social investment, it would yield handsome present worths even at fairly high discount rates. The Santa Maria, on the other hand, would require a larger social investment and yield comparatively small present worths. This difference is suggested most vividly by the contrast between the two internal rates of return: 55 per cent on the Green River program and 6 per cent on the Santa Maria project. Moreover, the redistribution of wealth under the Green River program would probably be preferred by most persons to that which would occur under the Santa Maria proposal. The latter, in comparison with the Green River program, would provide large subsidies to a few who seem to be relatively well off anyway, and would stimulate the development of an area which already has an average income per family higher than that in the Green River watershed.

On the other hand, the variability of the outcome—the chance of an outcome much poorer than is indicated by these estimates—is probably greater for the Green River project. Knowledge of the effect of conservation measures on yields in an entire watershed is none too firm. Also, while the social investment is estimated to be comparatively small for the Green River proposal because benefits exceed costs after the first three years, the net outlays *by government units* would be higher than for the Santa Maria project. The actual time paths of costs and benefits should be carefully inspected in the two cases . . . the two projects differ quite a bit with regard to scale of investment. Except in the context of additional projects and a specified budget, one cannot conclude that one should be accepted and the other rejected. For a particular budget, it might be that both should be accepted—or both rejected.[26]

Notice that McKean's discussion steers away from using a single measure for comparing the two programs. He tries to illustrate how

25 For the details of the Green River Watershed Program, see McKean, *Efficiency in Government*, chap. 11, pp. 185–213.
26 *Ibid.*, pp. 243–244.

TABLE 9.7 Suggested form of cost benefit exhibits, Green River Watershed Program as illustration (in 1948 dollars)

1. Present worth[a] (present value of outputs minus present value of costs)

	2½%, 50-year horizon	$550 million
	5%, 50-year horizon	310 million
	8%, 50-year horizon	151 million

2. Cost that would have to be covered by a national water-resources budget: Present value of the nation's investment stream[b]

	2½% discount rate	$7.3 million
	5% discount rate	7.1 million
	8% discount rate	6.8 million

3. Time paths of undiscounted benefits and costs (millions of 1948 dollars):

Streams	1-5	6-10	11-15	16 20	21-25	20-30	31-35	36-40	41-45	46-50
Total Benefits	29	98	166	233	262	265	267	267	267	267
Total costs	33	60	88	115	105	105	105	105	105	105
Installation costs	22	22	22	21	—	—	—	—	—	—
Federal costs	14	14	14	14	2	2	2	2	2	2

4. Variability of outcome
   Present worth "not likely" to fall outside this range $100 to $400 (million)[c]
   Present worth "extremely unlikely" to fall outside this range
                                                        −$100 to $600 (million)[c]

5. Effect on personal wealth distribution[d]
   Average value of land and buildings per farm-owner in watershed
      (1950) $5,000
   Average net benefit per principal beneficiary (in this case,
      per farm-owner) $4,900

6. Effect on regional wealth distribution[d]
   Average income per family in watershed (1950) $1,300[e]
   Percentage increase of income in watershed due to project   20%[e]

7. Basis for ranking, if required, to facilitate allocation of national
      water-resources budget[f]
   Internal rate of return (rate of discount which reduces present
      worth to zero)   55%

Source: McKean, *Efficiency in Government*, Table 14, pp. 206–207.

[a] If the exhibits are to be used for the comparison of this project with private investment, property and income taxes paid on private ventures should be allowed for; in this illustration, a rough allowance could be made by reducing the present-worth estimates by 50%.
   In the estimation of this figure, the venture is looked upon as though it were a large corporation. The corporate income tax, on the average, has been about 45% of net profits in recent years. The effective property tax rate has been about 1.5% of the market value of assets, which amounts to 25% of annual profit if property income is assumed to be 6%. Each tax should be deducted from income before the other is figured; and the combined rate is approximately 50%.
   [b] The nation's investment stream is the net excesses, in the periods in which they occur, of costs over benefits. In this case, these excesses occur in years 1 through 3. It is not clear just what budget is to be allocated, or what costs must therefore be

numerous types of information—including qualitative considerations—may be used to supplement intuition and judgment in evaluating water resource project proposals. Finally, he notes that the scale of the two projects is significantly different. This means that certain quantitative measures, particularly benefit cost ratios, either must not be used at all or used only with extreme caution.

ADMINISTRATIVE AND INSTITUTIONAL ARRANGEMENTS TO IMPLEMENT ALLOCATION DECISIONS

If we are to have effective program budgeting of natural resources activities, we shall have to provide for new institutional arrangements. In forging such arrangements, we should guard against overcentralization, which would be a poor substitute for today's possibly excessive fragmentation.

It appears doubtful that a natural resources program budget would have much impact without a good deal of centralization. Let me illustrate this point. The Bureau of the Budget has combined the submissions of different agencies into a six-year (more recently a four-year) natural resources administrative budget. But it appears that Budget officials are not close enough to these activities to make much use of the long-term budget; and with the fragmented control by various agencies they seem to find little use for it either. A natural resources program budget would make sense particularly if a strong argument could be made for setting up a Department of Natural Resources. However, while some centralization of authority regarding natural resources activities is surely

covered by the budget; here it is assumed to be these investment costs from the nation's standpoint.

c Such ranges are believed to be useful supplements to "best estimates" even though precise "probabilities" cannot be associated with them. If one insists on precision, the first range might be defined as that in which results would fall 75% of the time (if we could imagine repeated trial runs), the second range as that in which results would fall 90% of the time. These ranges are solely for illustrative purposes; the writer has not dealt with details of the Green River Program enough to have any "feel" for the variability of possible outcomes.

d These indicators of wealth distribution and effects of project on wealth distribution are merely illustrative. Present worth of benefits at 5% was used in estimating those subsidy effects.

e Increase in *local* income assumed to be 1.2 × net benefits expected to accrue locally from project.

f The internal rate should not be used as a basis for ranking interdependent projects, such as several possible sizes of a proposal. This figure (55%) was derived by plotting present worth as a function of the discount rate and then by interpolating to find the rate at which present worth appeared to become zero.

warranted, excessive centralization can bring serious disadvantages or costs. If lower level officials are left with very little authority, they lose their incentive to consider and propose alternative courses of action. This is especially important in the natural resources field, where so many decisions are made in regional offices.

Perhaps the principal way to guard against these hazards would be to use a program budget in such a way as to leave considerable authority at lower levels. If a Department of Natural Resources were to be set up, for example, a program budget would be a logical information system for departmental officials to use. But it might be introduced so as not to increase but actually to check the extent of centralization. That is, it could be set up mainly to help officials reach decisions and to enforce *major* program choices, but not as an instrument of detailed control. If used to enforce major allocative choices, it could be designed to permit considerable flexibility in other areas. The scheme should no doubt involve some sort of control over reprogramming or program change proposals. This would require some system of dollar thresholds; if a change would alter a program by an amount in excess of the threshold, central permission would be required. To ensure that lower levels retained some decisionmaking authority—for the sake of both flexibility and incentives—these thresholds could be set relatively high.

While we can see merits in efforts designed to facilitate the effective use of program budgets, we must also present a view that downgrades the importance and usefulness of program budgeting. This view holds that federal public works funds are subject to notorious pork-barreling rather than rational resource decisions as envisaged in benefit cost analysis and program budgeting. Therefore, it has been argued that because the political process does not permit rational natural resources decisions, there is little need for a program budget and the institutional changes to make it work.

We have no special insight on how easy it would be to do away with pork-barrel legislation in the natural resources field. As a matter of fact, we are not very optimistic. However, we do believe that program budgeting and benefit cost analysis can indicate some of the costs of excesses in pork-barreling and perhaps bring about a better blending of political and economic considerations.

Another argument points to the limited usefulness of program budgeting in the natural resources field. It pertains to the overwhelming importance of intangible, noneconomic values associated with natural resources activities. The reply to this criticism is colored by our optimism regarding the capability of dealing with noneconomic variables, and by our view of what we would like program budgeting to do for us. On the first point, my own attitude is that we shall never make progress in difficult areas of inquiry unless we try; on the second point, I merely want to remind the reader of the expressed philosophy of the book, perhaps best stated by Gene Fisher, that "the main role of analysis should be to . . . sharpen . . . intuition and judgment."[27]

Whereas it appears difficult to make a strong case for a Department of Natural Resources, a five-year program budget should be prepared. It would be used mainly as an information system to elucidate major allocative decisions. It would replace the relatively uninformative budget summary of Table 9.1. The main insurance against detailed control would be relatively high thresholds before permission was required for program change proposals or reprogramming. Even in the absence of a Department of Natural Resources it might be useful for the Bureau of the Budget to have what amounts to a Natural Resources Program Budget and use it in budget reviews with relevant departments. More important, the various departments with natural resources funds might be induced to modify their budget formats and exhibits in a way that would permit effective comparisons of resources activities and the integration of their budgets.

[27] G. H. Fisher, *The Role of Cost-Utility Analysis in Program Budgeting*, RM-4279-RC (Santa Monica, Calif.: The RAND Corporation, September 1964), p. 5.

PART III
IMPLEMENTATION AND OPERATION

Chapter 10

LIMITATIONS, RISKS, AND PROBLEMS

BY ROLAND N. McKEAN AND MELVIN ANSHEN

The type of program budget recommended in this book is not a simple proposal for improvement in public administration, easily designed, readily installed, promptly effective in operation. On the contrary, from initial concept to final implementation the project raises difficult and important problems. Unless these problems are recognized at the outset, the recommended innovation may invite overenthusiastic acceptance. This is likely to be followed by the discovery of deficiencies and limitations that could destroy confidence in the entire undertaking. Therefore, the purpose of this chapter is to report frankly on the problems, limitations, and risks of a program budget, and to suggest ways and means of alleviating some and removing others.

The discussion should emphasize one significant point made at the beginning of this book. The purpose of the program budget proposal is to redesign a basic management tool so that the quality and grasp of decisionmaking in the federal government can be improved. The proposal does not open the gates to a public administration utopia, nor does it contemplate the displacement of managerial imagination, judgment, or experience. The hard choices that are inevitably present in any effort to allocate scarce resources among competing claims will remain. Hopefully, they will be aided by a more appropriate and operationally meaningful organization of information on inputs and outputs, above all with information structured in relation to planning, decision, and implementation rather than, as is now generally the case, to assuring integrity in the use of appropriated funds.

Difficulties in the program budget will be examined under three headings: *conceptual*—those encountered in designing the program budget and relating it to the decisionmaking requirements of the executive and legislative branches of the government; *operational*—those related to managerial implementation of the program budget, particularly in the period immediately following its adoption; and *institutional*—those encouraged by bureaucratic or political pressures that are unavoidably present in any organizational setting, public or private. The description and assessment of problems, limitations, and risks will be followed by suggestions for coping with them and at least minimizing their impact and significance.

CONCEPTUAL PROBLEMS OF THE PROGRAM BUDGET

The meaning of the term "program budget" has not become standardized through general use. To some it suggests no more than a restructuring of budget exhibits, accumulating costs in more meaningful categories. This would suggest a budget organized in terms of categories that are closer to being true outputs than the older categories, which, as we see them in the current budget array, are generally inputs with some mixture of ill-related outputs, all heavily influenced by administrative and organization history. Those who hold this view judge such categories to be more useful because they contribute to better assessments of the implications of incremental changes to established programs.

To other people, a program budget implies a budget that employs a longer time horizon than is commonly found in the present federal budget with its forward projection limited to one year. Within the one-year horizon public officials commit themselves to purchase on the installment plan while examining only the size of the down payment. With the longer time horizon the full cost implications of alternative choices are less likely to be neglected (either inadvertently or deliberately).

To still others, the concept of program budgeting includes, in addition, the use of cost-utility analysis, a logical and measuring relation of inputs to outputs. Here the emphasis is on the analytical contributions of the program budgeting process and the consequent increased rationality and efficiency in the use of scarce resources.

Finally, there are those who understand the term to imply all the foregoing plus one significant addition: arrangements for enforcing the allocative decisions through appropriate implementation provisions. Such arrangements might, for example, include institutional reorganization to bring relevant administrative functions under the jurisdiction of the authority making the final program decisions.

With or without reorganization, there would be information reporting systems and shifts in the power structure to the extent necessary to secure compliance with program decisions by the agencies responsible for their execution.

As indicated in previous chapters, the program budgeting concept adopted in this book embraces all four of the items listed above. In other words we are interested in the organization of information for decisionmaking, and our view of decisionmaking is one that continues through implementation. To say this by way of description is not to solve the conceptual problem, however. In fact, it does not even fully define the problem. At best, it does little more than indicate the general approach.

What concept of program array constitutes an efficient design? How many programs should there be? What should their content be? What type of relationship to the decision process should the program structure embody? The central issue to which these questions lead is no less than a definition of the ultimate objectives of the federal government to be implemented through resource allocations. The framers of the Constitution did their architectural work in a similar context, of course, although the objectives they held in view were as much political as economic and, where economic, had a philosophic rather than managerial or operational character. The decisionmaking structure came later and, as we have observed before, under the influence of objectives other than rationality of choice.

Beneath what may be termed the technical problem of designing a new programming-budgetary array, composed of a specific set of programs that are in some sense end objectives and for the achievement of which resources are assigned, lies a conceptual problem. Its nature may be suggested by the question: What is the government trying to accomplish? As presented in Chapter 2, when this question was asked in the Department of Defense in the design stage of its program budget in 1961, a viable and acceptable answer was found in such categories as Strategic Retaliatory Forces, Continental Air and Missile Defense Forces, Airlift and Sealift Forces, and Research and Development. Within these categories it seemed meaningful to identify further breakdowns into such compartments as types of aircraft, unique missile systems, and discrete military or support activities. (See Chapter 5 for more

detail on this subject.) It is by no means clear that comparable
acceptable answers are readily forthcoming for the rest of the
federal government. As the political campaign in the fall of 1964
suggested, "What is government for?" can be a question of philosophy about which strong disagreements boil. The government is,
to be sure, concerned with education, welfare, transportation, research, and other familiar ends; but the nature of its concern must
be defined in terms of rational decision contexts as well as political-
philosophical considerations.

To take one example as a key to the puzzle, it is not just education with which the government is concerned. It is certain kinds of
education, certain levels of education, certain educational clients,
certain educational methods. The character of the decision process
must be influenced by the requirements created by these rather
specific concerns. It would then follow that the program budget
design most efficiently responsive to the needs of that decision
process is one that organizes information in a manner that is relevant to the decision process. After all, the main advantage claimed
for the program budget process over that of the present budget is
that it is designed in relation to the decision process and helps to
make it more effective by clearly defining the alternatives among
which choices must be made and by creating an information system
that permits analytical appraisal of costs in relation to expected
benefits. To bring this about, one must come to grips with such
conceptual issues as whether educational activities within an antipoverty program (such as skill training) should be dealt with in
the decision context of relief for the unemployed or the more
familiar framework of most types of educational activities not tied
to a special class of clients or a special kind of instruction. Above
all, it must be recognized that this is not a problem to be resolved
by a Solomon's wisdom. If there is a "right" answer, it will be
discovered only through study of the logic and logistics of the
federal decision process in the area.

The inadequacy of such study to date does not mean that the
public's business in allocating resources is handled carelessly or
inefficiently in the common sense of the terms. Inefficient management can be assessed on two quite different conceptual levels. (The
more common one appraises performance in implementing a determined decision. It asks whether a given objective has been achieved

with appropriate economy in the use of resources, with an absence of diversion or redundancy in application of assigned funds, and with an appropriate accounting for actions taken. The other concept, less commonly encountered, asks a quite different question: Should this decision be made at all? Or at least should it be made in this way, at this time, in this informational context? The question looks in two directions. The first considers alternative ends and alternative assignments of resources. The second considers what may be achieved in relation to what must be invested, which is what is often called cost-utility analysis. The concept requires a wealth, detail, and array of information altogether different from that called for in the narrow concept of efficiency. The precise character of that information cannot be determined before there has been more study of the entire decision process. This involves examining at least two sorts of complex issues. One is concerned with the kinds of decisions that public administrators should make, as a reflection of the ultimate objectives of the federal government at this stage of the nation's development. The other is concerned with the process of public decisionmaking: its scope, timing, and sequence.

As noted previously in this book, the initial step in designing a program budget for the nondefense sector of the federal government must come to grips directly with the conceptual issue, and the way to do so is to acquire a better understanding of the logic and the process of decisionmaking. The existing organization structure and existing decision practices may not significantly assist—in fact may only obfuscate—such understanding. The bureaucratic structure that is now in being and in operation is largely the product of a historic response to political pressures and expedient adjustments thereto, or in some instances, to haphazard acts of creation for the most part unresponsive to a planned analysis of the needs of efficient decision design. Considering the circumstances of its invention, there is little reason for the bureaucratic structure to reflect a logical decision-determined architecture. From this it also follows that the kinds of decisions made in the current annual budgetary exercise—their character, locale, timing, etc.—cannot be taken as reliable guides to future planning for a rationally ordered program budget. In fact, out of the existing structure and its operating habits must be expected resistance and opposition, corresponding to the familiar human disposition to protect established seats of power and procedures made honorable by the mere facts of existence and custom.

We should be careful to observe that this does not mean that in executing the recommended research the existing bureaucratic structure and the ways in which it gets its business done should be ignored or summarily rejected. We do suggest, however, that the first and most important task is to explore the fundamental issue of the objectives and functions in the federal government, the kinds of problems that arise and demand decision, the ordering of information that would effectively serve administrators confronted with these responsibilities. At a later stage due attention should be given to existing organizations and practices, both to discover additional clues to new insights into the resource allocation process, and to anticipate operating problems of the sort dealt with later in the present chapter. We must, in short, go back to fundamentals. It should be encouraging to note that this is what was done in the first stage of the work that led to the design of the program budget in the Department of Defense.

We emphasize, then, that the desirable decision structure emerging from such study might or might not resemble the existing bureaucracy. The possibility that a new program budget, if adopted and installed, might be implemented more easily or effectively through a new management structure is a separate issue not germane to the present discussion. There may be powerful reasons for retaining all, or most, of the existing structure while installing a new program budget. There are ways of accommodating process and structure that may be well worth using for a considerable period of time. In the long run, of course, it might be reasonable to expect an adjustment of structure to process, but this would not exclude a parallel adjustment of process to structure. Operational experience has a wonderful disposition to smooth jagged organizational interfaces when they are in a continual state of mutual abrasion. Again, we can observe that this process has been at work in the Department of Defense.

The heart of the conceptual problem described above is, of course, the fact that in many areas of government activity, including some in which expenditures in recent years have aggregated billions of dollars annually, few of the objectives have been clearly defined. In view of this circumstance, the recommended research would be pioneer work, subject to all the difficulties and vicissitudes that such an undertaking must confront.

A related conceptual problem must also be dealt with. A program budget structure can be developed around one or several definitional elements. One obvious possible structural element would be end objectives and subcomponents thereof. For example, this would correspond to strategic retaliatory forces being further divided into aircraft and missile systems in the military program budget. Another approach might be an attempt to distinguish between means and ends. This would come to grips with such questions as the classification of irrigation projects as means (to support agricultural development, for example), or as ends in themselves and therefore to be distinguished as discrete items for decision in a program budget structure. Other possibilities will need to be explored, including designs that bear no readily identifiable relation to the kind of distinctions suggested here.

In any event, it should be recognized that the initial program budget structure will need thorough testing in the early years of its use. It is certain that this design will call for amendment and modification (perhaps involving substantial change) as a result of experience in the decision process. Again, it is instructive that private business organizations that have installed information-decision systems resembling the program budget concept have commonly discovered a need to revise their systems in the light of practice as well as the changing nature of their own dynamic decision processes.

OPERATING PROBLEMS OF THE PROGRAM BUDGET

When we pass from the conceptual phase to the operating phase of the program budget, we confront a new series of problems. One of these transition problems is suggested by the gap between identifying a group of activities as an appropriate cluster for a single program or program element and actually bringing together the information applicable to making a program decision about the activity cluster. It will often be the case that activities that make a logical program package are currently scattered through several government departments, bureaus, and divisions. One illustration of such a situation is the international economic activities that can be discovered in a number of administrative units spread throughout the federal establishment. Other examples can be found in activities involved with the development, protection, and exploitation of natural resources; still others, in the field of educational activities. Operating techniques will have to be developed for identifying such elements and assembling them for program budget array and decision.

Doing this is no simple accomplishment. There is the initial task of discovering the relevant cells in multiple departmental budgets. This task, it may be anticipated, might be handicapped by potential bureaucratic resistance stemming from both the desire to retain power and status and the fear that duplications and inconsistencies may be revealed. The resistance arising in the public bureaucracy may be reinforced by opposition from the clients served by and benefiting from existing budgetary arrangements. It would be natural for them to fear any shifts, even of a statistical character, that might invite decisions less advantageous to their interests.

Probably a much broader range of difficulties should be anticipated as a result of the fact that things are not likely to work out neatly and promptly after the introduction of program budgeting. For a time many component cost estimates will probably be extremely poor, in fact may have to be achieved in a somewhat arbitrary fashion. Suddenly, instead of adding the costs of personnel for jurisdictional units with well-established identities and interlocks, personnel and their costs will be allocated among a new set of categories. This immediately suggests many difficult questions. What about personnel that service several different program elements? How should these costs be treated? Or what about operations and maintenance equipment and activities that serve several program elements? Public officials with middle management responsibilities must, perforce, make many of these cost identification determinations, and it would be unreasonable to expect that they will promptly understand what is wanted in a planning decision context and be motivated to deliver it. What this projects is a fair amount of initial confusion, error, and disappointment.

Troubles with the program element structure are also inevitable. One would like to design program elements so that they are relatively independent. In that fortunate case, officials could consider change proposals for the flood-control program element without worrying about repercussions on sewage disposal, disease control, fish and wildlife, recreation, grazing lands, and other program elements. Unfortunately, life is complex, and it is impossible to devise program elements (or even broad programs) that are not, in some degree, interdependent. This means that there should and will be considerable groping at first for an improved program-element structure. As a consequence, there may also be a certain amount of initial frustration with the whole decisionmaking apparatus. The interdependencies are also one of the reasons that a program-budget format should be accompanied by the use of such tools as cost utility analysis to aid program decisions. Thinking in terms of outputs can be clearer than thinking in terms of inputs (with inputs, the interdependencies can be overwhelming), but there are still important spillovers that must be traced out by special analyses.

Moreover, it is likely that the old budget structure will continue to exist side by side with the new one. Congress would in all likelihood wish to use the input categories to which it is accustomed. In addition, for some time agency officials would continue to need the old structure and the services of budgeteers familiar with it. The reason is that program-element costs, at least during the transition, would be so amorphous that although they would serve for broad allocative decisions, they would not serve for program management or "frying the fat" out of programs. For some inputs it may not be wise to constrain the amounts, program element by program element, yet still be desirable to constrain the total amount permitted. Cutting and managing such inputs may need to be done in terms of the old appropriations structure rather than of the new format.

With the two structures, however, there will develop large amounts of paper work, conflicts between program decisions and decisions about input categories, and difficulty in gearing the new system to an annual budget cycle. The nature of the paperwork is obvious, although people are likely to underestimate its extent. Conflicts between program decisions and input cuts may need explanation. As long as some decisions are made in terms of specific input categories, cutting across program elements, they can on occasion disrupt the program budget system, vitiate particular program change decisions, and cause considerable confusion.

Moreover, the possibility of such conflicts makes it desirable to gear the new system rather closely to the annual budget cycle. Other considerations also make this desirable. In principle it would be convenient to let the program budget be altered at any time and to eschew any budget ceilings or deadlines. In fact, however, there *is* an annual cycle (Congress is not about to authorize two-year budgets), and one should have cut-off dates and at least ball-park ceilings for the program budget as well as for the old style budget. Indeed, adjusting to the annual cycle and keeping it an orderly one may be the only way to preserve any energy and time for a serious look at the future program years.

In the longer run, there are other possible difficulties that should be considered. Program budgeting that includes a mechanism for enforcing central decisions may possibly be conducive to centralization of authority. There is no inherent necessity for such a relationship. It is possible to visualize, on the one hand, a decisive and powerful department head (or Bureau of the Budget) without program budgeting and, on the other hand, a decentralized system in which officials are motivated to make use of the information generated by a program budget. Nonetheless, looking at tradeoffs and interdependencies more systematically, making decisions in the light of these tradeoffs and interrelationships, and enforcing these decisions may make increased centralization appear to be more rewarding or less costly than before.

If program budgeting does not contribute any impetus to centralization, many of the following costs should not be charged to the budgeting system. They should be charged instead to whatever forces bring about increased centralization, and program budgeting will simply help decisions to be better than would otherwise be the case.[1] Even if program budgeting does lead to more centralization, of course, it will often be worthwhile. As an analogy, improved techniques for high-voltage transmission will probably lead to increased centralization in the production of electric power. But most people would agree that the net effects will be good, for the disadvantages will be slight (i.e., the costs of having this decrease in competition) and the gains large.

---

[1] If decisionmaking was *sufficiently* centralized, one might possibly prefer that decisionmakers work with poorer rather than better information, but in most parts of "democratic" governments this degree of centralization seems a little farfetched.

If program budgeting might facilitate the growth of central control, however, there are some possible long-run costs that should be weighed against the benefits. Perhaps more important, these costs should be considered in *designing* the system, so that steps can be taken to reduce the costs and increase the benefits wherever possible. Determining the appropriate degree of central control is a difficult task. In a small agency the long-run consequences could scarcely be serious, but in a comprehensive program embracing many activities these costs could be large. There are certainly ways to use program budgeting without excessive centralization (some of which will be discussed later), but the problems and possibilities deserve careful thought.

The nature of these problems can be illustrated in terms of a hypothetical natural resources program. Assume the program packages to be (1) Agriculture, (2) Water Supply and Use, (3) Forests, (4) Outdoor Recreation Capabilities, and (5) Grazing. Because decisions about these matters need to be coordinated, a "Secretary of Resources" has the authority to make final program decisions and enforce them. Approved programs are recorded in a five-year plan. The agencies responsible for the component activities are to submit change proposals whenever a change would increase total obligational authority or transfer resources in excess of designated thresholds. Below-threshold changes are to be listed, submitted to the Office of the Secretary of Resources (OSR), and periodically incorporated in the five-year plan. A reporting system enables OSR to detect departures from the approved program. To illustrate various points, we will keep referring to this hypothetical arrangement.

How it would work depends on many factors, one critical influence being the extent to which lower level officials continue to make significant decisions. If their authority thresholds are low, almost all decisions must be made at the top of the organization. If top management does not give relevant guidance, if lower levels devote their efforts to fighting the system, or if lower levels lose incentives, more and more decisionmaking authority may move upward to the OSR. Consider some of the possible effects of such a development.

One consequence could be the inadvertent suppression of alternatives, despite the fact that a properly functioning program budget should help officials to explore alternatives systematically. If the agencies responsible for the component activities (Water Supply, Agriculture, Forests, etc.) ended up with virtually no bargaining power, their dissenting and clashing views might have no impact. They might speak up, at least for a while, each urging its own position and making alternative proposals, but possibly with diminishing force and influence.

In this circumstance the views of one group (OSR) would come to play a larger role than before. These views are important, even when analytical tools play major roles, because in many government choices judgment has to be decisive. Suppose, for example, the Secretary of Resources was an unswerving proponent of irrigation but had relatively little regard for outdoor recreation. Cost-utility analysis could not settle this issue, because nonquantifiable considerations and uncertainties play too large a role. (The effects of outdoor recreation on personality adjustment and crime may or may not be extremely important; the development of "infant regions" by means of irrigation projects may or may not be of great value. The cost-utility analyst cannot measure these impacts.) Whatever OSR's particular convictions, centralization of authority might foreclose earnest consideration of some alternatives that vigorous interagency bargaining would air more seriously. In the long run, we would need both interagency rivalry and OSR coordination to flush out new alternatives and criticize obsolete functions.

If OSR began to control the sprawling activities in Agriculture, Water Supply, Forests, Recreation, and Grazing in much detail, simplifying its task would become imperative. Fast screening and disposition of alternatives and the use of rules of thumb would be required. In other words, if OSR took on too much, the cost of fully exploring numerous alternatives would become high, and fewer options would be designed and considered. Even if OSR expanded tremendously, its incentives might not be persistently strong without *effective* debate and criticism by the individual agencies.

Without effective bargaining power, the agencies might find *their* incentives to invent and urge alternatives weakened. If they could not get even a toe in the door on new activities, could not influence decisions, could not initiate studies or pilot projects to show how good their proposals were and how bad rival schemes were, they would find it less rewarding than before to think about innovations. Fretting about these matters requires effort. The lower the rewards and the greater the pressures for compliance alone, the less energy there would be to devote to designing alternative courses of action. Would the agencies find it rewarding to analyze choices that were to be made by someone else? In such circumstances the individual agencies might find it more rewarding simply to refrain from rocking the boat.

This influence could shrink the menu of alternatives considered in studies, research, and development pertaining to natural resources projects, investments, and operations. Central control of the studies program could result in harsh screening from a particular point of view. If only one group was out "looking for business," rather than several groups, a narrower menu of studies might seem worth authorizing. There would be only one customer instead of several to consider novel ideas. Thus, if one group and one long-range plan dominated the picture, another aspect of long-range planning (the exploration of unconventional ideas) might be partially sacrificed.

Another aspect is the tendency for analyses of alternatives to become "design studies." When a cost-utility analysis is begun within an agency, participants and successive echelons of reviewers perceive that their superiors frown upon certain alternatives. It seems useless, perhaps even risky, to put the strongest case possible for the unpopular alternatives. Gradually, the arguments against them are stressed or those alternatives are dropped from the study. The project turns into a design study—the design of one "required" system rather than an objective comparison of alternative courses of action.

These studies are still helpful as long as there are rival agencies, because the competition encourages alternative proposals. If the lower level agencies lose too much bargaining power, however, they may lose the motivation to stay in the study competition. OSR itself may become the only producer of studies. Yet these, too, may eventually become design studies. Persons assigned to prepare analyses will recognize what their superiors prefer. (If the Secretary is indifferent, his subordinates are likely to have preferences.) The course of action believed to be favored may be compared with "straw men," or the unpalatable alternatives may drop out of the study entirely.

Consider, also, investment and operations in the several program packages. If authority is too centralized, the five-year plan itself may discourage the quest for alternatives. It projects the approved programs for several years ahead. If the coordinating central group is to exercise control, departures from the programs must be appraised by the group. This means that changes become more difficult than they would be if only overall budgetary limits were being enforced. In other words, it becomes more costly or less rewarding for the organization to design numerous alternatives, consider them, and implement approved innovations.

Moreover, there is likely to be a trend toward proliferation of program elements—the compartments among which resource shifts require special permission. If the central group tries to manage the programs in detail, the responsible employees may feel their need for better "visibility" more keenly than the overall need for flexibility. They may keep shredding out more compartments or program elements, which helps higher authorities to see what is going on but makes resource transfers more difficult.

If there is excessive program control by one group, there are still other factors that may cause resistance to change. Any group that reaches decisions and records them in an official plan quite understandably defends those decisions and resists changes. Also, Congress is likely to complain about excessive reprogramming. Despite the old saying that a wise man changes his mind, most of us believe that frequent changes suggest scatterbrained decision-makers. In any organization dispersal of bargaining power is often required to effect extensive changes.

Other difficulties may develop if our hypothetical OSR is harried and short of staff or if the rival agencies are left with too little bargaining power. Central responsibility for programs several years ahead and a natural desire to keep the agencies from constantly reopening issues may convert what ought to be sequences of decisions into one-shot decisions. For example, choices about research on the conversion of salt water into fresh water, the advanced development of facilities, and investment in specific operational installations ought to be a sequence of decisions. But a long-term plan coupled with excessive centralization might aggregate the tendency to pick the "best" prematurely and become unnecessarily committed to that course of action.

Another long-run consequence of excessive central control of programs could be neglect of part of their impacts. This might strike with special force at one aspect of any proposal's costs and gains: uncertainty. The reasons are the same as those discussed earlier. The judgments of one group would not be as diverse as the judgments of several branches and agencies. One group would be keenly aware of and give emphasis to some contingencies, e.g., to the chances of a technological breakthrough in the desalinization of water. Another group might stress some other uncertainty, e.g., the extent of population shifts or the political feasibility of re-allocating water from irrigation to urban use, but have few doubts about technological developments. There are, in fact, uncertainties above all these and other factors. If bargaining among the groups plays much of a role in shaping program decisions, all these un-certainties are likely to be aired. If one group faces too few checks and balances, its convictions about the future may shape the deci-sions, and the full range of uncertainties is less likely to be considered.

Because of the possible neglect of uncertainties, it is often felt that program budgeting and increased centralization would give a conservative bias to the pattern of choices. In many instances program budgeting might be able to show officials rather formi-dable cost streams without being able to indicate in any tangible way the enormous gains that might be in the offing. This may seem to be a small danger, for pressures in government usually make officials feel potential benefits more keenly than costs. Nonetheless, we should recognize that the *attempt* to make decisions more rational and less responsive to bargaining pressures might intro-duce a conservative bias. Would the transcontinental railroad or the Panama Canal have made the grade in a regime of long-term program budgeting? In such a decisionmaking environment, would research and development or expenditures on education have fared as well as they have done in the past? Again, there is no inherent necessity of introducing an unduly conservative bias in government choices. It would have to come from misuse rather than from proper use of these tools. But the misuse of tools should be recog-nized as a possibility when designing or introducing them.

In addition, as suggested earlier, the magnitude of the task of central control may make it essential to simplify decisionmaking.

One natural way to simplify a decision is to disregard uncertainties. All of us, but especially those with complex administrative responsibilities, continually search for rules of thumb to simplify the process of choosing. It is tempting, indeed often imperative, to neglect the qualifications, the contingencies, the less probable outcomes. A slight dispersal of bargaining power, however (and this is compatible with achieving the major aims of program budgeting), may limit the tendency to shelve some of the uncertainties and simplify decisions.

A further reason why central control of programs may cause uncertainties to be neglected is that lower level groups may also become biased in favor of "safe" proposals. Consider, for example, projects that have high expected values but also a significant probability of turning out poorly. The costs of hedging against these uncertainties or of allowing for them are often hard to explain and justify. Such projects may not seem attractive to a cost-conscious central group. Or, if such proposals are accepted, they may involve overruns, which spell trouble and perhaps internal conflict for the agency. As a result, an agency may veer toward "safer" proposals, with less variable outcomes, but with lower expected values.

If experience developed along these lines, few offbeat studies would survive the screening process, and bold ideas might rarely seem worth exploring. In research and development, where costs and gains are clouded with uncertainties, there would be only one customer rather than several who might sponsor a proposal. If only a few types of ideas or only well-understood ideas could pass the test, explorations would be somewhat like walking down Main Street. In connection with R&D choices particularly, it may be advisable to implement program budgeting in such a way as to assure roles for a diversity of judgments.

Still another way in which program budgeting with central control might facilitate the neglect of uncertainty—although there is no inherent necessity of its doing so—is by increasing the extent of concurrent planning. Segregating the development costs, investment costs, and operating costs of a proposal ought to emphasize that these decisions can be made sequentially. Coupling them with central control, a one-group view of uncertainties, and pressures for a one-shot decision, however, may encourage the planning of these activities concurrently. This seems to happen with central control within branches or agencies; now it might occur in the management of broad programs. Just what is the correct course of action is never clear. Obviously, *all* activities should not be undertaken concurrently. Just as obviously, *all* activities should not be undertaken sequentially, with everything being reviewed every thirty minutes and everything else held in abeyance until each screw is put in place in sequence. Between these extremes the spectrum of possibilities is very wide, and we do not know what is optimal. Nonetheless, really major uncertainties should usually be cleared up before reaching interrelated decisions. Anyway, *if* we want greater awareness of uncertainties and less concurrent planning, a greater degree of decentralization may be called for. The kind of planning that is appropriate varies from one program to the next and from one situation to the next. This is clear in one's personal life. A business trip in which the objectives are crystal clear and the destinations are familiar can be planned and scheduled in great detail, with firm appointments and airline, hotel, and rental car reservations. An exploration of the Kalahari Desert or Arctic lands must also be planned carefully, yet in a very different manner. In the latter case the emphasis will be on planning for contingencies, not on planning for precise appointments and reservations. These two ways of looking ahead can be thought of as "Cook's Tour planning" and "Lewis-and-Clark planning."

In some government programs there are great uncertainties and good reason for trying to invent new courses of action. Objectives are unclear, and there is indeterminacy about human judgments. In other programs there are fewer uncertainties and less reason for hedging against them or exploring new alternatives. Objectives are relatively clear, and human judgment, although always fallible, can hardly stray far from the mark. In the former programs we need something akin to Lewis-and-Clark planning. In the latter we can use something farther along the spectrum toward Cook's Tour planning.

We should plan on the basis of projections that are as accurate as possible. For some programs an accurate projection is that population shifts and consumer demands are highly uncertain (although we will have best guesses), that technological breakthroughs may or may not occur, that certain programs may or may not have major impacts on juvenile delinquency and crime, that political developments affecting related programs are quite unpredictable, and so on. For other programs an accurate projection is that particular events and outcomes are quite likely to occur. Program budgeting and the accompanying control devices should be designed to accommodate these different situations. It should not be a procrustean bed that forces all decisions and activities to adjust to a single procedure and a single degree of central control.

Before ending this section, we would like to make sure that these issues are viewed in the proper perspective. In the discussion we have called attention to some costs or disadvantages that may be attributable, at least in part, to program budgeting. These should be kept in mind; but we must also keep in mind the shortcomings of the alternatives to program budgeting—for instance, the conventional one-year budget in terms of categories that are more nearly like inputs. In calling attention to the limitations and risks of program budgeting, we do not wish to obscure its potential benefits or the limitations of alternative ways of reaching budgetary choices. Similarly, it is appropriate to call attention to the unpleasant side effects of penicillin, but it would be foolish to allow this to obscure its benefits or the limitations of alternative medical treatment.

WAYS TO ALLEVIATE THE DIFFICULTIES

Thus far we have discussed the potential difficulties of program budgeting combined with central controls and the different kinds of planning that are appropriate in different situations. Let us turn now to the possible implications for the design of program budgeting systems. What might be done to avoid or reduce the difficulties and to facilitate the right kind of planning?

Accept diversity of arrangements. First, we should be well advised to accept a diversity of program budgeting procedures and not aim for a single arrangement that applies uniformly to all governmental programs or to all components of programs. A variety of arrangements would no doubt arise anyway, but this may be a virtue rather than a defect. Each arrangement should be specifically adapted to the individual situation.

Link program budgeting with the annual cycle. In principle one might like to avoid any announced budget ceilings, or "firm" programs, or deadlines for submission of change proposals. In this way any change proposals could be considered on their merits at any time; if the prospective gains from a change exceeded the prospective costs, the change would be incorporated in the program. However, Congress is unlikely to abandon the regular annual budget cycle. In addition, such a cycle may be better than the practicable alternatives because it produces a kind of orderliness that may be necessary and it gets decisions made.

Program budgeting needs to be linked with this cycle, so that decisions in terms of program elements do not conflict with decisions in terms of the appropriations categories, and so that decisions can be to some extent decentralized. Programs in their entirety need to be reviewed by lower levels, not just change proposals that initiators think are judicious to offer and not just change proposals taken one at a time. Such reviews have to be executed in the light of deadlines and ceilings, not ceilings that are inviolable in some mystical sense but ceilings and deadlines that give temporary guidance to lower levels. If program reviews are handled in this way and linked with the annual cycle, then (1) some of the work can be decentralized more effectively and (2) cuts in terms of the appropriations categories near the end of the cycle will not have to be deep slashes.

Try to maintain future flexibility. Although a five-year program is supposed to be flexible and provide specific mechanisms for change, it may make change more costly than before, in some ways that are obvious and others that are subtle. Whenever commitments should be postponed, it would be better not to record tentative decisions in the official programs. This could be done by leaving an empty place here and there or by inserting a tentative level of effort but not identifying specific activities. This is bound to occur occasionally (e.g., for basic research), and we are simply emphasizing that this is a good practice and one that should probably be adopted more frequently.

Keep "considerable" decisionmaking authority in the hands of lower levels. We cannot say what "considerable" decentralization of authority means, because it should vary according to the situation. We can discuss it, however, even if the meaning is imprecise. The intention would be partly to keep top levels from being overburdened with minor decisions so that they can focus their attention on the major ones, particularly major planning decisions involving interdependencies among departments or bureaus. The intention would be partly to maintain flexibility by making it simpler to reach certain decisions, make substitutions, and implement resource shifts. But the aim would also be to maintain lower level incentives to seek alternatives, to worry about uncertainties, and to criticize competing proposals.

The design of the program budget system can influence these matters. First and perhaps most important, the thresholds at which lower levels must get the central group's permission to make changes should be fairly high. There is no single figure that should apply to all programs, and any individual threshold should be adjusted as experience is acquired. But the magnitude of these thresholds is important because they play a major role in determining what decisions are left to lower levels, what decisions must be turned over to the central authority, and how much influence and bargaining power the lower levels have. Relatively high thresholds would give lower levels some influence and help maintain their incentives to keep "looking for business." To be sure, branches and agencies would have more leeway to make mistakes and to get at least a toe in the wrong door occasionally, but this would be worthwhile in the long run. Flagrant abuses could probably be deterred; the central authority could make an after-the-fact review, perhaps on a sample basis, of below-threshold changes and should have authority to punish such abuse by shifting functions from one branch to another.

Second and closely related, the conventional budget reprogramming "thresholds" and rules should be relaxed somewhat in comparison with present congressional requirements. The thresholds described above would apply to future program years, but if Congress retained the conventional budget also, reprogramming rules would apply to the current year and the fiscal year in the budget submitted to Congress. Again, although reprogramming cannot be free of central supervision, relatively high thresholds would help to maintain agency bargaining power, initiative, and incentives.

Third, where a diversity of judgments is especially desirable, as in the authorization of studies and exploratory development, the thresholds should be particularly high. Indeed, one can argue that a central program authority (like our hypothetical OSR) should give freedom to a diversity of lower level branches to allocate their budgets for studies and exploratory development. It might be worthwhile, that is, to accept some partial duplication and irrelevant research to insure against a review process that would make these activities consistent with only one view of the future. In areas such as basic research and exploratory development, the dollar amounts involved are typically relatively small. Therefore, the cost of duplication and irrelevant research would also be small.

Before we conclude this discussion of operating problems connected with the program budget, it is important to recognize at least one additional difficulty. The program budget structure recommended in this book requires forward projection of cost estimates for several years in all situations where the cost stream is an essential ingredient of a rational resource allocation decision. Perhaps a five-year projection might be taken as an acceptable general requirement for most programs, although shorter periods might be appropriate for some and longer periods for others (such as a major power, reclamation, and irrigation project; or a long-term commitment for federally financed highway development).

Public administrators and legislators have little experience in developing, evaluating, or using such extended-term cost estimates. The current practice in the case of most new, large activities is to estimate and request funding for only first-year costs, with hardly more than "blue-sky" or "pencil" projections for later time periods. As noted earlier, this has been done not only in the interest of avoiding difficult analysis of future requirements but also to take advantage of camel's nose tactics in winning support for proposals by publicizing relatively modest entrance expenses. Compulsion to think through the total cost implications of long-term undertakings and to give full exposure to their magnitude constitutes a significant part of the argument for the program budget. Rational decisionmaking in assigning such a scarce resource as budget dollars demands more than a knowledge of going-in costs.

The implementation of this new requirement will have to face up to the existing staff inexperience in the development of such cost estimates in terms of realism and validity. It will also call for strategies to overcome or counter opposition from those interested parties who prefer to hide or disguise the true long-term price tags attached to their favored projects.

Extensive educational efforts and strengthening of staff capabilities for cost estimating and analysis will be required in the executive departments, the Bureau of the Budget, and probably the staffs of at least some congressional committees. The major gains to be derived from the use of the program budget as an effective instrument for analysis, planning, and control will depend in large part on the quality of the data presented in the budget operation.

INSTITUTIONAL PROBLEMS OF THE PROGRAM BUDGET

Finally, some comment is in order about the institutional problems that should be anticipated in the design, installation, and operation of the program budget concept. We are dealing here with an operating instrument, not an exercise in arithmetic. The immediate significance of this observation is found in the proposed use of the new tool as the central device in the government's fundamental decisions about the objects and magnitude of federal financial support. This will inevitably be viewed throughout the organizational bureaucracy as a threat to existing, familiar, and manipulatable institutional arrangements. Such a view will by no means be confined to the executive branch of the government. Allied to each executive unit, as sponsors or clients, are legislative and private interests. To many of these interests the program budget will probably appear as a disturbing influence, if not as an outright threat. Its promise to provide better information that is better organized for better decisionmaking will not necessarily assure its welcome. It is unfortunately true that improved decisionmaking grounded in a more rational approach to the resource allocation problem will not be universally appraised as desirable progress. One of the characteristics of better decisions will be identification and possible removal of overlapping and redundant activities. Another will be exposure of ineffective or inefficient employment of resources. A third will be brighter illumination of the long-range cost implications of proposals with relatively painless initial expenses, and consequent harder screening with an accompanying higher rejection rate. And one should not overlook the threat to the existing organization structure and client relationships that many will sense as implicit in the program budget at some indeterminate time following its introduction.

In short, we should anticipate being confronted with the fact that the goals of an enterprise are not necessarily consistent with the goals of its individual component units or with the goals of individual administrators. This is in no sense an argument for withdrawing the proposal. It does, however, urge the importance of frank assessment of future problems and imaginative design of political, organizational, and social strategies to build support for the proposal in both its acceptance and installation phases, and to implement it in such a way as to maximize its usefulness.

In the Executive Office of the President, most importantly in the Bureau of the Budget, one should be able to count on understanding and strong support. Hopefully, key committee chairmen in both the Senate and the House may see in the program budget a decision tool that will help resolve the mass of information with which they struggle annually. Outside the federal government it should be possible to recruit active supporters for the proposal: among business leaders who know from their own management experience the importance of organizing comprehensive and valid information in a planned relationship to a rational decision strategy; among economic, political, and social analysts in business, trade associations, research institutions, and universities; and generally among all informed citizens who want to see their tax dollars used more purposefully and effectively.

Chapter 11

PROBLEMS IN IMPLEMENTING PROGRAM BUDGETING

BY GEORGE A. STEINER

The purpose of this chapter is to examine some of the outstanding problems in implementing program budgeting throughout the federal government.[1] Problems treated are only those that loom as most significant. We shall not be concerned here with technical operational issues.

There is no question about the fact that important milestones have been achieved in introducing program budgeting into federal budgetary operations. The question is not, Shall the use of program budgeting be expanded? It is rather, How fast and in what depth shall program budgeting be further used in the federal government?

The discussion of this chapter is not predicated on the proposition that we must revolutionize the budgetary process by making it all revolve about the single concept of program budgeting. Rather, it is that program budgeting embodies important characteristics that, when used appropriately, will improve the management of our government. In its usage, however, far better results are likely if its introduction is advanced in light of institutional and

[1] I want to expess my appreciation to the other authors of this book for their constructive suggestions, and to students of the subject whose ideas I have acknowledged in references to their works. In addition, I wish to thank the following officers of the Bureau of the Budget for their aid: William D. Carey, Executive Assistant Director; Samuel M. Cohn, Deputy to the Assistant Director for Budget Review; and Raymond E. Kitchell of the Management Improvement and Research Branch. Others who have contributed much to my thinking in the development of this chapter are Henry P. Caulfield, Jr., Director of Resources Program Staff, Department of the Interior; Winston W. Crouch, Pofessor of Political Science at the University of California, Los Angeles; Alan L. Dean, Associate Administrator for Administration, Federal Aviation Agency; Roy E. Moor, Administrative Assistant to Senator William Proxmire; and Murray Weidenbaum, Professor of Economics, Washington University, St. Louis. I am also indebted to Gerald Busch, Director of Planning, Eastern Region, Lockheed Aircraft Corporation, and to Harold Linstone and Harry Biederman of the Corporate Development Planning Staff, Lockheed Aircraft Corporation. To all these helpful critics I am grateful. Neither they nor their agencies, of course, can be held responsible for what I have written.

human realities as well as the multiplicity of purposes to be met in the budgetary process. Lao-tse advised more than a thousand years ago, "Govern a great nation as you would cook a small fish. Do not overdo it."

Any short examination of problems in carrying out program budgeting must be most incomplete. The budgetary process is so huge and complex as almost to defy description. It covers an exceedingly wide range of institutional phenomena and a bewildering mixture of human relationships that operate upon and within the institutional framework. The budget of the federal government is big in dollar numbers. It is even bigger when one considers the totality of human activities devoted to its formulation and implementation. It is still more monumental when one considers the implications of budgetary decisions and actions on people, basic U.S. policy, economic and political institutions, and foreign nations. The budgetary process of the federal government is truly of massive dimensions.

As the process proceeds, it draws into its orbit uncounted laws, governmental folkways and habits, the widest range of human capabilities, decisionmaking at all management levels, and the hopes and aspirations of millions upon millions of people. Each yearly budget exercise is different. As the players change, as the laws change, as the social and economic environment changes, and as human beings change, so does the process. Surface details change a great deal. The system as a whole, however, shows remarkable resistance to swift change.

Furthermore, the budget serves many purposes: "It is both a financial report and a plan for the future. It is also a request for legislation, since congressional approval is necessary if the proposals in the budget are to be carried out. Further, it is an important aid in the management and administration of the government's activities. Finally, it is an economic document, for it must take into account the many ways in which government taxation and spending affect the operation of our economic system."[2]

In this light, it is somewhat cavalier to treat problems of implementation so succinctly as is done here. The treatment is clearly more illustrative than definitive.

[2] *The Budget in Brief* (Washington, D.C.: U.S. Government Printing Office, 1964), p. 5.

A PROGRAM BUDGETING CONCEPT

Although previous chapters have discussed program budgeting concepts and have described some recent advances in great detail, it seems worthwhile to comment briefly on one concept here.[3] The principle of rationality in choosing among alternative courses of action is central to effective program budgeting, but the meaning of program budgeting is much broader. It embraces three major elements: structural, analytical, and informational.

The structure of program budgeting has several important features. Outstanding is the fact that programs are generally, although not always, end-product oriented. They are functional rather than a mixture of component programs, installations, equipment, maintenance and operations, research and development, and so on. Conceptually, these programs should be composed of all cost elements associated with their attainment.

Of great structural importance is the idea that meaningful programs should be concerned with specific objectives covering an appropriately long period of time. In government, past and current budgeting centers predominantly on short time periods. The modern concept of program budgeting emphasizes the long-range perspective. This is a framework within which short-range specific decisions are made. Behind current annual budgets there exists sophisticated long-range planning.

Programs differ, of course, depending on levels of decision-making. The President deals largely with programs encompassing broad functional areas, such as the antipoverty program, the agricultural program, the national security program, and the space program. At lower levels in the administrative hierarchy less comprehensive subprograms are required. This is a different structure from the one used in conventional federal governmental budgeting. It is also predicated on a much different philosophy from that of conventional budgeting.

The second major element in program budgeting is its analytical process. The heart of the process is emphasis on a systematic examination of alternative courses of action and their implications. This

---

[3] The following concept of program budgeting is from George A. Steiner, "Program Budgeting: Business Contribution to Government Management," *Business Horizons*, vol. 8, no. 1, Spring 1965, pp. 43–52, *passim*.

process has a variety of names, such as cost-benefit analysis, cost-effectiveness analysis, systems analysis, operations research, and others. In Chapter 3 the phrase cost-utility analysis was suggested. Being new, this phrase is probably less confusing than the others.[4]

We cannot here fully describe the analytical process, but a few comments are important. This tool systematically examines costs required to pursue a program and achieve the objectives sought. It also seeks to measure the benefits, gains, or advantages for achieving the objective by each alternative means chosen for examination. It is a concept requiring calculation of all major costs and benefits that make comparisons relevant. It makes comparisons of alternatives from measurements of a common denominator, usually money. It seeks to explore the important long-range implications of alternative decisions.

Cost-utility analysis is only one major tool in helping managers choose among alternatives. It is not at all inherent in program budgeting that cost-utility analysis "*makes* the decision for a manager" or is the sole basis for decision. As Fisher points out, cost-utility analysis plays a somewhat modest, though very significant, role in the overall decisionmaking process. Most major long-range planning decision problems are ultimately resolved primarily on the basis of intuition and judgment. What then is the role of cost-utility analysis? It is to sharpen this intuition and judgment. It is to ask the right questions and put them in a logical array of importance. It is to design, as scientifically as the question warrants, the most objective evaluation possible of the cost of alternative programs in relation to their values. It is a way of thinking. Cost-

---

[4] A semantic problem immediately arises, of course, in attempting to use cost-utility analysis to cover a broad analytical area. In commenting on this point, Alan Dean observed: "While all of these techniques have a potential role in cost-utility analysis (to use Gene Fisher's phrase) each is susceptible to distinctive definition and an effort should be made to appreciate the differences between the analytical techniques. For example, I see cost-benefit analysis as simply the effort to measure tangible and intangible benefits against the cost of achieving those benefits. On the other hand, cost-effectiveness analysis is usually most valuable in selecting alternative approaches to the achievement of a benefit already determined to be worth achieving. Operations research has acquired a specialized meaning as a field utilizing advanced mathematical techniques, particularly model building, as an aid to decisionmaking. I would doubt that we can replace references to the use of these specialized techniques by even as useful a phrase as 'cost-utility analysis.'" These are, of course, concepts that overlap in meaning. This is not the place to attempt a clear-cut line of demarcation among them; but the meaning of the term cost utility in the analysis of this chapter is, I think, clear.

utility analysis is a powerful tool for measuring the advantage of achieving an objective by the use of a dollar expenditure in one way versus another.

The third principal element in program budgeting is the data system to provide the information needed to accomplish the above two functions. The system must in the first instance, provide information that will aid in the specification of possible objectives. It must next provide the data required for choosing among alternatives. This means the collection of all pertinent costs to be incurred over a time period spanning the achievement of an objective. Benefits to be derived from the expenditure must also be calculated. They should be arranged in a fashion to help managers decide among alternatives. The information system must also provide appropriate progress reporting and control of actual expenditures.

Program budgeting in modern government demands an intimate interrelationship or fusion of budgeting and long-range planning. Both are indispensable elements of a sophisticated and comprehensive planning and budgeting system. Although each has different characteristics and functions in the system, they blend in operation. Robert S. Herman expresses their interdependence as follows: "Long-range planning without regard for the realities of annual budget implementation becomes an academic exercise of little operational value; budget-making which disregards the coordinated needs of the development plan tends to fragmentize the energies of the nation and to retard progress toward national objectives."[5] More will be said later about this matter.

DEVELOPMENT OF PROGRAM BUDGETING[6]

So much for the concept. A very brief sketch of the roots of the principal elements of the program-budgeting concept may now be in order as a useful perspective for what follows. Elements of pro-

[5] "Two Aspects of Budgeting," *Indian Journal of Public Administration*, vol. VIII, no. 3, July–September 1962, p. 319.

[6] This book is concerned with program budgeting in the federal government. The following treatment, therefore, deals only with the federal government. It is worthwhile, however, to pause and consider the fact that program budgeting not only has a longer heritage in state and local governments but is practiced rather widely. Early in this century local governmental reform resulted in budgetary procedures that can be considered predecessors to program budgeting. Many states now adopt program budgeting. See Eugene R. Elkins, *Program Budgeting*, Publication No. 14,

gram budgeting have been embodied in various parts of the federal budgetary process almost from its beginning. Applications were sporadic, however, until the 1930's, when both the Department of Agriculture and the Tennessee Valley Authority employed program budgeting.[7] Other federal agencies began to develop budgets on a program basis, and in 1949 the Commission on Organization of the Executive Branch of the Government (Hoover Commission) recommended that the entire budgetary concept of the federal government be refashioned by the adoption of a budget based on functions, activities, and projects. The Commission designated it a "performance budget."

Although the advice of the Commission was not followed completely, it did have an impact. The 1949 amendments to the National Security Act of 1947, for example, provided for performance budgeting in the Department of Defense. The Budget and Accounting Procedures Act of 1950 provided for an executive budget based on the functions and activities of government but did not use the phrase performance budget. In accumulating the FY 1951 budget, the Bureau of the Budget stimulated performance budgeting throughout government.

When reviewing this experience, the second Hoover Commission in 1955 re-emphasized its first recommendation and in the process "in the interest of clarity" used the phrase program budget rather than performance budget. This is what it recommended:

That the executive budget continue to be based upon functions, activities, and projects adequately supported by information on program costs and accomplishments, and by a review of performance by organizational units where these do not coincide with performance budget classifications.

Bureau for Governmental Research, West Virginia University, Morgantown, West Virginia, 1955. In 1963 a legislative committee of the State of California advocated that each budget be accompanied by a long-range projection of its consequences and by proposed long-range programs to keep abreast of state growth. See Assembly Interim Committee on Ways and Means, *Report on Long-Range Program and Budget Planning, Assembly Interim Committee Reports,* vol. 21, no. 5 (Sacramento, Calif.: Assembly of the State of California, January 7, 1963.) State and local government activities lend themselves readily to program budgeting. Program budgeting in these areas, however, is still far from reaching optimum utilization.

[7] Jesse Burkhead, *Government Budgeting* (New York: John Wiley & Sons, Inc., 1956), p. 134 and chap. 7.

That the agencies take further steps to synchronize their organization structures, budget classifications, and accounting systems.

That executive agency budgets be formulated and administered on a cost basis.[8]

Just about this time formal comprehensive long-range planning began to grow by leaps and bounds among the larger corporations of the nation.[9] The movement was reflected in the executive branch of the federal government with a lag of several years. A few important milestones in the development of program budgeting in the executive branch are presented to catch the flavor of this event.

In his budget presentation for FY 1952, President Truman said that the financial program of the government could not be planned in terms of a single year. It had to be prepared, in light of security, economic, and budgetary goals, for the next three and possibly four years ahead. Not until ten years later was his recommendation implemented in practice. Along the way, support was given to the idea by the success of the Department of the Interior with Congress in receiving approval for FY 1956 for its "Mission 66" (a ten-year program for the National Park Service). This stimulated interest among other agencies in long-range planning. Probably the first official comprehensive long-range projection of all federal expenditures was made in 1961. Judiciously waiting until the Eisenhower administration was ready to leave office, the Director of the Bureau of the Budget released his ten-year projection of all federal expenditures.[10] In the same year the Federal Aviation Agency placed all its programs on a five-year planning basis; it was probably the first agency to do so. Program budgeting was also introduced in 1961 in the Department of Defense with dramatic and far-reaching improvements in decisionmaking. This development was described in detail in Chapter 4.

In preparing the FY 1963 budget, a number of agencies at the suggestion of the Bureau of the Budget made five-year projections that were reflected in the budget-making process of that year.

[8] *Budget and Accounting* (Washington, D.C.: U.S. Government Printing Office, June 1955), pp. 13–14.

[9] See George A. Steiner, ed., *Managerial Long-Range Planning* (New York: McGraw-Hill Book Co., Inc., 1963), chap. I.

[10] *Ten-Year Projection of Federal Budget Expenditures,* Special Study, January 18, 1961 (mimeo.).

Similarly, in the preparation of the FY 1964 and FY 1965 budgets the Bureau encouraged budget preparation on the basis of long-range plans. In calendar year 1964 preparation of the FY 1966 budget proceeded in two broad stages. First, a spring preview was made on the basis of information about agency goals and programs through the decade. Second, in the annual fall budget submissions, agencies were asked to submit information covering the past year, the current year, and the next three succeeding years—a five-year time span ending in mid-1969.

The congressional voice calling for more factual bases for budgetary decisionmaking also has been growing louder in recent years, although it has by no means yet reached *fortissimo*.[11] Following are a few highlights of this development. The Eighty-Fourth Congress passed Public Law 801 (which will be discussed later), obliging those asking for new legislation of certain magnitudes also to present long-range plans. During the years since, a number of committees in both Senate and House have discussed and voiced approval of program-budgeting concepts. In 1963, for example, a Joint Economic Committee report concluded: "The Federal budget should be presented on a program basis. The program classification should be based upon an overall index system, such that appropriations requests can still be made on an agency basis by the functions performed."[12] This is not an isolated quotation but was based on a thorough analysis of the budgetary problem and elaborated at great length.[13] In a variety of documents Congress has approved and applauded the new budgetary procedures in the Department of Defense. One member of the House Appropriations Committee has said: "We have been talking in the past several years about program packaging with long-range cost projections. Basically my committee believes this approach is valid. Cer-

[11] For a more detailed history of efforts to reform budgetary procedure, see Joseph P. Harris, *Congressional Control of Administration* (Washington, D.C.: The Brookings Institution, 1964), chaps. 3 and 5.

[12] *The Federal Budget as an Economic Document,* 88th Cong. 1st Sess., Report No. 396 (Washington, D.C.: U.S. Government Printing Office, 1963), p. 9.

[13] *The Federal Budget as an Economic Document,* prepared for the Subcommittee on Economic Statistics of the Joint Economic Committee, 87th Cong., 2d Sess. (Washington, D.C.: U.S. Government Printing Office, 1962). See also *The Federal Budget as an Economic Document, Hearings before the Subcommittee on Economic Statistics of the Joint Economic Committee,* 88th Cong., 1st Sess. (Washington, D.C.: U.S. Government Printing Office, 1963).

tainly it has been, and I hope will continue to be, a very helpful tool to all of us. Many of the Members have been urging a program of this type for several years."[14]

Each year, for many years, members of Congress have advanced bills to reform the budgetary process. In the current Eighty-Ninth Congress, for example, House Resolution 42 has been presented by Congressman Lipscomb to help Congress better evaluate budgetary requests. In the Senate, Senate Bill 2 was introduced in January 1965, authored principally by Senator John McClellan but co-authored by a large number of Senators, "to amend the Legislative Reorganization Act of 1946 to provide for more effective evaluation of the fiscal requirements of the executive agencies of the Government of the United States."

This thumbnail sketch indicates growing pressure for comprehensive and systematic planning that covers a broad time spectrum and embraces program budgeting. This interest is in tune with the widespread efforts in industry to develop more scientific decision-making tools to help managers. No survey exists to measure how much program budgeting is actually performed now in the federal government, in the sense that the concept is used here. Parts of the process are used in a number of agencies. The pressure is for an ever wider adaptation. As this pressure persists, and it will, problems of implementation will expand. Some of the major issues should now be discussed.

BARGAINING IN THE BUDGETARY PROCESS

One important advantage of program budgeting is that it seeks to focus hard, pertinent, factual information at the appropriate points in the decisionmaking process where alternative choices are made. In this process, program budgeting brings to bear relevant economic, social, and technical considerations. These, however, must be mixed with political considerations in the final decision. It cannot be said that in a political democracy economic values have a higher relevance than political values. Both must be merged.

[14] Daniel J. Flood, "Responsibilities of the United States House of Representatives Committee on Appropriations," *The Armed Forces Comptroller*, vol. VIII, no. 4, December 1963, p. 21.

The forge of decision sets the degree to which each is ordered. The amalgam varies from decision to decision and from time to time. The interrelationships between quantitative and qualitative considerations also differ from case to case.

One dominant characteristic of our political democracy is fragmentation of, and checks and balances on, the exercise of power. Naturally the budget of the nation draws pressures from particular interest groups to make decisions to their satisfaction. These special interests focus at all stages and levels of the budgetary process. In fact, the budget is so important in the totality of national life that it attracts the strongest pressures that can be exerted in the political process.

Aaron Wildavsky, in a book dealing with political aspects of budgeting, summarizes this fact in the following passage:

The process we have developed for dealing with interpersonal comparisons in government is not economic but political. Conflicts are resolved (under agreed-upon rules) by translating different preferences through the political system into units called votes or into types of authority like a veto power. There need not be (and there is not) full agreement on goals or the preferential weights to be accorded to different goals. Congressmen directly threaten, compromise, and trade favors in regard to policies in which values are implicitly weighted, and then agree to register the results according to the rules for tallying votes.

The burden of calculation is enormously reduced for three primary reasons: first, only the small number of alternatives politically feasible at any one time are considered; second, these policies in a democracy typically differ only in small increments from previous policies on which there is a store of relevant information; and, third, each participant may ordinarily assume that he need consider only his preferences and those of his powerful opponents since the American political system works to assure that every significant interest has representation at some key point. Since only a relatively few interest groups contend on any given issue and no single item is considered in conjunction with all others (because budgets are made in bits and pieces), a huge and confusing array of interests is not activated all at once.

In the American context, a typical result is that bargaining takes place among many dispersed centers of influence and that favors are swapped as in the case of logrolling public-works appropriations. Since there is no one group of men who can necessarily impose their preferences upon others within the American political system, special coalitions are formed to support or oppose specific policies. Support is sought in this system of fragmented power at numerous centers of influence—Congressional committees, the Congressional leadership, the President, the Budget Bureau, interdepartmental committees, departments, bureaus, private groups, and so on. Nowhere does a single authority have power to determine what is going to be in the budget.[15]

Expansion of program budgeting must reckon with the entrenched interests focused on contemporary budget making. As noted in the above quotation, political influence is exerted throughout most of the budget-making process, in the executive as well as in the legislative branches of government. But Congress occupies a unique position in the entire process. Because so many critical budgetary decisions are made in Congress, and because so much that is done in the executive branch reflects the institutional and human forces at play in Congress, an examination of the budgetary process in Congress with respect to program-budgeting implications is now in point.

BUDGET MAKING IN CONGRESS

It is trite to say, but is nonetheless poignantly understood in the federal government, that "the President proposes and the Congress disposes." More precisely, Congress has the final responsibility, subject to constitutional limitations and the Presidential veto, to decide which activities shall be supported financially by the federal government and what amounts to distribute for them. A minor modification is the extent to which agency heads in the executive branch may fail to spend money appropriated by Congress or may shift funds in order to accomplish more or less than Congress had intended. The latter cases, however, are so minor in terms of the aggregate budget activities of government as to merit no further notice here.

Budgetary appropriation requests presented to Congress by the President are only requests, not final decisions on appropriations. Final decisions on actual appropriations, thus on expenditures, are made not in the pages of the official Presidential Budget Message

---

[15] *The Politics of the Budgetary Process* (Boston: Little, Brown & Co., 1964), pp. 130–131. Other writers on this subject have made the same point. See, for example, Charles E. Lindblom, *Bargaining: The Hidden Hand in Government*, RM-1434-RC (Santa Monica, Calif.: The RAND Corporation, February 22, 1955).

but in the halls of Congress, generally behind doors closed to students of budgeting as well as to the press, the public, and even the agencies that depend on the decisions for the flow of funds to carry out their assigned and desired functions.

Whereas Congress has the final authority, the executive branch can and does exert powerful pressures on Congress. The sheer magnitude and complexity of the executive budget limits congressional power over it. Despite the wide publicity frequently given to changes made by Congress in the budget presented by the President, important alterations are usually relatively few and minor. The exception is often, of course, for a program encountering a high degree of partisan or congressional hostility. One top executive of a major government agency expressed this point to me in the following way: "It is our experience . . . that the decisions made by the President upon recommendation of the Bureau of the Budget are far more significant and affect much larger amounts of money than those made by the Congress in its actions on the President's budget." The President does have enormous power, which he exercises, in seeking the concurrence of Congress with his budget requests. This is not surprising because the purpose of the Budget and Accounting Act of 1921 was to give him such responsibility and because the successful adoption of his budget requests is so important to the conduct of his office.

From a distance, the appropriations process—like the portion of an iceberg seen above water—appears to be simple in form and clearly defined. Very briefly, the budget is presented to the House of Representatives, where it is referred to the House Appropriations Committee. This committee divides the budget along agency lines into twelve to fifteen pieces, and it is never reassembled in Congress. Each appropriation bill is considered by a separate subcommittee, and after public hearings each subcommittee reports its appropriations bill to the full committee, where it is reviewed and revised. Then each bill is sent to the floor of the House for approval. Subsequently the same procedure takes place in the Senate. If differences exist between the two, a conference committee of the two Houses reconciles them, and a final set of appropriation bills is prepared for the approval of both Houses.

The details of what really happens in Congress differ from this popular account. The Budget Message of the President is submitted to both Houses of Congress simultaneously, and both Appropriations Committees (Senate and House) consider the bills during the same period. Hearings sometimes are conducted on a particular appropriation measure in the Senate before the House has completed action. Moreover, nothing in law—though much in custom—prevents the Senate from passing appropriation bills before the House does.[16] Generally, the Senate committee is in a position to begin hearings and report out bills within a few days after House passage. A great part of the hearings before the Senate committees are appeals to restore House cuts.

Appropriation bills are divided along agency lines, and the lines employed are usually redrawn slightly with each session of Congress. The House Appropriations Committee determines the demarcations each year. There are, however, some noteworthy exceptions. The Forest Service, for example, is in the Department of Agriculture (and is so shown in the budget), but the Service's budget is considered with the Department of the Interior. The Bureau of Reclamation is in the Department of the Interior, but the Bureau's budget is included in a Public Works Appropriations Bill, as is that of the Atomic Energy Commission. Defense Department appropriations can be found in the Defense Appropriations Bill, the Military Construction Appropriations Bill, and the Public Works Appropriations Bill.

Hearings vary in nature. Some are public, but some are not, especially where classified material is involved. Much material is simply submitted in written form for the record. In all cases the number and types of witnesses are limited, usually by the staff of each subcommittee speaking on behalf of its chairman. Rarely does the Bureau of the Budget testify, even though it typically helps the President make the final decisions on appropriation requests. (However, a decision was made in 1965 for the Director of the Bureau of the Budget and the Secretary of the Treasury to sit with the full fifty-member House Appropriations Committee for a comprehensive briefing and question-and-answer session on the entire budget of the President.) Agencies customarily testify. A high degree of

[16] This, of course, has been a matter of vehement debate on occasion between the two Houses. See, for example, *Congressional Record*, 87th Cong., 2d Sess. (Washington, D.C.: U.S. Government Printing Office, July 9, 1962), pp. 12898–12918, and (July 16, 1962), pp. 12762 ff. The question is essentially whether the force of custom has become as strong as law.

allegiance—both in appearance and in fact—is paid by the agencies to the President's decisions in the budget rather than to the agencies' own frequently higher requests.

The full appropriations committees and the two Houses rarely consider at length or significantly revise subcommittee decisions. A substantial appropriations measure frequently receives less than an hour's attention by the full committee. On the floor of the House and Senate the debate typically runs less than a day in length, and most of the recommendations of the appropriations committees are accepted by the two Houses of Congress. Case histories of recommendations show that in both Houses they are accepted nine out of ten times.[17]

Why is so little attention given to appropriations outside the appropriations committees? Why are the recommendations accepted with such comity? One reason is that members of the subcommittees possess a near monopoly of information on the bills, and great research is required to challenge successfully decisions made from such a strong position. Budget concepts, appropriation accounting, and agency budget schedules (along with the accompanying program and financial data) are complex and far from easy to understand. Subcommittee members have learned about them and in many cases have become experts through long background and experience in the budget process. Other members of Congress, frequently busy with other complex matters, have not had the time or the experience to become equally conversant with concepts and numbers or with program substance. Under such circumstances, members are reluctant to contest the usually unanimous subcommittee recommendations. Among other things, like all of us, they do not want to appear naïve or uninformed. Also, membership on the appropriations committees is highly desired, and dominant figures in both Houses are represented. In the Senate, subcommittee membership usually represents a substantial proportion of the full Appropriations Committee. There is a spirit of cohesion in these groups. One Capitol observer describes it in the House in

[17] Richard F. Fenno, Jr., found that out of 443 House Appropriations Committee recommendations, a total of 87.4 per cent were completely accepted. See his "The House Appropriations Committee as a Political System: The Problem of Integration," *The American Political Science Review*, LVI, June 1962, p. 323. Wildavsky, *The Politics of the Budgetary Process*, pp. 54–55, studied case histories of thirty-seven bureau recommendations and found just about the same results.

these words: "The House Appropriations Committee is an uncommonly self-contained group. Its fifty members exhibit a strong spirit of unity which crosses party lines and pits them against the Executive, the Senate Appropriations Committee across the Capitol, and the House of Representatives itself. They voice grave fear about the consequences of any differences among them. As one senior member has explained, 'If we don't have a bill that we can all agree on and support, we ought not to report it out. To do that is like throwing a piece of meat to a bunch of hungry animals.' "[18] The data on recommendations fully accepted hardly warrants the simile. Rather, it is nearer the truth to say that most basic congressional decisions on the budget are made in the executive sessions of the appropriations subcommittees.

The power of committee chairmen is majestic. Usually strong and decisive, fully aware of their power, and recognized as preeminent in their committee's jurisdictions by other members of Congress, these men have tremendous authority over the legislative enactments and appropriations of agencies in the executive branch. It is not at all unusual that those in executive agencies concerned with budgetary matters usually pay the greatest deference to these men whose decisions are vitally important to the agencies.

On what bases are the decisions made? To what extent do economic considerations determine economic decisions? What measures for decisionmaking are used? These are not easy questions to answer. The inside workings of the appropriations committees are not generally known. Very little exists in the literature on the subject. Some light may be shed, however, by a fleeting look at sources of information available to the subcommittees, the pressures exerted on the subcommittees, and an appraisal of how these pressures are reflected in decisions.

The executive agencies of government are major sources of information. Item-by-item justifications are prepared and presented to the subcommittees. Through hearings and other means of communication, fuller explanations are available to the congressional subcommittees as well as to other interested members. Lobbyists provide another source of information. Every government expendi-

[18] Douglas Cater, *Power in Washington* (New York: Random House, 1964), pp. 153–154.

ture benefits some group in the economy, and most groups are vocal and touchy about their interests. Many lobbyists are informed comprehensively on the programs in which their constituents are interested and are eager to provide Congress with information about the impact of specific expenditures on individuals, institutions, and regions. Constituents themselves, of course, supply information. Their views are heard in every congressman's office. Agents of Congress, including the instrumentalities of Congress such as the General Accounting Office, the staffs of the appropriations committees, and the staffs of the individual congressmen and senators, represent another lode of information. Finally, members of Congress do not come to an appropriation request newborn; they bring their own experiences, knowledge, and values to the decisionmaking process.

This last point merits further explanation. Individual congressmen and senators frequently have had many years' service on particular subcommittees and have thereby gained detailed knowledge of agencies under their purview. Many of these men have long memories of actions taken on particular programs in previous years. One member of the House Committee on Appropriations and of the Subcommittee on Department of Defense Appropriations has said:

Sometimes I feel that there are Members of our subcommittee who have a better grasp of the problems of the military services and the military posture of this country than many of the civilians and men in uniform making decisions in the Defense Department. Those of you who have been privileged, and this is a matter of personal opinion perhaps, to come before the Committee, I'm sure are familiar with what I have said over and over again, "that Admirals and Generals come and go like Greyhound buses before this committee, but we have to stay here and bear the brunt of what goes wrong in the Defense Department."[19]

In Congress, budget making is principally a political process. It is conducted in the political arena, for political purposes and political advantage. Congressmen represent their districts, and the interests of the districts are reflected in their decisions. But there are also other influences on congressmen. The results, therefore, reflect the balancing on political scales of a variety of forces, particularly in the subcommittees of the appropriations committees.

[19] Daniel J. Flood, "Committee on Appropriations," p. 19.

Members of subcommittees also accept roles and have perceptions that influence decisionmaking. One important characteristic of budget making today is that it is incremental. The base of measure is what was appropriated and spent last year and the year before. A philosophy of "holding the line," of withstanding pressures for appropriations increases, favors a process of permitting only marginal increases each year.[20] Such a philosophy is far from an equation of marginal dollars to achieve maximum advantage. It bears not on the achievement of long-range goals but on withstanding relentless pressures for annual budgetary increases. This philosophy is naturally reflected in the budget process that takes place in the executive branch before a presentation is made to Congress. Maurice Stans, Budget Director in the Eisenhower Administration, once coined a statement that reflected this. "Effective budgeting," he said, "is the uniform distribution of dissatisfaction." This has since been known as "Stans' Law."

While much of the budgetary process reflects this fact, there are notable exceptions. The programs of the National Aeronautics and Space Administration have been debated in terms of long-range goals, costs, and benefits—as also have been programs of the Department of Defense, the Federal Aviation Agency, and various reclamation and water projects. This does not mean, of course, that decisions with respect to programs of these agencies do not reflect important political considerations. They do. But the congressional budgetary decisions for these agencies in recent years have not been dominated by the old incremental philosophy.

[20] One student of the attitudes of Appropriations Committees describes them as follows: "Each executive official is seen to be interested in the expansion of his own particular program. Each one asks, therefore, for more money than he really needs, in view of the total picture, to run an adequate program . . . As an immediate goal, committee members agree that they must strike a highly critical, aggressive posture toward budget requests, and that they should, in principle, reduce them. In the words of the Committee's veterans: 'There has never been a budget submitted to the Congress that couldn't be cut.' There isn't a budget which can't be cut 10 per cent immediately . . . The workaday lingo of the committee member is replete with negative verbs, undesirable objects of attention, and effective instruments of action. Agency budgets are said to be filled with 'fat,' 'padding,' 'grease,' 'pork' . . . and 'soft spots.' The action verbs most commonly used are 'cut,' 'carve,' 'slice,' 'prune,' 'whittle,' 'squeeze,' 'wring,' 'trim,' 'lop off,' 'chop,' 'slash,' 'pare,' 'shave,' 'fry,' and 'whack.' The tools of the trade are appropriately referred to as a 'knife,' 'blade,' 'meat axe,' 'scalpel,' 'meat cleaver,' 'hatchet,' 'shears,' 'wringer,' and 'fine tooth comb.' Members are hailed by their fellows as being 'pretty sharp with the knife' . . . Executives are urged to put their Agencies 'on a fat boy's diet.' Budgets are praised when they are 'cut to the bone.' "

The most obvious, glaring deficiency of the congressional budgetary process is that the budget is handled piecemeal. There is no effort carefully to relate revenues and expenditures. There is no systematic effort to consider program requests on the basis of the advantages in spending additional dollars on one program as compared with another. There is no effort to look at expenditure requests in terms of coordinated future goals, needs, plans, or national conditions. The orientation is last year's base! The whole process is further removed from program budgeting because once the appropriations measures are passed in Congress, large supplemental and deficiency requests are then considered.

Nor is this all. The congressional process sets the tone for budget making in the executive branch. Predominant in the mind of every executive in the executive branch is getting requested appropriations through Congress. The final allocation is, of course, the prize. Everything else is merely preliminary. Strategies, procedures, policies, and appropriations requests are all developed with this in mind.

In this system there do exist barriers to any rapid expansion of program budgeting. However, as noted previously, there is a growing interest in Congress in program budgeting. Impediments to a rapid expansion of program budgeting exist in the executive branch and must not be underestimated. Before the discussion of some of the major ones, it may be interesting to review briefly the appropriations history of the National Environmental Health Center, which illustrates the fascinating play of complex forces on budget making in government. (Of course, any description of these forces, however complete, cannot properly picture the intermeshing of events and motivations.) This sketch may also illustrate how decision might have been made more quickly, with less frustration, and at lower cost, if careful program budgeting had preceded the proposal's introduction into Congress.

THE NATIONAL ENVIRONMENTAL HEALTH CENTER: A CASE STUDY

Early in 1962 a center was proposed to help achieve a long-range national objective of creating a more healthful environment for the American people. This center was designed to study air and water pollution; radiation, pesticide, and other chemical contamination of the environment; and occupational health problems. Initially, construction was to cost $33 million (including more than a half-dozen buildings), and some 1,600 people were to be employed. Eventually, the cost was estimated to be between $70 million and $80 million, and 4,500 people were to be employed. Because the first choice of location was in the Washington area, the National Capital Planning Commission became involved and had to relate the new complex to its year 2000 plan. Approval was finally obtained, and a decision was made to place the facility in the Washington area.

Because of various delays, the proposal missed the regular budget presentation for FY 1963 and was presented in the President's Health Message to Congress on February 27, 1962. The item was submitted to the Deficiency Subcommittee to the House Appropriations Committee, not the Subcommittee on Labor and Welfare, which would have had first review if it had been presented with other programs of the Department of Health, Education, and Welfare in the FY 1963 budget. The request was rejected. Funds were again requested for planning the center as part of the FY 1964 budget. This time the House Appropriations Committee recommended that the proposal be rejected. The Senate voted to go ahead with the project, but it was lost in conference.

Why? All sorts of reasons have been suggested. First, the Deficiency Subcommittee, which reviewed the matter in 1962, was not as familiar with affairs of the Department of Health, Education, and Welfare as was the Labor and Welfare Subcommittee. Also, the proposal was made at a time when controversy circulated in Congress about research grants in general and those for health in particular. In July 1962 a report was made by the House Committee on Government Operations criticizing the fiscal practices of the National Institutes of Health (NIH) and decrying the past actions of Congress, which had, since 1953, annually voted an average of 25 per cent more than the administration requested for the NIH.[21]

Controversy about appropriations for health continued into 1963.

[21] Richard Fenno, "The House Appropriations Committee," pp. 310–313. On the basis of a study made by the Committee's Subcommittee on Intergovernmental Relations, headed by Representative L. H. Fountain, Democrat from North Carolina, the House Committee charged that Congress had been overzealous in appropriating money for health research. The report said that NIH was hard-pressed

Hearings were held on the subject by the House Subcommittee on Public Health and Safety of the House Committee on Interstate and Foreign Commerce. The hearings disclosed some abuses, management problems, and difficulties of coordinating activities with other government agencies.[22]

Several other matters were operating against approval of the proposed center. Republican party policy at the time focused on efforts to reduce the administration's budget by pointing to the very substantial deficit entailed in approval of the budget as requested. The Subcommittee on Labor, Health, Education, and Welfare and Related Agencies to the House Appropriations Committee changed composition and took a more conservative turn. Disagreement also arose over the proposed location of the center.

Rockville, Maryland, was first chosen as the site, but the high cost of land and protest from the people of that area led to search for another location in the Washington area. Beltsville, Maryland, was then chosen. Strong efforts were made to locate the facility in North Carolina, West Virginia, and Ohio. Arguments were advanced, of course, as to why each of these locations was or was not the proper place for the new center.

The upshot was that Congress refused to approve the funds in 1962 and again in 1963. In 1964, however, Congress appropriated $1 million to be spent in FY 1965 for planning the installation, with the provision that it must be located at least fifty miles from Washington, D.C. This compromise was reached in the conference committee. How was it reached? The answer is not clear. It may be conjectured, however, that important in the decision of Congress was the fact that the District of Columbia was heavily saturated with research facilities and that other areas might profit from the stimulation of the center. Since none of the conferees had constituents in the Washington area, there were no political reasons for locating the center there.

---

to spend the additional money that Congress had authorized and was having trouble finding sufficient projects worthy of support. Furthermore, the report said NIH management was weak. See *Administration of Grants by the National Institutes of Health (Re-examination of Management Deficiencies)*, Twenty-First Report by the Committee on Government Operations, House Report No. 1958, 87th Cong., 2d Sess., (Washington, D.C.: U.S. Government Printing Office, 1962).

[22] *Organization of Public Health Service, Hearings before a Subcommittee of the Committee on Interstate and Foreign Commerce . . . on H.R. 2410*, April, May, and June 1963, House of Representatives, 88th Cong., 1st Sess., (Washington, D.C.: U.S. Government Printing Office, 1964).

POLITICAL EXIGENCIES OF PRESIDENTIAL DECISION

The President obviously considers many factors in decision-making. Of overriding significance is his leadership of the nation and the agencies of government, including Congress. Consideration of these matters has led Presidents to take action that, as a practical matter, dampens rather than stimulates program-budgeting concepts.

In 1962 President Kennedy, for example, became alarmed about the increasing total budget expenditure and the preliminary estimates for FY 1964. Total expenditure had risen from $76.5 billion for FY 1960 to $87.8 billion for FY 1962. He felt that to send to Congress what he would have considered a rational budget, consistent with his fundamental program and ideas, would have invited strong resistance in Congress and would possibly have triggered another major budget battle, in which he would have been placed on the defensive. This was the wrong position in which to find himself as President. As a consequence, all agencies were asked to reprune their FY 1964 budgets, and the President himself sharpened his budget pencil. As a result, some executive branch agencies that had been pressed to develop and improve their long-range planning became disillusioned and de-emphasized it.

In FY 1965 and again in the FY 1966 budgetary process, President Johnson operated under severe limitations, which on the one hand stimulated program budgeting, but on the other tended to repress it. The President has said emphatically that his concept of the "Great Society" is going to be a reality. He has also said emphatically that the major costs of his program will be met by reductions of lower priority programs and elimination of those that have become obsolete and should be abandoned. The President's FY 1966 budget held administrative expenditures to less than $100 billion. The result of this posture was that in preparing their budgets, agencies concentrated on cost reduction of FY 1966 activities rather than hammering out long-range objectives and programs to achieve them. Although the two things are not inconsistent, an administrator faced with the need for immediate and important budget cuts is considerably less inclined than otherwise to engage in the extraordinarily complicated job of acceptable program budgeting. A first-rate program-budgeting system would, of course, help. But this does not exist except in a few agencies.

There are other guidelines on which basic priorities can be formulated. In this environment it is difficult to get agencies to work hard on the kind of activity needed to make program budgeting effective. When the President's budget was made public early in 1965, speculation immediately arose as to the possible future costs of his Great Society, many programs for which were introduced in the Budget Message. Whatever his motivations, the President was reported at that time to have instructed agency heads not to discuss with anyone the future costs of the programs in the budget. It was pointed out that no agency head had any right to tie the chief executive's hands then for spending programs four or five years in the future.[23]

These are only two illustrations of the fact that the President is at the center of so many highly complex forces that almost anything he does is at a potentially high political cost. Naturally, he must consider his budgetary decisions in light of what other matters he wishes to advance or change. Although he himself may strongly support an expansion of the concept of program budgeting discussed in this book, it is possible and probable that he may on occasion be driven to take actions that may temporarily at least slow down its expansion.

LIMITATIONS ON MANAGERIAL DISCRETION

The degree of discretion of the top management of government —the President and Congress—is limited in budget decisionmaking. The limitations are of many types: economic, statutory, political, psychological, institutional. Because of these limitations, a new budget cycle does not present the opportunity for a fresh look at how money should be spent. The area of maneuverability is narrow, especially on the reduction side.

We have already noted the impact of a self-imposed total budgetary limitation that might be established by a President. Aside from national disasters, major national security crises, and extraordinarily powerful pent-up demands, administrative budget totals tend to push upward only against powerful forces aimed at "holding the lid on."

[23] Rowland Evans and Robert Novak, "Talk of Future Spending Banned," *Los Angeles Times*, February 4, 1965, Part II, p. 5.

Within the total administrative budget the bulk of expenditures is almost in the nature of fixed costs. Defense outlays take up well over 50 per cent of the total. Interest on the debt takes up another 11 to 12 per cent. Space research consumes 5 per cent. Agricultural commitments absorb 5 per cent. The multiplicity of other government functions must be accommodated in the approximately 25 per cent remaining. Within these functions, the same sort of embedded costs must be met. The result is that discretion to change major programs much more than marginally is generally absent except in unusual circumstances.

Statutory limitations narrow the margin of discretion. They cast a web of restraint about the whole budgetary process. They range from legislative requirements on a particular bureau that prevent an agency head from free decision to actions taken by Congress to impede free decision by the Chief Executive. A case in point is the Atomic Energy Act of 1946, which created the Joint Committee on Atomic Energy (JCAE). One careful student of the operation of the committee, Harold P. Green, has observed:

> It should not be assumed that the JCAE merely reacts to executive initiative; on the contrary, it has an aggressive program of its own, often in conflict with the program of the President or the AEC. Through its control over the process of congressional authorization of appropriations for the AEC, it frequently has been able to thrust its own programs upon an unwilling, reluctant, or not yet prepared executive branch. For example, the JCAE was the principal proponent of the Aircraft Nuclear Propulsion program, and succeeded for many years in forcing an unwilling executive branch to conduct this program. Indeed, the JCAE has made a shambles of the entire executive budgetary process in the atomic energy field.[24]

The JCAE has been able to exert its power within the executive branch. So much is this true that the JCAE often acts more like a high-level agency in the executive branch of the government than like a congressional committee.

In congressional budget making, appropriations are frequently made for a purpose specified by Congress. Whenever Congress

[24] "The Joint Committee on Atomic Energy: A Model for Legislative Reform?" *The George Washington Law Review*, vol. 32, no. 5, June 1964, p. 942. See also Green's *Government of the Atom: The Integration of Powers* (New York: Atherton Press, 1963); and his "Nuclear Technology and the Fabric of Government," *The George Washington Law Review*, vol. 33, no. 1, October 1964, pp. 121–161.

says that so many dollars are for this or that particular purpose, great problems arise in program budgeting. Classic illustrations are the funds appropriated by Congress to be spent for the B-70 manned bomber. The Department of Defense did not request all the money appropriated and, as it turned out, did not spend the sums authorized. This sort of resistance is not typical. Nor should it be expected, because earmarking "additional" funds for specific purposes of interest to Congress generally is met with sympathy by the agency concerned. Aggregate demands for funds in the non-defense area are so much higher than appropriations that congressional generosity is readily accepted even though it may not be directed to a favored program. The Department of Health, Education, and Welfare, for example, has been willing to try to spend the funds that Congress has for a number of years appropriated to the National Institutes of Health over and above the requests of the President.

Yet another way to look at the matter of discretion concerns the extent to which appropriations requests are really amenable to budgetary review. Murray L. Weidenbaum examined FY 1964 budgetary requests and related fixed charges of agencies (trust funds, treaty obligations, permanent special statutory requirements, continuing construction, and comparable other fixed requirements) to requested new obligational authority (NOA). For all agencies of government he found that only 58 per cent of requested new NOA was subject to effective review. He observed that for the national security agencies—Department of Defense, National Aeronautics and Space Administration, and Atomic Energy Commission —96 per cent of the expenditure authorizations was subject to annual review and control. In the other agencies, principally managing the domestic civilian programs, only 23 per cent of the request was really open to review. For these agencies, most expenditures are appropriated automatically. They result from commitments made in past legislation in Congress.[25]

Although this startling conclusion reveals the limits of current discretion associated with a program-budgeting program and also explains a fundamental basis for the incremental approach to

25 *Federal Budgeting: The Choice of Government Programs* (Washington, D.C.: American Enterprise Institute for Public Policy Research, February 1964), pp. 46–48.

budget decision, it is hardly persuasive in arguing against an expansion of program budgeting. Quite the contrary. The need for more program budgeting is glaringly apparent. A major contribution of program budgeting could be made at the point where Congress is considering the basic legislation that will in the future remove expenditures from managerial discretion. In theory, this is the critical point at which a program-budgeting system should have major impact. A new application of program budgeting might also serve as a worthwhile foundation for reviewing past legislative decisions that have committed so much of the annual budget and thereby removed so much of the annual appropriations from managerial discretion. Closer relationships between the executive branch and Congress in developing and using program budgeting would provide more discretion for both.

THE ROLE OF AGENCY HEADS AND PROGRAM BUDGETING

Expansion of the program-budgeting concept in the federal government must take account of the roles of agency heads. To be effective, program budgeting requires strong leadership. Securing and maintaining the required type of leadership in executive branch agencies of government is not an easy thing to accomplish.

Program budgeting is a system that permits and requires top executives to make decisions covering major programs in light of long-range considerations. This process is considerably different from the conventional incremental budget-making process in which the critical question is frequently how closely the allowable expenditure for next year can be held to that of last year. Because of the massive institutional stability of current budget making, any pressure to make more than incremental decisions or to change the locus of decisionmaking power requires very strong-minded top executives fortified by an information system to support decisions.

Program budgeting demands strong "economy-minded" top management of government agencies. The stress is on economy, not parsimony, and on making decisions about major programs. In a recent statement about the budget-making process the current Director of the Bureau of the Budget, Kermit Gordon, spoke approvingly of the following observation of Edmund Burke: "Economy is a distributive virtue and consists not in saving but in selection . . . Parsimony requires no providence, no powers of combination, no comparison, nc judgment."[26]

Gordon pointed out that proper budgetary decisionmaking was not simply a matter of increasing the federal budget in a "profligate" manner. We can, he said, do the many things that government must do at less cost if there is careful review of programs and weeding out of obsolete or lower priority programs. President Johnson observed in his Budget Message of January 1964: "An austere budget need not be and should not be a standstill budget. When budgetary restraint leads the government to turn its back on new needs and new problems, economy becomes but another word for stagnation. But when vigorous pruning of old programs and procedures releases the funds to meet new challenges and opportunities, economy becomes the companion of progress." The implementation of this philosophy requires hard decisionmaking and strong leadership.

It has been observed that three major reorganization acts had to be engineered through Congress before even a strong executive such as Secretary McNamara could assume the power needed to implement program budgeting in the Department of Defense. Despite these acts, it is doubtful if he could have maintained his power without the strong planning staff he built and supported. In newer agencies, such as the Federal Aviation Agency and the National Aeronautics and Space Administration, strong administrators (Najeeb Halaby in FAA and James Webb in NASA) have made major program decisions. In some of the older agencies, however, bureau chiefs have powers independent of the agency heads. Some bureau directors are appointed by the President and cannot be removed by the agency head. By congressional direction, different laws are administered by the bureau chief, as a bureau chief. Appropriations are made to him and his bureau. In theory, the agency head has power over the bureau chiefs, but in practice, by virtue of legislation as well as close personal relations with congressional committees, the bureau chiefs wield a power that is difficult if not impossible for agency heads to restrain. If an agency head does assert the power to make the decisions for the major programs of his agency, it cannot be assumed that his successor will have the

[26] "How Much Should Government Do?" *Saturday Review,* January 9, 1965, p. 25.

strength to maintain the power. Moreover, even if he has the strength, he may not choose to use it.

Making major program decisions may not always be the most popular course of action for an agency head. He may incur the opposition of his own subordinates, and not solely because he may be wresting decisionmaking from them. In government, as in other large organizations, people tend to advocate their own programs in preference to all others. One great attribute of program budgeting is that it presumably permits a top executive to view programs from the top of the administrative pyramid. This view permits a comparison of values that is impossible at lower levels. Beyond a single agency, however, is the vast potential political power exercisable by those who will benefit or be injured by a decision. The more important the decision, the greater is the shift in benefits from a program-level change. Opposition to a decision to reduce a program also tends to be greater than that for increasing a program. There are many reasons for this. Among them is the fact that a reduction of expenditures will directly and adversely affect particular interests. Whereas the adverse impact is concentrated, the advantage resulting from the reduction is spread over many people and groups and will not generate equally powerful political support.

Strong agency heads may also temper their determination because of uncertainties and difficulties in measuring advantage against cost and in finding answers to other formidable questions inherent in program budgeting. To illustrate, a variety of programs exist to aid less fortunate people—the food stamp plan, public assistance in many forms, and educational programs. There are also many subsidies scattered throughout the agencies of government to help people in difficulty. In the past the typical attitude has been that any incremental increase in such programs should be sought simply because the needs are so far beyond the nation's ability to meet them that any expansion is correct. There is another approach, however. It is to look at all the means of assistance and come face to face with some different questions. For example, if more food can be distributed, less cash may be required. To what extent is this feasible and desirable? If training programs can rehabilitate some of the destitute, to what extent should they be substituted for public assistance? Should marginal farmers be maintained or encouraged by incentives to enter the productive process in other areas? What is the real demand for aid to the less fortunate? What lower priority programs should be eliminated to help meet this demand? These are difficult questions to answer. There may not be firm answers to them, but to pose them and to seek answers demands a willingness to come to grips with program problems and not to remain inactive before a requirement presumably irreconcilable with the ability to finance it. The present administration is facing such questions. The point I wish to make here is simply that strong leadership in the top echelons of government is required to meet such issues and to select among the alternatives.

A nice question also arises concerning the extent to which Congress wants a powerful central planning staff in an agency and a tough-minded decisionmaker as the agency head. This question cannot be answered easily or briefly. It is true that newer agencies tend to be program oriented, with power centered in the agency head. On the other hand, institutional arrangements between Congress and the executive branch with respect to the older agencies—particularly those of the holding-company type—will probably be willingly changed only slowly.

The question also gets mixed up in the politics of a public versus a private position. Many factors influence what a congressman says publicly. On occasion, congressmen say one thing publicly and take a different position in the actual budgetary decisionmaking process. This is understandable. In such instances administrators in the executive branch obviously must be cautious about the candor with which they discuss a decision that may be criticized in public but that may nevertheless be received sympathetically in Congress. Congressmen sometimes are frankly pleased when an agency head assumes the burden of an unpopular decision so that the congressman may, within the confines of his executive sessions, underwrite the decision.

As noted previously, an outstanding objective of all executives in the executive branch is to get the appropriation that is sought. Doing this gives rise to a multiplicity of strategies in the budgetary bargaining process.[27] While it is always good strategy to be prepared with facts about costs and benefits, which should be available

---

[27] For an excellent account of strategies, see Wildavsky, *The Politics of the Budgetary Process*, chap. 3.

in a program-budgeting system, the factor influencing the budgetary process is often more political than economic. It may involve the stimulation of support within as well as outside the government, improving personal relationships with appropriations committee members, veiling expected future costs of a program, and in other ways using the machinery of government to achieve the objective sought. These are often acceptable strategies in a political democracy. They are realistic. They also create difficulties in implementing program budgeting.

Consider, for example, the problem of full disclosure of long-range program plans. In the nondefense area there are few programs that cannot be expected to require higher expenditures in the future. An expanding economy, a rising population, and a growing financial capability ensure this. On the other hand, the total potential, real, and supportable requirement for federal expenditures today could easily add another 50 per cent to this year's budget. The conventional approach to budget making in meeting this problem is one of holding the line and adding only as small a sum each year as will best satisfy the many pressures exerted and measure the political consensus.

With this in mind, the following conversation may be imagined between a congressman and an agency head:

Congressman X: Mr. Agency Head, it is my understanding that the legislation you are seeking will continue over a long period of time and will be of great future benefits to our country.

Agency Head: This is correct, Congressman X. We have tried to be forward looking in our program development.

Congressman X: I wish to compliment you on your advance planning. We in government must seek to understand long-range planning just as in a private company. You have, have you not, considered this legislation you seek within a long-range planning program for your agency?

Agency Head: Mr. Congressman, yes, we have tried to look ahead. As you know, it is difficult to see what will happen in the future. But our intent is to try to make decisions today in light of their future consequences.

Congressman X: Mr. Agency Head, has the President approved your long-range plans?

Agency Head: Mr. Congressman, I have discussed the long-range plans of my agency with the President, but only in very general terms. We have talked about a few of our major programs in light of the long-range future. The President, of course, is concerned with a considerably broader view than the specific programs of my agency. On the basis of my discussions with the President, I cannot say that he has either approved or disapproved our long-range plans. He has, of course, approved the present budgetary request and the legislation now before you to support it.

Congressman X: Mr. Agency Head, you are aware, are you not, that Public Law 801 requires that you provide Congress for each of the first five years of any proposed legislation with the expenditures and man-years of civilian employment required if the annual expenditures would exceed $1 million?[28]

Agency Head: Yes, sir, I am familiar with the provisions of Public Law 801. I would be most pleased to be in a position to provide this information concerning the present proposed legislation. Unfortunately, we do not have it. The future is so uncertain that I would not want to mislead Congress by providing grossly inaccurate data. You now have before you our estimates for the coming fiscal year. Because of our inability to see ahead very accurately, we propose giving to Congress the first year's costs and manpower estimates and providing other future estimates when we know more accurately what they are likely to be.

Now, why is Mr. Agency Head so reluctant to reveal his long-range plans if he actually has them? There may be many reasons. He does not want to commit the President to a long-range program unless it is a major issue that the President wishes to be identified with and to support. Because future costs will likely be considerably higher than those of today, such an estimate may conflict with conventional hold-the-line thinking and may provide ammunition for the opposition party. This is particularly true if the current budget registers a deficit. The agency may not really have very good estimates of future costs. What costs it does have may not agree with those Congress may have at hand. There are, of course, many other reasons. The point is not that agency heads should neglect long-range planning, but rather that problems may well

28 Public Law 801, "An Act . . . To Require That Certain Reports and Other Communications of the Executive Branch to Congress Contain Information Pertaining to the Number of Civilian Officers and Employees Required To Carry Out Additional or Expanded Functions," July 25, 1956, *United States Statutes at Large . . . 1956 and Proclamations*, vol. 70, 84th Cong., 2d Sess. (Washington, D.C.: U.S. Government Printing Office, 1957), p. 652.

arise in their candid revelation of such plans. This difficulty will undoubtedly restrain the development of institutionalized long-range planning as well as the thoroughness with which it is approached and reported.

OPERATIONAL PROBLEMS OF A PROGRAM-BUDGETING SYSTEM

As amply demonstrated in this and previous chapters, program budgeting is not a simple system, the structure, nature, and process of which is fixed, firm, and generally accepted. In its application it encounters problems that may be overcome in different, equally suitable ways. A number of these problems have been presented in preceding chapters. The objective in treating a few of them here, therefore, is only to add new thoughts and to re-emphasize major issues.

Fig. 1 shows one idealized format for a comprehensive planning system. To describe even briefly the many qualifications that one should keep in mind in translating this chart into practice would take the discussion too far afield. Even cursory examination and tentative acceptance of the chart, however, by those with only elementary knowledge of government must show many critical problems in implementing the system. Two problems will be noted here merely as illustration. One concerns definition of goals, and the other relates to problems in applying cost-utility analysis at critical points in the process.

Almost any major national goal—national security, economic growth, education, elimination of pockets of poverty, scientific and technical advancement—is so broad, and pursuit of it involves so many agencies, that a meaningful definition for the formulation of specific programs is difficult to achieve. Nevertheless, agencies must formulate subgoals that can serve as a basis for their own planning.

While much has been done in recent years to clarify both national objectives and those of major governmental programs,[29] there is no single set of goals that has been established as the basis

[29] See, for example, *The Report of the President's Commission on National Goals* (New York: The American Assembly, Columbia University, 1960); and Edgar O. Edwards, *The Nation's Economic Objectives* (Chicago: University of Chicago Press, 1964).

of governmental programming. At any one time the relationship must inevitably be loose between what national goals are conceived to be and the specific programs that an agency may designate as the means to achieve those objectives. The relationship will also be the subject of controversy.[30]

Lack of detail in broad national goal definitions can create difficult problems for agencies in determining subgoals. For example, the federal government has undertaken a program for the preservation and protection of migratory waterfowl largely in the interest of sportsmen. Congress is being asked to appropriate $12.5 million this year for acquisition of waterfowl refuge and breeding lands—some $5.0 million represents sale of duck stamps to hunters, and the balance is an advance on such receipts. Why? The precise goal is not clear, but it should be if cost benefits are to be developed convincingly in a program budgetary schema. Is the objective to have available one duck per hunter per day, week, month, or year in the year 2000? Is it to have so many ducks per GNP billion dollars? Is it to have so many ducks per 1,000 population? It is not clear precisely what the specific objective is or should be. If any one of these objectives is chosen, how is benefit to be calculated? Although one might possibly calculate the cost of having available a duck per week per hunter, measuring benefit is a most puzzling problem. A large number of programs in government face comparable difficulties. Even in the Department of Defense, cost-benefit analysis is not used in determining the level of expenditures in some major expenditure areas.

Another problem concerns ability to maximize benefits among marginal expenditures on diverse programs, such as strategic defenses versus the antipoverty program. How can one measure at what point benefit will be increased by the expenditure of a dollar to prevent poverty rather than the expenditure of the same dollar for strategic defenses? In theory, the government should increase its expenditures no further than the point where social benefit is the same from all government expenditures, per dollar of the expenditures, and is equal to marginal social cost. At this point the marginal social benefit is equal to the marginal social cost from individual expenditure. This concept, of course, raises the question

[30] For a discussion of this problem, see George A. Steiner, *Government's Role in Economic Life* (New York: McGraw-Hill Book Co., Inc., 1953), chaps. 10, 11, and 14.

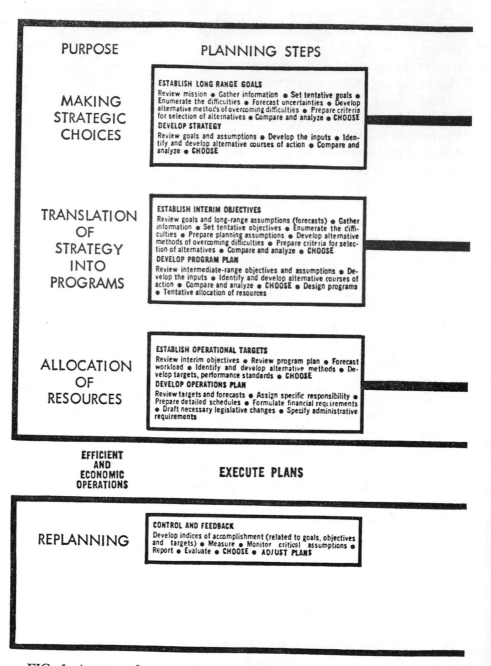

FIG. 1. A system for comprehensive planning. (Prepared by Raymond E. Kitchell; reproduced here with permission.)

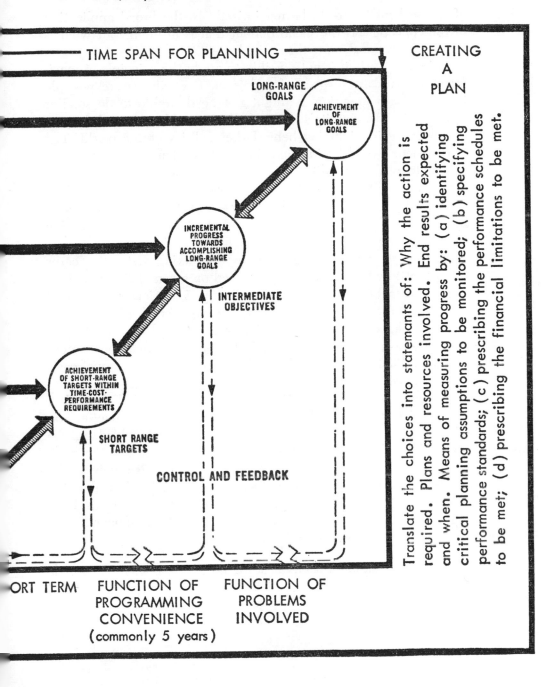

TIME SPAN FOR PLANNING

CREATING
A
PLAN

LONG-RANGE
GOALS

ACHIEVEMENT
OF
LONG-RANGE
GOALS

INCREMENTAL
PROGRESS
TOWARDS
ACCOMPLISHING
LONG-RANGE
GOALS

INTERMEDIATE
OBJECTIVES

ACHIEVEMENT
OF SHORT-RANGE
TARGETS WITHIN
TIME-COST-
PERFORMANCE
REQUIREMENTS

SHORT RANGE
TARGETS

CONTROL AND FEEDBACK

ORT TERM   FUNCTION OF   FUNCTION OF
         PROGRAMMING   PROBLEMS
         CONVENIENCE   INVOLVED
         (commonly 5 years)

Translate the choices into statements of: Why the action is required. Plans and resources involved. End results expected and when. Means of measuring progress by: (a) identifying critical planning assumptions to be monitored; (b) specifying performance standards; (c) prescribing the performance schedules to be met; (d) prescribing the financial limitations to be met.

of whose benefits are to be maximized? In the broad application of the concept it is the social benefit that is in mind. But what is that? Who is to calculate the social benefit?

Quite obviously it is not possible to apply the principle of maximization with any degree of precision. Even if it were possible to use it with precision, it might not be desirable to do so. For example, the community's estimate of its social benefit and the cost of achieving it might lag behind the realities of the world. The government would be justified, in the face of a national security threat, to push expenditures for defense much beyond what the community at the moment might consider a cost-benefit equilibrium. The principle, of course, is very rough. It remains a principle rather than a yardstick. But it is important in focusing attention on alternatives—costs as well as benefits.[31]

An important issue in the program-budgeting system concerns the extent to which choice can be based on a convincing quantitative cost-benefit analysis. As shown in Fig. 1, choices are required throughout the planning process; and, as has been clearly expressed in this book, cost-utility analysis is a strategic and important characteristic of program budgeting. But, clearly, all decisions cannot and should not be made on the basis of a quantitative array of costs and benefits.

Evaluating program effectiveness can be performed through a variety of methods that have different applicability depending on which end of the spectrum of decisionmaking is involved. At the pinnacle of decisionmaking, where the farm program, the antipoverty program, or the national security program is involved, the political test is of major importance. At the lower levels of decision the more rigorous tests embodied in cost-utility analysis have important applicability. In between are other tests—financial and administrative, for example.[32]

---

[31] For a fuller discussion of this principle, see Steiner, *Government's Role in Economic Life*, pp. 394–395. For another analysis, see A. C. Pigou, *A Study in Public Finance* (London: Macmillan & Co., Ltd., 1951), p. 31. For a different approach, see Howard R. Bowen, "The Interpretation of Voting in the Allocation of Economic Resources," *Quarterly Journal of Economics*, vol. 58, no. 1, November 1943, pp. 27–48. A different approach is that of Arthur Smithies, *Government Decision-Making and the Theory of Choice*, P–2960 (Santa Monica, Calif.: The RAND Corporation, October 1964).

[32] For a discussion of these tests, see Elmer B. Staats, "Evaluating Program Effectiveness," in Donald Bowen and Lynton K. Caldwell, *Program Formulation*

What program budgeting can and will accomplish is to push harder for quantitative facts on which to base decisions. The difficulty in calculating costs against appropriate advantages is not a threat to the wider use of program budgeting. Instead, present difficulties create a challenge—a challenge to press more strongly for more rigorous definitions of both costs and benefits. Whatever progress is made, much or little, is in the direction of more rational decisionmaking.

In government, as in industry, the most important decisions will always be made partly on the basis of the qualitative "feel" and value systems of the decisionmaker. The higher he is in the organizational chain and the more profound the decision, the greater is this nonquantitative part likely to play. One of the foremost practitioners of program budgeting, Charles J. Hitch, expresses this point as follows: "Obviously, there is an area of intuitive judgment involved in such considerations, but we want to give that area of judgment as much quantitative support as we can. What we need in requirement studies is less assertion and more analysis, fewer adjectives and adverbs and more nouns and verbs, and, indeed, fewer words and more numbers."[33]

Classification of budgetary items is a key to rational program budgeting. Unfortunately, however, there is no single grouping of expenditures that exists to implement program budgeting. Any search for an ideal is fruitless. Even if categories were established only for program budgeting, there would be no ideal, for one must also consider that different classifications of the federal budget may be needed to serve different budgetary purposes. While program budgeting may be adopted to improve decisionmaking, the classification best suited for this purpose may be ill-suited for operations. (This point is touched on in Chapter 10.) Furthermore, Congress insists that program-budget items, no matter how arranged for other purposes, must be translatable into state and congressional districts so that each congressman may be able to see the significance of budgetary change for his constituency.

---

and Development, Selected Papers on Public Administration, Institute of Training for Public Service (Bloomington, Ind.: Indiana University, 1960), pp. 62–76 (mimeo.).

[33] "The New Approach to Management in the U.S. Department of Defense," *Management Science,* vol. 9, October 1962, pp. 7–8.

There are, of course, difficulties in any budgetary classification. Moreover, there is nothing wrong in altering them from time to time. While coding problems may serve to restrain the ready expansion of program budgeting and may create other difficulties, in themselves they cannot be considered a serious barrier to expanding the concept in the federal government. There are ways to combine classes of budgetary items to serve different purposes.

BUDGET OFFICERS VERSUS PLANNING STAFFS

In government, as is the case in large business concerns, the need for a central planning staff group reporting directly to top management is becoming increasingly clear. Because of the growing complexities facing major government agency heads, such staff groups can be expected to grow in numbers and strength as a normal development of management. With the pressures of the Bureau of the Budget for more and better advanced planning, however, the expansion of these staffs may be accelerated. As they grow and flourish they will create organizational problems.

Long-range planning staffs in industry frequently have been considered a threat by both the functional central office and the decentralized line managers. In the better managed companies, however, these tensions are erased or are not important enough to create problems. In a government agency, as contrasted with a private company, these units may become the targets for pressure groups and individuals dissatisfied with agency goals and decisions. Two good illustrations of this sport occurred during recent wartime efforts when torpedoes were launched at the Program Staffs of the War Production Board during World War II and at the Defense Production Administration during the Korean War.

Long-range planning staffs in industry as well as in government have frequently come into conflict with budgeting officers. Problems of this nature in the Department of Defense have been partly eliminated because the Assistant Secretary of Defense (Comptroller) also supervises the major analytical work associated with program budgeting in the Office of the Secretary of Defense. But in many agencies of government the budget officer and the long-range planning and/or programming staff are not closely associated organizationally; they are separated, and problems have arisen between them.

Although some people may disagree, budgeting and program planning are clearly not the same thing. Budgets are important management tools, but they are only one part of a comprehensive planning process. It is true that budgets are concrete short-range manifestations of management's intentions to achieve long-range goals. But they are only a part of the planning process, which considers long-range goals and choices about how best to use resources to achieve them. Goals and strategies to achieve plans should not be framed on the basis of current budgetary decisions. This is not meant to exclude the fact that current budgetary requirements may reflect changes in longer range objectives and previously determined strategies to meet them. There is a close relationship between long-range goals and strategies and current budgetary decisions. Frederick C. Mosher explains the relationship in these words:

Planning involves first the conceiving of goals and the development of alternative courses of future action to achieve the goals. Second it involves the reduction of these alternatives from a very large number to a small number and finally to one approved course of action, *the program*. Budgeting probably plays a slight part in the first phase but an increasingly important and decisive part in the second. It facilitates the choice-making process by providing a basis for systematic comparisons among alternatives which take into account their total impacts on both the debit and the credit sides. It thus encourages, and provides some of the tools for, an increasing degree of precision in the planning process. Budgeting is the ingredient of planning which disciplines the entire process.[34]

Planning is more predominant, and current budgeting is more derivative.[35]

One reason for conflict between budgeting officers and central planning groups is purely professional and bureaucratic. In one agency of government the budget officer reports to an Assistant Secretary, and the planning office reports to the Secretary. The budget officer prepares the budget presentations and justifications for Congress and in the process makes decisions. More and more of the decisions that in the past were made by and through the

[34] *Program Budgeting: Theory and Practice* (Chicago, Ill.: Public Administration Service, 1954), pp. 48–49. For a detailed account of the interrelationships between budgeting offices and planning, see Burkhead, *Government Budgeting*, chap. 10.

[35] For more analysis of this point, see Robert A. Walker, "The Relation of Budgeting to Program Planning," *Public Administration Review*, vol. IV, no. 2, Spring 1944, pp. 97–107; and Robert S. Herman, "Two Aspects of Budgeting."

budget officer are now being made in the planning office, in close liaison with the Secretary. This loss of power, of course, generates friction. Budgeteers are not and should not be in the seat of decisionmaking power. Nor should planning staffs. Decisionmaking is reserved for line managers. But the line between recommendation and decisionmaking is often hard to find.

Controversy about duplication of effort has flared in several agencies. In one agency, for example, the long-range planning office wanted ten-year plans from major program officers. To satisfy Bureau of the Budget requests, in the past few years the budget officer has asked for five-year plans from major program officers. This has been for the most part a "costing-out" of current programs. If the long-range planning officer asks only a "costing-out" of current plans for ten years, clearly there is duplication of the first five years. This sort of information is not likely to be of great use to top management and is therefore unlikely to receive top management support. Yet if program officers are asked to think through carefully their evolving goals and the requirements to reach them, there is again a duplication with the budget officer request for the first five years. There may even be a conflict in the substance and procedures of the request. This makes everyone unhappy. There is no reason, however, why a long-range planning group cannot do its proper work in cooperation with the budget officer. More experience with program budgeting should resolve such problems.

A genuine managerial problem arises because the budgeting process is rather well institutionalized. Over a long period of time procedures, practices, and roles have been established. This is not true with a central planning unit. These groups are new and their roles and functions are not well established. Even if activities were clear and firm today, they would change tomorrow, for the work of a central planning group reflects the style of top management. A central planning group is doing the work of top management. It does it only because no top management of a large enterprise can do the job alone. As a result, some top managers do more of the work than others, and the operation of the planning group is tailored accordingly.

There is no more need for excessive friction between these two groups in government than in industry. The traditional budget process is in trouble and in need of change—important change. Sophisticated comprehensive planning is a process encompassing the work of both the central planning groups and the traditional budget officers. Each has a major part to contribute to the whole process. The discipline of the annual budget is a sobering frame of reference for planning. The merging of planning and budgeting is not something done at the top of the agency pyramid. It must begin at the base in all agencies of government. The budget groups, the planning staffs, and the program managers must work together as a team.[36] Better cooperation among these groups can and will add to the value of each in securing better management in government. The focal point of this book is that program budgeting (associated with long-range planning) rather than traditional budgeting will significantly help top management in the federal government to do a better job.

OPEN END STATE GRANTS-IN-AID

One possible new move away from program budgeting concerns comparatively unrestricted grants-in-aid to states. At the present time federal grants-in-aid to states aggregate around $10 billion annually. There are a few grants now made on a lump-sum basis, but the total is not great. A plan has been advanced to share a part of future potential surpluses of federal revenues over expenditures with the states through a system of unrestricted grants. One version of the plan would be to set aside around $2.5 billion to be allocated to states on a per capita basis.[37] This is not the place to argue the case for or against the plan. It is to the point, however, to observe that such a plan would remove a substantial part of federal expenditures from a program budgeting system of the federal government.

PROGRAM BUDGETING AND ORGANIZATION

The question of the interrelationship between organization and program budgeting has been discussed elsewhere, notably in Chapter 2, and will not be examined at length here. But the issue is a potentially important barrier to any expanded use of program

---

[36] See Elmer B. Staats, "Relationship of Budget Planning to Long-Range Planning," *The Federal Accountant*, March 1962.

[37] *Monthly Economic Letter*, First National City Bank, New York, December 1964, p. 140. See also an attack on this plan by Harley L. Lutz, "States & Surpluses," *Wall Street Journal*, December 28, 1964, p. 6.

budgeting in government and therefore commands a note here, however brief.

Program budgeting categories express in concrete terms the ends to be pursued. The assimilation of various activities into end purposes will be the beginning of a sort of synthesis of public policy that has been long overdue. The absence of it is costing a great deal. But to achieve this synthesis will precipitate rough controversy. The present "chest of drawers" type of organization cannot for long be compatible with program budgeting. In the long run, the institutional changes that program budgeting will involve may be substantial. It is true that decisions in some of the appropriations subcommittees are made by considering comparable major programs simultaneously, regardless of the location of the program among different agencies; but this is the exception rather than the rule.

It is not very realistic to expect any immediate wholesale reorganization of the federal government to incorporate in one agency the many scattered programs of the same type. There are numerous entrenched interests within and outside of government agencies that would find such reorganization highly distasteful. Undoubtedly great resistance would appear in Congress. In a study of water resource reorganization, James W. Fesler concluded in these words his estimate of congressional reaction to reorganization: "The indications that Congress cannot be appeased by any administrative arrangements so far devised simplifies our immediate task of drawing conclusions about national water resource administration. Until further political analyses disclose a way in which Congress might accommodate the patent need for more reasonable arrangements for consideration of water resource programs, we can revert to relatively apolitical modes of analysis."[38]

The answer to the problems of resisting organizational change is in several parts. To begin with, it is not necessary that all programs for water or education or transportation or health be incorporated in one agency. That would be impossible and not particularly desirable. If the major expenditure associated with any one of these or other comparable items were to be considered together, this would be enough. It should not be asking too much

---

[38] "National Water Resources Administration," *Law and Contemporary Social Problems*, XXII, Summer 1957, p. 468.

to provide this sort of aggregation for program decisionmaking in the executive branch. If it is done there, the congressional appropriations committees may find that a comparable view in the legislative branch of government may have important advantages. The success of program budgeting neither depends on nor requires great immediate reorganization of government. Some reorganization would indeed be helpful, but it would be better to get on with the job of introducing program budgeting, even though it might be a little less effective as a result of organizational problems, than to fail to act because of resistance to organizational change. It is probably accurate to say that if Secretary McNamara had tried to reorganize the Pentagon in conformance with program budgeting needs, he would still be reorganizing and the great progress that has been made in program budgeting would have never occurred. Over a long time period, as the benefits of program budgeting are demonstrated and as adjustments are made in administering the system, necessary organizational changes may be accommodated without exceptional pain.

The question of organization and program-budget aggregations, however, runs into a practical problem. To serve the interests of managerial responsibility and financial accountability, budget planning has to be structured along the institutional lines of agencies. When the executive and legislative branches approve appropriations and allocate funds, both must be assured that some responsible official is accountable for properly administering the funds. This is the basis for agency and bureau budgeting as well as for appropriation accounting. Although these requirements create problems in organizing for and implementing program budgeting, the difficulties can be and have been overcome.

In the meantime, research may push ahead to find methods to apply cost-benefit analyses for programs extending across agency lines. The role of the recently created Office of Economic Opportunity as a programming and planning office for governmental agencies engaged in the war on poverty is a new experiment in public administration that should be watched and studied closely. Other types of approaches also should be developed.[39]

[39] W. Edward Cushen, "A National Management Worksheet: An Aid to Strategic Planning," U.S. Department of Commerce, National Bureau of Standards, April 1964 (mimeo.), presents one pioneering approach. A different untried approach was suggested in Steiner, *Government's Role in Economic Life*, pp. 387–392.

ACCELERATING THE TIME SCHEDULE FOR PROGRAM BUDGETING

Program budgeting does require changes in the budgetary process and structure. It must, therefore, contend with exceedingly strong forces for maintaining the status quo. Institutions and habits of men do not change quickly, except under the pressure of exceptionally powerful drives. To introduce program budgeting too rapidly throughout the budgetary process might bring too drastic change and would not likely succeed. At the same time, the sluggish way in which we permit our budgetary process to change has been illustrated at various points in this chapter.

There may come a time when program budgeting can be importantly escalated in usage. If some large budgetary commitment is drastically diminished and a large gap appears between revenues and expenditures (a resolution of the farm problem or a major disarmament, for example), a sudden widening of the discretionary band of the top management of government will occur. In this event, program budgeting may be stimulated momentously to help make the decision about how the gap will be managed.

As we move ahead, there are many reasons for making haste slowly. We must develop clearer concepts of how long-range planning can and should be done in the government. There is a shortage of technically skilled people to undertake convincing cost-utility analysis. Many problems of classification and organization must gradually be tackled and solved. Many things must be done to improve the program budgeting system to be introduced as well as to ensure that whatever is done disrupts the operations of government only in a tolerable degree. Whatever is done must meet the test of program budgeting itself: Is the advantage worth the cost? Kermit Gordon states the matter nicely in these words: "The task of modernizing the federal budget will not be accomplished in one year or four. It is a continuing struggle, for the barriers are formidable and the pitfalls many. But it is an effort that should command the support and assistance of all who choose economy over both parsimony and profligacy."[40]

[40] "How Much Should Government Do?" p. 76.

SUMMARY AND CONCLUSION

This study examines the many impediments in the federal government to a rapid expansion of program budgeting and sophisticated long-range planning. Important barriers to a fast spread of such a system exist in both the legislative and the executive branches. In both branches there are many customs, procedures, philosophies, and methods that grudgingly yield to change, particularly quick change. One of the great stabilizing values to the preservation of our political democracy is resistance to sudden and revolutionary change in operations, except under the impact of threats to survival, such as military threats.

On the other hand, there are forces working for improvement in our budgeting and planning programs. During the past five years very important improvements have been made in the introduction of program budgeting and long-range planning. Not only the Department of Defense, but other agencies—AEC, Federal Aviation Agency, General Services Administration, and NASA, to name a few—have demonstrated the value of this system. Despite inertia in Congress for changing the budgetary system, it too has approved the concept and its growing utilization.

The enormously complicated job of managing the federal government makes administrators in both the legislative and executive branches more aware each day of the value of having more and better facts for decision even though in the end the decision may be made solely on political grounds. Both branches are hungry for the very type of information that a program-budgeting system, with its accompanying long-range planning, produces. They want this information because it is persuasive. There is growing recognition, too, that the more hard information is available, the more relevant and effective is the application of judgment to the decisionmaking process. Moreover, the extraordinary power for better management that a sophisticated planning system provides to large private business enterprises has been repeatedly demonstrated in recent years. The rapid expansion of long-range planning in industry is not and will not be without its influence in government.

The most powerful force working for program budgeting and long-range planning in government comes from a recognition of the great advantages of the system in permitting more rational decisions and better management of those decisions. The beauty of the system of program budgeting and sophisticated planning lies in the fact that it fosters better analysis of alternative courses of action. At the same time, it can reflect all the complex non-qualitative values that in a political democracy influence the man or the committee that must decide.

Chapter 12

THE PROGRAM BUDGET IN OPERATION

BY MELVIN ANSHEN

The discussion of program budgeting up to this point has largely concerned itself with problems of needs, concepts, and design. References to the resource allocation process in the federal government have been introduced to document and illustrate deficiencies in the existing budget structure and to suggest potential gains through adoption of the program budget. Other gains from full implementation of the program budget concept have been given only glancing notice. It may therefore be both useful and interesting to examine more fully the implications of the operation of this new budget design for organizations and individuals whose work would be affected by it.

Let us assume, for the purpose of this discussion, that a significant part of the federal government's resource requirement statements has been transformed into a program structure (still, of course, subject to evolutionary change). Let us also assume that the many intellectual, organizational, statistical, political, and administrative problems that have been described in earlier chapters have been resolved to the point that the program budget is a functioning, if imperfect, reality. In this setting, then, we raise the following question: How might the new structure be used by the executive and legislative arms of the federal government, and how might this use in turn extend a constructive influence beyond the federal establishment?

OBJECTIVES, PLANS, AND RESOURCE COMMITMENTS

The single greatest impact of the program budget in operation, and almost certainly the single greatest contribution, should be its encouragement and support of more rational assessment of ends and means, goals and resources, outputs and inputs. The comprehensive term for this range of activity is "planning." Not many years ago, any suggestion that the federal government might engage in planning was a disturbing notion implying centralized direction of the economy. Today, when planning has become one of the dominant characteristics of effective management in private business, it should be safe to suggest that the public sector of our society can also benefit from a more rational framework for viewing the future.

What we have in mind is simply the implementation of the proposition that in a dynamic environment those who do not anticipate and prepare for the future usually discover a crisis when the future becomes the present. Most of the nondefense objectives to which the federal government commits its discretionary spending (e.g., in the fields of foreign aid, education, research, space exploration, conservation, recreation, transportation, poverty, unemployment, and health) necessarily and inevitably involve long periods of time. One year's activity can never present more than a modest progress toward some final goal. Furthermore, the initial costs of most programs are usually low relative to the expenditures required to sustain progress in later stages. Unless resource commitment decisions are taken in the context of a long forward view, it is difficult to make rational choices among competing claims for scarce budget dollars, difficult to avoid the waste and inefficiency created by ill-judged or intermittent funding, and difficult to free annual budget-making from the negative influence of such costs and established clienteles.

With few exceptions, the present budget structure neither encourages nor assists an orderly, rational view of the future. It does not deny the possibility of planning, in our sense of the word, but it fails to organize resource utilization problems in a way that invites a planning viewpoint. Equally, it fails to organize cost information by a method that permits relating requirements to objectives. It should not be surprising, therefore, that a certain share of executive and legislative actions with respect to the budget resemble improvisation rather than informed decision. Nor should it be surprising that public administrators are often limited in their ability to make analyses of effectiveness and efficiency of the sort suggested in earlier chapters of this book.

A program budget structure of the general character of the one recommended here will not, it should be emphasized, in itself bring about an improvement in the federal resource allocation process. Indeed, it could result in accomplishing no change whatsoever, if officials in the executive and legislative branches of the government continued to think about ends and means within short time horizons and within the present organization design of the federal establishment. But the installation of a program budget could facilitate rational planning, could encourage its development, and could present relevant information in a form useful for its application in a planning context. By its comprehensive, integrated, and time-phased display of the costs associated with identified program objectives, it would make planning both possible and intellectually attractive. It would sharpen critical judgments and encourage the substitution of rational analysis for intuition.

How much progress in this direction would be achieved, and how fast, would be determined by the officials' recognition of the possibility of using program budgeting as a tool to improve resource allocation, and their desire to convert potential into reality. As earlier chapters have suggested, certain institutional and political considerations can be expected to act as drags both on acceptance of the new concept and on full employment of its potential. Nevertheless, with proper educational effort, effective leadership, and patience, it would seem reasonable to anticipate a progressive commitment to the use of the instrument. In time, the federal government should be greatly assisted in appraising the gains and costs associated with important program objectives. This process should be supported by progressive improvements in the quality of the data presented in budget projections and in the quality of the analyses through which the information is brought to bear on resource allocation problems.

The specific contribution of the program budget concept to realistic planning will be shaped by three characteristics of the recommended design. As indicated in the foregoing comments, the first characteristic is the forward projection of costs through an extended period of years. A second is the aggregation of budget items, many of which are presently scattered through a number of executive departments and bureaus. The third is encouragement of cost-utility analysis. Together, these characteristics should help to establish a decision grid, a decision time horizon, and a design for analysis.

These design elements should be viewed as evolutionary in response to operating experience and the changing needs of the executive and legislative branches. It would be unrealistic to assume that any initial program budget structure would in operation be found to be fully and continually responsive to the planning requirements of the federal government. The composition of individual programs will require revision as a result of knowledge gained through the annual budget-making experience. In some cases the initial program design may be too narrow; in others, it may be too broad. Changing economic and social circumstances through the years will create new resource allocation problems, which will in turn suggest new program structures.

Just what categories constitute the most useful programs and program elements is far from obvious. Earlier chapters on specific program areas brought this out vividly. If one puts all educational activities into a broad package of educational programs, he cannot simultaneously include school lunch programs or physical education activities in a Health Program, or include defense educational activities (such as the military academies) in the Defense Program. If one puts all transportation expenditures into a Transportation Program, he cannot at the same time put R&D on transportation into an R&D Program, or defense-oriented transportation outlays into the Defense Program. In short, precisely how to achieve a rational and useful structure for a program budget is not yet evident. Moving toward an optimal structure will inevitably be a gradual process.

Moreover, program budgeting will not prove to have the same degree of usefulness in every sector of federal activity. In defense planning, for example, program techniques are presently less useful in the area of General Support Forces than in the area of Strategic Retaliatory Forces and Continental Air and Missile Defense Forces. In the nondefense sector, program techniques may prove to be less useful in a Foreign Aid Program (because of incommensurable effects of alternative program elements) or in a Transportation Program (because of interdependencies with the rest of the economy) than in, say, a Health Program. We are sure to discover that we have much to learn about the most useful applications of program budgets.

Finally, only through a sequence of periodic planning exercises will an understanding develop of the planning projections appropriate to individual programs. A forward projection of five years may be judged appropriate for most programs at the outset. In

later years it will probably be found useful to extend the horizon
for a longer term in some program areas in which the full resource
commitment can be meaningfully appraised only over a longer
span of years. The important consideration, therefore, will be to
treat the program structure as a rough tool to be improved and
refined in response to evolving experience and changing needs.

It will be equally important in the operation of the program
budget to avoid rigidities in the planning process itself. As many
private firms have discovered, the value of long-range planning
is realized only if plans are kept flexible, subject to periodic assessment, amendment, and when necessary, scrapping. The view of
the future that supports today's planning decisions is a prospect
that changes with the passage of time—partly because the future
is seen more clearly as it draws nearer; partly because experience
in implementing the plan may differ from expectation; and partly
because new possibilities appear on the scene, some of which may
place a more urgent claim on resources. When a plan becomes a
strait jacket, it is worse than no plan.

It is precisely this concept of built-in flexibility in planning that
should overcome the objection to the program budget's forward
projection of resource requirements. Under our proposal, the executive will continue to present annual budget recommendations to
Congress, and the legislative branch will continue to make annual
appropriations. The power over the public purse will be unchanged
from existing procedure. In contrast to present procedure, however, annual appropriations will be recommended and acted on
with a knowledge of probable follow-on costs in the years ahead,
always subject to revision in future years. There is nothing auto-
matic about the decisions taken under a program budget. There
are no irretrievable commitments.

This point cannot be emphasized too strongly. The history of
the American people is one of dynamic response to a dynamic
environment. The program budget should facilitate this process
for two reasons. The first is procedural. As an integral part of each
year's budget exercise, forward projections of costs associated with
each ongoing program would be re-examined in the light of recent
recorded experience of expense and accomplishment, possible
changes in the magnitude and urgency of objectives, and general
budget constraints imposed by anticipated total revenue and total

expenditure ceilings. The second reason is analytic. When problems or opportunities appear, the program budget structure would encourage and assist more detailed comparisons of gains and costs phased through time. In this way the key areas of choice among alternatives would be illuminated for the executive and legislative branches.

In short, it is anticipated that the operation of the program budget and its support of a planning orientation for public administration will exert a powerful new influence on how the great problems facing the national government are organized for analysis and how officials think about these problems. As officials learn to use the new budget structure, and as the budget is improved and refined on the basis of operating experience, specific gains should be recorded in the rational assignment of resources to achieve desired goals. These gains should be realized in effectiveness and efficiency regardless of the political temperament of the administration in office. The proposed budget structure is essentially a politically neutral instrument.

ORGANIZATIONAL IMPLICATIONS OF THE PROGRAM BUDGET

One feature of the program budget proposal advanced in this book is the pulling together for planning purposes of related budget items wherever they are found throughout the government's administrative structure. How this can be accomplished, together with some of the schematic problems requiring resolution, has been illustrated in a number of earlier chapters concerned with such activities as education, transportation, health, natural resources, and space exploration. The observation has often been made that the recommended design of a program budget is not consistent with the existing organizational structure of the federal establishment, and that there is no necessity for compelling such congruence. What is required, it has been suggested, is a statistical crossover network that will permit the combination of activity costs into the specified programs—followed, after congressional appropriation decisions, by similar decomposition of program allocations back to the administrative organizations.

It should be recognized that some such arrangement is certainly feasible theoretically and probably feasible technically. But this assertion should not hide the likelihood that there will be difficult, perhaps deeply frustrating, issues to be resolved if a program budget structure is actually put into operation within the existing executive organization. The heart of the problem is the fact that the program budget in operation should not be a mere statistical game. Great strategic importance will attach to both the definition of program structure and content and the establishment of specific program objectives (including magnitude, timing, and cost). Only slightly less critical will be the probability that the functioning of the program budget will reveal wasteful duplications, overlaps, and inconsistencies created or permitted by the scatter of related activities through numerous executive departments, agencies, and bureaus. A closely related set of complications will arise from the fact that each existing unit in the executive branch has its interested counterpart in the House and Senate Committee structure. Finally, outside the government there stand the special interest groups of beneficiaries and clients who have developed relationships, understandings, and institutional and personal channels of influence, all mortgaged to the existing administrative structure and even to individual personalities in the executive and legislative branches.

One might conclude that the program budget could not function effectively in such an environment. Because wholesale revision of the federal structure in accordance with the logic of a program budget is clearly not going to be brought about in the near future, this judgment would be definitively negative for the budget's near-term prospects. Another conclusion, however—one that strongly appeals to the authors of this book—urges a realistic, moderate, and flexible articulation of procedures that would accommodate many of the demands of the existing administrative structure, on the one hand, and many of the requirements of an effective program budget performance, on the other.

There are at least three ways in which this suggestion might be carried out. In appraising operating feasibilities, one must start with a direct recognition of the central administrative task. The executive branch is responsible for proposing annual budgets to Congress, and it normally takes the initiative in defining objectives and recommending the allocation of resources for their achievement. Under the program budget concept, therefore, the executive branch would be responsible for proposing long-range plans and

for laying out, along appropriate time scales, the resource requirements associated with their phased implementation. This means
that within the executive departments and agencies the machinery
must be found for securing agreement on an array of programs
that all interested executives will support, defend, and following
congressional appropriation, implement effectively. To be specific,
if this country is to have a rationally determined set of long-range
programs for education, the plans of the many administrative units
presently concerned with fragments of the total educational effort
must be examined concurrently. Mutually acceptable educational
program objectives, costed and time-phased, must be hammered
out. And this set of programs, within the total spending proposals
of the President's budget, must be presented and justified to
Congress.

One way to accomplish this would be through the Bureau of
the Budget. Although the Bureau has exercised stronger leadership
in recent years than was its practice earlier, it could choose to
supply even more aggressive guidance and coordination. Such an
increased transfer of planning leadership from the departments
and agencies to the Bureau might not be accepted easily by those
who would see in the process a diminution of their influence, as
well as a slackening of the bonds that attach them to established
clienteles outside the government. Probably such change could
only be brought about through the strong determination of a strong
President. Skeptics should consider, however, that a similar transfer
has been accomplished since 1960 in the Department of Defense
under the leadership of a Secretary who undertook to plan the
allocation of resources for national security through a program
budget concept. If this approach were to be adopted, the staff of
the Bureau of the Budget would, of course, have to be expanded
in size, strengthened in planning capability, and to a degree
reoriented in its intellectual posture.

A second way to attack the problem would be through interdepartmental committees, one for each major program area, with
representation on each committee for all executive units with
relevant activity responsibilities. In this move the Bureau of the
Budget might reasonably supply the initiative and chair the committees, but the program conclusions would be committee decisions.
Critics of this approach have an obvious target in the general

reputation of committees for discovering viable compromises at a common denominator of mediocrity. But these groups would be primarily concerned with program planning decisions, not with operations, and there is a substantial history of the effective use of such interdepartmental groups in policy formulation assignments in the federal government. On the whole, the record is not so bleak as to forecast an inevitable dullness of performance. It is possible, indeed, to anticipate a growing loyalty by members to the program-design responsibilities of the committees, which should in time help lift sights above the tribalism of departmental attachments.

A third approach would retain the foregoing committee structure but place responsibility for chairing and strongly leading each committee in a high-level representative of the administrative unit that presently implements the principal assignment in the committee's area. In this design, for example, leadership of an interdepartmental committee in the area of education would be exercised by a top official of the Office of Education in the Department of Health, Education, and Welfare. This official would have prime responsibility for guiding the program-planning effort and for bringing about an effective coordination of the educational interests of all participants. The difficulties and potentials of the committee device would, of course, be present in this planning organization, and additional complications might be introduced by the assignment of a primary role to one agency. By way of rebuttal, it should be observed that the pattern has been used successfully in both public and private administration. There is no reason to conclude automatically that such a plan is impracticable.

All three possibilities have operating attractions as well as visible handicaps. Actual experience with a program budget would provide opportunities for experimenting with all three as well as with modifications and combinations. There is no overpowering need to insist on a single approach to the problem. What should be perfectly clear is that no simple solution is in sight. However, it should be equally clear that no insuperable obstacles stand in the way of experimentation and consequent evolution of several organizational schemes for making the program budget work.

A successful experience with the program budget in operation will probably lead in the long run to some restructuring of the assignment of responsibilities among the federal departments, agencies, and bureaus. Familiarity with inertia and resistance to change of any existing power structure, however, would strongly counsel against starting the installation of the program budget by suggesting a grand redesign of the executive branch.

Regardless of the kind of planning structure that may be found operationally effective, one critical need that must be emphasized is the requirement for continuing flexibility. This will be essential for mapping program objectives, timing, and costs in relation to evolving experience, the dynamic national and international environment, and the claims of important new programs that come into view after older programs have been given approval to go forward. The greatest danger in all planning is the threat that unimaginative minds will accept plans as rigid commitments. The value of planning is that it compels a long view. But the long view must be continually refreshed, and the basic intellectual attitude should be one that is prepared to modify plans in response to changing circumstances.

ANALYTICAL ACTIVITIES INTEGRAL TO PROGRAM BUDGETING PROCESS

Although there would no doubt be improvements in the planning process merely as a result of using a new program budgeting format and projecting resource implications over longer time periods, the full potential of the system can only be realized by expanding and strengthening the analytical effort to be used in support of the program budgeting process. This kind of effort should be applied at various levels, including the policy level. As indicated in Chapter 3, the techniques used would include cost-utility analysis, capital budgeting procedures, various kinds of macroeconomic analysis, and the like.

At the broad policy level, the main allocative considerations involve such questions as how much for welfare, for education, for natural resources, for defense, etc. Although the analytical tools currently available are very limited in their capability to come to grips with these broad allocative problems, they nevertheless can help to shed some light on the main issues and thus help to sharpen the intuition and judgment of the top-level decisionmakers. Undoubtedly the analytical activity in support of the decision process at this level should be located primarily in the Bureau of the Budget or in staffs organized for the committee structure described in the previous section. Although considerable analytical capability currently exists in the Bureau of the Budget, it would probably have to be supplemented, or at least reoriented in some measure.

To support the analytical effort at the broad policy level, capabilities would have to be expanded (or created) at lower levels. Within a given program area (e.g., welfare, education, space, defense), there is usually a wide range of alternative ways of attaining desired program objectives. Such ranges should be explored analytically with a view to seeking preferred alternatives. In the case of defense, for example, various analytical efforts are currently in existence in the Office of the Secretary of Defense (Office of the Deputy Assistant Secretary for Systems Analysis, Office of the Director of Defense Research and Engineering, etc.). These efforts are in turn supported by the analytical activities carried out by the three military departments in the form of planning studies and special analyses. Something akin to this arrangement would have to be established for the other major program areas.

It should be stressed again that introduction of program budgeting procedures, even though accompanied by the analytical techniques that have been discussed here and in Chapter 3, will not in itself provide final answers to problems or make decisions. Program budgeting is a tool that will assist the managers in reaching rational decisions on the critical resource allocation problems that they must face. It should help illuminate important elements of choice among alternatives and facilitate measures of performance. But it cannot serve as a substitute for management judgment, intuition, or experience.

IMPACT ON STATE AND LOCAL GOVERNMENTS

A successful experience with the program budget in the federal government cannot fail, as time passes, to exert a positive influence on planning and budgeting at the state and local government levels. This will occur for two quite different reasons. It will be useful to comment on the spillover influence, because part of the case for the adoption of the program budget in the federal non-defense sector is that the gains from a more rational allocation of resources will not be confined to the national government.

The first cause of the impact of the new federal budget procedure on resource allocation activities at lower governmental levels is the network of existing relationships that bind federal, state, and local funding in many important fields. In the fields of education, transportation, housing, and health—to name only four of the many areas of legally established intermesh—we are already committed to program-type planning and to joint allocation of funds subject to stipulated standards of performance and proportions of sharing. In areas in which this partnership relation exists, full implementation of the program budget concept at the federal level cannot be accomplished only by reference to allocation of federal funds. The problems to which federal appropriations address themselves are shared problems. Any analysis of goals and means must take into account both what states, municipalities, and other local districts do in cooperation with the federal government by way of matching funds and what they do with their own monies.

The probable result of this mutuality of interest resting on a foundation of legally determined relationships will be to encourage state and local governments to recast the relevant segments of their planning in conformance with the federal pattern. Perhaps a reasonable expectation might be that in the decade following the demonstration of the program budget's operating advantages, a strong movement will develop in many states and localities to adopt a comparable structure for resource planning, originating in those areas in which the national-state-local linkages are most important.

The second cause of a thrust of program influence from national to local levels will be the force of example. Although the states and cities have been markedly independent both in their disposition to retain certain established institutional and procedural arrangements in their administrative operations and in their inventiveness in creating unique new forms, in budgetary matters they have historically been much more disposed to conform to the national model. For example, budgetary staffs roughly modeled on the federal Bureau of the Budget have appeared in many states and lower governmental divisions. There is a simple explanation for this development. The institution has been discovered to be essential in the face of rapidly rising social and economic demands, complex pressures on officials, and proliferation of the range of governmental activities.

As the federal program budget demonstrates its ability to make a significant contribution to the rationally planned use of scarce resources, it should progressively influence the thinking of the considerable numbers of state and municipal officials and their staffs who find themselves increasingly overwhelmed by the complexity of the allocation decisions thrust upon them. No spectacular rapid changes should be anticipated by any realistic observer of local government habits. A decade is probably the minimum appropriate unit of time for measuring changes in such a sensitive area of administration. But anyone who has watched the evolutionary progress of rational attitudes and devices in the management of the public's business must have confidence that a useful administrative tool will sooner or later be put to work. We note in passing that there is a possibility that the federal government may employ familiar incentives to accelerate this progress.

THE FEDERAL BUDGET AND PRIVATE MANAGEMENT

The positive effects of the program budget in operation will not be confined to the public sector of the economy. Business managers have an interest in this development, which can be described in specific terms. The primary link between the use of the new budgetary structure in the federal government and its significance for private administrators is the planning function.

Although long-range planning has continued, at least until recent years, to be widely viewed as an undesirable, if not dangerous, occupation for the federal government, its status in private management is at the other end of the scale of values. For at least the last ten years management literature has been marked by an intense interest in the philosophy, techniques, and organization of long-range planning. Further, research in management practice has reported a growing planning activity in all companies studied. Conferences and symposia are regularly convened to stress the values of planning, to study technical and organizational problems associated with making planning an effective and profitable business function, and to report on successful planning experiences. This movement has been fueled by a broad recognition of two phenomena. The first is the acceleration of the rate of change in markets, in technology, and in interindustry competition. The second is management's grasp of the fact that it can exploit future opportunities and defend against future threats only by extending its forecasting horizon and its scheduled assignment of resources— physical, technical, financial, and human.

Closely linked to this development is a growing recognition of the important influence exerted on the private economy by the magnitude and direction of public expenditures. The cash budget of the federal government in 1965 was almost one-fifth of gross national product.[1] This relationship alone compels private management in many industries to pay careful attention to public spending. The significance is dramatically heightened, of course, in those industries that serve the government as a principal customer. The defense and space contractors are prime examples. Even in industries whose contact with federal expenditures is peripheral or indirect, there is mounting awareness of the relation between governmental activities and the ability of private managers to identify future opportunities and risks and to act appropriately.

The existing federal budget structure, with its absence of aggregation in related program packages and its one-year time horizon, handicaps private planning.[2] Both the size and the direction of expenditures in future years must be inferred from current budget objectives and levels. Because there is a marked disposition to underestimate or hide future costs associated with current federal programs (especially in connection with new activities whose reception by Congress is likely to be adversely influenced by such projections), private planners must work not only with a paucity of information but also, on occasion, with erroneous information. These deficiencies do more than lower the quality of decision-making in those firms that try to take the government's actions into account as inputs for their own administrative direction. Overall,

---

[1] If the administrative budget (a frequently used reference) is substituted, the amount is some $20 billion smaller, which makes the relationship one-sixth.

[2] See *The Federal Budget as an Economic Document, Hearings before the Subcommittee on Economic Statistics of the Joint Economic Committee,* 88th Cong., 1st Sess. (Washington, D.C.: U.S. Government Printing Office, 1963).

they cannot fail to contribute to unnecessary perturbations in the private economy, reflecting misdirection of investment, wasteful employment of resources, and ill-timed response to market demand.

The influence of an effective program budget operation on the quality of private planning should, therefore, be significant and positive. It will add in an important way to the volume of public information that serves to guide private decisionmaking in our mixed economy. In doing this, it will strengthen the ability of private managers to order the use of resources in an increasingly rational manner.

ANALYTICAL CONTRIBUTIONS OF THE PROGRAM BUDGET

Probably the least spectacular, although by no means the least important, contribution of the program budget in operation will be its assistance to those concerned with building through analysis an understanding of the dynamics of the American economy. Beneficiaries would include economic research and planning staffs in private corporations and trade associations, economists (and social scientists generally) in universities and research institutions, and those concerned with fiscal and credit policies in the Treasury and Federal Reserve Board.

As economic analysis has increased in sophistication, the attention of analysts has shifted from gross measures of activity levels and trends in major economic sectors (such as aggregate consumer spending, business investment, government spending, etc.) to the dynamic interactions among the parts of the system. Quantitative models of economic behavior, input-output grids, and income-flow networks illustrate this development. In its totality the development represents a broad effort to identify, as a basis for prediction, policy formulation, and control, the transmission of economic impacts through closed-loop systems characterized by multiple feedbacks.

Two problems confront the designer of such analytical constructs. First is the blueprinting of the mechanics of complex economic interactions. Second is the collection and application of economic data that will transform the designs into instruments of analysis. Obviously, the validity of the designs themselves can be tested only by the introduction of relevant data. The greatest deterrent to rapid progress in the whole field of econometrics has been deficiencies in the data.

A program budget would help to remove some of these deficiencies in the public sector. Projecting federal expenditures five years or more into the future within defined program channels would materially assist analytical exploration of economic prospects by helping to quantify some dynamic interactions that have hitherto been handled through gross estimates. Other gains will derive from the more precise identification of federal expenditures that are presently hard to trace through the budgets of multiple departments, agencies, and bureaus. The ultimate beneficiaries, of course, will be those who use the improved instruments for research and analysis aimed at adding to their understanding of economic behavior and thereby strengthening their ability to formulate policies that contribute to stable growth.

A realistic view suggests that the gains cited above are not going to be achieved in the first years of an operating program budget. A principal reason is that it is likely to take several annual budget planning experiences to remove errors or statistical softness in future cost data. It will take additional years to bring supporting information systems into consonance with program budget concepts. At the same time one should anticipate progressive evolution in the definition of programs. After the initial period of testing, validating, and acquiring expertise, however, the contributions of the program budget to economic research and analysis may well turn out to be among the most important positive results that the innovation helps to accomplish.

SUMMARY

The purpose and the content of this book can be summarized simply and briefly as follows:

1. A necessary and principal activity of the executive and legislative branches of the federal government is to allocate scarce resources among competing claims. This is a difficult and confusing task because requirements inevitably exceed resources, because relative urgencies are not easily determined, because the array of requirements is in continual dynamic evolution, and because avail-

able information about costs and performance is both imperfect and poorly organized.

2. The instrument through which the government's allocation decisions are made is the budget process. First, by its structure the budget strongly influences the framework of the whole allocation decision format. This means that the decisions that are made tend to be those that the budget requires to be made as a result of the form in which the program is cast. In the nondefense sector this form follows the executive organization of departments, agencies, and bureaus. Second, the program, as translated through the budget, supplies a character of information that influences the quality of decisions made by public officials. In the nondefense sector present programs do not gather related activities and do not project ongoing cost streams into future years.

3. As a result of imperfections in the organization and deficiencies in the quality of information in the present nondefense programs and budgets, decisions about the allocation of public funds to meet public objectives are often ill-judged, improvident, or poorly timed. New activities may be given initial funding without knowledge of long-term costs. Some important activities may find monetary support, while others of equal importance are not given appropriate consideration. It is difficult, often impossible, to build meaningful relationships of means and ends, costs and results. Because of the splintering of some activities among government units, the total scope of programs may be hidden, and duplications and overlaps may persist for years. All these examples of malperformance in the allocation process are primarily the result of a failure to encourage and assist more rational decisionmaking.

4. The problems described above are not insoluble. It is possible to conceive of a federal budget process differing from the existing one in design and quality that would contribute to better, more rational decisions bearing on the allocation of resources. Such an alternative has been recommended and described in this book. In concept and purpose it would resemble the program budgeting procedures begun in the Department of Defense in 1961 and used since then in that agency with increasing success as a decision tool.

5. Program budgeting starts with the decision process rather than with the historical organization of the executive branch of the federal government. It undertakes to organize information in a

manner that will encourage and assist improvements in the quality of resource allocation decisions. It does this by identifying the major objectives to which the government considers assigning resources and then organizing information in related terms. It also extends the time horizon of planning decisions by projecting costs through future years, in contrast to the present budgetary practice of estimating costs for only one year in advance.

6. The gains associated with the successful introduction of a program budget in the nondefense sector of the federal government in the first instance should yield better planning decisions. Comparison among alternative allocation patterns would be made more easily and with greater precision. Analysis of cost-utility relationships would be facilitated. Duplication and waste resulting from splintering related activities in multiple governmental units would be more readily identified and removed.

7. The gains achieved through a program budget operation would not be confined to a better administration of federal resources. Spillover gains should be anticipated in the adoption of at least some of the program approach in state and local government operations. Beyond this, the flow of information about federal expenditures would materially assist private business planning, which depends heavily in some areas, lightly in others, on information available through the federal budget. Finally, economic analysis, particularly that directed toward improving understanding of the dynamic, interactive effects of public and private expenditures, would be assisted by an operating program budget.

8. A number of conceptual, organizational, and administrative problems will have to be resolved prior to the introduction of a program budget in the federal government. A principal recommendation of this book is that studies should be initiated to explore ways and means of handling these problems. After the first introduction of a program budget, perhaps on a limited scale, it will be essential to anticipate an extended period of evolutionary modification and improvement in the structure of the program budget and in the budgetary process.

9. Implicit throughout our discussion has been the proposition that the program budget is a neutral tool. It has no politics. It is simply a method of organizing information to help officials who bear the responsibility for allocating public resources to make better decisions in accomplishing public objectives.

INDEX

INDEX

Administration, distinguished from programming, 54

Adult education: federal support of, 179, 190; program elements of, 192

A fortiori analysis, and uncertainty, 74

AEC. See Atomic Energy Commission

Agena, 143; budget category, 140

Agency for International Development, 9, 159n; and foreign policy, 39; health expenditures (1965), t214; support of education, 180; support of health services, 213, 220

Agriculture: and the federal budget, 19; price supports, 14, 32, 259. See also Department of Agriculture

AID. See Agency for International Development

Air Force, airlift and sealift, t153

Air pollution, 258, 271, 325; and program budget, 273

Air resources: in federal budget, 258, 266; in program budget, t265, 271; as program category, 257, t260, t261, t263

Aircraft, 93. See also Bombers; Long-endurance aircraft; Supersonic transport airliner

Airlift and sealift, federal budget (1965), t153

Airlift and Sealift Forces: DOD program, 34, 37–38, 42, 92, 287; effectiveness of, 49. See also Military Air Transport Service; Military Sea Transportation Service

Alford, L. P., book cited, 64n

Allocation: of appropriations, 58; of development costs, 130–133, 142–143; of federal transportation expenditures, 155. See also Consumer allocation; Supplier allocation

Alternative force structures, data presentation format, t95

American Telephone and Telegraph Company, and space program, 124

Analysis: in Department of Defense, 363; design of, 70; and the federal budget, 3–23; in program budget, 362–365; of programs, 48–52, 61–

78. See also Benefit-cost analysis; Cost analysis; Cost-benefit analysis; Cost-effectiveness analysis; Cost-utility analysis

Analysts: Air Force needs for, 104; functions of, 67–79

Anshen, Melvin, book cited, 28n

Anthony, Robert N., book cited, 63n

Apollo. See Project Apollo

Apollo Command and Service Modules, 120

Appropriations: decision process, 318–320; and program budgets, 57–58; 357. See also House Appropriations Committee

Army: airlift and sealift, t153; in DOD programs, 34, 92; and traditional budgeting, 29, 33

Army Air Corps, 81

Asher, Harold, report cited, 129n

Atlas, 93

Atomic bomb, decision to construct, 46

Atomic Energy Commission: health expenditures (1965), t214, t218, t239; and natural resources, t265; obligational authority and expenditures, t126; and program budgeting, 351; and space program, 122; support for basic research, 197; support for education, 179, 188

Aviation. See Civil Aeronautics Board; Federal Aviation Agency

B-70, appropriation, 331

Bangs, John R., book cited, 64n

Basic National Security Policy, 94

Benefit-cost analysis: in recreational resources field, 270; of Santa Maria Project, 273–280; in water resources field, 268. See also Cost-benefit analysis; Cost-effectiveness analysis; Cost-utility analysis

Berman, E. B., paper cited, 75n

Bierman, Harold, Jr., book cited, 64n

Bombers, and planning for missiles, 46

Bonneville Power Administration, and natural resources, t264

SELECTED RAND BOOKS

Baum, Warren C., *The French Economy and the State*, Princeton, N.J., Princeton University Press, 1958.

Brodie, Bernard, *Strategy in the Missile Age*, Princeton, N.J., Princeton University Press, 1959.

Dinerstein, Herbert S., *War and the Soviet Union: Nuclear Weapons and the Revolution in Soviet Military and Political Thinking*, New York, Praeger, 1959.

Dole, Stephen, and Isaac Asimov, *Planets for Man*, New York, Random House, 1964.

Dorfman, Robert, Paul A. Samuelson, and Robert M. Solow, *Linear Programming and Economic Analysis*, New York, McGraw-Hill Book Company, Inc., 1958.

Downs, Anthony, *Inside Bureaucracy*, Boston, Mass., Little, Brown and Company, 1967.

Halpern, Manfred, *The Politics of Social Change in the Middle East and North Africa*, Princeton, N.J., Princeton University Press, 1963.

Hirshleifer, Jack, James C. DeHaven, and Jerome W. Milliman, *Water Supply: Economics, Technology, and Policy*, Chicago, The University of Chicago Press, 1960.

Hitch, Charles J., and Roland McKean, *The Economics of Defense in the Nuclear Age*, Cambridge, Mass., Harvard University Press, 1960.

Horelick, Arnold L., and Myron Rush, *Strategic Power and Soviet Foreign Policy*, Chicago, Ill., The University of Chicago Press, 1966.

Hsieh, Alice L., *Communist China's Strategy in the Nuclear Era*, Englewood Cliffs, N.J., Prentice-Hall, Inc., 1962.

Johnson, John J., (ed.), *The Role of the Military in Underdeveloped Countries*, Princeton, N.J., Princeton University Press, 1962.

Johnson, William A., *The Steel Industry of India*, Cambridge, Mass., Harvard University Press, 1966.

Johnstone, William C., *Burma's Foreign Policy: A Study in Neutralism*, Cambridge, Mass., Harvard University Press, 1963.

Liu, Ta-Chung, Kung-Chia Yeh, *The Economy of the Chinese Mainland: National Income and Economic Development, 1933–1959*, Princeton, N.J., Princeton University Press, 1965.

Lubell, Harold, *Middle East Oil Crises and Western Europe's Energy Supplies*, Baltimore, The Johns Hopkins Press, 1963.

McKean, Roland N., *Efficiency in Government through Systems Analysis: With Emphasis on Water Resource Development*, New York, John Wiley & Sons, Inc., 1958.

Meyer, John R., John F. Kain, and Martin Wohl, *The Urban Transportation Problem*, Cambridge, Mass., Harvard University Press, 1965.

Nelson, Richard R., Merton J. Peck, and Edward D. Kalachek, *Technology, Economic Growth and Public Policy*, Washington, D.C., The Brookings Institution, 1967.

Pincus, John A., *Economic Aid and International Cost-Sharing*, Baltimore, Maryland, The Johns Hopkins Press, 1965.

Quade, E. S., (ed.), *Analysis for Military Decisions*, Chicago, Rand McNally & Company; Amsterdam, North-Holland Publishing Company, 1964.

Rosen, George, *Democracy and Economic Change in India*, Berkeley and Los Angeles, Calif., 1966.

Rush, Myron, *Political Succession in the USSR*, New York, Columbia University Press, 1965.

Speier, Hans, *Divided Berlin: The Anatomy of Soviet Political Blackmail*, New York, Praeger, 1961.

Whiting, Allen S., *China Crosses the Yalu: The Decision to Enter the Korean War*, New York, The Macmillan Company, 1960.

Williams, J. D., *The Compleat Strategyst: Being a Primer on the Theory of Games of Strategy*, New York, McGraw-Hill Book Company, Inc., 1954.

Wolf, Jr., Charles, *Foreign Aid: Theory and Practice in Southern Asia*, Princeton, N.J., Princeton University Press, 1960.

Wolfe, Thomas, *Soviet Strategy at the Crossroads*, Cambridge, Mass., Harvard University Press, 1964.